Japanese Democracy

BRADLEY RICHARDSON

Japanese Democracy

POWER, COORDINATION,
AND PERFORMANCE

WITHDRAW

Yale University Press
New Haven and London

Library of Congress Cataloging-in-Publication Data
Richardson, Bradley M.
Japanese democracy : power, coordination, and performance / Bradley Richardson.
p. cm.
Includes bibliographical references and index.
ISBN 0-300-06258-3 (cloth : alk. paper)
1. Japan — Politics and government — 1945- . 2. Democracy — Japan.
3. Political participation — Japan.   4. Political parties — Japan.
5. Decentralization in government — Japan.   I. Title.
JQ1681.R5   1997
321.8'0952 — dc20   96-22203
                                                         CIP

Printed in the United States of America

A catalogue record for this book is available from the British Library.

The paper in this book meets the guidelines for permanence and durability of the Committee on Production Guidelines for Book Longevity of the Council on Library Resources.

10   9   8   7   6   5   4   3   2   1

Contents

WITHDRAW

Preface   vii

List of Abbreviations   ix

1   Postwar Politics: Images and Questions   1

2   Political Culture and Electoral Behavior   12

3   Parties Under the "1955 System"   49

4   Party Fragmentation and Coalition Dynamics   74

5   Executive and Bureaucratic Power   95

6   Legislative Politics   127

7   Interests, Policy, and Power   152

8   Business Interests and Political Life   174

9   The Government and the Economy   200

10   Japan as a Bargained Distributive Democracy   240

Notes   267

Index   317

Preface

This book portrays Japan as a functioning democracy. Rule by a single party from 1955 until 1993, as well as the allegedly powerful bureaucracy and weak parliament, has led some scholars to describe Japan as having a "soft authoritarian" government. Others have criticized the supposed lack of governmental responsibility. They argue that the Japanese government does not behave in the same way as governments in other major industrial democracies. These critics of Japanese democracy are known collectively as revisionists.

There is a jarring difference between these portrayals of Japanese exceptionalism and the accounts of political life in Japan's newspapers and periodicals. There, politics is presented as a struggle among individual politicians, lobbyists, and bureaucrats and among highly competitive parties and interest groups, and the conflict seems to be widespread. The best scholarly works on Japanese politics repeat these themes. Even granting that Japan's record as a democracy has been marred by considerable public corruption, we see in these sources an overall picture of Japanese public life that looks much like public life in other industrialized countries.

In this book I address the revisionist claims and compare their version of Japanese politics with evidence from Japanese newspapers and government documents and a synthesis of scholarly writings. I mainly examine Japanese politics in the last decade of dominant party rule. I also describe the politics of coalition government since 1993 and find that the pluralistic patterns of politics under Liberal Democratic rule have been extended to the present. By and large I avoid comparing politics in Japan with an idealized view of American politics, which has been the source of some tenets on Japan's alleged exceptionalism. Instead, where I make comparisons, it is with parliamentary systems in other major industrialized democracies, which are a more suitable point of reference than the American political system, which is truly an exceptionalist case.

The Japanese press offers much better coverage of political details than the press in other major democracies, in part because newspaper reporters are attached to particular ministries, parties, and factions. I relied extensively on Japanese newspaper accounts of Japanese politics for this reason. The library of the Shimbun Kenkyujo of the University of Tokyo, to which I was introduced by Professor Hiroshi Akuto, was an excellent place to conduct newspaper research. Because there are so many citations of newspaper sources, I have omitted the *Shimbun* (newspaper) part of newspaper titles in citations. Newspaper articles translated by the Translation Section of the U.S. Embassy, Tokyo, which I also used frequently, are identified in the same way, that is, by using the abbreviated Japanese newspaper name.

I wish to acknowledge the help of several talented graduate and undergraduate assistants, without whose work this book could not have been completed. Aiji Tanaka, now an associate professor at Aoyama Gakuin University, did an enormous amount of the work leading to this book while a graduate student at Ohio State. Kazuomi Shiozawa, Mikinori Kobayashi, Kang Choi, Ki In Lee, Chang Oh, Jae Guk Jeon, Amy Weir, Erin Moore, Brian Carnahan, and Kent Kille provided invaluable research help. Karlene Foster's aid with tables and charts is deeply appreciated. I am also indebted to Masako Masuda of the Policy Study Group, Tokyo, and Junko Hasegawa of the National Diet Library for assistance with researching post-1993 politics. Professor Harumi Befu of Stanford generously shared his publications on theories of Japanese society, for which I am grateful. I am also obligated to Noboru Hatakeyama, former vice minister at the Ministry of International Trade and Industry, for help with research over the past two decades, including that for Chapter 9 of this book. Mary Pasti shepherded the manuscript through the editing process with great patience and many valuable suggestions.

I am always indebted to my wife, Barbara, for her patience and support and to Shotaro Ikegai and his family for their kindness and generosity in the early years.

Abbreviations

CGP   Clean Government Party (Komeito)
DSP   Democratic Socialist Party
EIB   Export-Import Bank
FILP   Fiscal Investment and Loan Program
JCP   Japan Communist Party
JDB   Japan Development Bank
JSP   Japan Socialist Party
LDP   Liberal Democratic Party
MAFF   Ministry of Agriculture, Forestry, and Fisheries
MITI   Ministry of International Trade and Industry
NLC   New Liberal Club
PARC   Policy Affairs Research Council
SDF   Self-Defense Forces
SDPJ   Social Democratic Party of Japan

I

Postwar Politics: Images and Questions

Japan is known the world over for its economic prowess and high-quality exports. Its politics are less well known. Yet since World War II, Japan has been a country of almost unique political stability. One party ruled for thirty-eight years, and during that time politics was predictable, and extremely rapid social change was accommodated without major political disruptions. Then, in 1993, after nearly four decades in power, the largest party split, and political life was thrown into a turmoil from which it has yet to recover.

In this book I address three questions embedded in the Japanese postwar political experience: First, was a dominant party system based on semi-institutionalized ties with interest groups and close relations with a strong bureaucracy conducive to democracy? Second, what led a seemingly invulnerable system to partially collapse in July 1993, and, relatedly, how can the currently fluid political situation be interpreted in light of the earlier stability? And third, what contributions have postwar governments made to economic success? Each of these questions addresses issues of major concern to students of contemporary Japan.

Democracy or Semiauthoritarian State?

A single conservative political party, the Liberal Democratic Party (LDP), won almost every national election and most local contests from 1955 until 1993. Under what is called the 1955 system, it was the majority party in the Diet and was divided from its opposition over foreign policy, security, and constitutional reform issues. From 1959 until 1993 the opposition camp included, in order from center to left, the Democratic Socialist Party, the Japan Socialist Party (later Social Democratic Party of Japan, or SDPJ), and the Japan Communist Party. These parties were joined in opposition to the LDP by the centrist Clean Government Party in 1967. (Throughout this book, I shall refer to the Socialist Party by its most recent designation.) The LDP was closely linked to a traditionally strong bureaucracy, and major interest groups were aligned with government ministries and the ruling party. Taken together, these three political actors decided political agendas.

Opinion is divided over the implications of the 1955 system. Some people think that it was not democratic. In their view, although the constitution of 1946 set forth a full complement of ostensibly democratic institutions, the style of politics remained semiauthoritarian. Others find the idea that Japan is a democracy acceptable. But the long exclusion of opposition parties and labor unions from direct influence over political agendas means to them that Japan under the 1955 system was an unusual kind of democracy compared with that of most other democratic countries.

My discussion of postwar politics is developed around two basic metaphors.[1] In one, postwar politics is depicted as highly centralized and integrated. I call this the vertical-integrative model.[2] According to the vertical view, a central bureaucracy dominated politics in close cooperation with the LDP and business. Relations among power centers were close and hierarchical. Opposition political parties, the Diet (parliament), labor, and local governments lacked privileged access to national power centers and were subordinated to central institutions.

In this vertical model, the bureaucracy is the main directive force in government. Ministries are the source of policy proposals, which later become cabinet bills and Diet laws; they also implement policy. Ministry officials are linked with interest groups via exclusive relationships characterized as either elitist or corporatist. Under the variety of corporatism preferred by supporters of the vertical approach, groups comply with ministry preferences, and group interests that do not contradict bureaucratic goals are indulged. Under the 1955 system the dominant conservative party, itself believed to be highly centralized, is seen as having been the handmaiden of the bureaucracy.[3]

Bureaucrats are Japan's natural political elite, according to the vertical metaphor. Officials, who are trained in prestigious universities, possess more policy expertise and social status than politicians do. Party elites work hand in hand with senior bureaucrats and business leaders in the establishment of policy priorities. Central ministries dominate local governments in a number of ways. National civil servants occupy local administrative positions; model laws suggested by the ministries determine local agendas; prefectures and local governments are fiscally dependent on national subsidies and tax transfers. Voters are manipulated by local social elites and machines so they will vote for conservative party nominees; that is, relationships between candidates and voters are hierarchical.

According to the vertical metaphor, Japan was led until 1993 by a politically and socially homogeneous cluster of senior officials, party leaders (many of whom had been bureaucrats), business executives, and heads of interest groups. In the early postwar decades there was an elite consensus on economic growth and opposition to communism that overrode other political concerns, including the interests of workers and consumers, and reinforced an existing structural tendency toward close elite relationships.[4] Political life was orderly under this set of arrangements, and the dominant characteristics of inter-actor relationships were hierarchy and deference.

According to the second, "horizontal-fragmented" metaphor for Japanese politics, power is fragmented, conflict is frequent, and issues are contested by parties, interest groups, and organs of government. In this view, the dominant party and the bureaucracy are part of a competitive multipolar system of power centers. Ministries influence agendas but do not by themselves dictate the direction of politics. Indeed, neither the ministries nor the conservative party (nor recent coalition governments) have completely dominated decision-making. Ministries are often constrained by the need to seek allies in interest groups and political parties.[5] Although different elements of government and politics are often closely related to each other by common interests, they still are frequently highly competitive.

The Diet, too, is at times a place of contention and interparty accommodation according to the horizontal metaphor. Ministerial proposals are modified in Diet processes more often than is assumed. The opposition parties occasionally exercise an informal de facto veto over legislative agendas. The Diet is frequently a focus of political dynamics and strategies involving groups outside the legislative domain. The timing and outcome of Diet processes are central to elite political recruitment and to election strategies and counterstrategies and sometimes occupy center stage on their own merits.

Interest groups compete for political access by seeking allies in political parties and ministries. Policies are formulated by temporary coalitions, with interest groups aligning themselves differently on different issues. Interest group relations with ministries are more clientelistic than corporatist; close ties and common interests exist but do not guarantee mutual concessions or agreement on all policy matters.

Governance is decentralized. Parochial power centers compete with national government organs and elites for political influence.[6] Inter-actor relationships are often renegotiated. The political climate is uncertain. Political parties are semi-institutionalized alliances or coalitions. Formal party organizations exist in all parties, but they only partially control internal political processes. Parties sometimes verge on collapse as the result of internal dissent. An intermittent tendency toward fragmentation and near collapse could be seen in the LDP. The Social Democratic Party of Japan was similarly divided at most times.

Much of this book is devoted to deciding which model better describes the era of LDP hegemony between 1955 and 1993. Although patterns are sometimes mixed, I am convinced that the horizontal metaphor provides the better fit. The horizontal model also fits the present political arrangements in Japan. Since the summer of 1993 single-party rule has been replaced by interparty coalition governments. But the patterns of competition and fragmentation observable during the period of LDP dominance are still visible. Intra-LDP competition has been replaced by interparty competition. Ministries and interest groups still have to address their pleas to multiple power centers. The substance of political alignments has changed, but politics has developed along lines not very different from those found earlier.

Political Science Models and Power

To determine the extent to which a vertical or horizontal metaphor fits postwar Japanese politics requires an examination of how power was distributed under the 1955 system and at present. We want to know whether political parties have been internally democratic or run by centralized elites. We also want to know the degree of pluralism in the party system — specifically, whether the LDP was accountable to parties in the opposition camp during its time in power. What checks and balances were present or missing in relations between bureaucratic ministries, prime minister and cabinet, and parliament are also central to understanding how the 1955 system worked. Finally, we want to know more about the quality of interest intermediation, including the extent to which citizens vote in elections on the basis of self-interest or simply ratified the power of incumbent politicians and social elites.

Political science has a number of middle-range approaches useful in characterizing power relations in Japanese politics. Although the various frameworks are concerned with political domains ranging from government institutions to interest groups, their classifications of power converge neatly. Most paradigms describe power as a continuum with centralization and concentration at one extreme and decentralization and dispersion at the other. Concentrated and centralized power is associated with concepts like elitism, authoritarianism, corporatism, and oligarchy. Dispersed and decentralized power is associated with concepts like pluralism, autonomy, democracy, and multipartism.[7]

Political scientists commonly associate dispersed power with democracy and concentrated power with nondemocratic government. Where power is dispersed, there is likely to be competition for political goods. Competition opens up political processes to different viewpoints, and outcomes are negotiated between different actors and coalitions. Dispersed power and widening of participation in decisions is believed to facilitate broader political representation.

Although power is one of the most important concepts in political science, identifying and measuring it is not easy. Power is often described in static or structural terms. Government institutions "have" power by virtue of constitutions, legislation, or tradition. Organization charts are used to determine whether parties are decentralized or centralized. Number of supporters or members, amount of wealth, and social status are used to assess the power of parties, interest groups, and elites. Parties that receive many votes and interest groups that have many members are powerful; those lacking these resources are weak. Power in all of these examples is identified on the basis of static attributes.

There are several problems with an attributional approach to political power. In real life, the interaction between political actors involves dynamic, situational, and relational dimensions of power not identified by the attributional method. For example, political parties may appear to be influential because they win an important election, but at the same time weak leadership or internal differences may prevent them from fully exploiting this advantage. Whether attributed political power is actually employed and whether it is employed effectively is thus questionable.

A related question concerns whether power is employed consistently in different environments. A numerically strong political party may discover that a weaker opponent is able to block its agenda on some issue by using procedural rules or enlisting powerful allies. On other occasions, the same party may be much more influential. A political actor's influence depends on the strength of its opponents and on other factors present or absent in different settings. Influence may also be employed or not in different settings because of different levels of interest in specific issues. Power is dynamic and varies in different contexts.

Power in the real world is a behavioral relationship between two or more individuals, groups, or institutions. As a result of the actions of another, a person or group does something he, she, or it did not intend to do; the one taking the initial action is more powerful, and the one responding in an unintended way is less so. How the political actors in a given system relate to one another in political processes, based on a review of different kinds of policymaking, is therefore the basis for saying conclusively which political actors are generally powerful and which are not. The static, structural characteristics of power — legal authority, votes, wealth, social status, and the like — are a useful starting point in identifying power relationships. But these characteristics have to be translated into behavior for power to be meaningful and measurable. Although institutions and other structures are important, processes are the key to understanding power.

Twin Political Dynamics

Looking at politics in terms of political process also brings into focus the frequency of conflict in Japanese political life. Japan is usually said to lack the conflictual style of American politics. In reality, conflict is far more pervasive in Japanese political life than has been assumed.[8] At every level, individuals and groups compete for influence. Interest groups criticize political parties, including those with which they are allied; business groups oppose farmers; small businesses distrust big businesses; ministries are paralyzed by internal and external disagreements; local politicians ignore higher-level authority; and individual politicians feud because of long-standing hatreds.

I have called the conflictual tendency in Japanese politics a "dynamic" because its intensity varies. Japanese politics is fairly quiescent, and political processes follow established routines in some periods. But political processes can also explode, causing episodes of extreme conflict. The result is sometimes crippling "immobilism": no legislative bills are passed or important decisions made because of the severity of disagreement.[9] During peak confrontations, the conflict dynamic can lead to fragmentation in Japanese political organizations. In the midst of the gravest confrontations, new intraorganizational factions or groups are formed, and conflict between old groups is intensified.

The Japanese tendency to have episodes of heightened conflict interspersed with periods of relative calm is not unusual. To some degree, all political systems have similar cycles of conflict versus stability. Japan, however, deals with conflict differently from other industrialized democracies. In other nations conflictual positions are usually negotiated without damage to existing institutions and procedures. As Arend Lijphart's work has shown, conflict in even the most divided societies — the compartmentalized Dutch and Belgian systems — can be dealt with through negotiation.[10] In contrast, in Japan, although conflict can be resolved through negotiation most of the time, sometimes a decentralized intergroup civil war can develop, with group enmities overcoming mutual trust. A mutual "amoral" ethnocentrism among competitive groups emerges which can, if sufficiently severe, lead to institutional collapse, such as that which took place in 1993. Conflict has a pathological potential in Japan, as we will see later in both intra-LDP and Diet politics. To recapitulate, the competition-conflict-fragmentation dynamic is a process in which political groups compete strenuously with each other. When group conflict occurs within organizations (for example, political parties), the organizations may lose their integrity through divisions and defections. When it occurs elsewhere, normal political processes lose their effectiveness through stalemates and immobilism.

In addition to the "conflict-fragmentation" dynamic, there is a second tendency in Japanese political processes and society: conflict is often constrained and controlled through consultation, coordination, and negotiation. In every conflict setting, individuals get together, often informally in behind-the-scenes meetings, to address their differences and attempt to negotiate some kind of agreement. The consultation may result in useful compromise or may simply produce a symbolic act of reconciliation sufficient to permit resumption of normal politics.

The processes of informal conciliation and integration are, like conflict, universal aspects of politics. Politicians everywhere consult with each other and try to handle conflict through informal contacts and negotiated agreements. What is striking in Japan is the scope and degree to which consultation and coordination are visible, at times semiformalized behavior. The frequency with which Japanese politicians consult using informal small group mechanisms is notable. In some cases, the procedures developed to respond to particular conflicts become institutionalized over time. Liaison meetings between top LDP officials and cabinet members are one example. Some of these institutionalized consultational processes contributed to the stability of the 1955 system and provided the channels and procedures needed to restrain otherwise strong centrifugal tendencies.

Political Culture

Japan's twin process dynamics are intimately related with its political culture. Although politics is driven by its own special rationales and is not culturally determined, culture still influences the forms of behavior visible in a particular system.[11] In fact, it is hard to balance the obvious importance of competition and conflict with the traditional notion that consensualism is the main driving force in Japanese political culture. There is, however, a Japanese-style competition that reflects native cultural preferences. It is best described as an amoral groupism in which — as in Edward Banfield's "amoral familism" — conflict is endemic, potentially very intense, and at times unresolvable by customary mechanisms. This tendency toward amoral groupism is increasingly recognized in recent Japanese historical and political science research.[12]

In spite of the frequency of competition and conflict in Japanese public life, order is also highly valued. The uncertainty generated by individual and group conflict is often immobilizing and debilitating. The well-known Japanese concern for consensus can, therefore, be seen as a behavioral response to conflict as much as a compulsion. In reality, both the outbreak of conflict and efforts to contain conflict are parallel continuing processes, in Japanese politics as in Japanese society at large.

The search for order and certainty leads to widespread inter-actor coordination as politicians try to stabilize otherwise highly conflictual relationships through carefully orchestrated compromises and through promotion of solidarity within relevant political groups.[13] Although politicians in all societies manage conflict and develop techniques of conflict control and resolution, conflict reduction and compromise occupy an especially valued place in Japanese political agendas.

Japanese politicians fight with each other endlessly; they also normally negotiate with each other and accommodate themselves to each other's concerns. Consultation, negotiation, and accommodation are pervasive and at times modify considerably the effects of differences in power between specific political actors. A search for order and certainty can also be seen in widespread efforts to institutionalize and routinize political processes. The development of elaborate policymaking machinery within the long-dominant LDP is an example of such a concern. Party politicians and groups endeavored to make their own futures predictable and to convert conflict-laden political processes into orderly routines through formulation of a dense architecture of procedures supplemented at times by informal norms.

Bargained Democracy

Critics from the vertical school of Japanese politics have lamented the lack of responsible, alternating party government in Japan. Their ideas are based on a British model of democracy whereby parties compete on the basis of platforms, and electorates choose the party that best serves their interests from a menu of party manifestos. The winning party then takes over central government institutions and responsibly carries out its manifestos in Parliament and through administrative actions. In the British model, critical decisions about how a democratic country is run are made at the top of the political system.

In an alternative view of the nature of democracy politics is a much more decentralized process. Interests and policy choices are bargained over at many decision points in a political system, rather than being negotiated solely through the mechanism of alternating, responsible parties. Most modern democracies have a mixture of both versions of democracy, but there are also major differences between types of political systems. A main theme of this book will be Japan's tendency to be closer to the bargained than to the programmatic democracy model (see Chapter 10). Many of the shortcomings of the vertical approach reflect a failure to realize the importance of the bargained decentralized nature of Japanese politics.

The Political Setting

The analysis in this book of Japanese political processes is set within a specific political context. For this reason, it is important to keep broad features of the postwar political setting in mind.[14] The Pacific phase of World War II ended with Japan's surrender in August 1945. For the next seven years, Japan was occupied by Allied forces under the Supreme Commander Allied Powers representing the United States, Britain, and other countries from the winning wartime coalition. Japan returned to the status of independent power in 1952 after accepting the terms of a peace treaty that removed most of its former empire. Only the home islands of Honshu, Kyushu, Shikoku, and Hokkaido (and a handful of smaller islands) remained under Japanese control. During the postwar occupation, Japan gained a new, more democratic constitution that forbade the use of military force. Various aspects of the economy and society were also reformed in order to diminish the chances of Japan's once again becoming a military power.

The end of the war also left Japan militarily vulnerable in a world divided into opposing camps by enmities between countries that preferred capitalism or communism. Japan entered the postwar era as an ally of the capitalist world in the Cold War, partly by preference and partly as a prerequisite to gaining independence.

Japan in the 1950s was beset by many problems related to the economy after the war, as well as by the legacies of the occupation. Between 1952 and 1955, Japan was run, as it had been during much of the occupation, by a coalition government made up of conservative parties. Hard-liners in the coalition wanted Japan to amend its Constitution, rearm, and restore central government authority over education and the police. Others argued in favor of economic development, self-defense based on a limited military force, and a modest reversal of occupation-inspired education and police reforms. Later, one conservative prime minister, Nobusuke Kishi, took a hard line on constitutional reform and police duties but was unsuccessful.[15] Attempts at reversion were resisted in what were the largest demonstrations of the postwar era; the 1950s ended in turmoil for this reason. Meanwhile, already supported by big business, the newly formed LDP entered into social contracts with farmers and small-business owners that would last for most of the coming four decades.

In the 1950s economic and industrial planning also took firm hold. The iron and steel industry received government bank loans for technological improvements. The coal, shipping, and power industries received the most help from the government's development bank, because plans called for development of industries that produced basic goods and services needed throughout the economy. At the same time, Japan began to repair relations with the international community by signing a peace treaty with many of its wartime opponents, concluding a bilateral agreement (but not a peace treaty) with the Soviet Union, and joining the U.N. Security Council.

The 1960s was the main period of high economic growth, as well as political stability. Two LDP prime ministers, Hayato Ikeda and Eisaku Sato, both former bureaucrats, ran the country for the entire decade. Politics was touched at times by a smoldering disagreement between the LDP and the Socialist Party over the U.S.-Japan Security Treaty and general foreign policy, including differences over a treaty of peace with the Republic of Korea. But the domestic political situation was relatively quiescent. Business entrepreneurs also chafed at intervention by a strong bureaucracy, and attempts by the Ministry of International Trade and Industry to preserve its power over the economy were rebuffed in the Diet on three occasions.

By the end of the decade, however, Japan was showing two consequences of extremely rapid growth: crowded cities and pollution. Over six thousand civic groups were formed to protest local quality-of-life issues or local development of new industrial zones. The issues motivating these movements, combined with dramatic shifts in city populations to the suburbs and to prefectures neighboring the largest cities, produced a leftward trend in city government that lasted well into the 1970s. The advent of local progressive government in the big cities, in turn, helped promote more adequate public pensions and virtually free medical care for older people. A package of pollution control bills also passed the Diet in 1971. Meanwhile, two big increases in the price of imported petroleum resulted in very high inflation, slow growth, and recession. Public works outlays were used to combat recession and added to the costs of new welfare programs to force government budgets into deficit.

In 1972, Japan was successful in having the Ryukyu Islands (including Okinawa) revert to Japanese control after seventeen years as an American military enclave. An agreement to have diplomatic relations with the People's Republic of China was also signed in 1972, followed in 1976 by a peace treaty. In the same period, trade disputes with the United States and other countries blossomed as Japan's exports of automobiles and other products became successful in foreign markets.

Japan in the 1980s was concerned more than anything else with the high cost of governance and related government deficits. A much delayed effort at administrative reform finally gained momentum under Prime Minister Yasuhiro Nakasone (1982–87). When the reforms were completed, free medical care for older people had been abandoned in favor of a system of limited payments. Administrative reform also led to the privatization of several public corporations, including the Japan National Railways, Japan Air Lines, and the world's largest single telephone system, Nippon Telephone and Telegraph.

Trade problems with the United States continued. In addition, even the winding down of the Cold War failed to persuade the Soviet Union or its successors to cede to Japanese control a handful of islands off Hokkaido that Japan claimed as *terra irridenta*. The biggest political event of the 1980s was the discovery in 1988 that many leaders of the LDP had indirectly accepted bribes from the Recruit Company in exchange for political influence. The Recruit scandal rocked the LDP and led the incumbent LDP prime minister, Noboru Takeshita, to resign. A subsequent mini-scandal forced Takeshita's immediate successor to resign, too, after only one month in office. A second major corruption scandal engulfed the LDP only four years later. Although the conservative party had been involved in scandals almost continually from the 1950s, the double scandals of 1988 and 1992 severely weakened it and led to widespread demands for reform. Conditions worsened when the party kingpin, Shin Kanemaru, was arrested and a fortune in gold bars was discovered in his home. Kanemaru's imprisonment removed the most capable political manipulator from the party while further damaging its reputation. Only a few months later a group from the Takeshita faction of the LDP left the party, forcing an end to LDP government in July 1993. Before the general election in 1993 the LDP held 275 seats. Party strengths in the House of Representatives after the election were as follows: LDP, 226 seats; SDPJ, 69; Renewal Party, 56; Clean Government Party, 52; Japan New Party, 37; Japan Communist Party, 15; Democratic Socialist Party, 15; and Harbinger Party, 13.

2

Political Culture and Electoral Behavior

One political party, the Liberal Democratic Party, dominated Japanese politics from 1955 until 1993. The LDP won a majority or plurality of the votes in national elections, and it maintained a majority in the House of Representatives until the 1993 general election. Among parties in industrialized countries since World War II, the LDP's record has been matched for longevity and system dominance only by parties in Italy, Norway, and Sweden.

The LDP is heir to a long tradition of conservative rule in Japan, having assumed the mantle of a conservative movement that dominated prewar politics. Conservative parties won most national elections even before the formation of the LDP in 1955, and conservatives or conservative independents have dominated most local elections since the war. Even the sudden success of three new conservative parties in the July 1993 general election extended the hegemony of the conservative movement, though at the expense of the LDP's continuation in power.

Voting in postwar elections has been remarkably stable on the whole. In most periods, interelection shifts in party support were fairly small. Voting patterns sometimes appeared frozen. Even at the individual level, where variation is often greater than that shown by aggregate election statistics, electoral choices were typically consistent for most voters.

Stability was the rule, but there have been some major exceptions. In the early 1970s the vote in large cities and their rapidly growing suburbs changed dramatically. The LDP also suffered sudden huge losses in national elections in 1989 and 1993. To explain both the long-term stability and the sudden change I consider four voting theories drawn from Japanese and foreign experience. I look at the effects of (1) occupational interests, (2) values, (3) psychological loyalties, and (4) mobilization of votes by candidate machines and labor unions. Each factor is relevant to Japanese electoral behavior. With certain qualifications, mobilization explanations are the most persuasive for most voters, although their effects are the hardest to document.

Whether a vertical or a horizontal model of Japanese politics best fits electoral campaigns and behavior is also important. Although Japan's acquaintance with elections dates to 1890, universal franchise for males did not come until 1925, and women were disenfranchised until 1946. Historically speaking, experience with the full franchise is relatively recent. In addition, accounts of prewar elections indicate that voting was often manipulated by local social elites.

Under a vertical model, electoral choices since the war would be similarly based on voters' deference to social elites or to voters' vulnerability to manipulation and their uncritical allegiance to community norms invoking support of a specific candidate. Under a horizontal model, elections would be seen as an exchange of voting support for representation of voter interests. Under a vertical interpretation, we would stress that during LDP rule Japan was dominated by one unified voting bloc. In other words, winning elections gave the LDP the power to single-handedly run the country. Under a horizontal model, we would look beyond national patterns to see whether election institutions and the organization of society in general resulted in decentralized party power. Because of the importance of discovering which view of electoral performance best fits Japan over the long run, most of this chapter deals with elections during the era of LDP hegemony. At the end of the chapter I will speculate about what the patterns during LDP rule suggest for the future.

Voting in national parliamentary elections exemplifies trends throughout Japanese electoral politics. The Liberal Democratic Party and other conservative parties were the main force in elections to the House of Representatives from the end of the war to 1990, as we can see in Table 2.1. Conservative support was divided between several parties before 1955. After the formation of the LDP that year, the LDP was successful until recent losses in the House of Representatives election in 1993, as well as the House of Councillors election four years earlier. The LDP's fortunes did, however, slowly decrease from the 1950s to the mid-1970s, with the result that the LDP and the parties opposed to it were nearly equal in the house in 1976–80, 1983–86, and after 1990. At

Table 2.1. *House of Representatives Elections, 1946–1990*

	Liberal Democrats	Social Democrats	Japan Communists	Democratic Socialists	Clean Government Party	Minor Parties/ Independents	Tc
1946	43%*	18%*	4%			35%	10
1947	52*	26*	4			18	10
1949	50*	16*	10			24	10
1952	66*	22*	3			9	10
1953	56*	28*	2			14	10
1955	63*	30*	2			5	10
1958	58	33*	3			6	10
1960	58	28	3	9		2	10
1963	55	28	4	7		6	10
1967	49	21	5	7	5	13	10
1969	48	21	7	8	11	5	10
1972	47	22	10	7	8	6	10
1976	46*	21*	10	6	11	6	10
1979	48*	20*	10	7	10	5	10
1980	51*	20*	10	7	9	3	10
1983	48*	20*	9	7	10	6	10
1986	51*	18*	9	6	9	7	10
1990	46	25*	9	5	8	7	10

Source: Data from Jichisho, Senkyobu, *Shugiin Giin Sosenkyo, Saiko Saibansho Saibankan Kokumin C* *Kekka Shirabe* (Tokyo, 1990).

Notes: Figures are percentages of the total vote. Blanks mean that parties did not have candidates in relevant election. The Democratic Socialist Party was formed in 1959 and fielded candidates in the follow year. Clean Government Party candidates contested national elections only beginning in 1967.

*Before 1955 the Liberal Democratic Party figure is based on votes for all conservative parties; the then Ja Socialist Party was split into two wings. From 1976 until 1983 New Liberal Club votes are included under LDP, and from 1979 on, Shaminren (Social Democratic League) votes are included under the Social De cratic Party.

other times in the 1970s and 1980s the LDP gained a few more seats. Today the LDP remains the largest political party despite its loss of majority status. If support for three recently formed conservative parties — Japan New Party, Renewal Party, and Harbinger Party — is added to the support for the LDP, we can say that conservatism remains the dominant force in Japanese elections. Two of the three parties are now part of an even more recently created New Frontier Party, which combines former elements of the moderate-to-conservative LDP with two former moderate centrist groups, the Clean Government and Democratic Socialist Parties.

Electoral change was, for the most part, modestly incremental. Unlike in Spain in 1982, Denmark in 1971–73, and Britain in 1974, change came slowly in Japan. Declines in the conservative vote in the 1950s and 1960s were small, not gigantic. A shaky stability characterized conservative voting in the 1970s and the 1980s.[1] How voting can be stable for so long and then suddenly change, as in the 1989 and 1993 elections, defies normal explanations of voting behavior.

In addition to a slow decline in the proportion of the vote going to the LDP in 1963–76, there were also some shifts in electoral support within the opposition camp. The Japanese Socialist Party (now the Social Democratic Party of Japan), which was expected to eventually gain power on the basis of trends in the 1950s, lost support after the mid-1960s. Socialist losses were matched by gains in Communist support and the appearance of a new party, the Clean Government Party. Henceforth, support for both the LDP and the opposition parties was stable with only occasional exceptions. The changes in opposition party voting patterns, however, meant that Japan had a larger and more balanced party system after 1969–72 than before.[2]

Elections are held for both houses of the national parliament, or Diet; governors and legislatures of prefectures; and city, town, and village mayors and assemblies. Elections for the House of Representatives take place every four years but can occur more frequently if the house is dissolved by the emperor upon the advice of a sitting prime minister. Until 1994 lower house elections took place in multimember districts (there was one single-member district). Constituencies in multimember districts had from two to six members to represent them, even though in amount of territory the districts were much smaller than most U.S. congressional districts. Each voter had just one vote. To win an election, a candidate had to have enough total votes to place in one of the top two, top three, top four, top five, or top six positions, depending on constituency size. The LDP ran more than one candidate in many multimember districts; other parties normally had only one nominee. Many of the 252 members of the upper house are elected in single-member "local" districts, but there are also some multimember local districts. There is also a nationwide constituency: 100 of the 252 seats are allocated to parties in this constituency on the basis of proportional representation. Like U.S. Senators, Councillors are elected for staggered six-year terms. Most of the districts are based on prefectures, which are intermediate-sized government units resembling U.S. and German states. Because elections for Councillors are held every three years, 76 prefectural seats and 50 national district seats must be filled at each election.

In 1994 the lower house electoral system was changed. Now there are 300 fairly small single-member districts; 200 additional seats are filled by proportional representation from regional multimember electoral constituencies. The changes were part of a political reform package proposed after several major corruption scandals. The feeling was widespread that competition between LDP candidates in multimember districts contributed to corruption by causing candidates to spend a great deal of money on wooing constituency support. Many people also felt that competition between candidates from the same party encouraged factionalism, which was also expensive. In addition to addressing these issues, electoral reform sought to reduce overrepresentation of the rural population, a longtime bastion of LDP support, by adjusting election institutions to better reflect the growth in urban electorates.

Societal Cleavages as Sources of Stability

The cleavage theory is the most venerable of the explanations for stable voting in industrialized societies. Sociologists define cleavages as deep, often societywide sociopolitical divisions that reflect the interests of people in particular social groupings. In the past, the main cleavages affecting voting have been class, religion, language and ethnicity, and region.[3] Even though Japan is more homogeneous than most countries where sociopolitical cleavages have been important, looking at Japan from the perspective of cleavage theory may provide insight into important aspects of Japanese elections. Occupational class, in particular, seems a likely candidate to be the basis of a sociopolitical cleavage.

Japan is a highly industrialized nation with many of the characteristics that would seem to favor the emergence of a "normal" class-based political cleavage. Occupations and other bases for class distinctions are as fully differentiated in Japan as in any industrialized society. Working-class and farmer-labor movements have existed for several decades, and working-class parties have been able to contest elections freely since 1945. There has also been a great deal of working-class rhetoric to stimulate class consciousness. Other things being equal, we would expect people in the middle class to vote for conservative parties — the LDP between 1955 and 1993 and the LDP and the New Frontier Party at present — and people in the working class to vote for Socialist or Communist parties.

Table 2.2 shows political preferences among Japanese voters in four major occupational groups: farmers, small-business owners, salaried workers, and manual laborers. Farmers and small-business owners make up the petit bourgeois component of the middle class.[4] They are property owners or managers of enterprises and could be expected to support conservative parties because le 2.2. *Party Support Within Different Occupational Groups, 1969–1990*

	1969	1972	1976	1980	1983	1986	1990
			Farmers				
eral Democrats	69%	71%	69%	80%	65%	85%	71%
al Democrats	3	7	9	4	5	5	15
n Communists		1		1	1	1	
ocratic Socialists	1	1	1	1	1	1	1
n Government Party	1	1	2	2	2		
er	8	2	5	2		1	
e / Don't Know	18	17	14	10	26	7	13
Total	100%	100%	100%	100%	100%	100%	100%
			Small-Business Owners				
ral Democrats	57%	59%	56%	57%	54%	62%	65%
al Democrats	10	10	8	9	5	4	9
n Communists	3	6	8	3	3	1	2
ocratic Socialists	4	1	2	3	4	1	1
n Government Party	3	3	3	5	4	4	4
er	4	5	3	2	1		
e / Don't Know	19	16	20	21	29	28	18
Total	100%	100%	100%	100%	100%	100%	99%
			Salaried Employees				
ral Democrats	25%	24%	22%	27%	26%	29%	33%
al Democrats	29	29	28	22	13	14	22
n Communists	4	8	3	3	4	2	4
ocratic Socialists	7	5	5	5	7	2	3
n Government Party	3	3	3	5	4	4	3
er	7	8	11	5	2		
e / Don't Know	25	23	28	33	44	49	35
Total	100%	100%	100%	100%	100%	100%	100%
			Manual Workers				
ral Democrats	23%	23%	28%	31%	26%	38%	31%
al Democrats	27	31	23	20	13	15	25
n Communists	3	6	5	3	4	2	4
ocratic Socialists	4	2	5	7	5	8	3
n Government Party	8	4	8	5	7	5	6
er	6	8	7		6	1	
e / Don't Know	29	26	24	35	39	31	32
Total	100%	100%	100%	101%	100%	100%	101%
N	2,461	2,468	2,371	2,427	2,342	2,372	2,269

ce: Akarui Senkyo Suishin Kyokai, *Shugiin Giin Sosenkyo no Jittai* (various years). The Akarui Senkyo Suishin ai (League for the Advancement of Clean Elections) is one of two groups subsidized by Japanese election authori- o monitor public attitudes toward elections. The other was the Komei Senkyo Remmei (Clean Election League).

s: All figures are percentages of the total sample. The LDP is a middle-class party; the Social Democratic, ocratic Socialist, and Japan Communist parties are nominally working-class parties. Information on the 1979 al election was omitted to avoid redundancy.

of their concern for private property and low taxes. In addition, farmers and small business owners, because they are self-employed, have no managers or supervisors. In other countries, these conditions are associated with conservative party support.[5]

Because salaried employees are often homeowners and sometimes have more education than blue-collar workers, they are usually considered members of the middle class. Although they are still subject to the authority of managers and supervisors, they would be expected to have middle-class concerns otherwise. Blue-collar workers have lower social status in most societies than salaried employees, are subordinate to managers at their place of work, and are often uncertain of continued employment. According to class theories of the vote, both their subjugation to authority and their economic vulnerability mean that we should expect them to prefer working-class parties, such as the Social Democratic, Communist, and Democratic Socialist Parties.

The electoral preferences of Japanese occupational groups fit class explanations of voting in some cases but not others. Farmers and small business owners were generally stably aligned with the Liberal Democratic Party or other conservative parties in the 1960s, 1970s, and 1980s. On the surface, this alignment suggests a propensity to vote for many of the same reasons as small bourgeois elsewhere.[6] For the moment, let us say that the farm and small-business vote seems to be anchored by economic interests much like those of middle-class Europeans.

But the relevance of a class cleavage explanation for voting in Japan disappears in the face of the partisan propensities of other large occupational groups. Until 1986 salaried workers supported centrist or left-wing parties more than conservative parties. Since "deviant" voting has existed among salaried workers in Japan as far back as the 1950s, other causes for these middle-class voters' support for working-class parties must be sought. Much the same contradiction exists for the many working-class voters who have increasingly supported the conservative movement (see Table 2.2).

Although we would expect social class to explain voting patterns in Japan, the partisan preferences of manual workers and salaried employees fly in the face of traditional theory. Factors that differentiate Japan from European countries have intervened, keeping a full-scale class cleavage from developing there. An egalitarian system of education and similarly egalitarian military conscription policies have existed in Japan since the late nineteenth century, so social inequalities found in Europe until World War I (and sometimes even later) did not exist in the same degree in Japan. In addition, sporadic suppression of the prewar labor movement, as well as the widespread incidence of company unions, have in some cases inhibited worker class consciousness and mobilization.[7] The cumulative effect of these experiences, plus somewhat unusual patterns of union mobilization, underlie the cross-cutting alignments of salaried and manual workers. If social class theory i for Japan, it applies only to farmers, some managers, and small busi ers, whose interests have in fact been strongly defended by the conservative movement. Manual workers and salaried employees in Japan do not fit class theory very well. Japan has voting based on economic interests but lacks a two-sided cleavage that might more solidly unite farmers and small business owners against a common class enemy.

Contemporary Japan also lacks other kinds of traditional sociopolitical cleavages. There is a sect-based party, Komeito, or the Clean Government Party. But the presence of this party does not indicate that broad religious cleavages are present in Japan. Nor does it indicate that religion is important to most Japanese. Buddhist sects clashed in the past but coexist peacefully today. Few Japanese are devout, and religious groups are not divided in half by a profound cleavage as between Protestants and Catholics or between Catholics and secularists in Austria, Germany, the Netherlands, Belgium, and Italy.[8] Although the Clean Government Party is an outgrowth of a religious movement, the party is not an expression of a nationally prominent religious cleavage. Japan also lacks the regional or ethnolinguistic diversity that motivates party loyalties in Spain, Belgium, and other places. There is a small Korean minority, whose members account for less than 1 percent of the population, a few hundred thousand immigrant workers, and a very small group with ties to an indigenous native group, the Ainu. Generally, then, Japan is a linguistically, ethnically, and regionally homogeneous country of largely secular persons.

Outside of the choices of farmers and small business owners, voting in Japan bears little resemblance to the predictions of social cleavage theory. Rather than having distinct links with broadly felt social cleavages, the demographic anchoring of the vote in Japan, though stable, seems to depend on other kinds of mobilization. As Joji Watanuki puts it:

> The relationship between social structure and voting in Japan across the postwar era has not been a clear-cut one. . . . Neither the British-style class voting nor the American-style socio-economic status voting exists in Japan. Instead, different kinds of broad occupation categories — self-employed vs. employee status, type of industry, enterprise size, and the types of organization tied in with a given occupation . . . are the important social structural predictors of the vote in Japan. Rather than a social cleavage model, Japanese voting behavior fits more of a mosaic or matrix pattern."[9]

In the 1960s, Watanuki proposed that Japanese voting patterns could be explained by the existence of a value cleavage between persons holding traditional cultural outlooks and those holding more modern views.[10] People subscribing to traditional values would tend to vote for conservative parties, whereas people with modern orientations would prefer left-wing or so-called progressive parties. In Watanuki's view, the value cleavage between the masses echoed a cleavage between conservative leaders who supported prewar political arrangements (that is, reinstatement of rule by the emperor) and opposition party leaders who strongly supported the postwar constitution (that is, rule by prime minister and Diet). Many conservatives, for example, abhorred leftist movements and viewed the polity in holistic or consensual terms, as is set forth in the 1956 Platform of the LDP: "The LDP is not a class party inviting internal schism . . . but a political party . . . that serves the interests and happiness of the people as a whole. . . . The LDP rejects the political doctrine of strife and destruction. . . . Based on the spirit of cooperation and construction . . . [it] seeks to eradicate evils while preserving just traditions and political order."

The value cleavage of the 1950s was represented in real-world preferences and concerns as well as in rhetoric and symbols. Many early postwar conservative leaders wanted to return to the prewar constitutional arrangements whereby the emperor was the head of state and the upper house of the parliament was an appointed body. Opposition party leaders and many opposition party followers, in contrast, were adamant opponents of these "reversionist" tendencies. For them a return to prewar political institutions would have meant a loss of the right for labor to organize autonomously, not to mention abandonment of other postwar constitutional prerogatives.

The concentration of support for the early conservative movement and later for the LDP in the rural bastions of conservative values added to Watanuki's impression that values were in some fashion intimately related to partisan preferences. Watanuki's cultural conflict model also fit the political and value preferences of the many people in the cities who preferred the postwar opposition parties.

After Watanuki put forward his value cleavage hypothesis, Scott Flanagan pursued the value interpretation of Japanese voting in a series of rich analyses.[11] Using people's responses to questions about obligation for favors, deference to superiors in the social hierarchy, and conformity to group norms, Flanagan has shown that partisan preferences correlate with value differences in quite a few cases. A values matrix explains roughly 15 percent of leftist voting, according to the most recent of his analyses, published in 1991. Flanagan's research also shows healthy correlations between "1955 issue positions" and values. He views value change as an explanation for shifts in party support since the war, although both he and Watanuki observe that the effects of the value cleavage have declined over time.

Watanuki intended the value cleavage as a Japanese equivalent to European-style social cleavages (which had a clear value component), but it is unclear how directly traditional and modern values have influenced voting for ordinary people. Values may help explain the substantial opposition party vote in urban areas, especially in the 1950s and 1960s, when urban dwellers felt self-consciously modern compared with their country cousins. But other factors — like union mobilization and the absence of close ties between conservative candidates and urban commuters — also encouraged urban opposition party support. And many explanations for rural conservatism do not depend on values. It is hard to identify a specific link between values and political behavior unless values are seen as a *barrier* to voting for some parties. Rural voters would probably seldom vote for a Communist, and to urban voters, conservative politicians who hail from farming areas look as out of place in the Diet as Mississippi good old boys look to Northern urbanites in the United States.

Nor does rural subscription to traditional values explain why Socialist and occasionally other opposition party candidates have always been successful in what otherwise appear to be traditional parts of the country. After the 1990 election, for example, 54 of Japan's 58 predominantly agricultural lower house districts were represented by Social Democrats.[12] Some of the Social Democrats were ostensibly elected because of their support for popular local issues and movements.[13] Others were endorsed by unions of schoolteachers and local civil servants or came from districts where progressive farm movements were well established. But these explanations seem inadequate to account for two out of three rural constituencies supporting at least one Socialist.

There is also ambiguity in the values data. Japan is culturally a more complex society than the values approach acknowledges. According to a forty-year series of surveys of Japan's "national character," endorsement of some values, such as a sense of obligation and a desire to continue the family name by adoption of a male heir (*yoshi*), has dwindled since the 1950s. In the early years after the war these were majoritarian values, but now they are the choices of only small minorities. In contrast, other value preferences, such as a desire for paternalistic managers, have hardly changed at all and remain majoritarian preferences by a substantial margin. Several kinds of feelings of interpersonal obligation have, in fact, shown a slight gain in support. Some elements of popular culture have received steady support ever since the war while other cultural norms have changed radically.[14] For values to be a useful explanation for party choice, an anchor for the vote, or a source of systematic change, value preferences should be more consistent and systematic across groups than is the case.[15] Alternatively it must be shown why some selected values count more than others politically. Other sources for stable voting patterns within the social mosaic must be sought.

Voter Psychology and Elections

In the United States political behaviorists have preferred a psychological to a sociological explanation of voting and therefore use survey questions to understand attitudes and motivations. Because parties were traditionally the most important and durable of the electoral objects to which people reacted, psychological partnership (called party identification) was and is the central concept of the psychological school.[16] Party identification has also been seen as driving European voting.[17] Although researchers have increasingly recognized the complexity of attitude-behavior linkages, party identification remains at the core of explanations of voters' preferences over time.

As originally formulated, party identification was expected to be inherited from one's parents and to remain stable throughout most of one's life span. Party identification was also expected to influence the direction of attitudes toward other electoral objects, such as candidates and election issues. Even though people could legitimately be swayed by these short-term phenomena while still preserving their traditional party ties, generally they stayed with the party with which they grew up. One reason for this persistence was the high emotional component of party identification. Partisanship was an affectively anchored loyalty and a lasting element of personal identity. Voting for the same party over many elections should actually strengthen identification with that party, barring other influences.[18]

The qualities of party identification make it a logical candidate to explain stable voting in Japan. In surveys in the 1960s and 1970s roughly two out of three Japanese indicated support for a party in response to American-style partisanship questions. Beyond this superficial fit, the picture for Japanese partisan loyalties was not very optimistic. The overall proportions of people identifying with a party have been among the lowest anywhere. The proportion of partisans self-identified as strong is also lower in Japan.[19] Most important of all, Japanese party attachments are less stable than those of partisans elsewhere. Only 59 percent of people identifying themselves as partisan reported the same partisan identity after one month, according to one study.[20] The figure for stable party identification was an even lower 54 percent in an adult sample interviewed over a longer period.[21] In both cases the Japanese figures were lower than comparable figures from the United States and Britain, even though the time between survey interviews was longer in the other countries.[22] Japanese psychological partisanship is clearly less stable than party loyalties in other advanced countries.

So far party identification does not seem to be a very good explanation of voting stability in Japan. Roughly half the population appear to be anchored in some way by party ties. But party attachments are seldom very intense, nor are they as stable as attachments in other known cases. If traditional partisanship theory applied to Japan, partisans could be expected to deviate in their vote decisions fairly frequently. With certain exceptions, however, that does not seem to be true. Many Japanese vote stably most of the time, perhaps because election issues do not stimulate them enough to deviate from what is otherwise mainly a habit.[23]

Initially, party identification theory was concerned with only the American setting. Scant attention was paid to the effects of general political culture on party loyalties.[24] Political culture refers to people's general attitudes toward the national political system and their own roles therein. Later research found that distinct political cultures were associated with different patterns in partisanship. French voters, for example, were both antipartisan and less prone than Americans to discuss politics within the parental home. Both conditions inhibited the development of party identifications among French adults in the early years after World War II.[25] Political culture was found to affect even how American partisans behave. A weakening of partisanship starting in the 1970s was linked to growing cynicism in the political culture after the Watergate scandal.[26]

Political culture is potentially very important to the nature of Japanese partisanship. Japanese voters, especially those living in large cities, are profoundly alienated from national politics. Surveys indicate that voters in Japan are less satisfied and less trusting regarding politics and politicians than their counterparts in most other democracies (Table 2.3). Only Italy has consistently matched or exceeded Japanese levels of distrust.[27] Investigations of youths' attitudes on political representation in various countries tell a similar story. In most cases, popular support for Japanese prime ministers and their cabinets has also been lower than ratings of governments in other countries.[28]

There are three plausible reasons for high levels of alienation toward national politics in Japan. The first is cultural. Alienation from remote political arenas and actors reflects a cultural preference for parochial relationships. Ordinary voters usually trust Dietmembers representing their local constituency but distrust national politicians.[29] Second, although most Japanese feel that the performance of national politicians is unsatisfactory (see Table 2.3),

Table 2.3. Japanese Political Culture in International Comparison

	Germany	France	Britain	United States	Japan
International Values Study, 1987–88					
Politics is important	40%	23%	26%	46%	54%
Leave politics to leaders	8	38	13	7	13
Interest in politics	50	39	51	69	56
Ideologically neutral	33	38	43	38	42
Satisfied with democracy	71	52	68	88	31
Political Action and Japan Studies, 1970s					
Trust in politics	69%		45%	31%	27%
Personal efficacy	27		37	59	29
Interest in politics	63		45	69	49
Affective neutrality	16		18	14	43

Sources: Tokei Suri Kenkyujo, *Ishiki no Kokusai Hikaku Hohoron no Kenkyu* (Tokyo, 1991), pp. 312–35; and 1976 Japanese House of Representatives election codebook available from the author and Political Action Study codebook available from the Inter-University Consortium for Political and Social Research archive at the University of Michigan.

Note: Figures are percentages of the total number of respondents agreeing with the statement or fitting the category. Italy is not included because of incomplete data.

supporters of traditional opposition parties have been disproportionately alienated. Their rejection of national affairs reflects frustration at their parties' seemingly permanent minority status.

Political alienation in Japan also reflects the prevalence of corruption scandals in national politics. Japan has experienced major corruption scandals intermittently since the war. Because these corruption episodes have involved LDP leaders more than opposition party leaders, the tendency for opposition supporters to feel more alienation than LDP supporters is intensified.

Weak and often marginal party identifications directly correlate with the alienated nature of Japanese political culture. One out of four adults who are not satisfied with politics lacks a party tie. Low political satisfaction also correlates with the most passive kinds of party loyalty.[30] The prevailing pessimistic mood of political culture also presumably influences party loyalties and the effects of loyalties on behavior in less directly measurable ways.

In addition to widespread cynicism about and dissatisfaction with national politics, many Japanese are emotionally neutral toward politics generally. In answer to thermometer questions — which ask respondents whether they feel hot, neutral or cool about something—more Japanese say that they feel neutral or don't know when asked about likes and dislikes of political leaders, major social groups, and political parties than do people in any other industrialized democracy (see Table 2.3). This tendency toward "affective neutrality" adds to the weakness of Japanese partisanship.

The weakness of partisanship in general and of its emotional component in particular suggests that some other attitude explains why Japanese vote habitually for the same party. One of the strongest predictors of the partisan vote in Japan until recently was whether people felt that the LDP was capable of governing Japan. This kind of attitude is called a party image. Other party images also correlate closely with partisanship in Japan.[31] Japanese partisanship is therefore more a cognitive evaluation than an affective tie. As a cognitively buttressed attitude, Japanese-style partisanship is a less secure anchor than an emotional commitment (like party identification) would be, even though it is obviously relevant to behavior.[32]

A second factor giving Japanese partisanship a cognitive nuance, at least until 1993, was the tendency of supporters of different parties to differ on certain quasi-ideological issues. Here ideology does not mean the familiar left-right concerns of electorates where competition between middle-class and working-class parties has been the central feature of political life. Rather, it has to do with deeply rooted attitudes regarding the postwar constitution and the use of military power.

The conservative camp and its progressive opposition were intensely divided in the early postwar years over whether to retain the constitution imposed by the occupying Allied powers. Some, but not all, conservatives favored development of military forces and, for this reason, urged constitutional revision: Article 9 of the postwar constitution forbade the use of force as an instrument of Japanese foreign policy, as well as denied Japan the right to possess armed forces.[33] The opposition parties, on the other hand, opposed constitutional change. The constitution granted labor unions the right to organize, which created a large base of support for the Socialist parties and which was deemed desirable on grounds of principle. Therefore, a preference for the postwar constitutional system, along with rejection of possessing military forces, became enshrined as opposition ideology. Rejection of a military alliance between Japan and the United States (allegedly the strongest and most influential purveyor of imperialism after the war) was another natural component of the leftist version of postwar ideology. The quasi-ideological rift was a strong component of party support in the 1950s. Partisan voters continued to divide along the same line in the 1970s and later, even though other issues were by then more salient.[34]

In summary, many Japanese are weak partisans or intermittent identifiers — not the type of voter expected where electoral patterns are normally stable. What actually happens is that people who identify weakly with a party, as well as those who waver, are often habitual voters. They are not sufficiently tied to a party to register as stable or strong partisans, but their regular votes for the party indicate a tentative party attachment.[35] Although the weakness and marginal character of party identification is very important, a partisan inertia has been typical in the Japanese setting.[36] To some degree, inertial voting during the period of LDP dominance was driven by cognitive rationales, including an appreciation of the LDP's competence to govern. But psychological structures are basically weak, so voters wandered when interest groups defected on major issues in 1989 and over the corruption scandals in 1993. That party ties are simply not very strong does not usually matter, because of habitual voting, but in high-profile elections, weak partisanship makes volatile voting possible.[37]

Mobilization and the Vote

To complete a picture of electoral motivation in Japan requires attention to voter mobilization. Efforts by electoral machines and unions to get out the vote for a particular candidate or party has helped make Japanese voting stable, even though interests and partisanship have also motivated voters.

Most Japanese have been exposed to candidates' electoral machines or related networks. Electoral machines consisting of locally influential people, local interest groups, and voters have existed in cities and small towns, as well as in the countryside, much of the time since the war.[38] Secondary organizations, especially labor unions, farm cooperatives, and small business owners' associations (including associations of shopkeepers), have also been part of candidate electoral networks, much as they have been linked with party organizations in Europe. Mobilization — the active seeking out of votes through personal ties or organizational memberships — has played a very big role in postwar election campaigns in Japan and will likely continue to do so.

A typical candidate's machine is a coalition of local social and political elites.[39] In rural areas, the usual coalition includes town assembly members, heads of farm or fishery cooperatives, and officers of other local groups, like voluntary firefighters. Hamlet heads might also be included. Sometimes the electoral organizations of prefectural and local assembly members have been used by parliamentary candidates to augment their own organizational strength. In some cases, a Dietmember's machine might even piggyback on a prefectural assembly member's electoral coalition.

Normally a candidate's electoral machine focuses on one geographical part of a constituency and consists at the most of a couple of hundred local leaders, but larger groups are sometimes seen. There were 315 municipal assemblymen, 26 mayors, and 11 prefectural assemblymen affiliated with Kakuei Tanaka's famous Etsuzankai organization in Niigata's third district.[40]

Most candidate machines have a formally organized component, a supporters' association, or *koenkai,* whose members are ordinary voters and whose staff are local social or political elites. In the past, supporters' associations were found more in cities than in rural areas, reflecting, among other things, the lower density of "natural" social relationships in urban areas available to politicians for use at election time.[41] Nowadays supporter associations have penetrated the countryside as well. One national newspaper reported in 1989 that forty million Japanese voters were enrolled in such associations, over half the electorate and roughly ten times as many as the number of members claimed by the LDP.[42]

Candidates' local machines have engaged in a variety of activities to maintain voter loyalty. National politicians appear regularly at local school athletic days, shrine festivals, and meetings of local interest groups. Local and national politicians respond to solicitations from communities and local groups to help support local events. Even after major corruption scandals in the late 1980s threatened many politicians' normal funding sources, incumbent Dietmembers were still making donations to support local festivals and other special events.[43]

The extent to which national politicians give money or some kind of token presents at election time in exchange for voting support, another typical practice, has never been known precisely, but it is believed to be widespread. My own interviews with local assemblymen indicate that politicians give more gifts at the time of their first candidacy than later, when they are better known and have established a record of representing their constituency. According to recent newspaper accounts, however, most incumbents still send presents to newly married couples and make donations at funerals when these events involve their supporters. Many Dietmembers hold parties for their most loyal supporters, and some pay most of the costs of trips to hot spring resorts for members of their supporters' association. One well-known national LDP politician owned a small fleet of buses to ferry supporters to hot springs in nearby districts.

Examples of the expenditures of an LDP and SDPJ Dietmember for mailings and various kinds of constituency gifts and donations were listed in a recent Japanese newspaper article.[44] The figures reported by both politicians total over $100,000, even in a year when no election was held. Roughly a third of their expenditures were for postage, and the costs of support association activities took another 20 percent. The remaining 50 percent was spent on donations to local groups for support of local events or on gifts to individuals in the form of wedding and funeral remembrances. Condolence offerings at funerals of supporters typically cost the Dietmember between $17 and $36 each time. Seventy dollars was a typical donation to the sponsors of a local event. According to the same report, a more senior LDP Dietmember was said to give condolence gifts costing as much as $140 and gifts at weddings costing as much as $210. These donations are made to demonstrate concern and feelings of obligation on the Dietmember's part in exchange for the favor of the voter's support. The costs to a junior and the costs to a senior member of parliament differ because persons of higher status must make gifts worthy of their position (a feeling undoubtedly espoused by followers, who expect to share in the success of their patron). A senior politician commented on the importance of gifts and donations to electoral mobilization: "One does not have to go to wedding receptions in person . . . but, in the case of funerals, it's good to go in person or have a representative there. If you forget them, there is no future for you. There have been incidents [after I failed to attend a funeral] when people said, 'There was nothing from you,' and then left my supporters' association."[45]

Some Dietmembers are renowned for their largesse. The last event held by Kakuei Tanaka's Etsuzankai was a weekend trip for eleven thousand people to Nukumi hot springs, in Yamagata prefecture, at a reported cost of 1.4 million dollars.[46] Another politician was said to sponsor three-day trips to Ise shrine for his supporters. As one Kanagawa Dietmember confided to me in an interview, "Personality is judged by how one observes the ordinary ways of the world." The ways of the world are costly for many politicians.

Frequent gifts and heavily subsidized trips are a Dietmember's way of demonstrating personal consideration and concern for supporters. Another way to demonstrate personal attention is by sending greeting cards. This is a common practice and also explains a large item for postage in the Dietmembers' accounts. Greetings are sent at New Year's and also in midsummer during the *chugen* season, a Buddhist time of remembrance. Even Dietmembers who travel abroad are expected to send greeting cards to their followers. Sometimes these number in the thousands.

The activities and expenditures for constituents help preserve the integrity of the electoral base of candidates and Dietmembers. Ordinary voters also gain the satisfaction of being recognized by an important person. Their vote is a commodity exchanged for psychological or material benefit. Evidence on politicians' use of financial largesse to woo constituents thus suggests that a vertical model of election mobilization applies to Japan. In this view, people of superior status cultivate support with displays of money and concern, which convince voters that the donor is a responsible person who observes the norms of Japanese culture regarding obligation and downward loyalty.

Another important part of securing a local base of support is representation of local interests, both those tied to a specific place and those tied to the occupations of the people who live there. Tanaka's Etsuzankai is an excellent example. Provision of public works projects in every corner of Tanaka's Niigata district was one of the reasons for his enormous electoral success. Some of the more costly and unusual projects captured national attention and became legendary. Construction of expressways and high-speed train lines with connections or station stops at rural towns, the provision of hot water systems in village streets to facilitate automatic snow removal, and linkage of an isolated town by tunnel to a prefectural road so that its residents could go out to work in the winter were among the better known of Tanaka's constituency projects.

Such efforts by Tanaka did more than just address local people's desire for improved public services and transportation. They also provided business for construction companies and jobs for construction workers. Nationally, substantial portions of the annual general account budget have been spent on local public works to shore up Dietmembers' reputations and develop the public infrastructure. In 1955 the portion spent on public works was 14 percent, in 1965 it ballooned to 22 percent, and in the mid-1980s the amount was still a hefty 13 percent. Public largesse in Tanaka's Niigata district helped Niigata prefecture move to first place nationally in per capita government expenditures for public works in 1983.[47] In the budget expenditures there are thus strong elements of a horizontal model of behavior as well.

According to Japanese survey results, at least one in every two voters has some direct contact with candidate-led campaigns. A slightly smaller percentage of the public say that they vote on the basis of the "qualities of the candidate" rather than "political party." Votes for candidate rather than party have been important to all parties; they have been especially important from the population groups most stably attached to the LDP and the conservative movement, such as farmers and medium- and small-business persons.

Candidate-centered campaigns depend heavily on face-to-face contacts between candidates (or their lieutenants) and their followers. From a voter's point of view, the most common form of candidate contact is by telephone. Making visits to people's homes to solicit votes has been outlawed in Japan for some time, in part because visits were often accompanied by a gift of cash or some other token present to indicate a candidate's appreciation of the favor of a vote. In contrast, telephoned requests for support are legal and are reported by as much as 41 percent of the public (Table 2.4.). According to 1990 data, other modes of informal personal contact included, in descending order of frequency, recommendations from friends and relatives (19 percent), requests from persons "interested" in the election (a euphemism for campaign workers, reported by 18 percent of respondents), and membership in supporters' associations (16 percent). Many of these contacts are likely made through home visits despite their illegal status. In spite of a widespread impression that the Liberal Democratic Party engaged in various kinds of vote mobilization more than other parties did, this was not true. For example, in 1990 it was Social Democratic voters who reported the most kinds of exposure to party efforts at mobilization, and, in any case, the overall variation between parties was not very great.

Campaign activities of community organizations, interest groups, and candidates' own support organizations reach even larger audiences. In the 1990 general election, 25 percent of respondents were exposed to endorsements of particular candidates from interest groups — for instance, from unions or business groups — and hamlet or neighborhood organizations (*chokai*), 29 percent reported receipt of a postcard from a candidate, 48 percent of the public had heard a candidate give a speech, and 49 percent had heard a candidate's greetings amplified by loudspeakers mounted on a truck or bus cruising constituency streets and roads. When all candidate-focused communications and activities are summed — those listed, plus radio, television, and newspaper announcements, posters and billboards, and the government's official election brochure — they accounted for 60 percent of reported exposure to the campaign. Only 9 percent of the respondents remembered specifically partisan aspects of the campaign, and the remaining 31 percent indicated exposure to contacts or communications that could have come from either parties or candidates.[48]

Past scholars forecast a decrease in candidate-focused voting as Japan modernized. In reality, candidate campaigns have become an increasing part of election communications.[49] By 1993 telephone solicitations had increased threefold compared with the number in the early 1970s, support organization membership had almost doubled, and interest group endorsements had increased by 36 percent. Some other campaign activities, such as requests from friends and receipt of postcards from candidates, increased in the 1980s only to decline to 1970s levels in the early 1990s.

The increasing visibility of candidate campaigns, especially the growing frequency of informal, word-of-mouth-based campaign activities, reflects changes in Japanese society. Postwar urbanization has taken people away from small communities at the same time that rural industrialization has

2.4. *Voters' Contacts with Candidates in House of Representatives Elections, 1972–1993*

	1972	1976	1979	1980	1983	1986	1990	1993
Personal Request								
ephone	12%	21%	26%	29%	40%	41%	41%	39%
relative or friend	17	16	18	23	25	26	19	18
activist	13	17	17	17	24	25	18	15
superior at work	2	3	3	4	6	8	7	3
Subtotal	44%	57%	64%	83%	95%	100%	85%	75%
p Endorsement								
ɔ	6%	8%	8%	11%	10%	9%	7%	7%
ess group	5	5	7	10	11	11	9	8
borhood group	4	3	6	4	4	6	5	4
group	3	4	4	7	5	6	4	3
ubtotal	18%	20%	25%	32%	30%	32%	25%	22%
bership in Supporters' Association	10%	14%	20%	15%	16%	18%	18%	16%
Campaign Exposure								
ved a postcard	25%	23%	34%	30%	33%	35%	29%	25%
ded a speech	47	52	59	48	42	54	48	44
d a greeting from a bus or truck	54	51	59	61	56	54	49	40
andidate statement	178	164	171	176	176	181	168	133
andidate poster	52	87	95	99	105	95	96	83
ubtotal	356%	377%	418%	362%	412%	367%	338%	325%

e: Data from Akarui Senkyo Suishin Kyokai, *Shugiin Giin Sosenkyo no Jittai* (various years).

Figures are percentages of the total number of respondents. Totals are much higher than 100 percent because
ɔle answers were given.

weakened the ties formerly fostered by proximity, longtime residence, and various modes of community and agricultural cooperation. Dependence on neighborhood mutual-help groups and farm cooperatives has also been weakened by rural affluence.[50] Candidates rely more and more on support organizations and explicit requests and endorsements, whereas they used to depend more on natural community solidarity, plus the influence of local elites. With candidate support organization activities and active use of social networks, traditionally intimate forms of social organization are being emulated in order to deal with the effects of modernization.[51]

The importance of candidate-focused campaigns is reflected in the substantial proportions of Japanese who answer that they have voted on the basis of candidate rather than political party. Replies to questions on the relative

Table 2.5. Candidate-Centered Choices in House of Representatives Elections, 1972–1993

	1972	1976	1979	1980	1983	1986	1990	199
Voted on Basis of:								
Candidate	38%	40%	46%	38%	42%	39%	37%	49%
Party	48	46	41	49	47	49	51	41
Considered Candidate's:								
Ability/Knowledge	52	44	46	47	50	53	49	50
Reputation/Name	28	35	36	38	36	36	41	39
Considered Candidate as Representative of:								
Local/Occupational interest	38	35	46	41	45	51	36	27
National needs	45	46	38	46	44	40	55	59

Source: Same as Table 2.4.

importance of these two factors (the question dates back to the late 1940s) show a strong but slowly decreasing concern for candidates until the 1970s, after which neither candidate nor party was consistently dominant (Table 2.5). Although slightly greater pluralities now usually vote on the basis of party, the reverse was the case in earlier years, and the candidate vote is still sizable and increased in the 1993 election, when there were suddenly three new, relatively unknown political parties.[52]

Surveys show that a vote on the basis of candidate means much more than an affirmation of a particular person's high social status. Among the reasons given for making such choices, a candidate's instrumental qualities, like "capability" and "knowledge," outweigh perceptions that the candidate has led an "upright life" or is a "source of local pride." Qualities associated with political competence are preferred over affirmations of a candidate's good character. Name recognition alone is less frequent, though fairly high in most elections (see Table 2.6).[53]

Candidate-centered campaigns and the candidate vote choice are part and parcel of an enormously important parochial theme in Japanese political culture (Table 2.6). Local elections nearly match national contests in appeal and, in rural areas, exceed them; and local (city, town, and village) politics are seen as closer to people's lives than national affairs are.[54] In addition, more people see elections for the House of Representatives as "dirty" compared with local elections. Local interest representation is the basis of the vote for up to 40 percent of the electorate in some surveys.[55]

A tendency to state that the candidate is the basis for a vote in Japan has *le 2.6. Cosmopolitanism Versus Parochialism in Japanese Political Culture*

	National	Urban	Rural	Farmers	Small-Business Workers	Salaried Employees	Workers
rest in Election							
·se of Councillors	13%	17%	9%	5%	10%	20%	14%
·se of Representatives	44	49	38	45	55	58	44
·Town, or Village Assembly	40	26	48	59	44	29	53
utation							
·onal politics is "good"	−5	−19	−1	+33	+6	−19	−11
·l politics is "good"	+24	+29	+30	+44	+25	+11	+22
·d on Basis of Candidate							
·se of Councillors	29	28	31	32	23	28	27
·se of Representatives	49	31	56	59	48	43	56
·ectural Assembly	57	46	61	63	72	57	59

ces: Akarui Senkyo Suishin Kyokai, *Dai-12kai Toitsu Chiho Senkyo no Jittai* (Tokyo, 1992); *Dai-ii Shugiin Giin Sosenkyo no Jittai* (Tokyo, 1991); *Dai-15kai Sangiin Giin Tsujo Senkyo no Jittai* (Tokyo, ɔ).

e: Under "Reputation" the category "good" refers to the percentage of all respondents who answered "The ·tation of —— politics is good" minus the percentage who answered "The reputation of —— politics is *"* Other figures are percentages of the total sample.

always been inversely related to election level. Candidates are more central in local assembly elections than lower house elections and least important in upper house elections (see Table 2.6). As the context of elections becomes larger, candidates become less important.

Overall, local candidate-dominated contests based on activation of interpersonal social networks and other informal contacts evoke more attention and more voter trust than campaigns initiated in more remote frames of reference. Contrary to earlier views that candidate mobilization and support were mainly the province of LDP candidates, candidate-focused communications are conspicuous among supporters of all political parties. Japanese political culture is, to a considerable degree, a parochial political culture.[56] Even though an electoral reform bill enacted in 1994 could bring greater party control over election campaigns and less emphasis on traditional mobilization centering on the candidates themselves, parochial factors will likely continue to be important.

The parochial nature of the political setting in which the candidate vote takes place has made a candidate's special vote-gathering techniques and appeals to local self-interest an effective anchor for the vote of many. The Dietmember for the local constituency is often a trusted and known ambassador to the outside world of national politics under these conditions. As the experience of Kakuei Tanaka affirms, even the taint of corruption until recently failed to stain the constituency appeal of candidates who looked after their supporters in the traditional way.[57] Local Dietmembers are normally trusted far more than politicians from other places.[58]

Why Japanese election campaigns have so often been dominated by individual candidates has long been a subject of scholarly concern. Many believe that the multimember district system — wherein candidates for the House of Representatives ran in districts represented by two to six members — was the cause of candidate-centered campaign mobilization.[59] It is also true, however, that *all* candidates, regardless of party, run individual campaigns and that this happens even where there is no competition with candidates from their own party. In the final analysis, individual candidate-run campaigns that depend on mobilizing small communities, sections of cities, individual companies, specific units of the farm cooperative movement, and labor union locals fit the highly personalistic and parochial nature of Japanese society.[60] The suitability of particular districts to mobilization is what underlies candidate-based choices, not the electoral system itself. Perhaps the small territory of lower house electoral districts also facilitates candidate campaigns. But even electoral mobilization in the prefecturewide House of Councillors districts centers largely on candidate-led campaigns. Because more than half the electoral constituencies established in the electoral reform of 1994 are small, single-member districts, penetrative mobilization by candidates will likely continue in many constituencies.

Labor unions and other large secondary groups play an important role in electoral mobilization in Japan, even where candidates are also important. Union locals, local farm cooperatives, small-retailers' associations, and other local groups have been part of many candidates' electoral coalitions. Where union memberships are spread across several constituencies, as sometimes happens, the unions have worked with the Social Democratic and Democratic Socialist Parties to allocate the votes of all union members in those districts — not just the votes of the union that recommended a particular candidate. That is, a candidate received support from members of several unions who resided in the candidate's district, as well as from members of the candidate's own union; elsewhere, members of that candidate's union vote for another candidate of the same party. In this manner, the discrepancy between the narrow territory of election districts and the wider distribution of union members' residences is dealt with in a rational way.

In small House of Representatives districts, votes by members of unions and other organizations are therefore either included in a candidate's mobilized base (if the members of an organization are concentrated, as occurs with miners' unions and some other organizations) or allocated by unions and parties working together. As election districts grow bigger, secondary organizations assume an even larger role in mobilizing votes. Labor unions and other secondary organizations have dominated mobilization in the national district of the upper house for much of the time since the war. Large, organized groups are also important in some prefectural districts in House of Councillors elections.[61] Under new lower house electoral arrangements that call for the allocation of more than two hundred seats by a proportional representation formula, large organizations can be expected to play a bigger role than in old-style lower house districts.

Interestingly, mobilization by unions also explains why salaried workers began to support opposition parties early in postwar Japan and in many cases continue to do so. Many white-collar and professional workers are members of unions of government workers, which have traditionally supported the Social Democrats. Quite a few white-collar workers in the private sector are also union members, for enterprise unions enroll employees up to the lower levels of management.[62] Both patterns contribute to the presence of white-collar workers in the ranks of supporters for opposition parties. Union mobilization — or, more correctly, the lack of it — also explains the presence of large numbers of conservative votes from blue-collar workers: they work in medium and small firms, which are not usually organized in Japan.

In spite of some clear linkages between union membership and voting preferences, the political role of unions is complex. The tendency for unions in Sohyo (association of government unions) to support the Social Democrats and for unions in Domei (association of private-sector unions) to support Democratic Socialists was well established until recent union movement changes.[63] At the same time, there was nothing automatic about these relationships. Some union movements — the teachers' unions are a case in point — were deeply split over which party to support, with some elements preferring the Social Democrats and others supporting another party. With the teachers, the alternative to the Social Democrats was the Communist Party. A substantial portion of the union movement has also been made up of independent unions, which lack systematic party alignments.

Still, whatever could be said in a systematic fashion about political alignments of labor unions in the past has been superseded by the establishment in 1988 of a pan-union movement called Rengo. A political movement affiliated with Rengo ran candidates in the 1989 House of Councillors election. Rengo has also supported existing parties in some elections, and some Rengo unions have maintained their traditional political identities and party alignments. Alignment of the two Socialist parties with different parties after the summer of 1994 has further complicated the union movement's push for a united leftist political camp. Nor do Rengo leaders feel comfortable supporting a governing coalition that includes the LDP, such as existed after June 1995. I fail to see a simple pattern in these events.

A third to a half of the electorate appear to be bound to candidates through social networks and other organizational ties with a highly parochial focus.[64] Secondary organizations also play an important role in electoral mobilization. But mobilization does not explain all voting in Japan. Candidate campaigns and secondary group mobilization directly explained 30–40 percent of the stable votes during the period of LDP hegemony. The remainder of the stable vote reflects some combination of occupational interests and psychological motives.[65] To see candidate support in the starkly simple way that I have presented it is itself somewhat misleading. Nor are the effects of machines and related activities on particular individuals always reinforcing. People can be exposed to different candidate machines or to social networks carrying different messages. Political life in Japan can be complex, and we must see its effects more as a matrix of stabilizing but complex influences than as simply individual-level stability.

Voting Change and Volatility

Fairly stable trends have been the dominant pattern in postwar Japanese voting. Some incremental shifts in the vote took place in certain periods. But there have also been a few episodes of intense volatility and change. Underlying these bursts of volatility were three kinds of voting choices: changes in votes because of environmental and local issues, volatility because of nationwide issues, and floating votes. Each example tells us something about the character of the Japanese voter.

Between the late 1950s and early 1970s the economy grew dramatically. High growth was itself accompanied by a shift in the occupation structure. More and more people went to work in manufacturing plants or took jobs in service occupations. Employment in primary-sector occupations (agriculture, for example) decreased from 48 percent to just 7 percent. Manufacturing plants invaded rural areas in search of labor, and many sons and daughters of farm families left the countryside to work and live in the cities, so cities and their suburbs burgeoned. In 1950 only a quarter of the population lived in cities of more than 100,000 people. By 1975 the proportion was 55 percent.

Growth was especially rapid in the suburbs of large cities, especially in the prefectures of Chiba, Saitama, and Kanagawa near Tokyo and in the prefectures of Hyogo and Nara near Osaka.

As people emigrated to the city and took up new occupations in the manufacturing and service sectors, they left the traditionally conservative voting milieu of rural districts and entered a new climate of opinion and met with requests from new organizations and candidates for their support. This change in environment was especially abrupt for those who went to work for large firms, where — more than in some environments — employment meant union membership and exposure to union appeals for support of opposition parties and their candidates. Partisan change was especially common among those in their twenties, who, according to psychological theories of voting, are vulnerable to new political appeals.[66]

As people moved to the suburbs and some older urban districts received an influx of residents, the electoral map of urban Japan altered. In both central city districts and expanding suburbs, votes for the Liberal Democratic and Social Democratic Parties declined and support for the Japanese Communist Party and the Clean Government Party increased. In part, these changes reflected the emergence of popular quality-of-life issues and efforts by the Communist Party and others to address them.

Massive economic development and related population movements affected local politics and local issues. After a decade in which local politicians welcomed investment and development, there was in the early 1970s a wave of antidevelopment and antipollution movements. Support for some movements led to election of local or even national representatives whose partisanship was a departure from local traditions. New local political issues also appeared in the periphery of metropolitan areas when extension of urban services, like paved roads and sewers, failed to keep up with home construction. Population mobility in the suburbs of big cities and some small cities correlated directly with replacement of local conservative leaders with government by an opposition party. Election of many opposition candidates to the Diet in the turbulent early 1970s reflected the same motivations and concerns.[67]

The difficulty of urban life itself affected some immigrants from rural districts in politically significant ways. Arrivals from farm areas and small towns, as well as small-company employees in general, were believed to have been attracted to the Soka Gakkai sect because of their sense of anomie.[68] The Clean Government Party, which is supported by the sect, gained votes among these population sectors through proselytization of neighbors, work companions, and acquaintances by Soka Gakkai activists.

Ichiro Miyake has studied the individual-level effects of change in the 1970s by examining the attitudes of people who grew up in rural conservative homes and later emigrated to the city or entered new occupations and social or economic strata. His findings show unambiguously that demographic trends and processes brought new political loyalties for many people.[69] Powerful forces of adult socialization or resocialization led those who changed jobs or places of residence to change political loyalties. These shifts, in turn, altered the electoral landscape of urban and suburban districts.

Other postwar electoral change — besides that instigated by population mobility and growth-related local issues — was the result of shifts in party support among interest groups. Normally, mobilization of the vote by interest groups was an important building block of stable voting. Earlier we noted that LDP candidates often allied themselves with local interest groups in their search for votes. Close ties between candidates and local farm cooperatives and shopping street associations (*shotengaikai*) frequently kept conservative voting blocs together.[70] Senior officials from the prefectural federations of these groups have run for office under conservative banners.[71] But interest groups are not bound to support a party if it does not represent their policy concerns. Events in 1989 showed the power of interest groups to detach votes that normally went to the Liberal Democrats and to send them in other directions.

Zenchu, representing the National Federation of Agricultural Cooperatives, was a longtime coalitional ally of the LDP.[72] Most domestic farm-product markets were protected from foreign imports as a result of this relationship. Until the mid- 1980s government farm-price subsidies were also favorable to farmers (see Chapter 7). In spite of close ties between farm interests and the ruling party, agriculture was under a state of siege in the 1970s and 1980s as LDP governments were repeatedly asked by American political leaders to open Japanese markets. Intense resistance came from interest groups and LDP Diet-members from farm areas, but the conservative governments gave in to U.S. pressure in some cases. A limited opening of the Japanese citrus fruit market was followed by agreements to lower import quotas on foreign beef.

When the United States asked Japan to open markets to foreign rice, farm group protests reached unusually high levels (see Chapter 7). For a while, the government continued to resist the American request, as had previous LDP governments. But in the months prior to the 1989 upper house election, the LDP leaders wavered, and by spring 1989 some degree of liberalization seemed to be in the offing. It looked as though rice market liberalization would follow declining rice price subsidies as a denial of farmer interests.

The farm cooperative leaders responded to LDP ambivalence by voicing adamant opposition to liberalization throughout the spring and early summer of 1989. Farm groups throughout the country echoed the same sentiments. In several prefectures the anti-LDP feeling of the farmers was buttressed by the nationwide antipathy toward the LDP after the Recruit corruption scandal.

In the late spring of 1989 group after group of local farmers were quoted as stating that they would not support the LDP in the forthcoming upper house election. Young farmers were especially critical of the Liberal Democrats, lamenting the result of their policies: the loss of a future agriculture. Anti-LDP movements were reported in March in eleven different rural prefectures — primarily in Tohoku, in the northeast, and Kyushu, in the southwest — even in areas that were usually bastions of LDP support. Later in the spring, farmers' groups opposed to the Liberal Democrats were reported in several other parts of the country.

Those in some prefectural farm cooperatives discussed running their own election candidates in the 1989 election, as the Rengo unions were doing.[73] Resentment toward the LDP's policy on beef imports was so strong in Kagoshima that the local farm groups considered this option.[74] So did the mandarin orange growers of Ehime prefecture. Opinion polls showed a substantial nationwide drop in rural support for the LDP.[75]

Discontent among farm interest groups was mirrored by small-business dissatisfaction over a newly imposed consumption tax. Owners of Japan's many small retail stores felt that the tax hurt business and was hard for them to administer. National leaders of such small-business groups as the Japan Chamber of Commerce and Industry opposed the tax long before the bill implementing it was passed in 1988, and they continued to do so after passage.

Once again matters came to a head as the upper house election approached and the Recruit scandal deepened. In spring 1989 decisions by small-business groups to vote against the LDP were reported in several parts of the country. In Hokkaido, 670 stores in the Tomakomai area's Federation of Shopping District Associations vowed to vote for candidates from other parties, as did stores in Asahigawa city in the same prefecture. A small-business group in Kumamoto prefecture with thirteen hundred member stores took a similar position.[76]

Opinion surveys bore out anecdotal accounts of interest group defections from LDP support in 1989. Whereas substantial majorities of farmers and smaller majorities of small-business owners usually supported the LDP (see Table 2.2), this was not the case in 1989. Farmers' support for the LDP dropped from 84 percent in the House of Councillors election in 1986 to 52 percent in the upper house election in 1989. Among small-business owners support dropped from 62 percent to 35 percent.[77] Although declines in LDP support induced by the corruption scandals could be seen within other occupational groups in 1986–89, the defections were nowhere near as severe as among farmers and small-business owners. Salaried workers' support for the LDP fell just 8 percent in 1986–89; blue-collar workers' support, only 2 percent. Electoral results in 1989 mirrored the trends in opinion surveys; LDP candidates did especially poorly in several of the most rural prefectures.[78]

Strenuous efforts by LDP leaders brought apathetic or alienated interest groups back into the fold in time for the lower house election in February 1990. Interest group defections during the House of Councillors election in 1989 were more of a protest vote than an indicator of total coalition collapse.[79] Still, it was clear from the events of 1989 that the LDP's vaunted coalition of interest groups was far from being the example of corporatist unity that it was sometimes asserted to be.[80] The events also attest to the degree to which the votes of a mobilized electorate are vulnerable to defections by the interest groups that normally organize electoral support. Although interest groups have usually been sources of stability in Japanese elections, their behavior in 1989 shows they can create sudden instability as well.

A sector of the adult population called floating voters — who float from party to party or between abstention and turnout — can be another source of electoral volatility. Although survey findings are limited in their ability to trace the floating vote, demographic patterns among people who do not have a preferred party can crudely locate it. Floating voters are consistently found more in cities than in the countryside. In the 1960s there was an unattached, apolitical grouping made up disproportionately of people in their twenties and older women who had grown up without the franchise.[81] Poorly educated people composed another grouping especially conspicuous for its lack of party ties. Salaried workers and blue-collar workers also reported apolitical preferences more than people in other occupational categories.

In the 1980s the proportions of unattached citizens among salaried and blue-collar workers continued to be high (see Table 2.2). In addition, the rejection of party ties among young people increased significantly. Although there has been some rejection of party ties in all age groups, half of young people became apolitical (Table 2.7). Cohort analysis formerly indicated a tendency for the proportion of persons reporting party loyalty to increase by the age of thirty; recent findings indicate that this pattern has attenuated.

The Electoral Changes in 1993

The mobilized vote in Japan is potentially volatile, then. This is the inference to be drawn from Miyake's analysis of voters who changed partisan allegiance when they moved from conservative homes and communities in rural areas to urban job environments where the Social Democratic and other parties were more popular. The changes in partisanship resulting from social

Table 2.7. Age Cohorts and Party Affiliation in Selected General Elections,
1969–1993

	1969	1980	1990	1993
20–29				
Liberal Democrats	27%	27%	28%	18%
Social Democrats	18	13	14	7
Japan Communists	4	5	2	4
Democratic Socialists	5	4	2	2
Clean Government Party	5	6	3	6
New 1993 parties	—	—	—	10
Other	7	8	0	3
None / Don't Know	34	36	51	50
Total	100%	100%	100%	100%
30–39				
Liberal Democrats	37%	39%	31%	31%
Social Democrats	22	12	17	13
Japan Communists	2	4	2	1
Democratic Socialists	5	3	2	1
Clean Government Party	5	7	4	6
New 1993 parties	—	—	—	6
Other	5	0	0	8
None / Don't Know	24	36	44	35
Total	100%	101%	100%	100%
40–49				
Liberal Democrats	42%	45%	41%	36%
Social Democrats	18	15	20	11
Japan Communists	1	3	3	3
Democratic Socialists	4	4	3	2
Clean Government Party	6	4	2	4
New 1993 parties	—	—	—	7
Other	6	0	0	8
None / Don't Know	23	29	31	29
Total	100%	100%	100%	100%
50–59				
Liberal Democrats	51%	52%	45%	42%
Social Democrats	11	13	20	12
Japan Communists	1	2	2	3
Democratic Socialists	4	2	2	2
Clean Government Party	6	4	2	4
New 1993 parties	—	—	—	6
Other	5	4	2	7
None / Don't Know	22	23	27	24
Total	100%	100%	100%	100%

Continued

Table 2.7. Continued

	1969	1980	1990	1993
	60+			
Liberal Democrats	56%	59%	58%	49%
Social Democrats	6	8	14	12
Japan Communists	1	2	0	1
Democratic Socialists	2	2	1	1
Clean Government Party	2	4	4	5
New 1993 parties	—	—	—	5
Other	4	0	3	5
None / Don't Know	29	26	20	22
Total	100%	101%	100%	100%
N	2,461	2,427	2,269	2,301

Source: Data from Akarui Senkyo Suishin Kyokai, *Shugiin Giin Sosenkyo no Jittai* (various years).

Note: All figures show percentages of respondents in an age group who indicate that they support a particular political party or who report that they are "apolitical" (have no party affiliation).

mobility jibes with information indicating that partisanship is only a weakly held psychological commitment for many Japanese. The events of the House of Councillors election in 1989 and the wavering of as many as one in three Japanese voters between party affiliation and apolitical status from one survey interview to another also suggest that the inertia in most voting conceals a very soft form of attitudinal partisanship.

Voting became volatile once again in the July 1993 general election. The election took place after defections from the LDP permitted passage in the lower house of a vote of nonconfidence in the LDP government. Rather than resigning, then Prime Minister Kiichi Miyazawa requested a dissolution of the lower house and called for an election. LDP defectors formed two new conservative groups; they also ran candidates in the forthcoming election.

The election results indicated a marked shift in electoral preferences since the previous general election in 1990. Overall voting support for the LDP declined from slightly over 45 percent of the popular vote (275 seats) to just over 36 percent (226 seats). The decline in support for the Social Democrats was even steeper. Before the 1993 election the Socialists received 25 percent of the vote (134 seats); after the election, just 14 percent (69) seats. After the election the LDP and new conservative parties held a total of 326 seats in the lower house, or 63 percent. This seemingly strange state of affairs, in light of the LDP's big losses, reflects two new trends: two new conservative parties based on former LDP members of parliament did very well in the elections (reflecting the strength of the mobilized incumbent-candidate vote), and one new party, composed of new conservative candidates, captured the urban protest vote that had formerly been the province of the SDPJ.

Analysis of aggregate patterns of the 1993 vote in all 130 lower house constituencies bears out earlier pictures of voting as well as explains what happened in 1993. First, the continuing importance of candidate-led campaigns in 1993 was apparent in the very high success rate of former LDP politicians who ran as candidates of new parties (as well as by the success of 223 candidates from the LDP). Outside metropolitan Tokyo and Osaka and a handful of other densely populated areas, voters followed former LDP Diet-members in 32 of 49 successful candidacies. Much of the success of the new parties outside large cities thus took the form of continued support for former LDP officeholders. New candidates — those who had never held office before — supported by the new parties were successful in only eighteen cases outside the major cities. A mobilization model continued to account for voting tendencies; defectors from the LDP survived with new party colors in a remarkable number of cases — a poignant indicator of the weakness of Japanese partisanship at a time when political reform had become enormously popular. Surveys showed that candidate preferences exceeded party preferences for the first time since 1979 (see Table 2.5).[82]

Second, the main examples of true electoral flux — that is, changing to new candidates and new parties — occurred in the large cities and adjacent areas, specifically in constituencies with very large numbers of voters. New candidates from the new parties were successful in Tokyo, Saitama, Chiba, Kanagawa, and Osaka, Kyoto, Hyogo, and Wakayama. New-party neophytes were also elected in Sapporo, Sendai, Nagoya, and Fukuoka — somewhat smaller cities. In quite a few cases these candidates displaced Socialist, not LDP, candidates.[83]

The voting shifts reflected the presence of four overlapping elements in electoral culture. Changes occurred in urban constituencies where alienation and protest voting could be expected from past experience. In fact, the districts where change to new candidates of new parties was most visible were the very same ones where change was greatest in the early 1970s: the suburbs of large cities. Because of the large numbers of voters, the districts where change occurred were also those where candidate contact with the electorate was likely to be least intimate. Many of the constituencies were mainly bedroom communities, so that long commutes to work virtually ruled out integration into local life, especially for men (many women are not employed outside the home).

Without local roots or strong ties to candidate machines, voters may well feel alienated. Voting on the basis of potentially fluid cognitive party images would be typical in these kinds of constituencies, as would floating votes. High levels of rejection of partisanship among young people — according to newspaper polls, the strongest supporters of the new parties — may also have contributed to the change in the 1993 vote.[84]

Just what soft partisanship may mean for the future depends on the incidence and impact of corruption scandals, the response to such events by party elites, and general trends in the economy. It is also necessary to determine the causes and significance of the extensive rejection of parties in Japan today. If widespread political distrust is only a superficial reaction to public corruption, voting inertia may reassert itself despite soft partisanship. But if cynicism and alienation are a more fundamental preference, considerable change is possible, especially if economic growth slows down. Further balkanization of party support is a plausible consequence of such a scenario.

Recent efforts by the LDP to develop new bases of organizational support are worth noting. The LDP wooed labor unions, women, and religious groups in 1993–94 in a preemptive search for new sources of support. Later, it held Tokyo: Getting to Know You meetings near major subway stations; there, LDP Dietmembers discussed women's political interests and other topics. The April Society was formed to entice from the new religions people opposed to the Clean Government Party, an affiliate of the New Frontier Party. The Clean Government Party was supported by the Soka Gakkai, a Buddhist sect. LDP leaders met with the heads of municipal, postal, and electrical workers' unions and leaders of the Rengo union movement to seek their support.[85]

Conclusion

I have described four partially overlapping models of Japanese voting — occupational interests, values, political psychology, and electoral mobilization — and six motivations for Japanese voters: (1) occupational interest (this mainly influences farmers and small-business owners), (2) a candidate's mobilization of support (people who live in rural and small-business districts), (3) weak but loyal psychological partisanship, (4) images (urban voters), (5) protest (educated urbanites), and (6) lack of political attachments (floating voters, who tend to be urban and poorly educated). The most efficient way to summarize the patterns of voting is to imagine two electorates. One is made up of people who are exposed to a particular candidate's local machine and who vote for him or her on the basis of favors and issues of local interest. Such a person may vote for the same party most of the time, but without feeling a strong party preference. If a trusted candidate moves to another party, as happened in 1993, this kind of voter may follow the preferred candidate and vote for a new party without considering party even relevant to the choice.

Some voters respond more to national politics and issues than to local ones. They tend to think more often of parties than candidates when they vote. These people, who tend to read newspapers and watch television to find out about issues and events, are infrequently exposed to a candidate's mobilization efforts; and like the locally mobilized voters described above, they, too, lack a strong party tie. Many of these people voted in the past to protest against the dominant party. Some are responsive to media-induced electoral moods, like those that develop after corruption scandals. Some even wander from party to party, as is shown clearly in the case of support for the Democratic Socialist Party.

Although most rural and many small-business voters can be found in the first electorate, not everyone in these two occupational categories fits the local mobilization model. Some fit the national-issue model better, and some are exposed to both local mobilization efforts and national issues. Urban voters, especially well-educated ones, are more likely to fit the national-issue model. But there are mixtures in this case as well. In reality, the models overlap, and the area of overlap varies over time. Some people vote for a local candidate for a long time, then are swayed by national events — such as corruption scandals — to vote for another party. The swings away from the LDP in 1989 and the corruption-dominated elections of 1976 and 1993 document movement of this sort between national/issue and local/candidate voting styles.

If we measure the different motivations for voting against the vertical and horizontal models of Japanese political life discussed in Chapter 1, we similarly find mixed patterns. The importance of organization and mobilization gives a strong hint of verticality to voting patterns. The role of candidates' financial largesse in keeping supporters content between elections could also suggest that manipulation (verticality) is more important than representation (horizontality). Survey evidence that sizable groups make voting choices solely on the basis of candidate reputations or name recognition has the same implication: a vertical style of electoral mobilization and response.

Yet the voter's concern to have local and occupational interests represented is legendary, as is shown by Kakuei Tanaka's pork-barrel style of constituency service and by similar evidence from other candidates' districts. A concern for representation is also signaled by the near majorities who say in survey answers that they vote on the grounds of self-interest in lower house elections. Constituency responses to economic development and pollution issues in the early 1970s, to farmer and small-business issues in 1989, and to corruption in 1993 also suggest a horizontal set of electoral concerns. In fact, Japanese politics is, arguably, unusually responsive to the interests of local constituencies and interest groups, as is evident in the large portion of the national budget normally dedicated to local construction projects, the enormous budget and off-budget allocations that used to go to LDP client groups, and the related power of interest-based LDP members of the Diet. Both image and protest voting conform to a horizontal model of political relationships.

Stable support from sectors of the population bound to the conservative movement by social contracts — which can reflect Dietmembers' efforts or a party's policy performance at the national level, or both — has a lot to do with the overall success of the conservative parties. These social contracts between the LDP and farmers and small-business people provide for an exchange of subsidies and jobs for votes.[86] There is, in fact, a striking element of continuity in the bases for party support in postwar Japanese society despite enormous social change. We tend to think of urbanization and industrialization as producing an urban middle class of salaried workers who are no longer integrated into the web of traditional political machines but who are, in many cases, members of company unions that supported Socialist parties. This was the implication of Miyake's evidence on the partisanship of urban migrants. We often fail to appreciate that urbanization did not produce a mass society of people working solely for large firms. Rather, Japan continued to be a mixed society, with some large enterprises and many small firms and farms. In 1950 there were 18 million farmers, slightly more than 1 million small-business owners, and 15 million small-business employees in an electorate of 47 million. By 1991 there were only 3.9 million farmers, but nearly 7 million small-business owners and 48 million small-business employees in an electorate of 89 million. The number who owned or were employed by small enterprises — in business, industry, and agriculture alike — has grown enormously (Table 2.8).[87]

Surveys indicate further that between one-third and two-thirds of those in the small-enterprise sector voted for conservative parties in the 1980s (see Table 2.8). These sectors are important to LDP and general conservative party strength. In the 1980s the LDP also made some inroads with both blue-collar and salaried or white-collar workers employed in large firms, although some in this sector defected in the 1989 and 1993 elections.[88] The electorate as a whole has been composed of very large occupational sectors bound to the conservative movement (by candidates' constituency machines and social contracts) and some social sectors that supported other parties.

Japan's electoral experience has profound implications for the shape of power in other realms of politics. The most obvious implication until recently was the sustenance of a fairly stable dominant party system through the success of conservative candidates who mined votes by intensive local electoral

Table 2.8. The Size and Reported Conservative Vote of Major Economic Groups in Selected General Elections, 1960–1993

	Farm Owners		Small-Firm Owners		Small-Firm Employees		Large-Firm Employees	
	Number	Cons %	Number	Cons %	Number	Cons %	Number	Cons %
1960	11.9	78	3.6	71	18.5	35	3.5	35
1970	8.1	74	4.6	57	32.7	38	5.8	22
1980	5.1	79	6.3	58	40.6	44	5.3	26
1990	3.9	77	6.6	63	48.4	43	6.6	25
1993	3.7	80	6.6	65	48.4	54	6.6	39

Sources: Prime Minister's Office, *Japan Statistical Yearbook* (Tokyo, 1960 and 1991); Asahi Shimbunsha, *Japan Almanac 1994* (Tokyo, 1993), p. 126; Komei Senkyo Remmei, *Dai-30kai Sosenkyo no Jittai* (Tokyo, 1964), p. 47; Komei Senkyo Remmei, *Dai-32kai Shugiin Sosenkyo no Jittai* (Tokyo, 1970), pp. 131–32; Akarui Senkyo Suishin Kyokai, *Dai-36kai Shugiin Giin Sosenkyo, Dai-12kai Sangiin Giin Tsujo Senkyo no Jittai* (Tokyo, 1981), p. 132; and *Shugiin Giin Sosenkyo no Jittai* (Tokyo, 1990 and 1994), pp. 252, 220.

Notes: Small businesses are classified, following a widely used standard, as firms having fewer than 300 employees. I assumed that firms of this size were individual or family owned, and derived the number of owners from the number of firms. The small-firm employees' LDP support rate was based on the non-unionized employee support rate, and large-firm employees' LDP support rate was taken from the figure for unionized employees. The same procedure was used for persons who supported one of the four conservative parties in 1993.

Figures for numbers of farmers, owners, and employees are in millions of persons. "Cons %" is the percentage of persons in the occupational group who supported the LDP in 1960–70, the LDP or New Liberal Club in 1986, the LDP in 1990, and the LDP, Renewal Party, Harbinger Party, or Japan New Party in 1993.

mobilization and appeals to voters' interests. Electoral volatility has also been important when it has occurred; volatile voting led to alterations in party system power in 1969–76 and 1993.

Electoral performance has other implications for the shape of national political power. Candidate electoral machines consist of relationships that channel the representation of local interests in national politics. Each candidate mines support in a sociopolitical enclave defined by constituency boundaries and the support networks of local elites, interest groups, communities, and neighborhoods. Intensive mobilization of local support by individual candidates has fragmented and parochialized interest articulation. This fragmentation, in turn, paves the way for the development of decentralized policy communities linking Dietmembers, interest group officials, and bureaucrats in a particular area of common interest (policy communities are discussed in Chapters 5, 6, 7, and 10). The fragmentation of power bases has also given individual members of parliament a resource that they would not have in a more centralized system. A Dietmember with a strong local base can offer cooperation on legislative bills or support for a faction leader in exchange for policy support in matters of constituency interest. Large political parties in Japan have been more decentralized than parties in most other industrialized countries because of these upward pressures.

3

Parties Under the "1955 System"

The long stay in office of the Liberal Democratic Party and its domination of national politics by working closely with the administrative bureaucracy — the system of government called the 1955 system — is one element in the vertical model view that political power has been highly centralized for much of the time since World War II. Had the party been elite run, internally consensual, and deferential to the cabinet and bureaucracy, the validity of the vertical model would be borne out. This is not the case, because of intraparty factionalism and major intraparty cleavages over China policy, national security, and the status of the postwar constitution, as well as many lesser issues, such as tax reform, farm policy, education policy, and political reform. The party's base of support was itself also very large and included many leading interest groups, some of which had mutually opposing policies. The decentralized nature of electoral power, combined with the openness of the party — the result of intense factionalism and policy cleavages — assured upward transmission of many local concerns from constituencies of varying kinds and interests.

The evidence for intra-LDP pluralism during the era of party dominance is strong. This important observation invokes a second set of concerns. If the party was divided by internal cleavages, how did it remain in power for so long? What organizational, ideological, or political glue held the party together from 1955 until 1993, and why did the party finally collapse partially in the summer of 1993?

It is also important to ask what the organizational patterns during LDP rule imply in a broader context. Does the LDP provide an organizational model applicable to most Japanese political groups or even political processes? How much do other parties and groups look like the LDP, and how much do current coalition governments resemble the LDP government? How does the LDP of the 1955 system compare with parties in other industrialized democracies, and what can be learned about Japanese politics from such a comparison?

These questions require an assessment of the formal and informal organization, processes, and procedures of the LDP and other parties. This chapter will be concerned with internal party processes and organization, with an emphasis on evidence from the 1980s to spring 1993. The partial collapse of the LDP in July 1993, interparty coalitions, and other aspects of recent partisan dynamics are discussed in Chapter 4.

Organization of the LDP

The Liberal Democratic Party was created in 1955 through the merger of the Liberal and the Democratic Parties.[1] Its formation followed a decade in which the conservative movement fragmented and recombined and party names frequently shifted. The LDP self-consciously modeled itself after the British Conservative Party and other European parties that had strong central institutions and permanent national and local organizations. In spite of an elaborate formal organization, the LDP has displayed more clearly than perhaps any other party in the industrialized world the importance of informal organization to the operation of formal institutions.

Factions were the most important of the informal groups. When the LDP was in power, factions collectively chose party and government leaders and supported candidates in elections. Local party factions and politicians' groupings also periodically challenged central party control. Informal policy groups and clusters of politicians with similar interests played important roles in party policymaking. Informal consultational processes at times replaced and often complemented formal procedures.

The formal organization of the LDP provides for a party executive composed of a president, a vice president (not always appointed), and an executive council (Figure 3.1).[2] There is also a secretary general, who assists the party president in the administration of party affairs. The secretary general is a major figure in the formation of legislative and election strategies. The Policy Affairs Research Council (PARC) is a large policy forum with its own internal organization, which includes a deliberative council, divisions (which are parallel to government ministries and Diet committees), investigative councils,

Figure 3.1. Liberal Democratic Party Organization, 1992

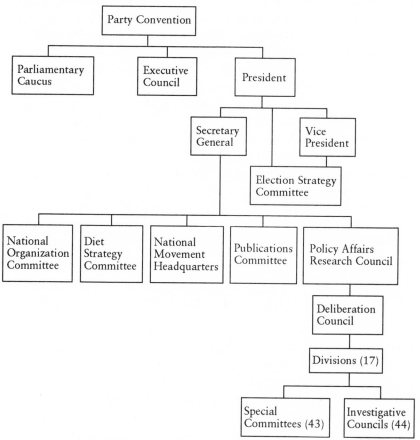

Sources: Seiji Koho Senta, *Seiji Handobukku* (Tokyo, 1992), pp. 179–83, for nomenclature; and Seizaburo Sato and Tetsuhisa Matsuzaki, *Jiminto Seiken* (Tokyo: Chuo Koronsha, 1986), pp. 188–89, for intraparty lines of responsibility.

and special committees. Top party officers — including the president, the secretary general, the executive council chair, the policy council chair, and the vice president — make up an informal decisionmaking group. Other elements of the national party hierarchy include Diet strategy, election strategy, national organization, and publications committees and a national movement headquarters. There are also organizational components of the party that include the LDP members of the House of Representatives and the House of Councillors. The LDP has forty-seven prefectural organizations and, under these, some local branches. In 1989 the party had nearly 3 million registered members.[3] The

LDP holds an annual conference, which brings together top officials and members of parliament, who constitute the party's nucleus, and people selected by the party's prefectural organizations.

The organization of the party is often described as an inverted pyramid despite the mass-level organizations. Local branches are inactive, and membership is nominal, indicating loyalty to a locally prominent politician. Policymaking is concentrated at the national level, and election management is also centralized, at least in theory. In reality, the party is more like two pyramids, one inverted and one standing on its base. The first describes the formal organization; the second, the importance of Dietmembers' informal political machines to informal party organization at the constituency level. Political machines have provided the party with extensive and intimate contacts among constituents, and the intensely personal nature of local electoral mobilization has ensured upward communication of local interests to national party councils. Other aspects of informal organization presented in this chapter complete the picture of a downwardly responsible party apparatus whose formal shape represents centralized party power.

Pluralism and Conflict in the LDP

The LDP was and is a political system. To some extent, this is true of all political parties. What made the LDP different was (1) the broad scope of its social base and (2) the formalized and institutionalized nature of important intraparty groups. The presence of several major and minor factions and multiple policy and interest groupings that competed with one another for positions and policies provide evidence for a horizontal interpretation of LDP power relationships.

The allocation of executive positions within the LDP was a major party function, as well as a source of intraparty conflict. During LDP rule, allocation was very important because internal decisions determined the selection of prime ministers and cabinets by virtue of the LDP majority in the Diet.

Until 1993, LDP factions were the main participants in the selection of party and government leaders and the most important of the party's several kinds of internal groups.[4] There were typically five to eight identifiable factions within the party and sometimes other minor groups as well. Although varying in size from 14 members to as many as 136, the factions were generally similar in character. The factions were groups of LDP Dietmembers who followed a particular senior politician. Faction members received a variety of benefits and supports, including appointments to senior party and government positions, in exchange for their loyalty to the faction. Factions also served as a power base for their leaders.

Politicians generally have three dominant concerns: getting reelected, obtaining top positions in the party, government, and bureaucracy, and influencing policy. The informal leader-centered factions in the LDP satisfied the second of these goals and played a role in the first. Their contribution to the third was less central, although interfactional competition affected policymaking at times.

Even though factions existed in part to resolve conflict, the LDP factions were also sometimes themselves centers of intense internal conflict. Intrafaction conflict reflected in part an inevitable clash between the personal ambitions and personalities of faction members, especially senior politicians near the top of the hierarchy of influence within the faction. Indeed, feuds between established or rising politicians were nearly constant. For example, a leader of the Takeshita faction, Shin Kanemaru, and the head of the faction, Noboru Takeshita, who had been political friends, turned into rivals in the late 1980s. They sponsored different clients for high posts, planned for different people to eventually inherit the faction, and initiated diametrically opposed succession strategies for the LDP leadership.[5] Other rivalries appeared in the late 1980s and early 1990s between ambitious, up-and-coming politicians within the Mitsuzuka, Miyazawa, and Watanabe factions.[6]

A perennial source of intrafaction conflict was the existence of subfactions led by would-be faction leaders. One example is the Watanabe group, the Onchikai, created within the Nakasone faction in 1979. Takeshita created his own "study group," the Soseikai, within the Tanaka faction in the mid-1980s with similar aspirations in mind.[7] On these and other occasions, those who supported certain senior politicians within a faction grouped together, and the formation of such a group signaled someone's ambition to become faction leader and eventually prime minister.

Conflict between subfaction leaders at times led to splits in factions, usually at a time of succession. When the death or retirement of a faction leader dictated a change, subfaction heads mounted aggressive campaigns for the faction leadership. The efforts connected with Takeshita's succession to leadership of the Tanaka faction in 1985–86 are a good example. Takeshita's formation of the Soseikai in February 1985, a subfaction thinly disguised as a study group, was the first step. Establishment of the Soseikai led to a yearlong struggle for factional leadership.[8] Eventually, the internecine competition split the Tanaka faction into two.[9] Although most factions have been stable over time, occasional faction splits (see Figure 3.3) are a reminder of the fragility of faction coalitions and the intensity of interpersonal and intergroup conflicts.

Sometimes factions were divided between junior and senior members. These intergenerational cleavages usually reflected younger faction members' feelings of distance from faction leaders. Junior members of the Miyazawa faction reportedly felt isolated from the group of mainly ex-bureaucrats who led the faction. In other cases, junior faction members were upset when they felt that the credibility of their faction was declining, as happened in the Nakasone faction when Yasuhiro Nakasone and other senior members were associated with the Recruit bribery scandal. The juniors were fearful that the accusations would weaken the faction's ability to get party and government positions for its members.[10]

Junior members could feel frustrated with faction leaders over other matters, too. At a breakfast meeting of the Hifumikai — a group within the Takeshita faction composed of members elected one to three times — the secretary general of the faction was criticized: "First-term Dietmembers in other factions have gotten assignments on such Diet committees as Construction and Commerce and Industry. Why didn't our faction take care of us? Also, even if we ask for support in our electoral district, no cabinet member comes to help us get votes."[11]

LDP factions were mainly concerned with personnel matters, but other important intraparty groups were concerned with policy, and policy cleavages in the LDP have at times been profound. Internal policy pluralism was the rule during most of the LDP's time in power. Considerable intra-LDP conflict reflected the presence of organized policy groups and zoku within the party. Policy groups like the Asian Problems Research Association and the Afro-Asian Problems Research Association, both of which were concerned with China policy, the now-defunct right-wing Seirankai, the liberal Hirakawa Society, the New Society Research Association, the Liberal Society Forum, and other groups contributed to intra-LDP policy pluralism at different times.[12]

Differences of opinion among the two China policy groups repeatedly stalled intraparty debate on Japanese relations with mainland China and Taiwan in the 1960s. These policy group antagonisms were stumbling blocks to achieving rapprochement between Japan and China in 1972 and to a Sino-Japanese peace treaty (one was finally signed in 1978).[13] Another intraparty group, the right-wing Seirankai, favored constitutional reform and a military role for Japan and opposed granting the right to strike to government labor unions. The Seirankai was opposed by a liberal group, the Hirakawa Society.

Internal groups advocating different directions in security policy and other issues often complicated Liberal Democratic policymaking in the 1970s. In the 1980s nonideological issues like administrative reform, a new tax system, and farmers' concerns dominated party agendas, and the LDP moved away from a politics of ideology. Recently, multiple political reform groups have participated in intraparty debates over election laws and related matters.

Groupings of LDP Dietmembers interested in specific policy areas were another source of intra-LDP pluralism. These groupings, which have existed since at least the 1960s, attracted a great deal of attention in the 1990s.[14] The clusters of Dietmembers were called *zoku* — roughly, "families" or "tribes." Members of zoku were concerned with specific special interests, such as agriculture, construction, small business, or education. Usually they occupied several positions on party or Diet committees in certain functional areas (those who held positions as parliamentary vice minister or minister in the same functional areas were also included in some accounts of zoku).

Two indicators have been used to designate Dietmembers' zoku attachments. One measure, the total number of a party member's assignments to special committees or positions in the party, Diet, or government, may indicate concentration and experience. But the number of committee assignments might mean only that a politician wanted to be viewed as doing something related to constituencies' main interests. A second and more convincing measure is a Dietmember's tenure on party or Diet committees in particular areas, which, in the case of long tenure, is a better indicator of commitment and expertise. Information on both aspects of zoku affiliation among members of the lower house is shown in Table 3.1.[15]

The zoku phenomenon points to the importance of the LDP's role in transmitting sectoral, regional, and local interests. After its formation in 1955 the LDP was aligned with many of Japan's most important interest groups and population sectors.[16] The party subsequently expanded its interest coalition by building ties with an increasingly broader constellation of interests. So inclusive was the scope of the LDP's interest coalition that the party was a "catch-all" party.[17] Although facilitating success at the polls, the diversity of interests served by the LDP sometimes made intraparty policy agreement difficult, especially at the party apex (see the discussion of farm policy in Chapter 7).

Organizational federations representing big business, farmers, and small business have been central to the Liberal Democratic interest coalition (Figure 3.2).[18] Interest groups representing narrower interests within these broad sectors — specific industry associations, beef farmers' and citrus fruit growers' organizations, and so forth — were likewise allied with the LDP. Several other major interest organizations, including the Association of Bereaved Persons, the Japan Medical Association, the All-Japan League of Environmental Hygiene Enterprises, the Special Postmasters League, the All-Japan Midwives Association, and the Rissho Koseikai (a religious organization) have contributed election candidates to the LDP cause.[19] Many of Japan's largest interest

Table 3.1. Liberal Democrats in the House of Representatives with Zoku and Committee Memberships

	Members with Zoku Positions		Members with Committee Tenure
	1963	1990	1980–89
Foreign Affairs	4	5	7
Finance	5	8	10
Commerce and Industry	4	8	15
Agriculture and Forestry	4	1	15
Education	2	4	11
Labor	1	1	13
Transportation	4	7	12
Construction	1	8	9
Defense	1	1	9

Source: Data from Seiji Koho Senta, *Seiji Handobukku* (Tokyo, 1990).

Notes: Numbers under "1963" and "1990" are the total LDP lower house members who (1) had five or more "zoku" positions such as Diet committee chairmanships/memberships or LDP PARC department or investigative council or special committee chairmanships/memberships in one area of specialization or (2), if they had occupied fewer than five total positions, the number of persons who had held at least two positions in the same area of specialization.

Members with committee tenure are those who held committee assignments for five or more years between 1980 and 1990.

Figures in this table are considerably smaller than those reported in Seizaburo Sato and Tetsuhisa Miyazaki, *Jiminto Seiken* (Tokyo: Chuo Koronsha, 1986), pp. 267–72; and Takeshi Inoguchi and Tomoaki Iwai, *Zoku Giin no Kenkyu* (Tokyo: Nihon Keizai Shimbunsha, 1987), pp. 295–364. Both lists were based on measures less restrictive than my own and on both houses of the Diet, whereas this table is based only on the lower house. Political appointees like ministers and parliamentary vice ministers were included in their calculations but not in mine, since these are not based on substantive expertise in some policy area in over half of the appointments I examined for the decade of the 1980s.

groups were customarily affiliated with or oriented toward the LDP; among the most prominent, only labor unions and certain religious groups were excluded from the LDP's base of support.[20]

Pluralism within the LDP had an obvious effect on internal decisionmaking. Policymaking had its own dynamic, with groups vying for influence over policy positions. At times, there were sharp divisions within the leadership. On some occasions, party leaders were called on to mediate between intraparty groups.[21]

Figure 3.2. Liberal Democratic Party Interest Group Coalitions

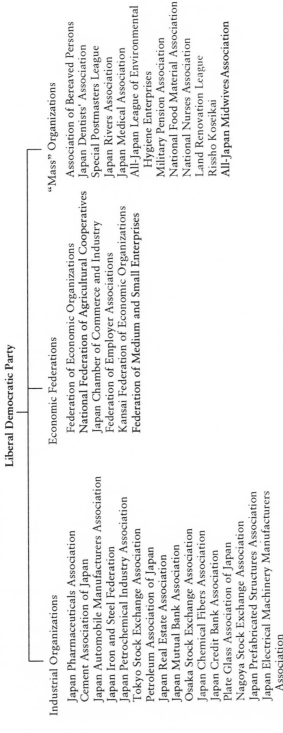

Liberal Democratic Party

Industrial Organizations

Japan Pharmaceuticals Association
Cement Association of Japan
Japan Automobile Manufacturers Association
Japan Iron and Steel Federation
Japan Petrochemical Industry Association
Tokyo Stock Exchange Association
Petroleum Association of Japan
Japan Real Estate Association
Japan Mutual Bank Association
Osaka Stock Exchange Association
Japan Chemical Fibers Association
Japan Credit Bank Association
Plate Glass Association of Japan
Nagoya Stock Exchange Association
Japan Prefabricated Structures Association
Japan Electrical Machinery Manufacturers
   Association

Economic Federations

Federation of Economic Organizations
National Federation of Agricultural Cooperatives
Japan Chamber of Commerce and Industry
Federation of Employer Associations
Kansai Federation of Economic Organizations
Federation of Medium and Small Enterprises

"Mass" Organizations

Association of Bereaved Persons
Japan Dentists' Association
Special Postmasters League
Japan Rivers Association
Japan Medical Association
All-Japan League of Environmental
   Hygiene Enterprises
Military Pension Association
National Food Material Association
National Nurses Association
Land Renovation League
Rissho Koseikai
All-Japan Midwives Association

Sources: Data from *Tokyo Shimbun*, February 6, 1989; and Seiji Koho Senta, *Seiji Handobukku* (Tokyo, 1990).

Note: Industrial associations are usually members of the Federation of Economic Organizations. Most of the "mass" organizations have many members, as the term indicates.

Divisions between the party elite and rank-and-file members were also fairly common. In the 1980s they disagreed on tax reform, farm policy, and several other issues. Party leaders sometimes had to give in to rank-and-file pressure and ratify policies initiated by informal groups within the party. The repeated accommodation of farm group demands provides one such example. In other cases, party leaders held the line against intraparty pressure. The party center prevailed in 1988, for example, when Prime Minister Takeshita and other party leaders pushed tax reforms through the Diet in the face of intense opposition from fellow party members representing regional and small retailers' interests. A generational cleavage between senior and junior Dietmembers was also visible upon occasion in the 1970s and later over issues related to political ethics and party survival.

Interestingly, although individual leaders of some LDP factions had reputations as hawks or doves on security issues, the factions themselves generally did not have strong ideological or policy coloring. Lacking cohesive opinions on most issues, members of factions and their leaders could be expected to refrain from involvement in policy matters. Nevertheless, competition for party leadership positions sometimes became entangled with policy processes. When that happened — particularly when extension of a party president's term was at stake or when a new LDP president was to be selected — factional politics became a part of legislative policymaking.

Careers and Conflict in the LDP

The long domination of political power by the LDP was in part contingent on election trends (see Chapter 2). But stable rule also depended on the integrity of party institutions and processes in the face of the competition within the party.[22] Some features of party life contributed to its organizational continuity and, therefore, to its ability to stay in power for thirty-eight years. Let us begin with the much maligned factions.

Factions, it will be remembered, are groups of followers of a particular politician. Before the formation of the Liberal Democratic Party in 1955, the most prominent conservative leaders, Shigeru Yoshida and Ichiro Hatoyama, each had personal followings. There were also some other leader-centered groups in those parties.[23] Soon after the formation of the LDP, factions appeared among followers and protégés of Yoshida and Hatoyama. This was the beginning of several faction lineages that have dominated LDP internal politics to the present (Figure 3.3).

In the 1950s factions reflected personal loyalties between party heavyweights and their followers. Because factions were identified by the name of

Figure 3.3. Liberal Democratic Party Faction Lineages, 1956–1993

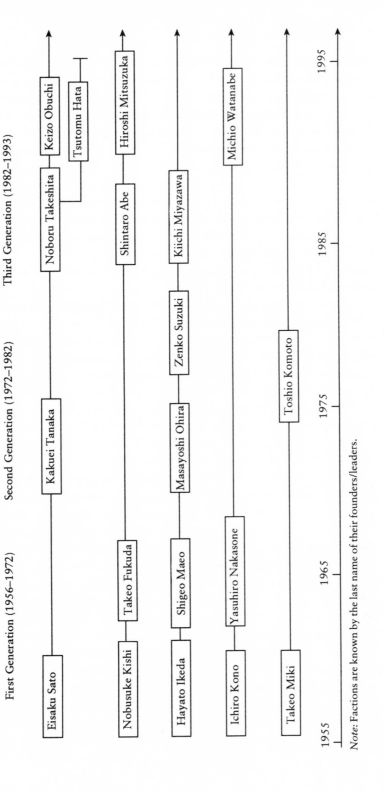

First Generation (1956–1972) Second Generation (1972–1982) Third Generation (1982–1993)

Note: Factions are known by the last name of their founders/leaders.

their leader (the Takeshita faction, the Nakasone faction), the belief that internal relationships followed a traditional patron-client model persisted. But the pure patron-client relationship was replaced over time by an organizational framework in which the faction leader was more a manager than a patron. This change makes it necessary to look beyond personal loyalties to determine the reason for factions' cohesiveness.

In spite of some changes in internal relationships, factions were always held together by the self-interest of members and leaders. Factions provided services for their members, and the members in turn were loyal supporters of the factions. Faction leaders used parliamentary votes controlled by their factions to launch coalition-building efforts to win top positions in party and government. The size of a faction, measured in number of members, was a bargaining resource to gain positions. Factions were the voting blocs from which party leadership coalitions were assembled.

Thus, as with other political coalitions, ordinary faction members and a faction's leader exchanged political resources. For LDP factions, the basic quid pro quo was, on the one hand, the provision of access to party and government positions and funding support for members and, on the other, members' support for faction leaders in contests for party leadership. Psychologically, factions reduced the uncertainty of members' political lives by making careers more predictable.[24] Over time, this intrafaction exchange of resources became at least as important to faction solidarity and continuity as personal loyalties and feelings, or even specific inducements by leaders to maintain solidarity, although these also contributed to faction maintenance.

Factions provided a variety of services and resources to their members above and beyond stable career expectations. Faction leaders and their lieutenants made campaign speeches in members' home constituencies and provided funds to help members with election campaign expenses.[25] Factions also sought party endorsement of incumbent members and newly sponsored candidates.[26] Even after the establishment of a proportional representation system in upper house elections in 1982, which theoretically might have enhanced the role of the party's formal organization, candidate positions on the party lists were said to be determined by factional interests.[27] Finally, faction leaders provided members with regular money allowances, which helped them maintain a constituency organization between elections. Leaders also provided their followers with New Year's gifts of money, or *o-mochi dai*, and gifts at the summer chugen season.[28] They helped members gain necessary access to represent the interests of their electoral constituencies. Even after 1993 some junior Dietmembers still thought that factions were important to their needs in regard to taking care of petitions from constituents.[29]

e 3.2. Business Contributions to LDP Factions and Subfactions in 1986–1993 (in millions
S. dollars)

essive Faction Heads	1986	1987	1988	1989	1990	1991	1992	1993
ka > Takeshita > Obuchi	6	15	11	10	7	6	NA	8
ki > Miyazawa	12	9	13	12	9	8	8	13
da > Abe > Mitsuzuka	20	20	17	18	35	12	14	13
sone > Watanabe	19	15	16	13	16	14	10	17
> Komoto	9	7	9	16	19	6	7	14

e: Data from Seiji Koho Senta, *Seiji Handobukku* (Tokyo, 1986, 1989, 1991), based on Jichisho reports.

Reported contributions to factions declined sharply after the 1975 reform. Newspaper exposés in the
s and 1990s suggest that much more was collected after the reform than was openly revealed.

The behavior of leaders also contributed to faction solidarity and stability.[30]
A faction head had to be able to raise money from important donors (Table
3.2) to pay for the faction office and meetings and to pay publication and
entertainment expenses, campaign subsidies given to candidates, and regular
allowances to faction members and their twice yearly gifts. However, reflecting mid-1970s changes in election funding laws and political corruption scandals, many sources indicate that after that date factions provided less monetary support for individual members' campaigns than in the past. Faction
leaders also needed to maintain solidarity within the faction by careful and
judicious management of political and material resources and energetic defense of the faction's interests in the coalitional politics of the party. Often a
faction leader was aided in these political tasks by lieutenants, who were
usually senior politicians themselves.

Most of the major LDP factions were formed in the 1950s and were passed
on to new leaders when a faction leader retired from politics or died (see
Figure 3.3). The stability of factions until the LDP's loss of power in July 1993
has reflected the importance of their functions. The most important function
until recently was the periodic selection of a party and government leadership
team. Even now, LDP factions exist, although most have reformulated themselves as study groups. According to some accounts, they still play a role in
party decisionmaking (see Chapter 4). The continuity of factions also reflects
the strong commitment of members to their factions. Like the lifetime employees of major firms, faction members seldom switched allegiance to a different intraparty group.[31]

Application of the social science concept of institutionalization provides
additional insight into the character of factions. Nelson Polsby uses the term

institutionalized to characterize an organization with (1) durability, (2) autonomy (that is, boundaries), and (3) internal complexity.[32] Having been in existence since the 1950s, the factions meet the test of durability. Because faction members rarely change factions, clear boundaries must exist as well. Factions also meet the criterion of internal complexity. Each faction had many of the organizational characteristics of a Japanese-style political party, including a hierarchy of formal offices (chair, vice chair, secretary general) and policy and election committees. Some factions even had a general affairs section, or secretariat. Often there were groups of junior, middle-ranking, and senior members (seniority being based on number of times elected to the Diet), plus an informal group of retired (or very senior) members who, like their counterparts in the party itself, provided counsel to faction leaders or championed faction interests as members of the party's supreme consultative council. Most factions also had informal power structures, for example, the "seven magistrates" of the Takeshita faction and the "court nobles" of the Miyazawa faction.[33] As already discussed, most factions had subgroups led by up-and-coming politicians.

The LDP factions also undertook a variety of regular activities that contributed to their organizational complexity. Meetings of officers and members were held regularly, in some instances as often as every week. "Study" meetings and dinners for members of different internal groups were also held regularly. Holding such meetings in Japanese-style restaurants (where customers sit on tatami mats and partake of *kaiseki* cuisine) has contributed to the image of Japanese "tea house" politics.[34] Summer retreats in mountain resorts provided another opportunity for faction members to get together and escape from the midsummer heat of Tokyo. In some factions new members were reportedly given special training—another routine.[35] Each faction also had newsletters and other forms of internal communication.

Procedural norms that developed over time contributed to the institutionalized character of LDP factions. A rigidly defined rule of seniority was used to select members for cabinet and party positions. By establishing exactly what kind of position a person would get after being elected a certain number of times, it helped prevent conflict among intensely ambitious people.[36] Faction members could be sure that they would receive certain kinds of appointments as they advanced in seniority. Faction leaders parceled out appointments in a predictable way. When the seniority rule was sometimes violated—when a junior member was promoted ahead of turn or when a senior politician entered a faction laterally—the ensuing uproar indicated its importance.[37]

Holding regular faction meetings encouraged a sense of solidarity among otherwise highly competitive people. Subgroups held special get-togethers, often dinner parties in Japanese-style restaurants.[38] These included separate meetings or study seminars for junior, middle-ranking, and senior members. Solidarity was easier to establish in these smaller groups than if the entire faction was present, and promoting solidarity among people with the same party tenure directly addressed the problem of intragenerational competitiveness, which was the only arena of competition left after strict application of the seniority principle. Dietmembers with different degrees of seniority had different interests. Faction members elected once or twice tended to be most interested in stabilizing their election base. Maintaining a positive reputation for the LDP was also important, because that would help their future campaigns as party-affiliated candidates. Middle-ranking and senior members were less immediately concerned about electoral support and more interested in the spoils of factional membership, that is, senior positions in official party organs, the Diet, and the government.[39]

Faction leaders' ability to handle appointments fairly is another key to promoting stability.[40] By not naming personal favorites to high positions, a faction leader could be known for having a "spirit of impartiality." A reputation for fighting hard to maximize the faction's share of top political appointments also helped leaders maintain factional solidarity and support. Leaders also gained legitimacy by donating money in culturally appropriate ways. The late Shintaro Abe was said to have handled gift giving with unusual judiciousness, thereby earning support from all members of his faction. He even made condolence gifts to faction candidates who failed to get elected to the Diet. Subfaction leaders also gave their followers money to cement their loyalty.[41]

The importance of factions to members' self-interest and, in turn, to faction durability was evident at times of transition. When factions lost their leaders or when leaders appeared to be losing their ability to provide access to top positions, observers described the factions as teetering on the edge of collapse.[42] Even though total collapse was rare, the fear of its happening could be common.[43] The factions were stable social structures, but their stability depended on their ability to continually serve members' interests.

Faction Competition, Leadership Coalitions, and Party Stability

To recapitulate: some of the considerable competition and conflict within the Liberal Democratic Party has been between institutionalized factions, which existed to provide members with stable career expectations. Like seniority norms in the U.S. Congress, the seniority system in the LDP made political life more certain and conflict less inevitable, at least within the factions themselves. Factions simultaneously enhanced and reduced conflict within the LDP. Because factions were institutionalized, competition between them was at times very intense. But the factions also stabilized party life. The same intraparty factions contested choices of top LDP personnel year in and year out with usually only minor, slow changes in the personnel involved in making choices. Faction stability lent an overall regularity to the behavior and expected behavior of important actors in intraparty political processes. Competition for top positions and expectations about this competition were stably structured, and this stability, combined with party procedures and norms, made orderly transfers of power possible despite occasional enormous intraparty conflict and centrifugal pressure.

Between 1955 and 1993 government and LDP leaders were chosen by coalitions of party factions. The coalitions were founded on agreements to support a particular leadership team in exchange for the allocation of several important positions to each participating faction. New LDP presidents were typically selected every two years in the 1970s and 1980s, although some had a longer or shorter tenure in office. A turnover in cabinet appointments took place even more frequently. In the first seven years of the 1980s Japan changed cabinets (but not prime ministers) on the average of once every twelve months. The LDP leadership coalitions were thus short-lived and were occasionally quite fragile. Coalition agreements could be renegotiated, and aspirant leaders were always waiting in the wings.

Cabinet tenure has been very short in Japan; in other countries this is often a sign of government instability. Cabinets were reshuffled annually in Japan between 1945 and 1993. In Britain, cabinets lasted for an average fifty months in roughly the same period. Given especially that the period of LDP rule was mainly a time of government stability, the frequency of cabinet replacement is striking. Italian and Japanese cabinets in the 1980s were of roughly equal durability, and Italy is usually said to be a country of unusual leadership volatility. The answer to this conundrum lies in the motivation for cabinet change. In Italy cabinets fell because of intense internal disagreements. In Japan they were replaced in allocating positions to new teams of aspiring politicians. We can conclude that frequent cabinet turnover in Japan indicates the importance of senior personnel appointments to politicians, not government instability.

When making leadership choices, the LDP functioned much like a multiparty system. When a cabinet reshuffle or change in party leadership seemed to be in the offing, each LDP faction developed a coalition strategy consisting of (1) efforts to form an alliance with other factions and (2) a slate of cabinet or party positions to be allocated to the faction in exchange for the faction's participation in a new interfactional leadership coalition.[44] As part of the coalition strategy, faction leaders cultivated relationships with members of other factions. Their goal was to acquire a sufficient number of allies among the large factions to end up in the winning coalition. The winning coalition was usually one that had, at a minimum, the support of a majority of the LDP Dietmembers; it was usually assembled from among the largest factions in the party. Sometimes precoalition alignments already existed, based on personal ties between faction leaders. One such relationship existed between Shintaro Abe and Noboru Takeshita in the 1980s.[45] In some cases, enmities between certain leaders precluded faction alliances. Because the LDP has always had its share of proud, ambitious leaders, maintaining good relationships was not easy. Long-standing grudges — such as the Kaku-Fuku (*Kaku*ei Tanaka–Takeo *Fuku*da) war of the 1970s and tensions between Takeshita and Shin Kanemaru and between Takeshita and Kiichi Miyazawa in the 1980s — were not uncommon.[46] Similar enmities between top politicians continue to exist in the LDP and other parties today.

Coalition negotiations typically took place between representatives of the individual factions and were moderated by the prime minister, a party elder, or the secretary general of the party. Eventually an agreement on a slate of government and party leaders was worked out. In the 1980s most or all of the main LDP factions participated. Earlier in the postwar period, a majority or "mainstream" coalition emerged from the coalition talks, and some factions were left out as "anti-mainstream" remnants.[47]

Party recruitment of leaders and cabinet members was governed by a mixture of formal rules and informal norms specifying when, how, and how often leaders would be selected.[48] On some occasions the LDP selected a president by vote in an extraordinary party convention. At other times an official party primary was held to eliminate all but the top candidates for the party presidency. On quite a few occasions a new party president was selected through informal consultations between the major factions. Sometimes this method was used even when the decision was later put to a vote in a party convention. One or more party elders or the party president himself managed this process. On twenty occasions in the 1970s and 1980s cabinet ministers were reshuffled in the same informal way. Table 3.3 shows the dominant method used in each choice of LDP president from 1972 to 1991.[49]

The expectations involved in forming (and removing) LDP leadership coalitions provide evidence of the regularized nature of intraparty processes. Usually there were tentative understandings within the LDP regarding the probable order of succession to the party presidency. Most of the time a particular generational window of opportunity existed for a small number of the leading

Table 3.3. Methods Used to Select LDP Presidents, 1972–1991

Year	Contenders	Method	Political Climate
1972	Fukuda, Tanaka*	Party convention election	Intense interfactional compet●
1974	Miki*	Informal talks	Prime Minister Tanaka accus● corruption
1976	Fukuda*, Miki	Talks and party election	Tanaka corruption scandal p weak prime minister
1978	Fukuda, Ohira*	Party primary	Intense interfactional compet●
1980	Suzuki*, Miyazawa, Komoto, Nakasone	Interfactional talks	Intense interfactional compet●
1982	Nakasone*, Komoto, Abe, Nakagawa	Party primary	Competition
1987	Abe, Miyazawa, Takeshita*	Interfactional talks moderated by prime minister	Moderate competition
1989	Uno*	Interfactional talks	Corruption scandal discredit party
1989	Kaifu*, Hayashi, Ishihara	Party election	Corruption scandal discredit party
1991	Miyazawa*	Interfactional talks	Moderate competition

Sources: Data from Asahi Shimbunsha, Asahi Nenkan (various years); and Nihon Keizai, May 28, 1989

Note: The years are those in which new prime ministers were chosen. The choice of a particular m● succession was dependent on the number of candidates, the predictability of the outcome, and the stabil● the general political environment. Sometimes informal competition for the presidency was intense, or the was in the midst of a crisis. Sometimes formal procedures were employed when consultations appeared fruitless because of intense competition.

*Winning contender.

party figures. The window was determined by expectations about (1) how long the incumbent would survive as party president, (2) how many credible aspirants (usually leaders of the largest factions) there were, and (3) whether and when a new generation of aspirants for office would make a challenge to replace the existing generation. The concept of leadership generations, or clusters of possible leaders classified by age — for example, Fukuda and Nakasone versus Abe and Miyazawa, Takeshita versus Mitsuzuka, Watanabe versus Ozawa, Hashimoto, and Kato — was used widely in the 1980s. Usually only the leaders of some of the large factions were expected to become party president and therefore were included in this group.

Contending faction leaders within an eligible generational cohort may have agreed on an even more refined order of succession to the party presi-

dency. It was rumored that such an agreement existed between Noboru Takeshita and Shintaro Abe when Prime Minister Nakasone resigned in 1987.[50]
One the "new generation" faction leaders—Takeshita, Kiichi Miyazawa, or
Abe—was expected to succeed as party president and prime minister after
Nakasone, simply because they were the heads of the three leading party
factions other than Nakasone's. Takeshita was the choice of the outgoing
party president, Yasuhiro Nakasone, perhaps because Takeshita's faction was
the largest and would inevitably play a major role in any succession talks. It
was said that Abe would succeed Takeshita if he agreed not to contest Takeshita's preceding him. Other factions began to consider who would be next
after that.[51]

Whether or not all the published rumors about private succession agreements are true, LDP leaders obviously paid a lot of attention to succession
issues and the pursuit of the prime ministership. Succession by age cohort
governed the expectations of the LDP members. Once again, the seniority rule
could dampen competition and conflict through its effect on leaders' ambitions and expectations.

When and how a party president had to step down was also a matter of intraparty understanding. A successful motion of nonconfidence or the failure of a
confidence motion can remove a prime minister before the end of a House of
Representatives term. These motions are made and voted on only in the House
of Representatives. Nonconfidence motions were not a preferred mechanism
for resolution of intraparty succession issues, although they were used this way
in 1980. Generally it was assumed that a party president would serve for two
terms at the most, or four years.[52] Most leaders in the 1970s and 1980s lasted
only one term. When a president had to step down was based on political credibility as judged by factions and their leadership. Failure of the party to do well
in a parliamentary election, extremely poor performance in monthly opinion
polls, or failure to move the legislative agenda of the conservative party
through the Diet or to deal with major problems effectively were all used to
discredit incumbents. Weak leadership performance prompted other factions
to try to terminate the incumbent leadership coalition and select a new leader.

Another norm at work—the "fair shares" norm—was evident in the tendency for most interfaction coalitions in the 1980s to be of the all-party or all-
faction variety. In all-party coalitions most or all factions received positions
roughly according to their size.[53] All-party coalitions reflected several factors
in combination, including an increased need for party unity after the electoral
losses in 1979 and 1983, as well as the application of the fair-shares norm in
selecting party leadership.[54] All-party coalitions were easier to establish in
the 1980s than earlier because explicit interpersonal rivalries (such as the

Kaku-Fuku war) and differences in leader ideologies and styles (which had produced mainstream versus anti-mainstream divisions earlier in the postwar era) had moderated by the late 1970s.

Internal Policymaking

The Liberal Democratic Party was a giant catchall party during its hegemony; it represented many diverse opinions and most important interest groups. Some degree of intraparty agreement on policies had to be achieved to preserve party integrity and to make it possible to vote as a bloc in the parliament. The goal of the intraparty policymaking procedures was to reach either substantive agreement on policy proposals or, in the absence of such agreement, tacit acceptance of the positions advocated by some section of the party. In case of irresoluble differences the goal was simply maintenance of legitimacy for the procedures used to develop decisions on controversial matters.

An elaborate set of institutions and procedures was developed to process demands from interest groups and accommodate pressures from zoku and other internal and external sources of policy proposals. The institutions included a kind of a intraparty legislature — the Policy Affairs Research Council — and three cabinetlike bodies: the PARC Deliberation Council, the LDP Executive Council, and the group of top LDP officers. A working hierarchy of institutions thus assured that final decisions or accommodations could be made in normal circumstances. These organizations and procedures, like the procedures for choosing leaders, were institutionalized over time.

Because the LDP and its predecessor parties dominated politics for so long, institutions and groups within the conservative party assumed particular importance in national policymaking. I have already suggested that the enormous LDP policy organ, the PARC, could be compared to a pre-parliamentary legislature.[55] In 1992 the PARC had seventeen divisions, which paralleled the organization of government ministries and the standing committees in both houses of the Diet (see Figure 3.1). The PARC divisions, like U.S. congressional committees, dealt with policies affecting broad functional divisions of government. The PARC also had forty-four investigative councils and forty-three special committees in 1991. The councils and committees dealt with more specialized policy matters, such as farm or small-business issues. Like U.S. congressional subcommittees, they focused on current problems and special issues. Subdivisions of the PARC even hold hearings on proposed legislation and issues related to legislative concerns. Their resemblance to congressional committees is closest in this sense. The Deliberation Council of the PARC might be compared to the plenary sessions of a legislature or a government cabinet. With the exception of the party leaders and the party executive council, the PARC, at least in theory, has the final word on intraparty policies.

By virtue of the LDP's pluralism, the PARC was a center of policymaking debate and policy coalition building. Linkages between PARC divisions, investigative councils, and special committees and the government ministries were numerous and had the net result of involving PARC groups and their related zoku in the early stages of policymaking.[56] Because a large share of the interest groups in society were part of the LDP coalition at some level, the PARC's role of screening or proposing legislative initiatives made it one of the most important institutions in politics.

Although policy discussions within the PARC served the important function of legitimizing party decisions and promoting the unity necessary for the LDP to operate as a disciplined corporate unit within the Diet, intra-PARC procedures did not always satisfy intraparty groups and the interests that they represented. Conflict sometimes surfaced within the party even after PARC deliberations were completed. Sometimes closure was invoked before sufficient intraparty agreement was reached or before LDP constituencies had weighed in. In the 1980s, LDP Dietmembers continued to disagree over health insurance policy, election system reform, tax reform, and defense policy even after policy proposals or legislative bills reached the cabinet or Diet. These disagreements distracted party leaders and kept them from moving forward with strategies focused solely on interparty legislative relations.[57] Similar intraparty differences occurred earlier over election system reform (1967), local tax law reform (1972), political funding law amendments (1975), antimonopoly law amendments (1975 and 1977), and the budget (1979).[58]

The great pluralism within the LDP often frustrated the efforts of the party's policy and executive councils to aggregate different positions. Party leaders sometimes found it difficult to make policy decisions that would preserve their own positions or the organizational integrity of the party. As a result, party pronouncements on annual budgets could take the form of unaggregated and unranked lists of demands from different interests.[59] The cultural goal of mutual accommodation enhanced the influence of diversity on party leaders. In some cases, even the existence of explicit procedures and institutional channels for handling conflict failed to result in decisions satisfactory to everyone.

Factions and Organization in Other Parties

Factions in the Social Democratic Party of Japan were at times even more fractious than those in the LDP. From 1951 until 1955 the SDPJ was formally divided into left and right ideological wings. In addition, factions existed which, like their LDP counterparts, were made up of Dietmembers who followed particular party leaders. Factions based on adherence to particular ideologies also existed. Some factions were both personal followings and ideological groupings.

Ideology was always much more important in the SDPJ and its factions than in the LDP and its factions. Generally, party factions and groups could be located on a left-right continuum (Table 3.4). Over time the SDPJ factions and groups have come more and more to reflect just ideological divisions. One authority has described intra-SDPJ factionalism in the 1980s: "The current practice is to designate factions as study groups rather than leader-follower groups. . . . Contemporary factions in the JSP [SDPJ] do not usually have obvious leaders, in the sense of single individuals behind whom the factions rally. These factions are vitally concerned with issues relating to the leadership of the party, but fundamental questions of party ideology . . . are also of pressing importance to them."[60]

The emphasis of SDPJ factions on ideology has led at times to party instability. Whereas factions in the LDP were highly durable, group fragmentation and recombination was frequent in the SDPJ. Whereas LDP factionalism resembled the institutionalized party system of postwar Italy, SDPJ factionalism more often resembled the French party system, where parties have dissolved and recombined within ideological camps. The LDP factions became institutionalized in the absence of strong ideological differences and by virtue of access to government positions. In contrast, the SDPJ factions were unable to offer their members access to government office; centrifugal strains were frequently generated by differences over ideology.

Factionalism has been less prevalent in smaller parties than in the LDP and the SDPJ. From time to time, factions have been reported in the Democratic Socialist Party (DSP). Leader-follower factions centering on Eki Sone and Eichi Nishimura existed in the late 1960s.[61] Later the DSP was divided between followers of Eichi Nagasue from "western" Japan and followers of Ikko Kasuga from "eastern" districts.[62] There was a sharp generational conflict over personnel appointments in the DSP in the late 1980s.[63] Other than these examples, there has been little indication of factional activities or interfaction strife in the fairly small Diet contingent of the DSP. Nor, in most periods, have factions been visible in the Clean Government and Japan Communist Parties.[64] The recent small conservative parties — Japan New Party, Renewal Party, and Harbinger Party — did not have factions, although there were some personal feuds. Large Japanese parties display a tendency to factional proliferation.[65] Small parties appear to be less prone to factional divisions.

Table 3.4. Factions in the Social Democratic Party

Groups	Representation in Party Executive			
	1982	1983	1986	1991
Government-Concept Study Group (Right-Wing)	2	7	8	10
"Intermediate Groups"				
Socialism Research Association	4	5	5	0
Left-Wing Groups				
New Life Study Group (Shinsei)	5	3	3	0
Former Katsumata Faction	6	4	3	0
Association for Creating a New Social Democratic Party (Socialist Association, Right Wing)	0	0	0	1
Ultra-Left-Wing Groups				
Socialist Association, Left Wing	0	3	2	0
Former March Society (Sangatsukai)	2	0	0	0
Nonideological Reform Groups				
Policy Research Group	0	0	0	2
Social Democratic Forum	0	0	0	3
New Wave	0	0	0	1
Total	26	28	27	29

Sources: Seiji Koho Senta, *Seiji Handobukku* (Tokyo, various years); *Tokyo Shimbun*, February 7, 1982, and September 8, 1983; *Mainichi*, January 22, 1986 (E); *Nihon Keizai*, August 25, 1989; *Yomiuri*, July 31, 1991.

Note: The total positions mentioned in press accounts varied in different years. Differences between totals for persons identified with factions and total number of executive positions are due to the presence of unaffiliated persons. Nine groups cited as existing within the party were omitted because they were not represented in the executive.

With the exception of the Communist and Clean Government Parties, party organization has been less complete within the traditional opposition parties than in the LDP.[66] All parties have executive positions and organizational units devoted to Diet strategy, party membership, party discipline, internal organization, and elections, as well as policymaking organizations.[67] Policymaking organs in the smaller parties have had far fewer internal divisions and sections than those in the LDP. With the exception of the SDPJ, the opposition parties have had less reason to develop large differentiated policy organs than the LDP, because their interest group base has been much smaller. The many constituencies of the LDP and its long stay in power contributed to the proliferation of institutionalized subunits. The smaller parties also lacked the members to staff complex internal policymaking bodies.

Conclusion

The decentralized and fragmented nature of faction and policy group power in the LDP during its hegemonic period has been a key feature of postwar Japanese politics. Centrifugal tendencies within the party and the centrifugal and parochialized nature of electoral competition made LDP-dominated governments less authoritarian than they might otherwise have been. There is little evidence for a simple vertical model of politics in the area of party organization.

Penetration of the traditionally dominant party by interest groups and a related flow of policy proposals from the rank and file to the party center through the institutionalized processes of the PARC was facilitated by the general fragmentation of party power in the LDP. Even the much maligned factional system helped provide access. Bureaucrats and others knew that regular Dietmembers, who were more accessible than the political movers and shakers, could appeal to senior faction members for assistance on behalf of special interests.[68] Power distributions within parties, and within intraparty groups, has conformed mainly to a horizontal model of politics.

The internal structures of the LDP (and, to some extent, the SDPJ) are an interesting mélange of both European-style party centralization and American-style party decentralization. European parties, such as Socialist and Christian Democratic parties, established highly centralized and complex formal organizations from the beginning. Their organizational style was mobilizational.[69] These parties also had party branches nationwide and sometimes many affiliated secondary associations. Parties often went beyond their organizational bases in unions and churches to establish local organizations encompassing many kinds of social and recreational activities.[70]

American parties and European Liberal parties have a very loose form of organization; their structure mainly consists of the small nuclei of party officials at different levels of government. The parties lack local membership branches, and American parties usually have no equivalent of the card-carrying members typically found in European parties. Nor are the different levels of nuclei connected hierarchically. Their nonhierarchical nature has led one scholar to call the American parties stratarchies.[71]

The formal organization of the LDP conforms to the European centralized type, with its multiple formal central and local organs and overall dense organization. In fact, the Policy Affairs Research Council of the LDP is an unusually inclusive party institution and has no counterpart in the political parties of other major industrialized countries. On the other hand, the LDP is more decentralized than European Socialist and Christian Democratic parties.[72] Nor does it resemble the centralized British Conservative Party, which was its model. The politics of factions, policy groups, zoku, and local political machines actually made the LDP in its heyday resemble a stratarchy more than its formal organizational centralization and density would suggest. Much the same is true today, despite the partial eclipse of the factions and zoku. The same may be true for the SDPJ, although it has probably been somewhat more centralized than the LDP. Both parties, however, are more responsible to their local organizational bases (local constituency interests in the LDP and unions and local constituencies for the SDPJ) than the typical European case. Interestingly, the large parties in Japan have developed an informal federal structure. We could say that they best resemble the postwar Italian Christian Democratic and Socialist Parties.[73]

A striking feature of Japanese party organization is the importance of informal groups and relationships. Factions, coordination bodies, zoku, and the machines of local politicians are all unplanned social formations, even though they may have taken on formal, institutionalized characteristics. Party organization in postwar Japan is somewhat unique in this regard and once again resembles only postwar Italy in its degree of informal but also highly structured factionalism.[74] Factionalism in both countries has existed for highly utilitarian reasons but each also reflected practices more in tune with society and culture than the organizational paradigms of most Western parties did. All parties, wherever they are, have important informal characteristics. But in Japan and Italy informal relationships were conspicuous and formalized to an unusual degree.

Under LDP rule, party fragmentation was one reason why the political system was more decentralized than its European counterparts. Even though Japanese politics has recently changed in ways that could not have been predicted earlier, many party characteristics will not change. Even though parties with new names shared power in 1993–94 and still other formations may appear, fragmented, decentralized rule will prevail.

4

Party Fragmentation and Coalition Dynamics

The Liberal Democratic Party was stable and institutionalized between 1955 and 1993. In spite of frequently intense internal competition and conflict, it retained its organizational integrity for nearly forty years. Then, in 1993, two groups of LDP Dietmembers defected to form new parties. The defections and associated events threw the LDP and Japanese politics into virtual disarray in 1993–94. At least two dozen new intraparty and interparty reform groups, several splinter groups, and one new multiparty movement were formed within only fifteen months. How can the contradictions between the LDP's long rule and elaborate organizational arrangements, on the one hand, and its sudden partial collapse and related organizational chaos since 1988–89, on the other hand, be explained?

Political parties are coalitions as well as organizations, and it is in this fact that the reason for the partial collapse lies. Coalitions can last a long time and develop highly institutionalized structures. Under some conditions they are also very fragile and may collapse. Even though a party organization appears to be firmly established, continuation depends on whether party politicians continue to believe that the party should exist. Japanese party factions, faction-based intraparty and government leadership coalitions, and interparty government coalitions all share some of the same characteristics, although only the first two are normally expected to develop complex organizational forms. If coalitional agreements fall apart, organizational superstructures become less meaningful or even irrelevant. Historically, LDP politicians gained government positions and policy influence in exchange for accepting party policies and procedures and the faction system. As long as the coalition met members' needs, the party continued to exist. When the party and its leadership lost credibility in 1992–93, the party's raison d'être was weakened. For the LDP members who defected, it failed entirely.[1]

The LDP, which was formed in 1955 by joining two conservative parties, debuted in the midst of intense conflict in the conservative movement. Criticism by business that the ongoing disagreements and struggles for power of conservative politicians were disrupting effective government contributed to its formation. Since its formation the coalitional nature of the new party was visible in the periodic crises that threatened its existence. Loss of confidence in party leadership, coupled with internal factionalism and group conflict, brought the LDP near collapse several times. Intraparty troubles were so severe in 1980 that two LDP factions abstained from voting on an opposition-sponsored nonconfidence motion, which therefore passed the Diet. Before this, the Liberal Democrats' long domination of the lower house meant that nonconfidence motions were normally unsuccessful. This event, and the secession by LDP politicians who formed the small New Liberal Club in 1976, exemplify the severe internal conflicts and fragmentation that have intermittently threatened the party's existence.

Intraparty conflict and reactions to that conflict have contributed to opposing dynamics in the LDP. One dynamic is the persistence of party institutions and procedures that promote integration and solidarity. The other is an intermittent tendency toward fragmentation and crisis. The patterns visible in the LDP are also seen in the SDPJ and occasionally in other parties and organizations. Sometimes Japanese parties and organizations are highly stable coalitions; at other times, fragmentation and conflict make them volatile and potentially self-destructive. A similar dynamic and potential for collapse can be seen in interparty coalitions.

LDP Crises and the Coalition Dynamic

The Liberal Democratic Party is a coalition that has existed to serve the interests of its members, its leaders, and its interest group constituency by winning elections, formulating public policy proposals, and providing a system for recruiting party and government leaders. By working together, party politicians were able to gain office in the Diet, in party organs, and the government, represent constituencies, and formulate policies that advanced the principles of the dominant intraparty groups. The existence of the party served both the substantive interests of constituencies and a general desire among conservative politicians for orderly career advancement.

A concern for predictability also led to the formation of a variety of intra-party groups. Yet these groups also contributed to intraparty conflict and uncertainty. Sentiments among faction and policy group members generated such intense feelings that cleavages became nearly unresolvable. Interfaction and policy group conflict threatened the very existence of the party.

Between 1955 and 1993 party crises disrupted party affairs from time to time. Party collapse was forecast, and LDP politicians considered forming new parties. The most severe crises were sparked by intense factional opposition to Prime Minister Kishi's hard-line leadership (1960), criticism of Prime Minister Tanaka's involvement in multiple corruption scandals (1974), cabinet defections during the latter part of Prime Minister Miki's shaky tenure (1976), disputes over Prime Minister Ohira's leadership (1979–80), and intraparty tensions over the Recruit and other corruption scandals in the late 1980s and early 1990s. Less severe but still major conflicts took place in other years.

LDP crises developed in a more or less predictable pattern and as a counterpoint to the stable features of the LDP discussed in Chapter 3. Major crises most often resulted from a loss of credibility on the part of the party leadership. When Nobusuke Kishi's handling of revisions to the U.S.-Japan Security Treaty in 1959–60 resulted in abandonment of legitimate Diet procedures and the largest antigovernment demonstrations in postwar history, other LDP leaders maneuvered to repair the damage and dump Kishi. In 1974 a major corruption scandal undermined the credibility of the party president, Kakuei Tanaka, and it caused subsequent problems as well. In 1988–93 two major corruption scandals discredited the core party leadership. In 1976, 1979–80, and 1993 other crises were similarly fueled by the vulnerability of the party presidents Miki, Ohira, and Miyazawa. Some of the crises were aggravated by differences between mainstream and anti-mainstream factional coalitions and by intense internal policy differences.

External problems, such as LDP electoral declines and severe disruptions in Diet processes, also contributed to intraparty crises. Election losses added to the disequilibrating forces in 1974, 1976, 1979, 1989, and 1993, much as conflict in the Diet and on the streets of Tokyo added to the LDP's problems in 1959–60. The LDP dynamic of periodic internal crises and strong centrifugal tendencies was intertwined with external as well as internal political dynamics.

Two sets of events in the mid-1970s serve as good examples of intra-LDP crisis development and demonstrate the party's fragility long before 1993. Kakuei Tanaka became party president and prime minister of Japan in 1972 in a contested succession. Early in his premiership Tanaka engineered a rapprochement with the People's Republic of China that was opposed by many in the party; in fact, the rapprochement was carried out with the help of the opposition parties in the Diet. Opposition by important conservative groups in the party continued throughout Tanaka's time in office.[2] Many felt the party lacked a clear policy direction under his leadership. Tanaka's inclination to make quick decisions — indeed, impulsive, swashbuckling, populist leadership style in general — was also widely criticized. He was not a university graduate and lacked the elite credentials and bureaucratic background of most of his predecessors. His background was not a direct issue in his loss of intraparty credibility but undoubtedly contributed to the general controversy.[3]

Intraparty differences under Tanaka's rule crescendoed in the spring and summer of 1974. LDP Dietmembers who had been elected only one or two times were worried about the effect of problems in the party leadership on their future electoral chances.[4] The LDP's failure to stem declines in electoral support in the House of Councillors election in July added to the general malaise. After the election, eighteen members of parliament voted blank ballots in opposition to Tanaka's chosen candidate for House of Councillors president. In the same month Takeo Miki resigned as party vice president to protest Tanaka's leadership. Takeo Fukuda, a party leader and an avowed enemy of Tanaka, resigned from his post as finance minister for the same reason. Miki and Hayato Ikeda had similarly resigned to protest Prime Minister Kishi's arbitrary handling of the Police Duties Bill of 1958. Resignation by two senior cabinet members was an unusual and serious event in formal consensus-prone Japan, and these resignations by two party leaders dealt Tanaka a hard political blow. Rumors of splits in the party surfaced. The head of a right-wing policy group, the Seirankai, proposed formation of a new party.[5] The typical components of a party crisis were all present: leaders' loss of credibility, intensification of factional strife, anxiety among junior members of the party, and rumors or proposals of a party split. Prime Minister Tanaka finally resigned after a prominent magazine article implied that he had used public office to become rich. Later in 1976, Tanaka was the central figure in a bribery issue; his subsequent indictment and conviction brought off-and-on tensions in the party over nearly a decade.[6]

Miki replaced Tanaka as party president and prime minister in late fall 1974. The choice of Miki reflected in part his public image as a clean politician at a time when the party's reputation was suffering from the allegations of corruption involving Tanaka. But Miki was a maverick, and his faction was small, which limited his influence within the party. Complaints against Miki surfaced less than a year after he took office, motivated by both factional competition and perceptions that his leadership was weak. Miki was especially criticized for being conciliatory with the opposition parties. (Because of the LDP's thin majority in the Diet, he had sent feelers to the Socialist Party leadership, which led the SDPJ chair to suggest a coalition with the LDP.)[7] In typical crisis fashion, junior members of the parliamentary party formed groups advocating party reform. Later, party elders said that Miki's wobbling leadership was the party's "worst crisis since its formation in 1955" and proposed party "modernization" under an all-party leadership team. Secretaries general at the prefectural level took up the same theme.[8] Again, as under Tanaka, the possibility of a party split was openly discussed.

New groups and new proposals for courses of action proliferated as the crisis mood increased in the fall of 1976. Rank-and-file party members in the upper house proposed a declaration to reaffirm the LDP's anticommunism in refutation of Miki's "soft" stance. An All-Party Structure Establishment Council (APSEC) was formed, supposedly with support from more than 70 percent of the LDP. Arguments broke out between Miki and his opponents in the cabinet. Party elders formed a new cross-factional reform group, the Senyukai. Chairs of nineteen prefectural-level party federations proposed an extraordinary party convention to select a new president. In October the APSEC proposed Takeo Fukuda as Miki's successor, alleging that Miki had failed to carry out traditional LDP policies, curried favor with the opposition, was indecisive, and failed to consult with others.[9] After the party received the lowest share ever of the national vote in the general election in December 1976, Fukuda replaced Miki as prime minister.

LDP reactions following major corruption scandals in 1988–1993 were similar to those in the mid-1970s crises. Leading politicians lost credibility after accusations that they had profited from purchases of Recruit Company stock on the basis of insider information or accepted bribes from Sagawa Kyubin, a large trucking company. Junior LDP Dietmembers formed several intraparty reform groups out of frustration with the party leadership:[10] the forty-eight member cross-faction, Free Renovationist League, and a reform-oriented policy group, the Heiseinokai. The latter was also formed in response to creation of a right-wing group, Association of Persons Concerned over Basic State Problems.[11] A number of other groups were also active at this time, including the Hirakawa Society, named after the Tokyo location of the LDP headquarters, the Liberal Society Forum, the Utopia Study Group, and the Liberal Reform League.

The creation of reform and anti-reform groups was symptomatic of anxiety. As the party began to lose credibility and formerly secure careers seemed in doubt, different groups sought some solution to party problems. As in past crises, starting a new political party was a consideration. The Takeshita faction leader Shin Kanemaru met Social Democratic and Democratic Socialist leaders to discuss formation of a new middle-of-the-road party combining moderate elements of the LDP and the two Socialist parties.[12] LDP politicians also reportedly met with Democratic Socialist and Clean Government Party leaders to discuss other new combinations.

The 1988–1993 crises forced top party officials to resign and culminated in defections from the party; these, in turn, deprived the LDP of its majority in the Diet, ending its single-handed domination of politics. The LDP prime minister Noboru Takeshita had to resign in 1989 because of his involvement in the Recruit scandal. The LDP prime minister Kiichi Miyazawa, whose leadership was characterized as very weak from the beginning of his term in 1991, was forced to step down in 1993. With help from centrist and moderate left parties the previously unthinkable event of a non-LDP coalition government became reality in August 1993.

Defection from the LDP and the formation of new parties in 1993 had several motivations. Some who left the LDP were frustrated by the failure of Prime Minister Miyazawa to carry out political reform in the face of the party's loss of credibility in the corruption scandals: some saw reform as merely a political necessity; others believed that it was worthwhile in and of itself. There was also an element of opportunism. Ichiro Ozawa, a former rising star inside the LDP and a follower of Shin Kanemaru, left the LDP to expand his personal influence, as well as to promote reform. Ozawa said that politics must be "modernized" by eliminating the LDP. In a sense, the actions of the former Takeshita faction Dietmembers (including Ozawa) who established the Renewal Party represented the spread of LDP factionalism beyond the party's boundaries. (This rump factional group led by Tsutomu Hata and Ozawa stayed in the LDP for several months after its formation but left the party after political reform became mired in intraparty disputes.)

Specific events and loss of leaders' credibility contributed to each LDP crisis. Factional competition was also a factor in several cases. But the LDP crisis dynamic went beyond interfactional competition. Factions attempted to take advantage of events that were causing alarm among party politicians and therefore added to the general anxiety. In each case, severe intraparty conflict, perceptions of failed leadership, and election losses all contributed to a growing feeling that the party's very survival was threatened. Members of the LDP openly suggested in each case that a party split was in the offing. Internal policy disagreements added to the leadership crises. The conservative movement was sharply divided in the 1950s over revision of the postwar constitution and security policy, a cleavage mirrored again in the 1970s in debates on China policy.[13] Both ultraconservative and moderate groups (such as the Hirakawa Society led by Kiichi Miyazawa) were formed in this later period.

The fragility of the party coalition was further demonstrated by the outbreak of hostilities between the national party and its local components. In the most recent crisis (1988–93), several local LDP federations took up the protest against the central party leadership and passed resolutions demanding party reform and accountability. One prefectural organization threatened to secede from the party.[14] These actions concurred with the anti-LDP sentiment among farmers and small-business people in spring 1989.

Later in 1989 prefectural delegations at the annual summer meeting of representatives of party chapters reiterated demands for party reform. Nine LDP members of the Fukuoka prefectural assembly also asked for "en masse resignation of all LDP officers suspected of Recruit scandal involvement."[15] Similar demands came from members of the Nagoya city assembly and the Kagawa prefectural assembly. The same sort of local protests had been made during the LDP crises of the 1970s.

Local disagreements with the national leadership at times of crisis reflected the stratarchical nature of local-national party relations even in normal times. National-local squabbles over parliamentary and gubernatorial nominations during the era of LDP hegemony were routine and sometimes involved national and prefectural factions along with the formal party organs. In 1991, for example, the secretary general of the party (Ozawa) and some members of the Tokyo metropolitan prefecture party disagreed over the choice of a nominee for the governorship of Tokyo.[16] Incidents like that occurred with every major postwar election.

Cleavages within local party groups were fairly common as well. Divisions among the LDP representatives in the Saitama prefectural assembly were said to have helped ensure the reelection of left-independent Governor Yawara Hata in 1988. A split within the LDP headquarters in Yamanashi prefecture in 1990 reflected the lack of support by the chair, Shin Kanemaru, for the incumbent prefectural governor, Komei Mochizuki.[17] The LDP party coalition had internal fractures at all levels, and they widened during party crises.

Although the LDP survived multiple crises and internal conflicts and maintained its institutional integrity in a "perils of Pauline" fashion, it existed by grace of its coalitional support. Until 1993 the payoffs of positions and power and, for some, ideological opposition to communism, along with the party procedures that constrained conflict, held together an otherwise fragmentation-prone political movement.

Coalitions in the Social Democratic Party of Japan

The LDP model of a semi-institutionalized but highly fragmented coalitional structure can be seen elsewhere in Japanese politics. Fragmentation not unlike that in the LDP was often evident in the second largest party, the Social Democratic Party. Indeed, even though the SDPJ has always been considerably smaller than the LDP, the number of factions and intraparty ideological groups has often been greater. In normal times, then, the SDPJ could be described as more fragmented than even the LDP. Social Democratic factions and policy groups also split and regrouped fairly often. For example, the Socialist Association, the largest left-wing group in the party, split in 1986 over the New Declaration (a party move toward greater realism on policy issues). Forty of the 50 members of the Socialist Association on the 134-person party secretariat resigned.[18]

An internal fragmentation pattern like that of the LDP was apparent in the SDPJ in 1989–90 and later when party reform groups of junior Dietmembers were formed and local party organizations rebuked the party center.[19] Although the SDPJ did not lose credibility to the same degree as the LDP, by the early 1990s more than ten new groups had been established as party members struggled to redefine themselves in light of the rapidly changing conditions of Japanese politics.

A generational divide like that in the LDP was a prominent feature of the ongoing divisions in the SDPJ. For example, sixty SDPJ members of parliament elected for the first time in the 1990 election established two important new groups, New Wave and New Power. Not long thereafter, New Wave members requested that the party leadership resign, blaming them for the past failure of the SDPJ to gain power. New Power members criticized the party leadership for election losses in 1991. Like other reform groups, however, New Wave was divided on certain issues only a few months after its formation.

Several other intraparty policy or reform groups — Social Democracy Forum, Action New Democracy, Sirius, New Generation Political Forum, Leadership 21, and Society 91 — were also formed in the early 1990s.[20] In a 1992 report, *Nihon Keizai* stated: "With the successive establishment of new policy groups centering on young Diet members, the SDPJ is showing signs that its factional composition will become fluid. . . . Responding to the distrust in politics over the Tokyo Sagawa Kyubin case, and arguments for political reorganization in labor circles, this may be the spark that ignites an explosion on the opposition party side."[21]

Meetings were also held at several points in late 1992 to discuss possibly setting up a new middle-of-the road party, which would include parts of the

Hata-Ozawa group from the LDP, the right-wing of the SDPJ, and centrist parties. Fissures, generational challenges, and centrifugal dynamism were not properties of the LDP alone.

Party Organizations Under Stress

The fragmentation dynamic already in evidence in the LDP in autumn 1993 accelerated in the face of the many ongoing problems. Several people left the LDP in December 1993; and in April 1994 three small new parties were formed: Future, with five former LDP Dietmembers, Blue Clouds, with three former Japan New Party Dietmembers, and the Liberal Party, with former LDP members and independents. LDP defectors also formed two more small groups, Reform Club and Reform Federation.[22] The LDP lost seventy-four Dietmembers through defections or death between the general election in February 1990 and mid-1994. Fragmentation could be seen both within and outside the LDP, as the 1955 system as a whole began to crumble.

By October 1993, the LDP was divided into two main camps, a reform group and a conservative anti-reform group, as well as many smaller groups. The conservative or anti-reform group, called the Dietmembers' Liaison Council for Promotion of Political Reform, was opposed to changing the lower house election system, even though the existing multimember districts were widely criticized as a source of factionalism and corruption.[23] The camp favoring party and election system reform, called the Dietmembers' League for Promotion of Political Reform, was led by former Prime Minister Toshiki Kaifu.[24]

Many other groups of varying sizes and persuasions appeared and disappeared as Dietmembers aligned and realigned themselves in the ongoing debate over political reform. In addition to joining groups to express their own preferences, LDP politicians wanted to be on the winning side when the party reformed itself or at least recaptured a semblance of its former integrity and credibility. Other groups emerging in 1993 included the Democratic Politics Study Group (seventy members), Asian Security Study Group, Society to Think Cautiously About Public Subsidies for Political Parties (sixty-four members), Party Politics Research Group, and Committee for the Renewal of the LDP. One group without a name began meeting in September to formulate a reform program to counter that of Ichiro Ozawa, which indicates the intensity of anti-Ozawa feeling within the remnants of the LDP.[25] At different times several other groups were identified, too. The number of overlapping groups is noteworthy.

Intraparty reform and antireform groups proliferated into 1994. Some were set up by people who supported different views on reform, others by first-term Dietmembers who wanted to replace the traditional factions with new organizational structures. Some LDP Dietmembers, including junior MPs whose Diet tenure was short, were also active in cross-party groups, such as the New Century Association, an anti-Ozawa group that sought support from alienated Dietmembers within and outside the LDP. The New Century, founded to promote a transfer of power to younger members of the LDP, was led by a trio of LDP leaders in their fifties. Some in the party saw the New Century as a precursor to a new faction, castigating its three leaders as "class A and class B war criminals," a reference to the Allied war crimes trials after World War II.[26]

There were fissures in the SDPJ during 1993–94 as well. A group called the Democrats was formed in January 1994 from SDPJ moderates and members of two small parties, the United Social Democratic Party and the Democratic Reform Party.[27] A left-wing group, Taiyo (Sun), remained active and opposed SDPJ participation in the Hata cabinet.[28]

The proliferation of new LDP groups was one of several factors contributing to the decline of the existing LDP factions in 1993–94. The involvement of top party members — including faction leaders — in corruption scandals reflected poorly on the factions. The defections of nearly fifty LDP members and subsequent LDP losses in the 1993 election also presented problems for the factions. Loss of power meant, too, that neither the party nor its factions provided a certain career trajectory. The decision of big business to discontinue money contributions to the LDP further deprived the factions of a traditional raison d'être, the distribution of funds to followers.

The factions came under direct fire in proposing party reform. Shortly after the resignation of the Miyazawa government, LDP Secretary General Seiroku Kajiyama announced that a self-appointed interfaction leadership group, the Council for Party Unity and Advancement, would choose a new party president. Junior LDP Dietmembers heckled Kajiyama and accused him of perpetuating old-style party politics. The call to end the faction system was repeated when LDP party president Yohei Kono and party secretary general Yoshiro Mori met with first-term and second-term Dietmembers in August.[29] Eventually it was decided that LDP Dietmembers and prefectural organization representatives should elect the president by secret ballot.[30]

Indications of faction decline notwithstanding, faction leaders still influenced the course of party events at times. To retain power, the heads of all five major factions began holding regular meetings to discuss party policy in January 1994. They cited the current LDP leaders for "depriving the party of its dignity" by giving in to the Hosokawa coalition on rice imports and budget matters.[31] In April the faction heads called for a reshuffling of LDP leaders.

Although most factions had responded to repeated calls for their elimination by creating study groups, they still continued to hold meetings and conduct other factional activities under the study group umbrella.[32]

Other efforts at LDP reform also had mixed effects. When the incoming party president Yohei Kono chose new party leaders in August 1993, he included several senior politicians from the traditional factions. A challenge by rank-and-file Dietmembers to Kono's use of the seniority principle in this decision led to a promise to "consider" allowing junior members to enter the leadership group. The Supreme Advisers of the party, a group of former prime ministers, actually defended the factional system on the grounds that it "keeps order within the party." Nor was a decision made by Kono on a proposal to the party's political reform headquarters of a mandatory retirement age. The Supreme Advisers criticized the idea, and nothing was decided on the issue.[33]

Interparty Coalitions

After the LDP's loss of power in July 1993, Japan entered an era of coalition government. Three coalition governments were formed after that time, each with parties from the right, center, and left in different combinations. Because intra-LDP conflict led to partial collapse of a party coalition in the past, the degree of stable government that can be expected now from interparty coalitions is questionable. The turn to interparty coalitions does not bode well, given the possibility of intraparty fragmentation. Nor does experience provide a convincing clue to the future. In many countries multiparty coalition governments have been both stable and very unstable depending on conditions. Italy after World War II and France and Germany before the war had frequent cabinet changes. The Netherlands, postwar Germany, and Scandinavia provide examples of more stable multiparty coalitions. Postwar Japan has shown a mixture of patterns. Governments between 1945 and the formation of the Liberal Democratic Party in 1955 had both periods of stable rule and instances of volatility.[34]

Efforts to form interparty coalitions before the LDP's recent troubles are relevant to the question of where Japanese politics will go from here. Old coalition attempts and new interparty coalitions share some characteristics. Even intraparty leadership coalitions in the LDP offer some insight into Japanese-style coalition behavior, although ideological diversity has normally been less of a problem within than between parties.

The reduction in 1976–80 and again in 1983–86 of the LDP majority in the Diet to a handful of representatives, and the LDP's minority status in the House of Councillors after 1989, resulted in several proposals for interparty government coalitions (Table 4.1). The only actual governing coalition,

Conservative/Right	Center	Progressive/Left
		SDPJ-DSP-CGP or SDPJ-JCP alliance debated (1971)
		SDPJ right-left split over SDPJ-JCP cooperation (1972)
DSP moots coalition with part of LDP (1972)		
		SDPJ-JCP fight over outcastes and other issues (1975)
		SDPJ-JCP coalition plans stalled by policy fights (1976)
	DSP-CGP-SDPJ coalition plan stalled over including JCP (1977)	
	Opposition-center efforts to form government coalition fail (1980)	
	Social Democratic League open to coalition with some LDP factions (1982)	
	DSP angry with CGP but will continue some cooperation (1982)	
LDP-NLC Coalition (1983–86)		
DSP open to coalition with LDP if leader changes (1984)		
CGP open to coalition with LDP on three conditions (1984)		
LDP-DSP leaders secretly discuss policy alliance (1984)		
	DSP-CGP unity disrupted by disagreements (1982–84)	
	DSP-CGP leaders secretly discuss policy alliance (1984)	
	SDPJ and CGP make commitment to consult on coalition (1985)	
	Denki Roren union urges opposition party "unity" talks (1985)	
LDP courts DSP after House of Councillors election loss (1989)		
	Four opposition party leaders meet to discuss future coalition (1989)	
	Four-party Coalition Government Consultative Council formed (1989)	
LDP secretary general proposes LDP-SDPJ "grand" coalition (1990)		
LDP leader proposes "grand" coalition to DSP, CGP, and SDPJ (1992)		

Sources: Nihon Keizai, January 15, 1972, June 25, 1977, February 17 and 18 and June 6, 1982 (E), February 10 and 20, April 27, and November 1, 1984, June 8, 1985, November 19, 1989, March 23, 1990; *Yomiuri*, December 2, 1976, April 8, 1989, February 16, 1992; *Asahi*, August 30, 1971, June 10, 1975, January 13, 1985; *Tokyo Shimbun*, April 24, 1989, March 3, 1992.

however, was the conservative cabinet in 1983–86, comprising Liberal Democrats and New Liberal Club members. This coalition had several characteristics favorable to survival. The LDP-NLC coalition was established more than anything else to provide the LDP greater leverage within the Diet committee system. A payoff to the NLC came in the form of cabinet minister appointments. Forging a coalition was also facilitated by the ideological compatibility of NLC members with many in the LDP. Although there were personal enmities and rivalries between NLC leaders and some LDP politicians, ideological differences were not a barrier to a government alliance.

Proposals for coalitions within the opposition camp during LDP rule were a different story. Many such alliances were proposed in both the 1970s and 1980s. Formation of opposition governments had been discussed even in the 1960s. An alliance of conservative breakaway groups, centrist parties, and Socialist parties — one like the coalition government in the summer of 1993 — was proposed as early as 1975. But the chances of a coalition government were remote until the gap between the LDP and the opposition forces in respective numbers of Diet seats became narrower in the 1970s. No alliance was successful, even though a variety of coalition formulas were considered: right-center (LDP-DSP-CGP), middle-of-the-road (CGP-DSP–"right-wing" factions of the SDPJ), and center-progressive (DSP-CGP-SDPJ or DSP-CGP-SDPJ-JCP) (see Table 4.1).

Several kinds of events usually set the stage for coalition talks or speculation about coalition building. When LDP electoral fortunes reached lows in 1976–80 and 1983–86, right-center coalitions were mooted by the two center parties, the Democratic Socialist and Clean Government Parties. At other times, when the LDP was discredited by scandals, the center and left opposition parties discussed possible coalitions among themselves.[35] After major LDP losses in the upper house election in 1989, some LDP members approached the SDPJ and center parties to propose a grand coalition of all parties except the Japan Communist Party. In 1980, when the LDP temporarily lost its Diet majority after passage of an opposition party nonconfidence motion, the center and progressive parties attempted to form a coalition government but failed. Consolidation of the labor movement in the late 1980s was also perceived as increasing opposition chances for successful takeover of the government and led to interparty coalition talks, including some discussions sponsored by the unions.[36]

Possible interparty governing coalitions were discussed a great deal, but none was formed involving parties opposed to the LDP until 1993. Interparty enmities, like factional rivalries in the LDP, frustrated some coalition attempts. Relations between the Social Democratic Party of Japan and the Democratic

Table 4.2. Interparty Mayoralty Coalitions, 1976–1991

	1976	1979	1983	1987	1991
LDP-Center	38	98	194	219	189
Center (DSP-CGP)	3	5	13	13	6
Left (SDPJ-JCP)	35	38	23	14	13
Center-Left	83	61	51	43	31
LDP-SDPJ	2	3	2	2	7
Right-Center-Left	10	39	78	114	121

Source: Records of the labor-union-supported Chiho Jiji Sogo Kenkyujo.

Notes: LDP-center coalitions included LDP-DSP-CGP, LDP-DSP, and LDP-CGP coalitions. Center-left coalitions included SDPJ-CGP, SDPJ-DSP, SDPJ-CGP-DSP, SDPJ-DSP-JCP, SDPJ-CGP-JCP, CGP-DSP-JCP, and CGP-DSP-SDPJ-JCP coalitions. Right-center-left coalitions were three- to five-party combinations including the LDP, one or both center parties, and one or both left parties. Figures are raw numbers of electoral coalitions in coordinated national, city, town, and village elections.

Socialist Party, which split off from the SDPJ in 1959, remained cool even into the 1980s, despite intermittent discussions of a rapprochement.[37] On at least one occasion, relations between these parties were complicated by intra-SDPJ and intra-DSP leadership rivalries.

Ideological cleavages within a party also affected coalition possibilities. The left-wing Socialist Association usually opposed any coalition between the SDPJ, with which it was affiliated, and the two center parties, DSP and Clean Government Party. The center parties usually indicated that they would feel more comfortable in a coalition with only the right and center elements of the SDPJ. Proposals for opposition party coalitions traveled a rough road because of these alignments. The absence of a real opportunity to form a government (except briefly in June 1980) was also a major deterrent to cooperation.

Proposals for multiparty governing coalitions frequently failed, but there were still many successful multiparty coalitions on specific issues and bills in the Diet. The Democratic Socialist Party and the Clean Government Party cooperated with the LDP on several legislative bills in the House of Councillors after the LDP lost its majority there in 1989. Local election coalitions were even more numerous (Table 4.2). Of the city mayors elected in partisan elections in 1991 a high percentage — 77 percent — were supported by multiparty coalitions. Of the mayors elected between 1976 to 1991, 62 percent were supported by coalitions that included the LDP, and 27 percent were supported by coalitions that included both the LDP and the SDPJ. It is important to note that coalitions involving the SDPJ and the Japan Communist Party, as well as center-left coalitions of the DSP, Clean Government Party, SDPJ, and sometimes the Japan Communist Party, declined in number over time, whereas LDP-center coalitions increased by leaps and bounds. As we can see, coalitions were formed even between ideologically opposed partners at times, either because practical alternatives did not exist or because the agreements were forged between ideologically close intraparty groups, or both. Political parties have been able to work together on at least a temporary basis.

Since the major party upheaval in July 1993, partisan politics have been very unstable compared with all but the most fractious periods under LDP hegemony. Japan has had three interparty coalition governments since August 1993. The first brought together Dietmembers from the three new conservative parties — Japan New Party, Renewal Party, and Harbinger Party — plus the Democratic Socialist, Clean Government, Social Democratic, and two other small parties. The coalition was led by Morihiro Hosokawa of the Japan New Party. The second coalition government was led by Tsutomu Hata and consisted of the same parties as before minus the Harbinger Party; it succeeded the Hosokawa cabinet in April 1994. Both the Hosokawa and Hata cabinets were formed on the basis of opposition to the LDP. In June 1994 the Hata coalition cabinet was replaced by a coalition cabinet of the LDP, Harbinger Party, and SDPJ. The Socialist Tomiichi Murayama became prime minister. The pattern and shape of power were largely unchanged. Under the new coalition governments cooperation between parties replaced the cooperation between coalitions inside the fragmented LDP (Figure 4.1).

Policy divisions were a problem in the Hosokawa and Hata government coalitions, much as they had been in past efforts to form anti-LDP coalitions. The Hosokawa coalition of five major (and three tiny) parties was united by opposition to the LDP and concern for advancing political reform. But there were differences on defense and security policy, tax reform, nuclear power, electoral reform, and the proposed shape of a new party system (Table 4.3). Reflecting long-standing preferences, the SDPJ, and sometimes the Harbinger Party, opposed sending the Japanese Self-Defense Forces (SDF) overseas under U.N. colors. Its stand against remilitarization also led the SDPJ to oppose foreign deployment of the Self-Defense Forces to rescue Japanese nationals in overseas emergencies. The Renewal Party, in sharp contrast, favored a new, more assertive foreign policy for Japan. Overseas deployment of the Self-Defense Forces to support U.N. missions was one component of the proposed Japanese role. Similarly, the SDPJ, DSP, and Clean Government Party wanted income tax cuts, but the Japan New Party favored higher taxes in order for Japan to prepare for an aging society — one with an increasing proportion of

Figure 4.1. Intraparty and Interparty Coalitions, 1990–1995

Government

Opposition

1990–1993

LDP Factions

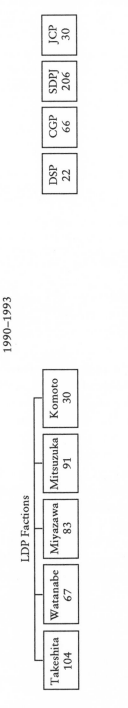

| Takeshita 104 | Watanabe 67 | Miyazawa 83 | Mitsuzuka 91 | Komoto 30 |

| DSP 22 | CGP 66 | SDPJ 206 | JCP 30 |

1993–1994

Multiparty Coalition

| Renewal 56 | Harbinger 13 | Japan New Party 41 | DSP 22 | CGP 76 | SDPJ 137 |

LDP Factions

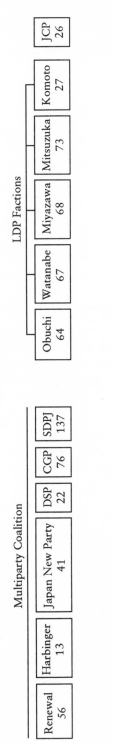

| Obuchi 64 | Watanabe 67 | Miyazawa 68 | Mitsuzuka 73 | Komoto 27 |

| JCP 26 |

1994–1995

Multiparty Coalition

LDP Study Groups

| Obuchi 64 | Watanabe 67 | Miyazawa 68 | Mitsuzuka 73 | Komoto 27 | SDPJ 137 | Harbinger 13 |

New Frontier Party

| Japan New Party 41 | DSP 22 | CGP 76 | Renewal 56 |

| JCP 26 |

Note: The number in each box is the number of Dietmembers in the party or faction.

Table 4.3. Party Divisions on Issues Under Coalition Government, August 1993–April 1994 (Hosokawa Cabinet)

Proposed Action	Japan New Party	Renewal Party	Clean Government Party	Democratic Socialist Party	Social Democratic Party of Japan
Creation of Small Election Districts	-	+	+	unk	-
Cabinet Reshuffle	unk	+	+	-	-
Formation of a New Party	+	+	+	-	-
Income Tax Cut	-	unk	+	+	+
Overseas Use of the Self-Defense Forces	unk	+	unk	unk	-
Liberalization of Rice Imports	+	+	+	unk	-

Sources: Nikkei Weekly, August 23, September 20, and December 13, 1993, February 28 and March 31, 19‹

+ = favored proposed action. - = opposed proposed action. unk = unknown.

older people. Coalition leaders were also prepared to accept an end to trade barriers on rice imports even though the SDPJ opposed them.

New as well as old issues divided the coalition parties. Political reform posed dilemmas, especially concerning the type of election system to be used in future House of Representatives elections. Quite a bit of the organizational support for the SDPJ came from trade unions whose members were spatially dispersed. The party therefore wanted a new election system with more large districts based on proportional representation. The Renewal Party and the Clean Government Party opposed this formula. Both parties (or their incumbent Dietmembers) had strong local organizations; their support was concentrated and more suited to a small district system than to large constituencies. The SDPJ differed with other parties over the closely linked issue of the shape of a new party system. The SDPJ wanted Japan to have three or four parties, one of which would be center-left; this would enable the SDPJ to maintain its influence in national politics. The Japan New Party, Renewal Party, and Clean Government Party wanted to form a single large party to oppose the LDP. As Table 4.3 illustrates, the coalition parties had shared views on some issues but not others.

Formation of the next coalition government, the Hata government, was preceded by an agreement between the participating parties on various general policy directions. But the agreement was expressed in bland generalities. The coalition members said only that they were willing to "work with the United States and South Korea" on the issue of North Korean development of nuclear weapons, "promote welfare policies" to cope with an aging society, and "continue administrative and tax reform." In fact, there were divisions over each issue.[38] More concrete policy positions could not be forged in a short time because of interparty differences. The LDP-SDPJ coalition that assumed control of the government in June 1994 would have had similar difficulties had the SDPJ not agreed to accommodate itself to LDP policies, though at the cost of alienating its own left wing.

Not just issue differences repeatedly frustrated coalition efforts to formulate a common policy under both the Hosokawa and Hata governments. Close personal ties and personal enmities between leading politicians also orchestrated relations within coalitions, as they did earlier in coalitions of LDP factions. To some extent, personal ties were congruent with left-right policy differences, dividing the coalition into a conservative camp (Renewal and Clean Government Parties and part of the Japan New Party) and a moderate camp (DSP, Harbinger Party, and the right wing of the SDPJ). For example, Ichiro Ozawa (of the Renewal Party) was so close in both personal and policy terms to Yuichi Ichikawa of the Clean Government Party that the positions they supported were dubbed the Ichi-Ichi line (from *Ichi*ro-Yu*ichi*). Ozawa also has close ties with both the Clean Government Party and Rengo, the united union movement.[39] Enmities between Renewal Party leader Ichiro Ozawa and leaders in the moderate camp were a defining element in the division of the coalition parties into two groups. Animosities between Ozawa and the SDPJ were especially strong when, as happened several times, Ozawa publicly chastised the SDPJ. The SDPJ actually left the Hata coalition temporarily when a plan by Ozawa to form a new parliamentary group that excluded the SDPJ came to light in May 1994.[40] Those who rejected participation in any new party formed by Ozawa even formed a Japan New Party splinter group.

Personal ties also could be at work in relations between the Harbinger Party and the Japan New Party. An initially close working relationship between the heads of the New Party and the Harbinger Party, Hosokawa and Kisayoshi Takemura, induced the parties to consider a merger. But relations cooled after the two leaders became enemies because of both personal and policy differences. (For one, Takemura wrote a book on Japan's international prospects to compete with a book on this subject by Ozawa.) Their differences are part of the reason that the Harbinger group supported the Hata coalition but refused to join the Hata cabinet.[41] Interpersonal relationships are extremely important in Japanese politics and require a delicate balance between individual ambition and viewpoints and deference to others to work effectively.

In 1994, amidst the confusing proliferation of intraparty and cross-party groups, Japan moved toward formation of a new party system. The first steps toward the formation of a new conservative party were taken when the Renewal, Clean Government, and Democratic Socialist Parties and most members of the Japan New Party created a parliamentary group called Kaishin (Reform) in May 1994. Kaishin was succeeded in September 1994 by a similar parliamentary union called Kaikaku (Reform); the names have the same meaning.[42] In early December 1994 the same group of parties joined together to form the Shinshinto (New Frontier Party).

Establishment of the new party did not end internecine bickering among some of its members. Other problems arose from the inability of the Clean Government Party to move easily into the new party. Local chapters of the Clean Government Party depend on links with its religious founder, the Soka Gakkai, and do not want to abandon their organizations to participate in a new party. For the moment, the Clean Government Party is de facto divided into two, a parliamentary group within the Shinshinto and a federation of local parties that run candidates in local elections under the Clean Government banner.

A group calling itself the Democratic League has also formed within the Socialist party; its objective is to create a center-left party to parallel the Shinshinto. If current plans succeed, Japan will ultimately have two conservative or conservative-centrist parties, the Liberal Democratic and New Frontier Parties, and a center–moderate left party, to be called either the Democratic Party or the New Liberal Party. The proposed party is seen as a "third force" to oppose the "new conservatives" in the LDP and New Frontier Party.[43] There will also be a rump left-wing cluster of the remaining parts of the SDPJ and the Japan Communist Party. The two conservative parties are unlikely to coalesce in the foreseeable future, although events in 1993–95 indicate that virtually anything can happen. The current status and historical roots of the 1994 party system are shown in Figure 4.2.

Conclusion

The partial collapse and loss of power of the LDP in 1993 reflect processes of internal conflict and intermittent centrifugal fragmentation long visible in the party and present in other large Japanese political organizations as well. Japanese politicians form or join small-to-medium groups to advance their careers, to promote constituent and group interests, and to advance personal or group ideologies. Similar motivations are present in the formation and maintenance of political parties. Parties, however, normally contain several smaller, often institutionalized groups, which contributes at times to

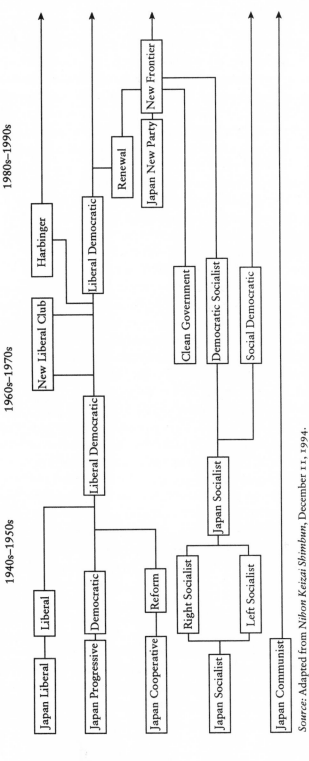

Figure 4.2. The Party System, 1946–1996

1940s–1950s 1960s–1970s 1980s–1990s

Japan Liberal — Liberal

Japan Progressive — Democratic

Japan Cooperative — Reform

Right Socialist

Japan Socialist

Left Socialist

Japan Socialist

Japan Communist

Liberal Democratic

New Liberal Club — Liberal Democratic — Harbinger

Clean Government

Democratic Socialist

Social Democratic

Renewal

Japan New Party — New Frontier

Source: Adapted from *Nihon Keizai Shimbun,* December 11, 1994.

Note: The processes of fragmentation and recombination have been simplified; only nineteen of the sixty parties listed in the source are shown here.

intense internal conflicts. In the case of the LDP, factions became institutional-ized and engaged in highly structured, but also bitter, competition. Japanese political parties are coalitions that contain strong internal centrifugal forces.

Throughout the history of Japanese politics there has been a struggle to contain and bridge conflict, which has a pervasive tendency to occur. Recent important changes in the political geography notwithstanding, the politics of new parties and coalitions will continue to resemble the highly conflictual interfactional politics within the LDP during its long rule. Whether Japan will again have single-party hegemony by a group as internally institutionalized as the LDP is doubtful. Neither the LDP nor the new New Frontier Party have yet achieved a level of internal organizational integrity sufficient to indicate a stable future. Moves to create a new moderate left-of-center grouping that includes most of the SDPJ are laden with uncertainty as well.

Besides the important changes that have taken place in the party system there has been some ideological realignment. Party realignments and coali-tional agreements between parties traditionally on the right, center, and left have changed the political map. But the new coalition governments have each resembled former LDP governments in their internal mechanisms. Like earlier faction-dominated LDP cabinets, the new cabinets have been based on a coali-tion of several smaller component groups. The content of coalitional politics has changed, but governance based on decentralized power continues.

The ability to form or maintain coalitions depends on a common set of variables. Factors such as (1) relative party strength (that is, what party com-binations could contribute most to the coalition outcome in numerical terms), (2) electoral appeal, (3) ideological and policy compatibility, (4) cooperation or opposition from intraparty groups, (5) interpersonal rivalries or friend-ships, and (6) interest group support have all affected coalition chances. The influence of these factors is in no way surprising, although it is at odds with coalition theories that stress mainly the importance of numerical majorities.[44]

What is striking about Japanese politics — as well as about politics within other former Cold War allies — is the disappearance of ideology as a unifying force within parties and as a dividing force between parties. What new cleav-ages might anchor (and divide) future party movements is uncertain. Although the Hosokawa and Hata coalition governments stumbled frequently because of issue differences, those differences were either resolved (political reform) or eventually made redundant (by a realignment of SDPJ views on foreign and security policy when the SDPJ entered a governing coalition with the LDP and the Harbinger Party). It is precisely the lack of important interparty differences that could contribute to electoral volatility among floating voters, as in 1989 and 1993.

5

Executive and Bureaucratic Power

Japan has formally democratic institutions, including an elected parliament (Diet) and a prime minister, who is selected by the parliament. Once selected, the prime minister is given explicit policymaking authority and is expected to play a leadership role vis-à-vis the parliament. At the same time, the prime minister and the cabinet ministers, whom the prime minister selects, are responsible to the parliament. The prime minister and the cabinet (known collectively as the government), or individual cabinet members, can be removed by a vote of nonconfidence in the House of Representatives.

As in any country, the actual working of government institutions in Japan has depended on the nature of informal political power, as well as on formal constitutional mandates. The distribution of power within and between parties, and between parties and interest groups, has affected executive and legislative performance, even though it is not part of constitutional arrangements. According to the vertical model, the long domination of politics by the Liberal Democratic Party meant the absence of checks and balances. One proponent of the vertical model has even described postwar Japan as a "rigged one-party system."[1] Under this system, power was held by a triad of elite groups, and decisions were made by a centralized elite and passed downward.[2]

Recent research on policymaking presents a different picture of Japanese rule, including a more complex and qualified view of the performance of the prime minister. In this view, coalitions of political parties, government ministries, and interest groups (including unions and businesses) are participants in policy processes that are not dominated by any one political actor. Prime ministers are neither perennially weak nor consistently dominant; executive authority, including that of the bureaucracy, is variable.[3]

Three questions are central to an evaluation of LDP governance. First, under LDP hegemony did prime ministers exert strong leadership on the basis of both their constitutional grant of authority and single-party dominance? Or were they constrained by informal power centers, as is so often the case in modern democracies? Second, did the party in power exert control over the bureaucracy?[4] Are there circumstances that made the ministries responsible to the LDP and other parties in parliament? Or did long-term rule, coupled with a strong bureaucracy, produce a cooperative, semiauthoritarian style of policy formulation?[5] Third, if relations between power centers appeared democratic and pluralistic, was the outcome centralized programmatic democracy or decentralized bargained democracy?[6] Each of these questions concerns the relations between different formal (government) and informal power holders. We must also ask what can have happened or be expected under post-1993 coalition governments. The best way to answer questions about power relations is to examine policymaking processes.

How informal power centers and government institutions interact in different policy arenas can tell us what power relations really exist. In the case of administrative policy decisions, proposals are approved, amended, or rejected by such senior ministry officials as division chiefs, bureau heads, administrative vice ministers, and ministers. The policy process ends at the vice ministerial, ministerial, or cabinet level if a ministry or cabinet rule is to be formulated, revised, or discarded. Legislation follows a longer path, involving not only administrative policymaking processes — when bills are originated or drafted within a ministry — but also cabinet review, political party review, and, finally, a parliamentary decision.

Building support coalitions is an important part of policymaking. Policy proposals inevitably affect individuals or groups with different points of view. Regardless of whether decisions are made by majority rule or consensus or simply approved by senior officials, policy sponsors have to enlist the support of other political actors to have their ideas accepted. Successful passage of an important administrative rule requires acceptance by the relevant divisions and bureaus of a ministry or, at times, a coalition involving more than one ministry.[7] To pass a legislative bill requires, in addition, the support of a coalition of enough members of parliament to reach a majority decision. Because the LDP commanded a majority in both houses of the Diet until 1989, most coalition building took place within the policy institutions of the party. The specifics of an issue were normally discussed extensively within the Policy Affairs Research Council before a major bill was submitted to the Diet. Intra-LDP policymaking processes were critical to the fate of political issues and contributed to the development of highly specialized intraparty policymaking institutions. The opposition parties also participated in policymaking at times. Interparty coalitions were not unheard of, even under the dominant party system. After the LDP's loss of power, interparty governing coalitions became a necessity.

Development of strategies and counterstrategies are part and parcel of coalition politics, regardless of whether processes are centered in the bureaucracy, the ruling party or parties, or some other combination of political actors. Policy sponsors often make a trial proposal to determine the degree of support among relevant individuals or groups. They also try to determine the extent and location of opposition, for opponents to proposals engage in similar strategies and moves. If support is inadequate at an early stage or if opposition is too great, a proposal may be abandoned. Alternatively, a proposal may be amended to enhance support or at least neutralize opposition. At any point along the way, a proposal may die owing to lack of sufficient support or intransigent resistance. Legislative proposals have been withdrawn even in the midst of Diet proceedings in response to too much opposition or in exchange for passage of a higher priority bill.[8]

The Government: Leadership Versus Constraint

Once selected, the prime minister and cabinet have substantial formal powers. The constitution entitles the prime minister to appoint the members of the cabinet, the only limitation being a requirement that a majority of cabinet members must be civilians and Dietmembers. The prime minister and the cabinet are empowered to propose legislative bills; and the cabinet is also in charge of the administrative branch of government in the task of formulating and implementing legislation. Under LDP rule, the prime minister's authority was enhanced by virtue of his being the leader of a permanent majority party. In 1983–86, the only time before 1993 that the LDP was not sole hegemon, the prime minister was also president of the LDP, because the LDP at that time was the dominant party in a coalition government with a small splinter party, the New Liberal Club. LDP dominance, plus its close business ties, led observers to the conclusion that politics was ruled by three closely linked elites — senior leaders of the LDP and the government, top bureaucratic officials, and heads of major business interest groups.[9] In reality, the prime minister was enormously constrained in the exercise of his powers during the LDP era by intraparty factions and policy groups, interest groups affiliated with the LDP, and, in some cases, minority parties in the Diet.

Observing elite behavior during the period of LDP hegemony is a lesson in coalition politics. Under LDP rule, the prime minister was the temporary head of an intraparty, interfactional coalition. Because the prime minister can be removed from office by the lower house of the Diet if political support in that body wanes, survival during the LDP's hegemony required that a prime minister and his government maintain intraparty support. Factional competition was consequently pervasive. An LDP prime minister was the constant target of strategies by other factions that sought to weaken his credibility and increase their own status. Exposure to faction and policy group challenges made him abnormally vulnerable. The result was limited, sometimes weak leadership.

Prime ministers were exposed to a variety of attacks by factional opponents. Some were based on substantive policy grounds. In that case, when an LDP prime minister took a stand on a controversial issue, other LDP politicians sought to unseat him by arguing for alternative policies. This happened at a critical juncture in early postwar Japan when Prime Minister Kishi's formula for a revised U.S.-Japan Security Treaty was challenged by others within the LDP elite. Both Kishi's choice of treaty renewal options and his management of the issue were criticized.[10] In a similar case in 1983, Prime Minister Nakasone was denounced within the PARC Foreign Affairs Investigative Council after he proposed that the Self-Defense Forces be prepared to blockade the straits adjacent to Japan as part of an upgrading of maritime defenses. Members of the anti-mainstream Suzuki and Komoto factions called Nakasone's ideas a "virtual declaration of war."[11] Although LDP factions were usually concerned mainly with party and government positions, policymaking was still affected by interfactional conflict.

Prime ministers were also criticized by other party leaders for their alleged lack of competence to govern. Factional opponents frequently questioned an incumbent prime minister's skill at managing party or Diet processes. Nakasone's leadership ability was widely criticized within his own party in 1987, for example, when LDP tax reform measures that he had advocated were abandoned because of intraparty disagreement and adverse election results. The failure of the tax bill led Tanaka and Komoto faction leaders to predict the early demise of Nakasone's prime ministership. Their predictions came true later that year.[12]

LDP leaders were also criticized if they failed to consult widely with other LDP leaders or failed to show sufficient concern for their factional allies' feelings. In 1985 the vice president of the LDP, Susumu Nikaido, criticized

Prime Minister Nakasone for making commitments to the United States without consulting party officials, accusing him of "rushing ahead alone" on trade policy commitments without considering the opinions of LDP leaders who opposed his policy. In fact, Nikaido was offended by Nakasone's lack of proper deference. Nakasone's prime ministership depended on a coalition whose mainstay was the Tanaka faction, the largest in the party. Nakasone's failure to consult was annoying to Nikaido because he was one of the heads of the Tanaka faction. (Nikaido later attempted to take over the faction, so he may also have discredited Nakasone as a ploy in his strategy to attain power.)[13]

Long-standing enmities between faction leaders affected incumbent prime ministers' influence. Former Prime Minister Takeo Fukuda once challenged the Nakasone government's ability to deal credibly with political ethics problems because of Nakasone's dependence on a coalition with the Tanaka faction to stay in power, and Tanaka had been indicted for taking bribes so that a Japanese airline would purchase Lockheed aircraft. Fukuda's real reason was his longtime hatred for Tanaka. Tanaka had defeated Fukuda for the party presidency in 1972, and later, Masayoshi Ohira had taken the prime ministership away from Fukuda with Tanaka faction support.[14] Both events embittered Fukuda.

Prime ministers developed strategies to cope with frequent opposition by other factions. Some prime ministers tried to extend their stay in power by saying that they wanted to achieve particular policy goals before leaving office. For example, Prime Minister Nakasone promised in 1986, when his term as party president was coming to a close, that he would carry through reform of the Japan National Railways "during his administration" and pushed that policy goal to the forefront of his political agenda. He denied that he was using railroad reform to stay in office, although that was his purpose.[15]

Winning elections was another way to stay in power. Prime Minister Nakasone's call for a double election in 1986 was an effort to lay the groundwork for staying in office. The LDP had done unusually well in double elections in 1980, but not as well in a stand-alone lower house election in 1983. This experience encouraged party leaders to consider a double-election strategy again. Nakasone's proposal was initially opposed by the Fukuda and Komoto factions, which wanted to deny him the advantage of that strategy.[16] When the LDP did well in the elections, Nakasone was able to gain an extension of his tenure as LDP president and prime minister.

On other occasions, the LDP's weak record in an election gave rise to a factional challenge to an incumbent leader. When the LDP did poorly in the general election in 1979 after Prime Minister Ohira proposed a value-added tax, Ohira's leadership was criticized by opposing factions. The following spring, when two anti-Ohira factions abstained from voting on a nonconfidence motion in the Diet, Ohira was forced to resign.

Scenarios such as these illustrate the intense factional competition faced by an LDP prime minister. Factional politics placed an enormous pressure on prime ministers to toe the line in policy and other matters. The vulnerability of prime ministers to being pushed out of office in the factional game was sufficient to restrict their freedom of choice in matters of state. Much the same kind of vulnerability can be expected from coalition governments today, especially those comprising parties with diverse ideologies.

Because of its catchall character and related ideological pluralism, the LDP usually had multiple internal policy cleavages. In the 1980s, for example, the party was divided over defense issues, tax reform, the "green card" postal savings tax exemption issue, health insurance for older people, liberalization of imports of farm products, and the reform of lower house election constituencies.[17] Even when an LDP prime minister agreed with one or another of the policy camps in his own party, his freedom of policymaking action was constrained by his basic dependence on an intraparty coalition of factions to stay in office.

LDP cleavages took several forms. Factional competition and substantive disagreements over issues fed on each other in intraparty processes. Sometimes intraparty divisions reflected differences between free-floating, unstructured opinion groups. More often than not, however, loosely structured groupings of like-minded people soon turned into organized groups. As a result, several organized, policy-oriented study groups were active within the LDP at any given time; some exist even now after the party has lost its dominant status. Examples of the divisions over issues, such as the intraparty stalemate over China policy, were discussed in Chapter 3.

Intraparty zoku were also the basis for some divisions, especially those concerning such special interests as farm subsidies and protected farm-goods markets. The presence of zoku enhanced party influence in specific policy arenas but simultaneously diminished the ability of the party to provide overall policy leadership or set unified policy priorities.[18] The LDP zoku were also related to policy communities. Policy communities were another kind of institutionalized policymaking group linking elements of the LDP with their counterparts in ministries and interest groups in ways that restricted party elite power.[19]

A group of semiretired former LDP leaders was intermittently a source of constraint on prime ministers during the period of LDP rule. The Supreme Advisers — an unusual group in the context of political practices in other industrialized countries — included former prime ministers and party presidents, former party vice presidents, former House of Councillors presidents, and, at times, former secretaries general, chairs of policy councils, and chairs of executive councils of the party. The existence of such a group reflects both the Japanese deference to age and high status and a desire by up-and-coming politicians to have former leaders safely out of the way, assigned to a largely ceremonial position.

Ceremonial status aside, the Supreme Advisers occasionally functioned as a sounding board, much the way the prewar *genro,* elder leaders, were consulted on major issues even after their retirement from active political life. The blessings of the Supreme Advisers conferred legitimacy on government decisions, especially controversial ones. The group's judgments could also be a source of constraint on LDP governments, especially since four former prime ministers were still alive in the 1980s. (The number of former prime ministers alive at one time was higher in the late 1970s and 1980s than before, because after 1972 most prime ministers served only one term in office. In the mid-1980s Kishi, Miki, Fukuda, and Suzuki were all active.) The role of the Supreme Advisers seems to have been mainly reactive; they did not initiate policies, although some advisers criticized the prime minister or other party leaders on occasion. In 1987, Fukuda and Nikaido rebuked Prime Minister Nakasone and other party officials for failing to consult with party members on a pending Diet tax bill.[20]

Government-LDP Consultative Council (GLCC) conferences were another potential mechanism to constrain the prime minister.[21] These meetings provided a forum where positions taken by the ministries and cabinet and those taken by the policymaking organs of the party could be reconciled. Policy demands from interest groups, passed on by the PARC, could be presented there, as could policy positions that originated within the party itself. Influence in the GLCC sessions was bidirectional. For example, the LDP succeeded in inducing the cabinet to abandon a proposed tax reform package in 1987 through discussions in the GLCC, even though abandonment amounted to a political setback for the Finance Ministry and its cabinet supporters. At other times, the government side prevailed, as when the cabinet succeeded in reducing the subsidized rice price against party wishes the same year. Which group was dominant—the cabinet or the LDP—depended on the issue and the patterns of support or opposition.

The ministries influenced the prime minister and the cabinet. As in most political systems, there was a kind of structural dependence between the ministers and the ministries they were appointed to supervise. The political leaders of Japan depend on the administrative bureaucracy to supervise the economy and to conduct other matters of state too numerous or complex for the cabinet to manage. Because the cabinet and prime minister have only a limited staff, much of the policy research needed by the central organs of government is performed within the bureaucracy. The bureaucracy with its large, permanent staffs is well suited to collect and analyze information. Policy implementation brings ministries in direct contact with problems relevant to government. Ministry officials normally deal with interest groups and others in fields where both information and advice based on long specialization are available.

The dependence of the government on the bureaucracy is induced in part by limitations on the scope of party control over ministerial appointments. In each ministry only the positions of minister and parliamentary vice minister are held by political appointees. In the United States, Britain, and France there is direct party control over a much greater range of bureaucratic appointments than in Japan.

In theory, Japanese cabinet ministers have the authority to decide on internal personnel assignments, which could be a means of control over the ministries to which they are assigned. But the matter of control over appointments is hard to trace. According to Yung H. Park, consultations over appointments took place regularly between ministry bureaucrats and LDP cabinet ministers in the cases that he studied. Civil servants deferred to ministers' views in these discussions or anticipated ministers' preferences in their choices.[22] Chalmers Johnson and others have likewise described interventions by LDP politicians in major intraministry appointments.[23] Both journalistic reports and academic accounts suggest, however, that ministry preferences generally outweighed ministers' in personnel choices. Some ministries have norms that dictate promotion paths, and these seem to be insulated from influence by political appointees. Control over administrative appointments within ministries is a matter in which bureaucrats, not politicians, probably hold the upper hand.

An unusually frequent turnover in ministry portfolios (compared with other countries' governments) during the LDP's stay in power favored upward ministry influence. The desire of LDP factions to have as many of their members as possible fill prestigious ministry positions kept ministers' terms short. Most ministers held office for only one year because of the pressure for rotating opportunities. One year was not long enough for the appointee to grasp many of the details involved in running a ministry or to learn how to deal with a staff of several thousand. In most countries there are much longer terms; the conditions in Japan make learning the job even more difficult.

All these factors not infrequently made LDP cabinet ministers hostage to their respective ministries in policy matters; the advent of coalition government has probably not brought a change in this area. Upon occasion, ministers aggressively defined their policy priorities or intervened in intraministry personnel matters, but they were influenced by their subordinates more often than not, even though they were nominally in charge.[24] Ministers (the prime minister as well) were sufficiently dependent on the bureaucracy for information, advice, and cooperation in handling the myriad of details involved in policymaking and policy implementation that acceptance of the views of ministry officials was common. Cabinet ministers needed cooperative relationships, even at the cost of exerting their own influence. Savvy ministers might have cooperated, too, in hopes of advancing their influence in national politics.

The emergence of zoku within the LDP may have balanced the power equation between party and bureaucracy compared with earlier in the postwar era.[25] "Zoku" Dietmembers were appointed to ministerial portfolios in one of three cases during the 1980s and presumably brought experience in the substantive affairs of the ministry to the job. In view of this trend, perhaps the vulnerability of LDP ministerial appointees has been overstated. Still, many appointees held office for only one year, so it is unlikely that very many mastered the internal politics of the large bureaucratic organizations to which they were assigned.

Different ministers had differing degrees of influence. LDP heavyweights were usually assigned to important ministries and often stayed there for two or three years — longer than normal appointees — enabling them to provide stronger leadership than one-year officeholders could. The heavyweights usually had prior experience in one or more of the major ministries, which gave them background in dealing with the bureaucracy that those who had yet to hold such an assignment or who had only served in a minor ministry for a year.[26] Usually the more experienced appointees had much more assertive personalities than ordinary LDP Dietmembers. Often they were former senior bureaucrats who had entered the LDP after long ministry careers. Whether ministers received their assignments because they were heavyweights or sought posts to add to their résumé, they had more potential for party control than ordinary Dietmembers.

Whatever the relationship between ministers and their ministries, most ministers represented their ministries in public statements and cabinet meetings and championed ministry interests. LDP ministers of agriculture, forestry, and fisheries, for example, opposed agricultural liberalization and at times even set themselves against LDP prime ministers and other cabinet members as a result. (It is possible that political logic required having agriculture ministers make pro-farmer statements to satisfy farm groups, which would free the prime minister and other cabinet members to take counterpositions for consumption by the international community or some other constituency.) There were other confrontations between LDP ministers over the 1985 defense budget allocations. These tendencies for ministers to publicly assert their ministry's views could equally well have represented (1) the influence of strong intraministry policy arguments, (2) dependence of appointed ministers on bureaucrats' cooperation to get specific things done, or (3) appointment of a zoku member as minister. These factors were probably all present most of the time.

Even opposition parties exercised some direct or indirect checks on the policymaking influence of the prime minister and cabinet during the years of LDP domination. They sometimes effectively vetoed positions taken by LDP governments on high-profile issues in the Diet, for example, several public security laws, defense budgets, and income tax cuts (see Chapter 6).[27] Interest group lobbies likewise were sometimes able to force a reluctant prime minister or cabinet to give in to their demands, even when this meant abandonment of a prime minister's policy commitment.[28] In the 1980s, the efforts by prime ministers to please the United States by opening the market for agricultural imports were sometimes abandoned or postponed owing to farm group opposition. Small-business opposition similarly derailed plans to revise the Large Store Law, even though the government did succeed in limiting the effect of the existing law. Interest groups often worked through supportive policy communities; government leaders were pressured from multiple sources.

The bulk of the evidence indicates that the policymaking powers of LDP prime ministers and cabinets were severely constrained during the period of LDP hegemony. The need for cooperation from other political actors and the general fragmentation of informal political power made prime ministers and cabinets vulnerable to influence from multiple intraparty and extraparty sources. Restraints on executive power are not unusual in large, pluralistic democracies. But the extreme factionalism in the ruling party in Japan and the extensive institutionalization of intraparty policymaking activities invoked an unusual level of downward responsibility. Although the revisionist view that Japan had weak leadership is true, the weakness was the result of responsibility to too many power centers, not an indicator of irresponsible government.

There is also a cultural preference for leadership that is not overly autocratic. Although many people in authority are autocratic — founders and heads of large corporations are a case in point — leaders whose style involves consensus seeking earn more praise than those who are more arbitrary. Criticism from opponents along such lines was another potential source of constraint on LDP leaders. The weight of this norm was evident in the favorable public reception of Prime Minister Hayato Ikeda's low posture; his autocratic predecessor, Nobusuke Kishi, was frequently condemned. Intraparty criticism of Nakasone's aggressiveness can be similarly contrasted with the positive feelings about Noboru Takeshita's consensualism. Takeshita was known for his tendency to slowly and carefully consult with all participants in important decisions, even at times including opposition party politicians in his circle of contacts.[29]

Taken together, an impressive array of informal forces limited the exercise of independent power by most prime ministers between 1955 and 1993. There were occasionally strong leaders, and there are some differences in LDP leadership related to time and context, as I will demonstrate shortly.

The Role of the Prime Minister

Compared with democratic countries like Britain or France, post–World War II Japan has had extremely weak leadership. The prime minister has an important part in public policy making. But prime ministers took the lead less often than might be expected in view of the long dominance of the LDP and the authority granted the prime minister in the constitution. Decentralized and fragmented informal political power substantially limited executive options.[30] An inventory of the different roles played by the prime minister validates this point by showing how prime ministers and their cabinets have been constrained.

The prime minister's primary function in many policy settings was that of an arbiter — a neutral overseer of negotiations among opposing individuals or groups. When important ministries disagreed among themselves or when one or more ministries disagreed with some element of the ruling LDP, there was no easy method for resolving the conflict. Efforts were made to bring the contestants together under the supervision of an arbiter of superior political status. Quite a few times during LDP rule the arbiter was the prime minister himself.[31] The neutrality of the prime minister or other leader both facilitated a face-saving solution to a political impasse and legitimated the process and its outcome.

Arbiters were frequently used. In fact, the prime minister's role as arbiter reflects the general social practice when parties to a conflict are equal in status and unable to reach a compromise. Arbitration was the option when LDP supporters of rice price supports were opposed by the Ministry of Finance; the prime minister or some small group within the government or party leadership arbitrated in several of these conflicts.[32] Arbitration was also employed when the foreign and finance ministers and the head of the Defense Agency took different positions on a proposed defense budget. Finance Minister Takeshita claimed that financial resources were too limited to cover the proposed outlays, Foreign Minister Shintaro Abe was worried about the effects of the decision on U.S.-Japan relations, and Defense Agency Director General Masaharu

Gotoda sought higher expenditures on defense. The issue frustrated efforts at resolution owing to its zero-sum nature, as well as the difficulty of settling disputes among equals, and was therefore referred to Prime Minister Nakasone. The prime minister eventually ruled in favor of the Defense Agency and the Foreign Ministry. His superior status legitimated his ruling.[33] The constitution, the facts of political power, and general social practice supported his adoption of an arbiter role.

Besides arbitrating, the prime minister and cabinet members ratified decisions made within the bureaucratic ministries or within the policy organs of the LDP. A ratifier role was assumed when decisions fell clearly within the jurisdiction of a particular ministry or agency and were not otherwise politicized. In such a case, a ministry official might consult with a cabinet member in advance, especially if a proposed action had policy implications above and beyond the specific competence of the ministry. The main role of the minister became basically one of ratifying or approving a decision made elsewhere. There was little direct cabinet or prime ministerial involvement in policymaking. When a prime minister agreed with the decisions of the Defense Agency on choices of new weapons, when the cabinet approved the long-term research and development targets of the Ministry of International Trade and Industry (MITI), and when cabinets have accepted Ministry of Finance views on microeconomic policy matters (like the routine allocation of budget funds to different ministries), they were essentially confirming decisions made by lower-level government units.[34]

So far, the role of the government elite seems to have been more reactive than assertive. In some situations, however, the prime minister has provided leadership. Most of the postwar prime ministers committed themselves to a major foreign or domestic policy goal, usually reflecting an incumbent's desire to be remembered for at least one major policy accomplishment. This explanation fits Kishi's plan to amend the U.S.-Japan Security Treaty (1957–60), Ichiro Hatoyama's commitment to rapprochement with the Soviet Union (1956), and Eisaku Sato's desire to normalize relations with South Korea (1965) and have Okinawa revert to Japanese control (1972). Other prime ministerial commitments have had a domestic focus, such as Hayato Ikeda's resolve to double incomes (1960), Tanaka's proposal to develop peripheral parts of Japan (1972), Nakasone's desire to complete administrative reform (1982–87), and, in a less substantive sense, Noboru Takeshita's idea for a "hometown" Japan (1988).

Some prime ministers have had very strong views on fiscal priorities, intervening in budget-making decisions normally controlled by the Ministry of Finance or another political actor. Intervention by the Liberal Democratic leadership and/or prime minister has probably been most common in macro-budgeting decisions — those where national economic directions are at stake. Especially strong and determined leaders also single-handedly forced their ideas on the Finance Ministry. Kakuei Tanaka had a practice of calling middle-level ministry officials to task for particular decisions and was consequently called a computerized bulldozer.[35] Prime ministers and cabinet ministers have taken stands on other issues, too, depending on their personal style and the political situation. See, for example, two events in 1963: Ikeda's oversight of the proposed Anti-Monopoly Law revision and Minister Hajime Fukuda's sensational appointment of Zennai Imai over Shigeru Sahashi as MITI vice minister.[36] Their objectives reflect at times a strong commitment to a particular policy goal. Some prime ministers were concerned about the power of their office. For example, Nakasone planned a reorganization of the Prime Minister's Office and used consultative councils to expand the prime minister's direct access to information on critical issues. He also used high-level consultative councils on political and education reform and economic reorganization to legitimize his own positions and bypass ministry roadblocks to change. In some areas this was successful; in some it was not.[37]

The context in which different prime ministers served affected their style of leadership. Michio Muramatsu believes that pressure from the United States on trade issues helped prime ministers during the 1980s be more "presidential." Their efforts to meet U.S. trade requests led them to insist on cooperation from ministries; this further diminished the power of the economic ministries, already weakened by financial deregulation and loss of import licensing powers. Nakasone's bypassing of bureaucratic ministries and LDP policy organs by using special consultative councils, such as the Second Provisional Administrative Affairs Reform Council, also contributed to the presidentialization of Japan's leadership.[38]

Even strong leadership did not always prevail over the forces marshaled by other political actors. And sometimes when commitments prevailed, they came at a high political cost. With Yoshida's commitment to limited rearmament, Hatoyama's normalization agreement with the Soviet Union, Kishi's revision of the U.S.-Japan Security Treaty, Tanaka's normalization of relations with the People's Republic of China, and prime ministerial commitments to health insurance and tax reform in the 1980s — to give several examples — the prime minister's position was strongly opposed from within the LDP or by other conservatives.[39] Power struggles between factions — like the intraparty struggle over the ratification of a revised U.S.-Japan Security Treaty in 1959–60 — gave rise to opposition to prime ministerial initiatives.[40] Recurring factional struggles in the LDP and inherently fragile coalitions among Dietmembers made assuming a strong leadership role or making a policy commitment risky for the prime minister. Indeed, much of the dynamism of postwar elite politics reflected the almost constant internecine struggle for power within the conservative movement. The pattern of constrained leadership continues today, but now the focus has moved from intraparty to interparty differences.

The Administrative Bureaucracy

According to democratic theory, the administrative branch of government should be subordinate to an elected legislature and an executive body and should mainly implement their policies. In the present industrialized democracies, practice is usually quite different from theory. The administrative branch is often at least partially independent of legislative and cabinet control. In Japan the power of the bureaucratic ministries is especially great because of legal, structural, historical, and social factors.

Japan has twelve major ministries, plus several agencies attached to the Prime Ministers' Office that are almost equivalent in importance to the major ministries. The most significant of the agencies are General Affairs, Economic Planning, Defense, Science and Technology, Environment, National Land, Hokkaido Development, and Okinawa Development. Each is headed by a minister of state, as are the major ministries.

Laws have established the ministries and agencies and assigned functional jurisdictions. Among other things, the ministries collectively possess authority to regulate more than eleven thousand different kinds of activities.[41] The Ministry of International Trade and Industry alone is empowered to regulate and supervise economic activities by 109 separate laws. MITI is assigned oversight of the economic health of many industries, supervision of small-business cartels, the monitoring of product quality control, regulation of patent rights, and preservation of industrial safety. Between the 1950s and the 1970s, MITI also administered an import license system; in some periods the ministry also controlled licenses for new factory construction. Although MITI's powers have declined recently, it still has authority in many areas. MITI is an excellent example of the Japanese tendency to combine regulatory and other functions in one institution, unlike the American tendency to separate regulatory organs from general administration.

Besides law, another source of ministry influence is the existence of permanent research staff who provide expertise and gather statistical and other information to guide and support policy decisions. Bureaucrats collectively develop highly valuable competence in complex areas of governance. Some help regulate the aviation industry (the job of the Transportation Ministry), plan multibillion-dollar budgets (Ministry of Finance), or develop high-tech defense systems (Defense Agency). In contrast, and unlike their American congressional counterparts, members of the Diet do not have significant research staffs. They are often dependent on the ministries for even basic information in areas of their own legislative interest. In spite of the zoku, LDP Dietmembers still have less opportunity to develop expertise on complex matters than ministry officials do.[42]

Higher-level bureaucrats, too, have somewhat limited opportunities to develop individual technical expertise. Ministry officials at the upper-managerial level are rotated every two or three years, both to inhibit sectionalism and to encourage them to acquire general competence. They also spend at least one tour of duty outside the ministry. So the lower-level bureaucrats, who stay in a section, have the most specialized knowledge; they are sometimes called walking encyclopedias (*ikijibiki*) for this reason. Some scholars also note correctly that ministries depend on external groups, such as industry associations, for detailed information, which makes it possible for interest groups to influence agendas.

A tendency to have a powerful bureaucracy is part of historical tradition. The bureaucracy has had a large role in government at several points since its formal inception in the late nineteenth century. A vigorous administrative bureaucracy was anticipated in the Prussian-inspired constitution of 1890. Ministers of state were made politically responsible to the emperor, rather than to the Diet, which in practice made them responsible only to themselves and each other. The bureaucratic ministries were also central in the development of a modern economy and military in the late nineteenth century and again in the 1930s and 1940s, during the era of military expansion. They played a pilot role in early industry development because of a shortage of resources and trained persons.[43] Japan entered the postwar years with a legacy of wartime bureaucratic controls. Even though the prewar Diet was at times very assertive and party politics influenced governments in some periods, the prewar institutions encouraged bureaucratic authority.[44]

Japanese social traditions also have favored a strong bureaucracy. Because the government leaders who established the modern bureaucracy in the late nineteenth century assumed that officials in the government ministries would play a guiding role in national development, the top positions were filled by elites educated specifically for government service in the foremost Japanese universities. Recruitment of the products of an elitist educational system reinforced the influence and status of the bureaucracy before the war and continues to do so today, just as it does in France and Britain.[45]

It is often assumed that some ministries are more important than others

(Table 5.1). Allocations of Foreign, Finance, and International Trade and Industry Ministry portfolios to party heavyweights, other portfolios to less-influential politicians, lends credence to such a view. So does the presence of undersecretaries to the prime minister representing foreign affairs, finance, international trade and industry, and the national police. The Finance, Foreign Affairs, and International Trade and Industry Ministries are also those where elite university graduates most often seek employment, and the functions performed by these ministries are critical to national economic health and security. The Finance Ministry controls national budgets and has a strong say in tax policy, which gives it a solid basis of authority. In contrast, some other ministries, like Posts and Telecommunications, mainly perform necessary services and play less of a central policymaking role. All ministries perform important functions, however, as is shown in Table 5.1, where the size of ministry budgets, numbers of assigned personnel, and regulatory powers necessary to perform ministry tasks often contradict traditional views of their relative status. Some observers feel that the power of specific ministries shifted in the 1980s to favor the Ministries of Construction and Labor over the Ministries of Finance and International Trade and Industry.[46]

Currently scholars hold three views on the role of the Japanese bureaucracy. One group sees the bureaucracy as playing an enormous and often decisive role in policymaking. Ministry dominance of a highly centralized policymaking process has even been characterized as a kind of "soft authoritarianism."[47] MITI has been singled out as a dominant player in the economic sphere and is widely viewed as having made policies based on its own version of economic rationality and on contacts with business, especially before the 1970s. The Ministry of Finance has likewise been seen as dominant in its own domain of fiscal policy, though losing power with financial liberalization. According to the second view of bureaucracy, ministry officials have interacted extensively on relatively equal terms with other political actors. Mutual accommodation has been the central theme of these interactions; the relationship is termed "reciprocal consent" in one study.[48] The third group of scholars believe that economic ministry influence has been limited to setting general frameworks in place. Bureaucrats are unable to control specific industry decisions in this version of "state-society" relations, and sometimes ministerial power is subject to party control.[49]

Satisfactorily sorting out the extent of bureaucratic versus party or group influence in all issue settings is impossible. But there are some indicators to where ministries are normally influential and where their influence is often curbed. For example, data on submission and passage of legislative bills indicate the influence of a bureaucratic agenda setting. Comparing the number of

Table 5.1. *Status of Ministry Versus Function-Related Needs and Support*

Ministry	Number of Personnel	Budget (in billions of U.S. $)	Number of Regulations Administered	Number of Consultative Councils
Group I				
Foreign Affairs	4,525	5.8	53	2
Finance	78,633	168.5	1,387	17
International Trade and Industry	9,299	7.9	1,986	33
Group II				
Transportation	38,478	8.3	1,893	11
Justice	50,453	4.7	172	7
Education	137,570	49.3	333	17
Agriculture, Forestry, and Fisheries	54,942	26.6	1,427	14
Construction	24,493	45.0	910	9
Home Affairs	579	147.1	134	3
Group III				
Health and Welfare	76,567	118.2	1,221	22
Posts and Telecommunications	307,503	.3	319	5
Labor	154,887	4.5	631	14

Sources: Prime Minister's Office, *Japan Statistical Yearbook* (Tokyo, 1994); *Nikkei Weekly*, January 10, 1994; and unpublished government records.

Note: "Status" is reputational: I is high, II is moderate, III is low.

government-proposed and Dietmember-proposed bills demonstrates that a substantial proportion of the legislation considered in the Diet is originated or at least drafted by the bureaucracy. (Both ministry-initiated and ministry-drafted bills end up in the Diet as government-sponsored bills.) Specifically, about two-thirds of all bills dealt with by the Diet from 1952 to 1990 originated in the government—that is, ministries or cabinet (Table 5.2). Regardless of whether bureaucrats initiated or drafted bills at the request of the cabinet, their perceptions of problems and solutions influenced legislative proposals—in the 1980s, all annual and special budget bills, three major tax reform bills, bills to alter food and drug standards, health insurance bills, pension bills, and several election reform bills.[50] The ministries had an additional edge where bills dealt with technical matters unfamiliar to ordinary politicians.

Claims of pervasive bureaucratic influence based on these statistics on legislative input are at least partly misleading, however. Where bills affected chief LDP concerns, opposition party commitments, strongly felt group interests,

Table 5.2. Government Bills Versus Parliamentary Member Bills, 1952–1989

	Government Bills	Member Bills	Proportion of Government Bills to Total (%)
1952–59	2,057	1,976	51
1960–69	1,614	746	71
1970–79	1,208	680	64
1980–89	948	472	67

Source: Calculated from Naikaku Hoseikyoku unpublished documents.

Notes: The figures under "Proportion" indicate the percentage of all bills considered by the Diet that were cabinet bills. The data begin in 1952 because Japan resumed control of its affairs in that year, after the Allied occupation.

some quality of life, social welfare, and pocketbook issues, or macroeconomic decisions, some or all stages of decisionmaking were usually politicized. Compelling party or group pressures were the rule in these settings, even though the bureaucracy still prepared the bills.[51]

Influence aside, ministries make many administrative rules that have the force of law. Much Diet legislation has been very broadly conceived — some argue that ministries draft bills very vaguely to discourage litigation against the government — and this comprehensiveness has allowed ministries to formulate rules and regulations suited to specific settings and needs and even their own preferences.[52] Ministries use these ministerial regulations and other kinds of administrative devices to "legislate" extensively — that is, to make rules that govern private behavior. The cabinet performs a similar quasi-legislative function, utilizing the vehicle of cabinet ordinances and rulings. The resulting administrative rules are probably a better indicator of bureaucratic influence than the number of government bills submitted to the Diet, for it is sometimes hard to pinpoint who initiated specific ideas.

There are many more regulations than laws (Table 5.3). In 1993, for example, there were 410 new or revised cabinet orders (*seirei*) and 673 new or revised ministry regulations (*shorei*) but only 98 new or revised laws.[53] Ministry regulations have increased relative to Diet laws as the result of a decline in legislative output starting in the 1960s.

The Japanese practice of administrative "legislation" is far from unique, even though it is often described this way. Similar examples of bureaucratic legislation exist in other industrialized democracies, especially where the administrative side of government has a longer tradition than the legislative. In

Table 5.3. Legislation Versus Regulation

	Number of Laws	Number of Regulations	Ratio (laws: regulations)
1946–55	2,417	3,525	1:1.5
1956–69	2,371	5,298	1:2.2
1970–79	1,208	5,570	1:4.6
1980–89	1,335	5,837	1:4.4

Sources: Calculated from data provided by the Naikaku Hoseikyoku; and data from *Shugiin, Sangiin, Gikai Seido Hyakunenshi*, vol. 7: *Kokkai Gian Kemmeiroku* (Tokyo: Okurasho Insatsu Kyoku, 1990).

Notes: Figures indicate numbers of new or revised laws and regulations in each time period. The table covers the Allied occupation, which was a time of unusual legislative activity due to the large volume of reform legislation requested by the occupation authorities.

the United States many regulations are issued by independent commissions or agencies, such as the Federal Communications Commission and the Federal Aviation Administration. But the scope of bureaucratic lawmaking through ordinances is widely said to be very great in Japan.

Ministry policies are frequently enforced by a system of understandings and influence called administrative guidance (*gyosei shido*), whereby ministries persuade private-sector actors or local governments to comply with their policies by indirect means. One kind of administrative guidance occurs when ministry powers embodied in specific legislation are applied to new uses not necessarily part of the original mandate. The authority to regulate one activity is used implicitly or explicitly to gain compliance in a second area. Guidance is thus usually a form of supervision and control that relies on the threat of some legally imposed sanction rather than coercion per se.[54]

Another possible source of ministry influence is the practice of *amakudari*, or "descent from heaven," by which private-sector firms hire retired bureaucrats for their experience and contacts. With one important exception, there is little evidence of strong outside influence from former bureaucrats appointed as advisers in Japanese firms, either in Japanese newspaper accounts or in academic writings. In the standard view of Japanese business, there is a stress on the relative isolation of management teams from outside influence, which is symbolized by the appointment of senior company officials and few outsiders to boards of directors.

National Personnel Agency reports indicate that 208 senior bureaucrats retired to private-sector positions in 1993.[55] Most were from the Ministries of Finance, International Trade and Industry, Construction, Education, and Posts and Telecommunications. Many of these people took positions as advisers or directors, and it can be assumed that they were hired for their contacts and the prestige that their presence gave to the companies.[56] In one exception to this generalization, there are quite a few former Finance Ministry officials in influential positions in Japanese banks. A disproportionate number of retiring bureaucrats who descend from heaven are from the Finance Ministry — 66 in 1993 and 58 out of a total 203 in 1994. Their destination is more often small banks than Japan's leading so-called "city banks," and banks receiving officials don't do any better than those who do not, according to one source.[57] It is also important to remember that there are more than 1,200 firms listed under the major firm category in the Japanese stock market; this means that appointments of ex-bureaucrats would each year only produce directorships in one tenth of the major firms. It is doubtful if there are enough ex-bureaucrats to make appointments on as widespread a basis as some press accounts suggest.[58]

Many former ministry officials have shown up in the LDP's Diet contingent ever since the war, however. At the beginning of the 1980s, one in every three Liberal Democrats in the House of Representatives was a former official, and one in five was a former central ministry bureaucrat. Fifty-two former national bureaucrats were LDP Dietmembers in 1990. Proportions of former national bureaucrats in LDP governments and top party positions have been even greater, especially before the 1980s. Between 1960 and 1980, about 40 percent of cabinet portfolios were held by former bureaucrats, and in thirty-two of the forty-six postwar years, ending in 1991, the prime minister was a former bureaucrat. Former bureaucrats also usually occupied the top three positions in the LDP.[59]

Consultative councils are yet another potential source of ministry influence. There are 154 of these councils attached to the different ministries and agencies of the central government. By the 1980s the councils were widely believed to contribute to a two-way process of communication and influence between interest groups and ministries or agencies, although earlier they had been seen more as instruments of ministry control and domination.[60]

Traditional arguments for bureaucratic dominance were based on the assumption explicitly or implicitly that the bureaucracy functioned as a monolith or at least in terms of individual ministry initiatives. Seemingly limitless examples of independent ministry actions reported by Japanese newspapers also encourage an impression of ministry dominance. (A small subset of these actions is identified in Table 5.4.) Ministries have some latitude in generating

Table 5.4. Independent Decisions by the Ministry of International Trade and Industry, 1952–1990

Foreign Market Interventions

1952 MITI Curtails Raw Cotton Imports Because of Slow Textile Market
1952 MITI and the Ministry of Transportation Ask the Ministry of Finance to Help Subsidize Plant Exports
1959 MITI Develops Liberal Foreign-Exchange Policy
1972 MITI to Simplify Procedures for Expansion of Imports
1973 MITI to Strengthen Emergency Tariff System as Trade Negotiations Weapon
1976 MITI Changes Approval Procedures to Increase Automobile Imports
1987 MITI to Continue Restrictions on Automobiles Exported to U.S.

Plans and Development Programs

1953 MITI to Develop Rationalization Program for Basic Industries
1955 MITI to Present Plan for Industrial Infrastructure Development
1972 MITI Presents National Plan for Relocation of Industries
1972 MITI Finalizes New Capital-Liberalization Plan
1973 MITI Develops Comprehensive Energy Acquisition and Usage Plan
1973 MITI to Develop Program for Survey of Underseas Manganese Deposits
1986 MITI to Promote Development of Ultrasonic Passenger Airplane

Industry Structure Policy

1973 MITI Intends to Reorganize Oil Development Companies into Three Groups
1973 MITI to Establish Public-Private Liquid National Gas Corporations
1973 MITI to Establish Corporation for Import of Lumber and Nonferrous Ore
1976 MITI to Reorganize Cement Firms Ten Groups Owing to End of Cartels
1981 MITI Develops Five-Year Plan for Stockpiling of Rare Metals
1981 MITI Surveys Sites for Construction of Nuclear Power Plants
1983 MITI Develops 1984 Facilities Investment Plan
1984 MITI to Reorganize Cement Industry into Five Groups
1986 MITI Targets Thirty Areas for Change of Local Industry Structure
1986 MITI to Permit Construction of New-Type Textile Facilities

Domestic Market Interventions

1952 MITI Formulates Price Subsidy System for Iron and Steel
1952 MITI Proposes Subsidized Steel Purchase-Sale System
1952 MITI to Subsidize Coal to Spur Iron and Steel, Fertilizer Industries
1976 MITI to Establish Raw Materials Policy Committee to Counteract Shortages
1976 MITI to Control Price Inflation in Petroleum Industry by "Guidance"

Continued

Table 5.4. Continued

1984	MITI Requests Textile Industry Firms to Curtail Production of Polyester Cloth
1985	MITI to Discontinue Stockpiling of Aluminum Ingots
1987	MITI Coordinates Semiconductor Production, Guides Investment
1988	MITI Promotes Sharing of Consumer Information in Textile Industry

Other Policies

1972	MITI Decides to Abolish Foreign Aid with Strings Attached
1985	MITI to Foster Export Industries in Developing Nations Through Aid
1985	MITI Establishes Program to Dismantle Old Nuclear Power Plants
1990	MITI Sets Plant Export Standards to Prevent Use in Chemical Warfare
1990	MITI to Approve Revolving Credit System for Credit Cards

Sources: Nihon Keizai, May 14, 1952, July 3 and 22, September 10, October 3, 1952, June 4, 1987, November 12, 1972, December 3, 1972, May 16, 1973, October 2 and August 7, 1976, March 24, 1981, June 15, 1983, August 2, 1984, November 11, 1984, June 18 and October 3, 1985, April 10 and July 16, 1986, May 13, 1990; *Yomiuri,* September 4, 1952, January 15, 1959, December 31, 1987; *Tokyo Shimbun,* June 23, 1973, May 15, 1981, December 1, 1988; *Jiji,* November 6, 1952; *Sangyo Keizai,* May 21, 1953; *Jiji Shimpo,* September 29, 1955 (E); *Asahi,* June 16, 1973, October 5, 1986; *Nihon Kogyo,* June 12, 1973, February 2, 1976, May 3, 1985; *Nikkan Kogyo,* July 12, 1973, October 2, 1976; *Mainichi,* December 5, 1972; *Sankei,* October 31, 1972.

Note: MITI actions shown here are a small, representative sampling of the vast number of MITI actions reported in the economic press.

policy. On the other hand, they do not operate unilaterally when it is necessary for more than one ministry to formulate policy. Indeed, just the opposite has been the case; while independently powerful and assertive in some instances, ministries have often been circumscribed by bitter interministry or even intra-ministry conflicts. This was stipulated in a Japanese newspaper: "Of course, there is a weakness on the side of the bureaucrats. . . . They are unable to decide anything on crucial matters because of their jurisdictional strife."[61]

The frequency of interministry conflicts must be understood in order to put the role of the bureaucracy in proper perspective (Table 5.5). Even reputedly strong ministries like MITI have been involved in sustained arguments over policy with other ministries. Both jurisdictional and substantive differences can be at issue. Disagreements over cartel policy are one example. The Ministry of International Trade and Industry has at times advocated restricting competition between firms to promote healthier Japanese industries. Some MITI programs were opposed by the Fair Trade Commission, a government organ set up under the Allied occupation to combat monopolies and other market abuses.[62] In this case, different laws created areas of potential jurisdic-

Table 5.5. Disagreements Between Ministries, 1952–1990

Disputing Ministries	Issue
Differences over Policy	
MITI–Bank of Japan	Proposed creation of an automobile industry in Japan
MITI–Fair Trade Commission	Company mergers and cartels policy
MITI–Finance Ministry	Tax depreciation of robots
	Tax incentives for depressed industries
	Establishment of high-technology-development corporation
Finance Ministry–Posts and Telecommunications Ministry	Withholding of postal savings deposit interest
Finance Ministry–Transportation Ministry	Use of airport passenger tax for airport improvement
Finance Ministry–Defense Agency	Defense levels, plans, budget
Differences over Jurisdictions	
MITI–Finance Ministry	Intellectual property rights
MITI–Foreign Ministry	Establishment of foreign public relations section within MITI
	Stationing of MITI officials in overseas embassies
MITI–Welfare Ministry	Pollution problems and responsibility
MITI–Posts and Telecommunication Ministry	Jurisdiction over the information industry
MITI–Transportation Ministry	Jurisdiction over oil pipe lines
MITI–Agriculture, Forestry, and Fisheries Ministry	Food codes
Home Ministry–Education Ministry	History textbooks in Japanese schools

Sources: Eugene J. Kaplan, *Japan: The Government-Business Relationship* (Washington, D.C.: U.S. Department of Commerce, 1972); *Asahi*, August 8, 1982 (E); *Mainichi*, October 6, 1982, September 19, 1984, and February 24, 1985; *Nihon Keizai*, July 23, 1982 (E), October 31, 1983, October 3 and October 5, 1984 (E), March 25, 1985 (E), June 29 and August 13, 1986; *Yomiuri*, July 14, 1982, May 24, 1983, November 11, 1990.

Note: Disputes listed here are a small sampling of the total number of interministry disagreements.

tional overlap as well as different policy commitments for the ministries. Accounts of civil-military, army-navy, and intraservice rivalries before and during World War II indicate that interministerial and intraministerial conflict is a chronic feature of the Japanese political landscape.[63]

Ministries also compete over which will undertake new administrative functions. MITI's fight with the Ministry of Posts and Telecommunications over supervision of the emerging telecommunications equipment industry is an example.[64] The same two ministries have also disputed control over which controls the telephone lines connecting computers. There are many other examples of territorial ambitions on the part of specific ministries, with some ministries "colonizing" new administrative units by dispatching their own officials for temporary duty. This explains why, for example, the Science and Technology Agency is heavily staffed by officials from other ministries.

Differences of opinion between ministries sometimes reflect deeply embedded, long-standing policy cleavages that have virtually ideological status. The responsibility of the Ministry of Finance for the national purse (both revenue collection and preparation of the annual national budget) is a case in point. Ministry officials are loath to spend money or to place restrictions on revenue. The ministry has often opposed MITI proposals for new tax exemptions for specific industries for this reason. Because each of the ministries recruits its own staff, policy differences like these are enshrined over time. Responsibilities and jurisdictions turn into sacred causes. Cultural values favoring in-group solidarity encourage such ministerial parochialism.[65]

Other longtime differences divide ministries internally. In the 1950s and 1960s one faction of MITI preferred domestic industrial development and therefore supported protective tariffs and quotas. The internationalist group within the ministry opposed trade barriers to maintain access to foreign markets. There have likewise been differences in the Finance Ministry among officials concerned with budget making, revenue collection, and deficit spending, respectively.[66]

The term Japan, Inc. was coined by Western journalists who attributed Japan's great strength as a trading power to the leadership of ministries like MITI and the close relationship between Japanese government and business interests. But interministerial and intraministerial cleavages belie the existence of a monolithic bureaucracy that runs a coalition of ministries and business. Viewing the bureaucracy—especially the major economic ministries, Finance, MITI, Transportation, and, sometimes, Construction—as both influential in policymaking and internally pluralistic is more realistic. Although interministry conflict is not present in every example of bureaucratic policymaking, where it is present, it imposes limits on the autonomy of individual ministries.

Thus far I have emphasized the prevalence of pluralistic, conflictual relationships in the cabinet and the bureaucracy. But there is extensive coordination and consultation at all stages of policymaking, not just conflict (Table 5.6). The Japanese preference for extensive, informal consultation modifies ministry authority, as well as constrains other actors' influence. Inter-actor

Table 5.6. Permanent and Ad Hoc Coordinating Groups in Japanese Policymaking

Intraministry and Interministry
Administrative Vice Ministers
 Conference
Comprehensive Security Ministers
 Conference
Conference of Economic Ministers
Ministry-Cabinet Legislative Bureau
 Meeting
Chiefs of Ministry Secretariats
 Meeting
Ministry Bureau Directors Meeting
Council for Comprehensive Security
National Security Council

Government-LDP
Government-LDP Liaison Council
Government–Ruling Party External
 Economic Measures Promotion
 Conference

Coalition Government (1993–95)
Representatives Council (Hata and
 Hosokawa Governments)
Policy Directors Council (Hata and
 Hosokawa Governments)
Council of Responsible Persons
 (Murayama Government)
General Council (Murayama
 Government)
Policy Coordination Council
 (Murayama Government)

LDP
Party Executive
Supreme Advisors
PARC Division Heads Conference
Special Committee on Diet Testimony
 Law Revision
National Tax System Promotion
 Conference
Faction Secretariat Heads Meeting
PARC Division Heads Meetings*
Chairs / Vice Chairs of PARC Foreign
 Affairs Research Division

Interparty
Conferences of Secretaries General
Diet Policy Committee Chairpersons
 Meetings
Diet Steering Committee Directors
 Meetings
Political Ethics Council
Parliamentary System Reform
 Consultative Council
Tax System Consultative Council
Party Heads Meetings
Party "Top Officers" Conference
Election Law Fixed Number
 Correction Consultative Council

Sources: Nihon Keizai, June 19, 1982, February, 18 and April 23, 1983, July 30 (E) and December 20, 1985; *Mainichi*, March 14, 1982, May 9, 1983, April 6, 1984, September 7 (E) and November 18, 1986; *Tokyo Shimbun*, January 20 and June 12, 1982, February 23, 1983, May 22 and August 4, 1984, December 8, 1985, April 5, 1986, April 25, 1991; *Yomiuri*, July 10 and 16, 1982, November 7, 1983 (E), January 6 and February 2, 1984, June 17, 1987, July 2, 1988 (E), December 6, 1990; *Asahi*, April 3, 1982, February 23, 1984, June 2, 1985, June 10, 1986; *Sankei*, June 13, 1986, February 19, 1987. See also additional source citations relating to coalition government coordination groups in text.

Note: With the exception of coalition government councils, most other coordinating groups are from the period of LDP rule. A few groups transcend both eras and/or have been replaced by similar groups under coalition governments. Interparty policy teams in specific policy areas have also existed under coalition governments.

*Sometimes PARC division heads have participated in special consultations on particular issues. One example was the meeting of the defense, foreign affairs, and judicial affairs division heads during formulation of a state secrets law proposal in 1985 (*Nihon Keizai*, April 10, 1985).

coordination is a political necessity in any society, but in Japan it assumes unusual prominence.[67] Widespread, at times ritualized, consultation tends to make political processes more inclusive and more responsible than would otherwise be the case.

Coordinating groups exist to sound out opinions and try to reach agreement at each point in policymaking processes that involve cabinet and bureaucracy, as well as elsewhere in the political arena. If agreement is not possible, partial acceptance of a policy initiative is sought among as many individuals and organizations as are relevant and feasible. Within the bureaucracy, intraministry consultations at the level of division and bureau director and interministry meetings of administrative or parliamentary vice ministers have been the typical coordination points for policy proposals. In these discussions ministry officials endeavor to gain support from their colleagues and counterparts. They also begin fairly early in the course of developing a policy to look for support from members of parliament, traditionally Dietmembers from the ruling LDP. Dietmembers themselves sometimes take the initiative in these discussions by asking ministry officials to include a desired subsidy or proviso in a forthcoming law proposal.[68] Consultative councils of ministries also serve as coordinating points for the adjustment of ministry, interest group, and sometimes party views.[69]

Cabinet members themselves are appointed to task teams to deal with specific issues or policy areas. Ministers concerned with economic policy, such as the heads of the Ministries of Finance, International Trade and Industry, and Agriculture, Forestry, and Fisheries, are frequently asked to join these teams. Meetings of administrative vice ministers fill a similar function. Ad hoc informal bridging efforts to hold policy coalitions together, integrate participants in new coalitions, or reduce conflict between opposing coalitions are also common. Some of these became institutionalized, for example, the meetings between LDP leaders and top ministers in the LDP-led cabinets.

During the period of LDP rule, there was coordination at several levels in the party organization: within PARC divisions and committees, between LDP deputy secretaries general (each selected from a major faction), and within the loosely defined group of top party officers, including the vice president of the party (when this post was filled), the secretary general, and the heads of the Executive Council and PARC. Secretaries general of the major factions met when issues divided the party to the point of immobilism and when the outcome of a factional struggle depended on obtaining consensus over policy — during the final stages of tax reform in 1988, for example. Discussions between the prime minister or other party officials and the Supreme Advisers also took place regularly at these and other times of intraparty disagreement.

The LDP leadership and the government or cabinet also consulted regularly during the latter years of LDP rule. Everyone present was from the same political party. The LDP leaders represented the constituencies, including rank-and-file Dietmembers and affiliated interest groups, and the LDP cabinet ministers represented the ministries.

Consultation followed a variety of formally and informally defined paths. Several groups set up to provide opportunities for consultation at different points in the policymaking process are listed in Table 5.6.

Since the advent of multiparty coalition government, consultation and coordination have become even more important than before. The first two post-LDP governments, led by Morihiro Hosokawa and Tsutomu Hata, respectively, established a Representatives' Council (Daihyosha Kaigi) to advise the prime minister; it was made up of the secretaries general of the five main coalition parties. There was also a two-branched ten-person Policy Coordination Council (the branches: Seisaku Kanjikai and Seimukanjikai) consisting of heads of the policy organs and Diet strategy committees from each of the five parties. These coordinating councils, which provided policy inputs supplementing those of the cabinet itself, appeared to operate in the fashion of the earlier government-LDP liaison conference.[70] Working groups were also set up in such areas as administrative reform and tax policy.[71]

The third post-LDP coalition government, headed by the Socialist Tomiichi Murayama, established coordination organs like those of the earlier coalitions. A Council of Responsible Persons (Sekininsha Kaigi), made up of the secretaries general of the coalition parties, was supplemented by a General Council (Innai Somukai), composed of sixty Dietmembers, twenty from each party. The party-cabinet liaison system from LDP days was revived to coordinate relations between these bodies and the cabinet. There is also a Policy Coordination Council made up of heads of coalition party policy councils and representatives of coalition party Diet policy committees and five special policy teams in important issue areas (administrative reform, welfare, agriculture, tax policy, and macroeconomic policy). In addition to these multilevel contacts, the leaders of the three coalition parties meet regularly each Monday.[72]

Consultation is a universal part of politics. It is also a cultural imperative in Japan. In spite of abundant conflict, the political system contains pervasive efforts at coordination. Appreciation of this organic tendency in Japanese political processes is essential. Because of consultation, policy outcomes reflect more than the working out of simple configurations of adversarial power (even though power relationships are also a basic factor in most policymaking scenarios). The best scholarly treatment of consultation describes it as an expanding process by which progressively more relevant participants are sequentially added to a moving bargained consensus.[73] Still, lingering conflicts abound. Sometimes even the hierarchies of coordinating groups disagree internally or with each other. Here are some recent examples: A working group of the Hata-coalition Tax Reform Committee disagreed over deregulation of agriculture after opposition from business and the Ministry of Agriculture, Forestry, and Fisheries; Finance Ministry officials and coalition party representatives in a Hosokawa-coalition working group were stalemated over tax cuts; SDPJ and LDP representatives on the Policy Coordination Council differed over security policy; and the Policy Coordination Council of the Hosokawa government claimed that it was relegated to the "mezzanine" while the Representatives' Council decided policies.[74]

Governments and Bureaucracies in Other Countries

In a rating of executive power in the five major parliamentary democracies — Britain, France, Germany, Japan, and Italy — the postwar prime ministers of Japan, including both those during LDP hegemony and those now, were closer to the weak end of the scale.[75] Governments in Britain and France were much stronger than those in Japan in both formal power and informal influence. British prime ministers are heads of centralized political parties and can appoint their own cabinets with less pervasive fuss and calculation than always occurs in Japan. They can also influence cabinet and parliamentary agendas using the party whip and control of patronage to maintain party discipline and sway cabinet ministers.[76]

Britain probably has the single strongest executive. The two-level government of Fifth Republic France comes next, and even though the authority of French prime ministers is inferior to presidents', they have considerable influence when they are from the same party as the president. The French executive — president and premier together — is clearly very strong. German chancellors' influence on policies and appointments is also superior to operative executive power in Japan. Still, Japanese prime ministers were apparently stronger than Italian premiers, who have traditionally experienced even more severe constraints from decentralized, fragmented power relations than Japanese leaders have. Many of the factors described in this chapter as affecting central power relations in Japan exist in other political systems, but their proportions and mix are different.

The characteristics of public bureaucracies also vary in different major industrialized democracies. These variations have implications for evaluating the role of the Japanese bureaucracy.

1. The bureaucracy is much smaller in Japan than in other major countries. As befits the lower levels of taxation and expenditure in Japan, there are roughly half as many civil servants relative to its workforce as in the United States, Britain, and Germany and considerably fewer than in France. Probabilistically speaking, more Americans, British, French, and Germans will come in contact with public officials during their lifetime than Japanese will. More will have relatives and acquaintances in public service, and more will be dependent on the bureaucracy for social services in the European cases than in Japan. As an institution, the bureaucracy is a larger part of society in the other major democracies than in Japan — a fact usually ignored in discussions of the official Japanese establishment.[77]

2. The extent of the government's power to make political appointments varies, too. In 1990, after the last election won by the LDP, 47 LDP Dietmembers were appointed to cabinet or subcabinet positions. A British majority party appoints more than 100 people to senior government positions. In France, approximately 500 positions are filled by appointment, roughly ten times the figure for Japan.[78]

3. The presence of quite a few former bureaucrats in LDP Diet ranks is believed by many to have facilitated ties between the ruling party and the ministries during the era of LDP rule. It is true that former bureaucrats dominated the prime ministership and many postwar cabinets, especially before 1980. But in some European parliaments there are considerably more bureaucrats than in the Japanese Diet. In 1990 former bureaucrats accounted for less than 10 percent of all Dietmembers. In Germany the figure was 37 percent; in France, as high as 53 percent in the 1980s. The social status of former bureaucrats in these European countries is also very high. In France, they are recruited from an educational system that is, if possible, even more elitist than the Japanese.[79]

4. The ministry consultative councils found in Japan are found nearly everywhere else, too. Specific figures are available only for France, where there are 500 councils, 1,200 committees, and 3,000 commissions, compared with the 154 ministry consultative councils in Japan. France also has a more extensive administrative regulatory system. The 11,000-plus regulatory rules and 1,834 laws in Japan are more than matched by the 125,000-plus laws, decrees, and directives in France.[80]

Each figure cited here is a fragment of information about very complex institutions. The statistics are mentioned solely to cast doubt on the frequently unqualified assertions that the Japanese bureaucracy is unique in its high status, relations with conservative political parties, extensive regulatory powers, and social impact. The ministries are, however, unique in one way: they are remarkably free from external judicial accountability, as Frank Upham has documented persuasively and in appropriately great detail.[81] In contrast, ministries in Italy and France and, to some degree, in Germany are subject to administrative law, administrative courts, and other nonparliamentary forms of authority over legislation. In France, for instance, "the barrage of internal control mechanisms includes a network of Administrative Tribunals, headed by the Council of State and the Mediator's Office, which are judicial bodies with the task of judging allegedly administrative abuses against the citizen. The Court of Accounts and the Financial Inspectorate look into the financial irregularities of the administration."[82] In Italy, legislative grants of authority, as well as legislation in general, are highly specific. In Japan, legislative grants of authority to administrative bodies are generally just the opposite — very vague and lacking in specificity — and the only review of legislation is provided by the Cabinet Legislative Bureau, a government unit staffed by officials seconded from the ministries. There is serious scrutiny in the Japanese case, but it is limited to a search for legal and constitutional precedents; other matters are left to the general court system. The story of Japan's uniqueness stops here until more information is available.

Conclusion

Evidence that executive and bureaucratic power is constrained in ways not indicated by scholars of the vertical governance school accords with my central thesis that Japanese politics was pluralistic even during the long period of LDP rule. Before 1993, Japanese political elites were limited in their options by LDP factionalism and internal policy divisions. Pressure from interest groups and opposition parties also at times constrained party leaders' ability to exploit LDP control of the government. Internal divisions and the politicization of many issues constrained the traditionally influential bureaucracy as well. Decisions reached by the mutual accommodation of multiple political actors were common. As I will summarize in Chapter 10, Japan and Italy lie together at the opposite end of a continuum of the centralization of political control; at the other end is the Westminster model of party government so often cited by denigrators of Japanese-style democracy. Japan has a bargained democracy, even if it generally lacks a Westminster-style programmatic democracy.

Ministry influence has declined since World War II, according to many sources.[83] Ministry of Finance officials have less influence over budget allocations than in the past because of revenue shortages and deficit financing constraints. In some years, the need for zero-ceiling budgets has restricted the options of the Finance Ministry and, therefore, its ability to independently shape government priorities. A view that MITI's powers have declined is also widespread.[84]

Influence on the LDP side of the ministry-LDP equation grew during the same period, according to many observers. Many feel that as time went on, the LDP became an increasingly effective policymaking body. Some assert that the party had replaced the bureaucracy as policy innovator and agenda setter until its recent loss of power. Finance Ministry officials have reportedly lamented that the Government-LDP Consultative Council had become the "real Budget Bureau," and the party's Tax-Reduction-Problem Subcommittee the "real Tax Bureau." The ability of the LDP to overrule Finance Ministry budget decisions supposedly exemplified these changes.[85] A belief that LDP zoku were growing in influence was an integral part of this argument. Whether in the form of zoku or not, there is ample evidence of party constraint on ministry power. As one senior Ministry of Foreign Affairs bureaucrat said to me in 1994: "Whether the political parties or the ministry position is most important depends on the case. If the parties are deeply concerned, they may come to us for advice. But they still decide on the basis of their own views. If it is a matter of little concern to them, or if there are foreign pressures, or if international agreements take precedence, then they come to us for help and advice. Sometimes they come back as often as fifteen or twenty times if it is a matter where they need expertise."

Tracing the interactions between the cabinet, LDP groups, and other political actors heightens awareness of the importance of horizontal power configurations in Japanese political life. Political demands were often fragmented, reflecting both a parochializing culture and a decentralized electoral process. Power within parties was also decentralized because of extensive factionalism and, in the case of the LDP, deep policy cleavages plus the development of an enormous intraparty policymaking apparatus. A compulsion to consult widely also led to inclusion of political actors outside the core of top bureaucrats and party leaders.

Political life has been more decentralized in Japan than in major European parliamentary systems despite nearly four decades of single-party rule. Many factors have contributed to the weakness of the political center. Barring a massive change in the effects of electoral reforms, which is not expected at present, these factors will not disappear under coalition government. Although intraparty electoral competition will be eliminated under a single-member district system, penetrative electoral mobilization and parochialization of political demands will not be eliminated. In spite of widespread assumptions to the contrary, it is naive to assume that parochial influences on politics will be eradicated so simply. Because of the greater diversity of the current multiparty coalition, its members may exert even more influence over the prime minister and cabinet than was the case under sole LDP rule. But other factors — such as the relative lack of experience among ministers in the first two post-LDP coalition governments — may have an opposite effect.

6

Legislative Politics

Most observers see the political role of the postwar Diet as negligible.[1] Although it occupies a central place in the constitution, many consider it a ritualistic body and say that the ministries have dominated policy initiation and, therefore, legislative agendas. The Liberal Democratic majority in the Diet from 1955 to 1993 meant that bills submitted by the LDP-dominated ministries and cabinet had a strong chance of passage. These conditions, together with the weakness of the opposition in the Diet under the 1955 system, have allegedly permitted the Diet to ratify without amending the many bills submitted.[2] One scholar bluntly describes the limited role of the Diet: "There is no clearly polarized competition between genuine alternative governments. There is, instead, a permanent majority party and a number of fringe parties which act as gadfly critics of the established power."[3]

A few scholars have taken a more positive view. Some saw the early postwar Diet as a place of interparty accommodation.[4] In 1976–80, when the LDP and the opposition were nearly equal in strength, the Diet moved toward even more inter-camp accommodation, according to one study of the period.[5] Other researchers concluded that in the 1970s and 1980s the Diet was a much more important legislature than its reputation indicated.[6]

How the Japanese Diet worked given a strong bureaucracy and dominant party system is central to our concern with the distribution of power in postwar Japan. The vertical view is that LDP governments dominated the Diet, reducing its processes to ritual. The horizontal view would be that there was a give-and-take between the political parties during LDP rule and, relatedly, between the prime minister and cabinet and the Diet. Which interpretation is accurate is the question. It is also important to see whether legislative practices under LDP hegemony have changed today under coalition government.

How the Diet has performed is also significant in a comparative perspective. Different types of democracies have major differences in legislative styles. Some legislatures make policies. The U.S. Congress is the best example; it initiates many important legislative proposals. Most parliaments, in contrast, mainly react to policy proposals initiated by the government or bureaucracy. Britain and France fit the second model; Germany lies somewhere between them and the U.S. Congress.[7]

Using newly available data on the processing of parliamentary bills, I will demonstrate that the influence of the Diet since World War II has been underestimated. The Diet has been more than a rubber stamp, even though the way it works is very different from idealized versions of how legislatures should perform. Although the amount of work actually accomplished in the formal sessions of the Diet was not always large, the Diet was still the fulcrum of important political processes. Political parties developed multilevel strategies to have bills passed or rejected in order to enhance their electoral credibility and to respond to party and interest group constituencies. Success or failure in the Diet also affected recruitment within the ruling party, with the result that events in the Diet influenced who led Japan.

The Diet and the Legislative Process

The design of government institutions was influenced by the Allied occupation, so the postwar parliament only partially resembles prewar institutions. The lower house, the House of Representatives, bears the same name as the prewar lower house. But its status is more clearly that of a popularly elected institution. Before the war the cabinet was responsible solely to the emperor. The House of Representatives now functions more like the British House of Commons in its relations with the government. A majority of cabinet members must come from the Diet, and the prime minister, cabinet, and individual ministers can be removed by a vote of nonconfidence or a failed vote of confidence in the lower house. The postwar House of Councillors is an entirely new institution; it resembles the U.S. Senate, both because it is an elected body (unlike the prewar House of Peers) and because its members are elected for six-year terms on a staggered basis.

Both houses have a permanent committee system. The standing committees parallel the government in their organization; fourteen committees directly correspond to ministry functions, and the other four are concerned with cabinet affairs, audit, discipline, and steering. Several special committees correspond to government agencies attached to the prime minister's office or address special problems, such as disaster plans and coal policy. In the upper house, positions as standing committee chair are apportioned on the basis of party representation. During most of the era of LDP rule, lower house committee chairs were LDP Dietmembers. Lower house committee chairs were appointed by the speaker, upper house committee chairs by the president of the House of Councillors.

The committees affecting the overall performance of the Diet by far the most are the steering committees of both houses. It is here that the schedules of Diet proceedings are decided, including the schedules for debates and votes in both Diet committees and plenary sessions. Decisions in both committees are made on the basis of unanimity among the committee directors, one of whom comes from each party. The unanimity rule is perhaps the single most important feature of the Diet and gives minority parties a potential veto over legislation. The steering committees can control the movement of legislation. A committee chair, in consultation with the committee directors, can decide when to consider a bill and how much time will be devoted to its debate. However, once debate has begun, a single party can still move to close the debate and take a vote, and if the party holds a majority, the bill can be passed by the committee without full debate. This is called the forced or snap vote.[8]

According to statistics on the numbers of government bills — that is, those proposed by cabinet or prime minister — the prime minister and cabinet have in fact played a strong role in Diet legislation. Typically two of every three bills considered in most Diet sessions between 1952 and 1989 originated within the cabinet and were initiated or drafted by bureaucrats (see Table 5.2). Clearly, the cabinet and bureaucracy dominated inputs to the legislative branch of government. A high percentage of government bills passed the Diet, too. Bills drafted within the bureaucracy and sponsored by the cabinet accounted for 84 percent of the bills passed by the Diet in 1952–89. On the basis of this information alone, it would appear that the role of the Diet was subordinate to that of the cabinet and the ministries.

An analysis of the outcomes of government bills qualifies that view, however. Several kinds of Diet actions are concealed by simple statistics on government bill passage. Bills sent to the Diet can be (1) passed without amendment, (2) amended, (3) abandoned, or (4) postponed. Under LDP dominance, government bills were seldom defeated or rejected outright, although actions

Table 6.1. Actions on Government Bills in LDP-Dominated Diet Sessions,
1952–1993

Years	Total Number	Percentage Passed Without Amendment	Percentage Amended	Percentage Postponed	Percentage Abandoned
1952–59	1,426	62	22	8	7
1960–69	2,017	56	16	11	17
1970–79	1,208	58	19	11	10
1980–89	1,335	62	12	25	5
1990–93	436	74	7	14	6

Sources: 1952–89 data from *Shugiin, Sangiin, Gikai Seido Hyakunenshi*, vol. 7: *Kokkai Gian Kemmeiroku* (Tokyo: Okurasho Insatsu Kyoku, 1990); 1990–93 data from Politics and Parliamentary Affairs Division, National Diet Library.

classified under (2), (3), or (4) may have constituted de facto rejection of some or all of the content of specific bills. Of the 6,422 government bills considered by the Diet between 1952 and 1993, just over 60 percent passed in the session in which they were initially presented without modification or delay (Table 6.1). Another 15 percent were amended owing to some kind of opposition to the original government proposal, and the remainder were postponed until later sessions (13 percent) or abandoned (10 percent). Sometimes bills were postponed or abandoned because the Diet ran out of time. (In a few cases, Diet sessions were very short, sometimes lasting less than one week; then, most or all bills were postponed for lack of time. But general statistical trends are not affected by this.) Sometimes they were deferred as part of an agreement between the ruling and opposition parties to consider another bill or bills in the current session. Sometimes postponement or abandonment meant explicit rejection, with the result that the bill was either dropped completely or rewritten and resubmitted. Although a high proportion of the output of the Diet originated within the government, the Diet acted on government bills in different ways, including some suggesting a moderate degree of activism in legislative processes.

The information in Table 6.1 also indicates that LDP dominance did not completely deny the opposition a legislative role even in the 1950s and 1960s, when Diet representation favored the LDP even more than it did later. There are examples of amendments, postponements, and abandonment of government bills in all periods — not excluding the time in the late 1950s when the LDP was led by the controversial and autocratic Nobusuke Kishi. Although the Diet is usually said to have been a more conciliatory place in the 1970s and later, the record of the early years is still significant, especially with regard to amendments. More bills were actually amended in the 1950s than in later decades. Perhaps LDP leadership changes after 1960 resulted in more constraint or more accommodations with the opposition before bills were drafted, so that less had to be done in the Diet.

When I analyzed legislative actions on 320 legislative bills that attracted major media attention in 1960–89, I found once again that interparty accommodation was fairly common and, in this instance, conformed to the impression that conciliation increased after the 1970s. The Diet was often a remarkably intense arena of interparty conflict and associated efforts at accommodation. Important actions were taken in the Diet — or in political processes outside the Diet but closely related to Diet debates — by parties determined to have favored bills passed or disliked bills modified or abandoned. Both the Liberal Democrats and the opposition developed strategies to affect Diet outcomes based on their long-term relation as majority and minority, respectively.[9]

Table 6.2 presents the different kinds of Diet actions taken on major legislative bills from 1960 to 1989. One in every eight important bills was dealt with by forced votes in which Diet committee votes were initiated by the LDP without minority party consent to closure of debate. A slightly larger proportion of major bills resulted in boycotts — refusals by opposition parties to participate in Diet deliberations. The opposition also employed filibusters to delay decisions that they did not like; sometimes they successfully postponed debates to a later Diet session. Boycotts and filibusters often followed forced votes, pointing to the importance of procedural actions in the Diet. In the Diet under LDP rule and even now under coalition rule, procedures are often used to stall and block legislation. Control of the movement of a bill through the Diet is preferred over substantive debate. This tendency partly reflects the impact of the unanimity rule of the Diet steering committees on the way the Diet is run. The opposition parties have used this rule, plus procedural actions within committees, to manipulate schedules to give disliked government bills little or no time on the docket. The result is that a disproportionate amount of the political maneuvering in the Diet focuses on setting the legislative timetable.

Forced votes, boycotts, and filibusters were a feature of intense interparty confrontations over proposed major legislation in the Diet. Many of the conflicts were subsequently mediated by lower or upper house speakers. Many other bills were dealt with by informal, behind-the-scenes conciliation between party representatives. Often conciliation led to substantive amendments to bills. In the 1960s a few controversial bills were passed with attached

Table 6.2. Disposition of Major Bills in the Diet, 1960–1989

		Conflict Tactics		Conflict Resolution		
Years	Total Number	Forced Votes	Boycotts/ Filibusters	Mediations/ Conciliations	Amended Bills	Withdrawn Bills
1960–69	121	14	16	13	21	8
1970–79	98	13	14	10	37	8
1980–89	101	12	18	5	36	20
Total	320	39	48	28	94	36

Source: Asahi Shimbunsha, *Asahi Nenkan* (Tokyo, the years 1960–90).

resolutions, which have the same general purpose as amendments, though not the same legal effect. Eleven percent of the major legislative proposals were abandoned. Amendment or abandonment was the final disposition of 40 percent of all the important bills that I reviewed.

Ministries themselves withdrew and redrafted some important bills for submission to a later Diet session. These changes and re-submissions are additional evidence of the capacity of the Diet to influence legislation. They also show that the role of the bureaucracy in legislative processes could be one of give-and-take where important LDP or occupational concerns were at stake. The tax reform of the mid-1980s discussed in Chapter 7 is one such example, as were the special measures law for industry promotion that MITI repeatedly re-submitted in the early 1960s and revision of the Anti-Monopoly Law, which was debated at various times.

Intercamp disagreements over (1) national security policy, (2) the interests of party clients, (3) political autonomy, (4) consumer interests, and (5) LDP manipulation of Diet rules resulted at one or another time in sustained, sometimes bitter parliamentary confrontations (Table 6.3). Indeed, the opposition's frustration over permanent minority status led to resistance to many government proposals that might not otherwise have been opposed. Loss of access to preferred informal channels of contact with the LDP during periods of serious confrontation produced more alienation, further separating the parties to the conflict and giving rise to extreme, often violent behavior.[10]

The opposition parties also rejected LDP bills simply to preserve their own parties' solidarity. Internal pressure was a frequent motivation for Socialist Party actions in the 1950s and 1960s. On one occasion, SDPJ backbenchers insisted that party cooperation with the LDP on a National Holidays Bill had to be balanced by opposition on other bills, so the SDPJ opposed three subsequent bills related to Japanese participation in the Asian Development Bank, an issue of little substantive importance to the party at that time. On

Table 6.3. Major Conflictual Legislation in the Japanese Diet, 1960–1990

Year	Bill	Reason for Opposition
National Security		
1960	U.S.-Japan Security Treaty	Differences over Japan's military role
1967, 1969	Defense Agency Bill	Same
1967, 1969	Self-Defense Forces Bill	Same
1971	Okinawa Reversion Treaty	Same
1972	Defense Agency Bill	Same
1972	Self-Defense Forces Bill	Same
Autonomy and Postwar Values		
1961	Anti-Violence Bill	Memories of prewar suppression
1965	Japan-Korea Treaty and bills	Opposition to prewar imperialism
1969	University Administration Bill	Concern for autonomy in education
1973	Tsukuba University Bill	Autonomy in education
1974	Teacher Supervisor Bill	Same
1974	Yasukuni Shrine Bill	Opposition to traditional values
1978	Korean Shelf Agreement	Opposition to renewal of imperialism
Interest Group and Consumers Representation		
1962	Coal Industry Bills	Labor union interests
1965	ILO Treaty and related bills	Concern for rights of labor
1969	Japanese National Railways Fare Increase Bill	Defense of consumer interests
1975	Postal Rate Increase Bill	Same
1975	Alcohol and Cigarette Price Bill	Same
1978	Narita Airport Security Bill	Support for oppressed farmland owners
1986	Japan National Railways Privatization Bill	Labor union interests
1987	Tax Reform Bills (6)	Defense of consumer interests
LDP Usage of Diet Rules to Force Bill Passage		
1961	Agricultural Basic Law	LDP forced vote
1961	Election Reform Bill	LDP rejection of SDPJ amendment
1978	Budget	LDP rejection of opposition amendment
1981	Budget	Response to LDP forced vote
1989	Budget	Same

Continued

Table 6.3. Continued

Other Issues		
1976	Budget	Overlap with Lockheed bribery scandal
1982	Election System Reform Bill	Small party fear of proportional representation system
1982	Tax Reform Bills (2)	Tanaka corruption issue

Source: Asahi Shimbunsha, *Asahi Nenkan* (Tokyo, various years).

another occasion, the Socialists formally opposed amending the election law to provide for proportional representation in House of Councillors elections. The opposition was pro forma but led the LDP to resort to a forced vote in the upper house. This incident is an excellent example of the complexities in interparty and intercamp relations in the Diet. The SDPJ need to satisfy its most extreme factions for the sake of party unity led to formal intransigence and hence to conflictual formal action even when some party factions supported a moderate position.[11]

The amount of conflict in Diet debates on major bills in 1960–90 varied a great deal. The most severe conflicts led to sustained interparty tensions and hostile behavior. Often these conflict scenarios began with LDP violation of parliamentary norms or other LDP tactics, including forced votes and manipulation of the Diet schedule or meeting locations to confuse the opposition or even keep them from participating in debates. Although intercamp feelings were often hostile, as long as the LDP allowed Diet deliberations to proceed according to a schedule agreed on by all parties in advance of the Diet session, the opposition parties normally did not employ disruptive tactics. But once the LDP resorted to a forced vote, the opposition parties usually turned to boycotts, filibusters, the "cow walk" (walking slowly to the front of the Diet chamber to deposit a written vote — which could stretch out voting for several hours), and other delaying tactics. Such scenarios repeatedly led to temporary suspensions of Diet proceedings.

Confrontation in the Diet was at times self-sustaining. Initial conflicts over some legislative proposals led to continued interparty hostility lasting for several days or even several weeks or months. Because the LDP was in many cases loath to pass bills without the opposition parties' presence and participation, conflicts usually brought Diet processes to a standstill. Confrontations on one bill could spill over into debates on legislation that had nothing to do with the initial source of conflict. Bills that might otherwise have passed the Diet without a major hitch became hostage to sustained conflicts. Debate and passage of other proposals was delayed because of preoccupation with controversial bills and the parties' use of procedural tactics that prolonged the conflict. Only four of forty-four bills on the docket were debated and passed in two short sessions following the giant intercamp battle over extension of the U.S.-Japan Security Treaty in 1960, to give one example.

Interparty conflict over important bills has been fairly constant despite the gradual development of a more benign pattern of legislative interaction than prevailed in the earlier postwar period. Confrontation in the 1950s and 1960s was perhaps an inescapable result of both ideological polarization and opposition politicians' memories of prewar suppression. Conflict in the Diet moderated somewhat in the late 1970s, when the ruling party and the opposition were nearly equal in strength, only to return intermittently in the 1980s. As can be seen in Table 6.2, there were roughly the same number of forced votes and opposition boycotts and filibusters in the 1970s and 1980s as earlier. (Forced votes abated temporarily during the period of nearly equal power.) Even though interparty differences had moderated on many issues by the 1970s and 1980s, disputes over the Lockheed scandal and related issues of political ethics and disagreements over national railway reform and some other proposals were marked by a return to earlier patterns of confrontation. Confrontations in the Diet happened now and again, even though the conditions underlying conflict in the 1950s and 1960s were changed or no longer relevant. Episodes in later years reflected the continued frustrations of a seemingly permanent legislative minority, the need of the SDPJ to maintain party solidarity (the presence of the left-leaning Socialist Association often resulted in party support of extremist positions), and the severely alienating effects of corruption scandals involving the LDP. As before, conflict at times reflected a breakdown of normal procedures of interparty accommodation.[12]

Resolution of confrontations in the Diet was never easy. In some cases, the speaker of either the lower or the upper house met with representatives of the political parties to mediate disagreements. Sometimes the speaker took a symbolic step, including his own resignation, to coax the opposition parties to rejoin Diet deliberations. Substantive differences were also addressed through mediation at times, including negotiated abandonment of objectionable bills. Major disagreements over laws affecting defense, pensions, farmers, and national holidays, opposition to an LDP-supported bill to compensate former landowners, conflict over an International Labor Organization ratification package, and some other disputes were resolved in this fashion. Altogether, nearly thirty cases of mediation resulted in abandonment of major bills between 1960 and 1989. Other kinds of consultative actions were taken when an impasse was reached on Diet legislation, depending on the case.

Efforts to resolve Diet conflicts took place both within the Diet and through informal channels external or tangential to the formal Diet procedures. An example of the former was increased use of coordination by the directors of the lower and upper house steering committees to resolve differences or set schedules for debate. Ad hoc consultative committees, which brought together party heavyweights and specialists to seek compromises on difficult issues, were also set up frequently (see Table 5.5). This was the option chosen to handle the post-1976 Lockheed scandal, revision of the Diet testimony law (1982), political ethics issues (in several years), tax reform (1987), and several other issues. Extralegislative efforts to resolve conflicts included informal meetings between party leaders from both camps, "secret" agreements between the LDP and the SDPJ, and negotiations led by LDP heavyweights.[13] When the house speakers mediated a substantive or face-saving compromise between opposing parties, they normally used informal channels.

Some major disputes over bills ended in mediation and resumption of procedural debate. Once the Diet resumed normal functions and ruffled feelings over a violation of parliamentary or cultural norms were dealt with, bills or treaties that had generated interparty or intercamp confrontations were often passed without further controversy. Diet procedures and recognition of their legitimacy sometimes concerned the opposition parties as much as the substance of bills.

Many disputed bills, including some that provoked considerable conflict, were simply postponed for future consideration. As Table 6.1 shows, the percentage of postponed government bills increased to one quarter of all bills in the 1980s, up from a much lower 8 percent in the 1950s. Postponement did not necessarily mean extinction. It permitted emotions to cool off and allowed time for informal negotiations and sometimes revisions to the original bill. Postponed government bills thus fit a pattern of advance and retreat: they were submitted to test the response, postponed when there was too much opposition, then reconsidered (sometimes after changes) when the climate in the Diet was improved. Ratification of the International Labor Organization convention is an example. First submitted in 1962, the treaty and related domestic reform bills were withdrawn or postponed in two Diet sessions and were finally passed after a three-year delay and after amendments were made to the related domestic legislation.[14] Several antiviolence bills were submitted and withdrawn or postponed in the same fashion. Proposals on government secrets (1985), on increases in Japan National Railways fares and health-care payments (1972), and on increases in postage, liquor prices, and cigarette prices (1975) were similarly withdrawn. In 1985 a proposed amendment to the Public Offices Election Law was withdrawn after widespread opposition in all political camps.

Tax reform is a more recent example of the advance-and-retreat processing of highly controversial bills. In this case, divisions among LDP Dietmembers also hastened withdrawal of the offensive bills. The bills were redrafted by the Ministry of Finance, and a new legislative package was sent to the Diet the following year. In a few other instances, the retreat was permanent: a bill or bills were withdrawn. Newspapers sometimes use the term *withdrawal* when abandonment was the formal action of the Diet. This may be confusing, but the important point is that the Diet took some kind of action as the result of opposition pressure. This happened twice in 1968 when an LDP-supported election law revision bill and several education proposals were abandoned owing to heavy SDPJ opposition.

Yet another form of withdrawal was less specifically tied to the substance of some of the bills under negotiation. Rather, it demonstrated interparty accommodation. The LDP and the opposition agreed on a quid pro quo whereby one or more bills were removed from the docket in exchange for passage of a different bill or a package of several bills. An example is the acceptance by the opposition in 1979 of the LDP budget bill in exchange for withdrawal of nine objectionable bills pertaining to other matters.

Quid pro quo exchanges did not always result in the permanent withdrawal of bills. Sometimes they led to alterations in bills or other actions. In the 1980s two budget bills and a tax reform package were handled by these strategies. Typical quid pro quo exchanges are listed in Table 6.4.

Noncontroversial Bills and Legislative Coalitions

The occasional confrontations in the Diet attracted a great deal of press attention. However, many bills were accepted or even supported by the opposition, as well as the LDP. Some bills were endorsed by interparty coalitions; others were not controversial. In the 1950s and 1960s, even though Dietmembers were polarized on many issues, self-interest sometimes produced alliances between parties that were otherwise enemies. In some cases, opposition strategists wanted their party to gain credibility by supporting popular bills or bills that addressed broadly felt issues, even if support came at the cost of a temporary alliance with the LDP. This happened with coal-mining legislation (1961), the Basic Agricultural Law (1961), amendments to the Basic Law for Medium and Small Business (1963), and some other legislation that affected broad economic sectors. In the late 1970s unemployment assistance similarly received multiparty support.

Even coalition agreements between the Liberal Democratic and Socialist Parties were not unheard of, despite their disagreement over many issues. The SDPJ supported government bills to increase railway fares in some years

Table 6.4. Quid Pro Quo Accommodations in Diet Legislative Processes, 1960–1990

Year	LDP Advantage	Opposition Advantage
1962	Election law passed	Objectionable bills withdrawn by LDP
1962	Budget passed	Three objectionable bills withdrawn
1965	Japan-Korea treaty ratified	Treaty-related bills withdrawn
1966	Holidays bill passed	Foundation Day removed from bill
1967	Two defense bills passed	Mine safety bill supported by LDP
1968	Civil service bill passed	Public employees' salaries bill amended
1968	University administration bill passed	Diet committee chair changed
1969	Japan National Railways fare increase passed	Telephone rates frozen
1972	"Normalization" of Diet	Defense budget cut
1973	Health insurance bill passed	Amount of premium increase lowered
1977	Three major bills passed	Two bills to be held over for future debate
1984	Budget bill passed	Income tax reduction for wage-earning housewives
1984	Nippon Telephone and Telegraph reform bill passed	Pension bill passed
1985	Budget bill passed	LDP to "study" tax cuts
1987	Tax bill amended	Favorable tax reform action by LDP

Sources: Asahi Shimbunsha, *Asahi Nenkan* (Tokyo, various years); and *Asahi*, September 26, 1984.

because that would raise railway workers' salaries, but they opposed similar proposals at other times in defense of consumer interests. The two major parties also agreed on one annual budget (1977) because the SDPJ supported a section that would increase coal mine safety measures.

LDP-SDPJ coalitions were exceptional and occurred only where there was unusual overlap in interests. Right-center coalitions on major bills based on some combination of the Liberal Democratic, Democratic Socialist, and Clean Government Parties were more common than other ideological coalitions because the parties had similar positions on foreign and national security policies. Although ideological differences precluded SDPJ and LDP cooperation on many issues, policy differences were smaller where the more centrist Democratic Socialist Party and Clean Government Party were concerned. For example, the Democratic Socialists joined with the LDP in 1965 over a rapprochement between Japan and the Republic of Korea (in the face of strong opposition from the SDPJ) and supported the LDP on a later (1977–78) treaty covering oil rights on the Korean shelf. Right-center coalitions were even more common in the 1970s and included agreements on domestic legislation: a bill defining the responsibilities of school principals (1974), reform of an election and political-funding law (1975), an annual budget (1977), and an amendment to the bill naming the imperial era (Gengo; 1979). More recently, there have been right-center coalitions to support defense legislation (1980), health insurance and pensions (1980–85), administrative reform (1983–84), contributions to the Persian Gulf war (1991), and use of Self-Defense forces in U.N. peacekeeping operations (1991–92).

In the 1950s, 1960s, and 1970s parties agreed on somewhere between one-quarter and one-third of major issues that came before the Diet. Joint support of legislation by the LDP and the more moderate or centrist of the opposition groupings (Democratic Socialist and Clean Government Parties) or "grand" coalitions involving the LDP and the SDPJ, sometimes along with other parties, were an important part of Diet processes. Some of the agreements were forged in interparty negotiations after initially strong disagreement—additional testimony of the contribution of the Diet to a functioning government.

Some major Diet legislation was noncontroversial from the start. Legislative proposals in this category usually addressed an obvious and clearly legitimate problem. One example was national disaster legislation in 1961: fifteen emergency bills passed the Diet with broad support. However, the SDPJ insisted that the word "emergency" be removed from some laws because it evoked the spirit of prewar legislation directed toward control of dissidence. (The LDP was rightly seen by the Socialists and others as the heir to the prewar conservative leadership, which had suppressed leftist movements.) Among other examples were several laws dealing with coal mine safety (1967), petroleum industry law reforms (during the oil crises of the 1970s), drug legislation (1979), organ transplants legislation (1979), and revision of laws regulating businesses affecting public morals (1984). In each case, legislative objectives were so universally supported that interparty agreement was easy. A large majority of routine (that is, not major) government bills also passed through the Diet without eliciting conflict.[15]

Japan is not an exception in this regard; unanimity is common in both the British and German parliamentary systems. There is also agreement on many bills in the U.S. Congress.[16] For us, knowing that quite a bit of Japanese legislation was consensual counters an image of the Diet as a locus of perennial irreconcilable conflict. Interparty agreements on bills imply, further, a degree of activism that goes beyond the stereotype of the Diet as a do-nothing body.

The Diet's Multiple Roles in Japanese Politics

Besides working collectively to make laws, Dietmembers work as individuals who represent local constituency interests in meetings with ministry officials. They press the officials to include the proposals in budget bills or other legislation. Typically, local politicians and a Dietmember form a petitioning group to visit ministry officials, as the following account from a personal interview in Kanagawa prefecture describes.

> We never had a primary school serving this district, even though the matter had been discussed for years. The X hamlet and our own hamlet leaders were never able to get together and agree on where to place the school, even when there were opportunities for support in Tokyo. Finally we prevailed, in part because the Honorable Mr. A [the Dietmember] came from here. We hamlet leaders and a delegation from X hamlet met with the mayor and accompanied him to Tokyo to Mr. A's office in the Dietmembers' building. After formalities, he accompanied us to the Education Ministry and the Construction Ministry to talk to the officials involved. It helped that this area had one of its local sons as Construction Minister, although Mr. A's ties with the prime minister's faction helped, too. This is the way we got a new school here in this hamlet.

Dietmembers perform an important representational role by articulating local interests in meetings with bureaucrats. Dietmembers also have an input into prospective legislation before bills go to the Diet, either because they initiate visits with bureaucrats or because bureaucrats coordinate policy proposals with PARC committees and, via them, with LDP zoku. Opposition party and LDP Dietmembers both engage in this activity. Individual Dietmembers were also involved in cross-institutional policy communities, which included government bureaucrats and organization officials concerned with particular sector or group interests. These communities provided another opportunity for Dietmembers to make inputs into pre-legislative bill-drafting processes.[17] Both LDP and opposition party Dietmembers were active in policy networks, although the former were probably more influential while the LDP was in power.

The Diet performs functions as a corporate legislative body above and beyond its function in processing legislation. Ministers and ministry officials are regularly asked to defend their policy positions and decisions in the Diet. The most active and public forum for Dietmembers' interpellations is the lower house Budget Committee, meetings of which are regularly reported in the national media. Interpellations make government processes more visible to the public, even though they are often very ritualized.[18]

In many senses, the Diet is a focal point for other political processes. Elections, intraparty recruitment of top leaders, and intraparty policymaking — all important processes in their own right — are also related in some key way to events in the Diet. The political centrality of the Diet contrasts sharply with the common notion of the Diet as an insignificant organ of government.

Parties use Diet procedures to favor their own interests. The unanimity rule in the two Diet steering committees means that legislative agendas are open to contestation by all parties. Because the time allotted to plenary sessions of the Diet is fairly limited, setting the times when bills will be debated in committees and plenary sessions is important for both supporters and opponents of specific bills. Delaying a bill could result in its abandonment or postponement. Delaying a bill might also keep the Diet from having time to debate another bill later on the agenda.

Party strategies regarding the timing of deliberations have been part and parcel of an extensive political game reflecting the importance of the Diet agenda. Parties dedicate themselves to passing or resisting passage of controversial bills. Efforts to arrange schedules for specific bills to advantage one or another party or faction have been one route to this end. A spokesman for Prime Minister Nakasone once said, "We will extend the [Diet] session this time long enough to make the opposition parties sick!" The goal of the LDP was passage of a health insurance premium increase that the opposition parties opposed. The purpose of the LDP strategy was to wear the opposition down in an extended Diet session where several other important bills would also be debated. Some LDP leaders favored a long Diet session the next year (1984) for the same reason, others a short session in order to kill an unpopular election reform bill. The opposition parties followed the same strategy as the second LDP group, although they aimed to kill a pension bill instead of the election reform bill.[19]

Legislative timing strategies are an example of how informal activities overlapped with formal channels in parliamentary management. Party timing strategies are often discussed in joint meetings of party leaders or subleaders, including meetings of the secretaries general of the five main parties. Most of these meetings take place outside the Diet's formal institutional apparatus.[20] Political parties supplement institutional processes with their own informal actions to a significant degree. All the parties take Diet processes very seriously.

Not just the timing but the substance of Diet legislation is often negotiated in meetings that take place outside formal Diet processes. According to one source, the House of Representatives spends only 67 hours in plenary session per year, in contrast with 1,468 hours for the British House of Commons, 844 hours for the U.S. House of Representatives, and 430 hours for the German Bundestag.[21] In Japan formal committee meetings are often brief as well.[22] The brevity of formal debate highlights the importance of consultations outside formal sessions. In some cases, special interparty consultative groups are set up to discuss a bill or legislative package. Informal contacts between Diet-members and leaders from different parties are also common.

During the LDP's hegemony both the ruling and the opposition camp formulated multilayered strategies to address the implications of events in the Diet for other arenas of politics, and vice versa. Party elites and others undertook Diet tasks for the purpose of achieving both specific legislative goals and secondary goals in some other context. Prime ministers, for example, tried to enhance their credibility as LDP leaders by getting important bills passed in the Diet — much the way an American president earns high approval ratings for legislative successes in Congress — which might pave the way for them to continue in office, a different political arena from the Diet.[23]

Legislative credibility was important to executive survival in Japan under LDP rule. A Nakasone faction leader one summer used the hint that there might be a dissolution of the Diet as a tactic to ensure the faction leader's survival as prime minister. At the time, it was clear that the opposition parties did not want an election and would probably urge continuation of the Diet session. But the opposition would be forced to accept an extended session and to debate (and perhaps accept passage of) several major legislative bills that they opposed and wanted postponed. Nakasone would appear to be an effective parliamentary leader if the bills were passed, which would enhance his chances for staying on as party president, even though other factions wanted him to quit.[24] Bolstering Nakasone's reputation was the motivation for the plan.

The Nakasone incident shows how LDP factional politics sometimes spilled over into Diet strategies. On another occasion, the anti-mainstream factions in the LDP were aligned with the opposition parties on the timing of a Diet session in order to thwart the mainstream factions' party presidential election strategy. The purpose of the mainstream factions' strategy was, as in the example above, to have bills passed that would make the incumbent prime minister appear more credible.[25] Many other examples of multilayered strategies can be cited, including, on occasion, LDP extension of Diet sessions to assure passage of bills that would enhance LDP electoral credibility and, more cavalierly, to have time to reshuffle the cabinet, and to synchronize the Diet session with a party presidential election.[26]

LDP influence on legislative policy was sometimes qualified by differences between the cabinet and the party. Although the prime ministers and cabinet ministers who ran the government between 1955 and 1993 were Liberal Democrats in almost every instance, cabinet ministers and party leaders still represented different organizational constituencies. Party leaders were concerned with policies emerging from internal party organs and supported by interest group constituencies. Cabinet members tended to represent the concerns of the ministries that they headed.[27] Disagreements among elites from the same political party arose from these different primary concerns. Sometimes the party capitulated; on other occasions, the prime minister and cabinet did.

Divisions within the LDP frequently had to be addressed before the party could mobilize the necessary support to push legislation through the Diet. Until recently, LDP Dietmembers almost always voted as a bloc. When the LDP was in power, deviations from party discipline in the Diet were rare, unlike in the U.S. Congress, where individualized voting is practiced. Reaching a consensus or modus vivendi was therefore a necessary step toward maintaining party discipline once a bill reached the Diet. Intraparty divisions were so great on such issues as tax and electoral reform that years went by before the party was sufficiently united for legislation to be sent to the Diet. Several times major bills were postponed or withdrawn as the result of party disunity. Complex coalitions and alignments involving elements of the party and other political actors within and outside the Diet sometimes emerged in these cases.[28]

The influence of the opposition parties on Diet processes during the LDP reign depended to some extent on whether the four main parties — Democratic Socialist, Clean Government, Social Democratic (formerly Japan Socialist), and Japan Communist — could agree on particular bills. In the 1980s opposition party unity on tax reform, health insurance, and political corruption strengthened their position in Diet debates. Unified stands resulted in LDP accommodation to their demands in two out of the three instances. In contrast, unresolved differences between the middle-of-the-road parties and the Social Democratic Party on defense legislation and on privatization of the Japan National Railways contributed to opposition camp weakness. The government's railway bill package eventually passed the Diet with middle-of-the road party support, and the best a divided opposition achieved along the way was postponement of the bills. A tacit LDP-SDPJ agreement on adoption of proportional representation in House of Councillors elections deprived the opposition of the benefit of a unified front on still another important 1980s issue.[29]

Complex checks and balances were evident at times when the LDP or the opposition parties, or both, were divided over issues and when groups of Dietmembers were allied with an element of the bureaucracy. In 1986, for example, the Finance Ministry took the same position as some of the opposition parties in deliberations over abandonment of tax shelters for small investors (the Green Card issue). A league of LDP Dietmembers and the Tax System Research Council of the LDP opposed this alliance. In the same Diet session, an alliance of the LDP Special Committee on Public Works and the government Economic Planning Agency endorsed higher public works outlays opposed by the Finance Ministry. Later that year, the LDP's PARC, the party's leadership, and the government opposed tax reduction (because of revenue shortfalls caused by a slow economy), whereas some rank-and-file LDP Dietmembers and the entire opposition camp supported tax reduction. Finally, in 1984, the Tanaka faction of the LDP decided to support a controversial health insurance reform bill while other factions of the LDP and an LDP Dietmembers' league (Association for People's Medical Care for the Twenty-first Century) opposed the bill along with the opposition parties, the Japan Medical Association and the Japan Dentists' Association. These cases show that because the Diet is part of a larger political process and because political actors have different interests, unexpected and complex alignments develop.[30]

The participation of the parties in a complicated interactive political game centered on the Diet is further indicated by the presence of extensive cross-party contacts. Informal behind-the-scenes meetings between the LDP and the opposition parties were important to intercamp accommodations throughout the period of LDP rule. Opposition party leaders and even rank-and-file parliamentarians discussed issues with their counterparts in the majority party, even when the formal stands of the parties were not openly conciliatory. Meetings of Diet policy committee chairs from the various parties are another example of how channels outside the Diet were used to address deliberations in the Diet.[31] So-called pipelines also existed between LDP politicians and opposition party officials. The following report illustrates both kinds of activities:

> There are many *ryotei* [Japanese-style restaurants] in Tokyo's Akasaka area, which lies at the foot of the hill where the Diet building stands. . . . Talks were held in these settings on March 25 by LDP, SDPJ, CGP, and DSP Diet policy committee chairmen under the pretext of a birthday party for LDP Diet policy chairman Kajiyama. A similar meeting was held last year. At this year's meeting the overseas dispatch of the Self-Defense Forces to support U.N. peace-keeping operations was discussed. At last year's meeting Kajiyama asked the others' cooperation on the provisional budget bill. . . . On March 30, LDP Vice President Shin Kanemaru met with SDPJ upper house Budget Committee member Kubo and others from the SDPJ for three hours at Kicho, a restaurant in the Ginza district. The topics of discussion included proposals for opposition Dietmember trips to North Korea.[32]

Close personal ties between people like the LDP faction leader Kanemaru and SDPJ Secretary General Makoto Tanabe, or LDP Secretary General Roku-suke Tanaka and Secretary General Saburo Tsukamoto of the Democratic Socialist Party were often reported. Informal meetings of party heads took place during the Suzuki, Nakasone, Takeshita, and Kaifu administrations, as well as behind-the-scenes contacts between individual LDP and opposition members in the Diet chamber lobbies. In recent years private meetings between representatives of the Liberal Democratic, Democratic Socialist, and Clean Government Parties decided the fate of bills pertaining to the consumption tax, Japanese participation in the Gulf war, and U.N. peacekeeping operations.[33]

Informal cross-party discussions of legislation have taken place over the years, and policy coalitions have likewise included opposition party Dietmembers. In the 1960s an alliance of the National Mayors' Association, MITI, and the SDPJ succeeded in having legislation passed for the rehabilitation of municipalities in coal-mining districts.[34] (At the time, mining communities were suffering from the long-term decline of the coal industry.)

The Diet in Time and Space

Major changes took place in the distribution of power within the Diet in the 1970s and 1980s. The LDP had a comfortable majority in the Diet from 1955 to 1976, even though its proportion of total seats dropped from 64 to 55 percent during that time. From 1976 to 1980 it had a very thin majority. The ruling and opposition camps had relatively equal strength. With the reduction of the majority to a very narrow margin in 1976–80, there were changes in the style of legislative policymaking. Reallocation of parliamentary committee chair assignments was one result. The procedural norms of the Diet also changed to favor easier resolution of legislative conflicts. Central in the new arrangements was what Ellis Krauss calls the practice of "concurrent majorities, or simply a tendency to seek broad inter-party agreement on controversial bills through consultation." The growing neutrality of the lower house speaker and the increasingly central role of meetings of directors of Diet steering committees in negotiating interparty compromises likewise favored smoother processing of bills.

The changes in the 1970s were reflected in the disposition of major bills (see Table 6.2). The number of major bills that were amended or withdrawn nearly doubled from the 1970s on, relative to the 1960s. (Table 6.1 showed that proportions of amended bills to *all* government bills declined over time; these data do not contradict the increasing tendency for the Diet to amend *major* bills after the 1970s [shown in Table 6.2], because the statistical base is different.) What appears to have happened is a move toward greater accommodation on the major bills before presenting them in the Diet and less frequent amendment of minor bills, which could reflect greater LDP and ministry anticipation of opposition concerns or the presence of more consensual issues than in earlier periods.[35] The role of the Diet relative to the executive also changed, albeit more modestly: 92 percent of the major laws passed by the Diet in the 1960s were based on government bills; the figure was 85 percent in the 1970s; and it declined to 80 percent in the 1980s.

The proportions of successful member bills related to major legislation have also increased. Member bills, which are legislative bills introduced by political parties or groups of Dietmembers, have had a special function in the Diet. The opposition parties customarily sponsored member bills to present their own version of desired legislation. The bills were usually doomed from the start, for they were not supported by a parliamentary majority. But submission of opposition member bills often led to LDP action on a government bill, such as an amendment or even withdrawal of an unpopular bill. According to my analysis, at least 30 percent of all major government bills in 1980–90 were matched by opposition member bills. Member bills were significant in parliamentary processes, even though passage was unlikely. The growing legislative strength of the opposition parties contributed to the increasing importance of member bills relative to government bills. Still, member bills never dominated the legislative agenda to the extent seen in the United States, where 96 percent of bills passed by the Congress are member bills.[36]

In addition to the cited shifts in the relative power of parties, several other factors contributed to improvement in interparty relations in the Diet. Changes in the legislative agenda favoring nonideological over ideological issues helped facilitate interparty and intercamp accommodation from the early 1970s on. "Valence" issues were, as a result, increasingly common in Japanese elections, whereas "position" issues declined. (Candidates or parties take identifiable stands on position issues; on valence issues they simply try to appear more credible or capable than their opponents.)

By the 1970s the positions of the LDP and other parties were also more centrist on ideological issues (even though there were still LDP hard-liners on China and security policy). The LDP trend away from ideology was uneven. Moderation on ideological issues prevailed under Tanaka (1972–74), Miki (1974–76), Fukuda (1976–78), Ohira (1978–80), and Suzuki (1980–82) and again from the Takeshita (1987–89) era forward. There was a gap in the long-term trend during Prime Minister Nakasone's stay in office (1982–87), when efforts to boost the defense role of Japan were pursued.

The center parties—the Democratic Socialist and Clean Government Parties — took a cooperative stance toward the LDP that reflected in part their hopes for participation in a coalition government. The advent of the next generation of Dietmembers also contributed to a more accommodationist Diet by the 1970s. Conservatives with attachments to prewar political institutions and opposition party members who held memories of prewar suppression of leftist parties and unions were gradually replaced by younger members. Assumption of LDP leadership by accommodation-oriented politicians like Masayoshi Ohira (1978–80), Zenko Suzuki (1980–82), and Noboru Takeshita (1987–89) also promoted interparty cooperation during their terms in office.

With the end of the "nearly equal" period in 1980, power relations in the Diet seesawed. The LDP dominated the Diet in 1980–83 and again in 1986–89, although it needed the help of the New Liberal Club in 1983–86 to control key Diet committee chair assignments. Finally, in an unprecedented development, the LDP became a minority party in the House of Councillors after the 1989 "earthquake" election, which the opposition parties collectively dominated. Full coalition government came to Japan after the July 1993 election, although the LDP continues to have the largest number of representatives in the Diet.

Under coalition rule the Diet has been both different and similar, compared with the Diet under LDP hegemony. The ratio of amended and postponed bills was much higher in the 1993 autumn Diet session than in a normal session under LDP rule. The number of amendments and postponements resulted from intense struggles over political reform in the months following the inauguration of the new coalition government. Cleavages on security policy between the SDPJ and other coalition parties were an additional factor in Diet disagreements.

A tendency for formerly disciplined and united party voting blocs to fragment emerged on important votes, beginning with the nonconfidence vote that unseated the LDP cabinet in June 1993. Eighteen SDPJ Dietmembers abandoned their party's commitment to the ruling coalition to vote with the LDP to stall coalition-backed political reform bills in January 1994. When the Socialist Tomiichi Murayama was selected as prime minister in July of that year, sixty Dietmembers voted against their party or abstained. In the past, party discipline was much more effective than in the fluid political situation of 1993–94.

The LDP was the main opposition party between August 1993 and June 1994. Although unaccustomed to being the opposition in the Diet, it rose to the occasion and employed procedural tactics formerly the preserve of the SDPJ and its allies during the era of LDP rule. The LDP used procedural rules in the upper house Special Committee on Political Reform to keep reform bills in committee in early 1994.[37] Later, the LDP boycotted debates on the 1994 budget to force disclosure of possibly improper uses of money by then Prime Minister Morihiro Hosokawa.

The government coalition was likewise influenced by procedural consider-ations. Although some coalition leaders wanted to railroad political reform bills through the Diet, others cautioned that "that kind of bill [election system reform] was never railroaded even when the LDP had a majority," and "we cannot allow four railroadings [of these bills at every level of the Diet sys-tem]."[38] Accommodation between the ruling coalition and the opposition followed informal channels like those described above for the period of LDP hegemony.

There seem to be two basic types of democratic legislatures. The first type makes laws; it has been termed legislative. The second type, which includes most parliaments, mainly deliberates on legislation proposed by an executive and only influences laws; it has been termed deliberative.[39] The criteria for deciding whether a legislature fits the former or latter type are the degree to which (1) the dominant source of legislative proposals is internal or external to the legislature, (2) external bills are altered within the legislature, (3) the ruling party's rank-and-file loyally defer to party leadership, (4) parliamentary or congressional committees are independent, and (5) parliament has control (audit, supervision, or control) over the administrative bureaucracy.

Evidence suggests that the Japanese Diet is fairly close to the deliberative or law-influencing type of legislature. It mainly processes bills initiated by the cabinet and bureaucracy, much like the legislatures of Britain, France, and most other countries with parliaments. But there is also evidence that the Diet is more activist than some parliaments: 97 percent of government bills submit-ted to the British parliament are enacted into law. The success rate for govern-ment bills in France was 82 percent; in West Germany, 87 percent. The same figure for Japan was a much lower 84 percent in the 1950s and an even lower 74 percent in the 1980s.[40]

Diet-centered political processes also tend to be slightly more activist than with a purely deliberative legislature with regard to participation by rank-and-file Dietmembers and the proportions of government bills amended, aban-doned, or postponed. Most bill amendments in the British House of Commons are made by cabinet ministers, who are the top officers of the party in power. In Japan the process is more decentralized.[41] The opposition parties in the Diet propose amendments in the form of member bills, and the parties collectively negotiate on amendments using the differences between the original and mem-ber bills as a starting point. The considerable amount of intraparty policy deliberation described earlier also indicates that a moderately activist evaluation of the Diet is indicated even for the period of LDP rule. Though closest to the deliberative end of a continuum of legislatures, the Diet legislates more than a parliament of the purely deliberative type does.

My interpretation of the significance of the Diet rests heavily on a view that intraparty and interparty processes outside the formal Diet processes are as important as (or more important than) the processing of legislation in formal Diet channels. There have simply been too many behind-the-scenes consultations and deliberations within party groups like the PARC to think otherwise. Although we do not yet have systematic information on how often Diet committee sessions involve substantive debate, one careful study has indicated that committee members do not participate much in deliberations. Instead, committee directors debate issues, but we still do not know much about how often.[42]

Much of the analysis of the LDP-dominated Diet has explicitly or implicitly compared it with the U.S. Congress, hence the impression that the Diet was a very weak legislature. Yet the American tradition of an independent, activist legislature is an anomaly. Few, if any, parliaments play as central a role in policymaking as constitutional arrangements and tradition make possible for Congress.[43] But parliaments, including the Diet, are not quite the inert bodies that proponents of a dominant bureaucracy theory of policymaking would argue for. Japan joins postwar Germany and Italy as an example of a moderately activist parliament.

Legislative Policymaking in Japan

Policymaking in the LDP-dominated Diet was more meaningfully competitive than proponents of a vertical model would accept. Two political blocs and several different political parties with different ideologies and views have faced each other in the Diet and tried to gain advantage over the others through its processes. Party members tried to pass or thwart legislation and to counter the influence of their opponents. To accomplish their goals politicians developed strategies to enhance the influence of their party relative to that of other groups; they also developed strategies to achieve political goals outside the Diet that interacted with their legislative strategies.

What is striking is the extent to which Diet processes were competitive even in the face of long-term dominance by the Liberal Democratic Party. The LDP frequently sought to maintain its legitimacy and credibility by avoiding too high-handed a posture with its opponents in the Diet. Although on occasion resorting to one-sided forced votes to expedite Diet processes, it still often chose to preserve orderly Diet processes by making concessions to the opposition. Both the procedural necessity of interparty consensus on legislative agendas and cultural norms favored accommodation.

The opposition parties met LDP assertiveness with strategies and tactics that utilized Diet rules to delay debate and votes on disliked bills. Sometimes the opposition parties boycotted Diet sessions, refusing to participate in debates on current bills. Trade-offs between the political camps involving withdrawals of bills disliked by the opposition in exchange for opposition participation in the Diet or passage of a bill important to the LDP were fairly common. Amended bills were more numerous than might be expected in a dominant party system. The Diet, together with political processes centering on but not inside the Diet, functioned as a forum for discussion and for negotiated amendment of government proposals. It also functioned as a brake on government initiatives when bills were withdrawn in a process whereby the opposition parties exercised a de facto veto. On the other hand, the Diet is deficient in one respect: not having controls over the administrative bureaucracy such as exist in some parliamentary frameworks.

The LDP was in no sense especially benign in its dealings with the Diet. Rather, LDP concern for the legitimacy to be gained by adhering to institutional norms dictated that it seek a modus vivendi with the opposition. Consensual procedures reflecting the Japanese cultural heritage also led it to take an accommodationist path. Because of accommodation the horizontal model of power relations could be observed in the Diet far more than might have been expected. Vertical domination by the government supported by a unified LDP was rare on issues that mattered to large political constituencies. Highly politicized issues were handled in horizontal-type processes, and the power of the cabinet, ministries, and the Liberal Democratic Party was qualified as a result. The configurations of power looked more like those in a multiparty system with alternating coalitions than like those in a political system with single-party domination.

Understanding that there were accommodationist trends in Japanese parliamentary life in the era of LDP dominance should not blind us to the one-sidedness of policies. Although political processes were more responsible than has heretofore been acknowledged, conservative governments and ministries still set agendas, and other actors mainly reacted to them. Decisions on social policy have reflected the partial exclusion of the left and the labor unions, especially in the early postwar years. Policies were very different from those in European nations where Socialist-led governments or Socialist participation in ruling coalitions led to the earlier development of comprehensive social supports. In dominant-party Japan, policy agendas reflected conservative positions, just as long-standing dominance by Socialist parties over many years influenced legislative agendas in postwar Norway and Sweden.[44] In each case an important political force was at least partially excluded from participating at critical stages in agenda setting and policymaking, even though legislative pluralism often prevailed.

7

Interests, Policy, and Power

Although interest groups are found in all political systems, their relations with the government vary. Two partially overlapping schemes are used by political scientists to describe these variations. One is the corporatism-pluralism continuum. Under corporatism, some groups have close, privileged relations with government bureaucracies or ruling parties. Under pluralism, there are many power centers, which compete for policy influence. A second continuum is used to describe whether interest groups seek political access mainly through bureaucracies or through legislatures. The extent to which interest groups are represented via legislative action or bureaucratic intervention, or some mixture of both, is the key distinction.

The relevance of corporatism and pluralism for Japan has been hotly debated in political science research. Chalmers Johnson and, early on, T. J. Pempel have endorsed the corporatist interpretation, asserting that cooperative links existed between some interest groups, central ministries, and the Liberal Democratic Party to the exclusion of other sectors.[1] Another group sees Japanese interest intermediation as more pluralistic than corporatist. Michio Muramatsu, Ellis Krauss, and Richard Samuels are most prominent in this important and growing school of analysis. Case studies by Haruhiro Fukui, John Campbell, Michael Donnelly, Naoki Kobayashi, and others have also shown many arenas of Japanese interest group politics to be pluralistic.[2]

Still others, like Aurelia George, emphasize that Japanese politics is a mixed system, with elements of both corporatism and pluralism.[3]

Corporatism has to be defined precisely to differentiate it from some forms of pluralism. Having very close, mutually accommodating relations between interest groups and government is one definition of corporatism; this is one sense in which the term is used in Japan. Interest groups are, in effect, incorporated into public political processes. Interest group participation in ministry advisory councils implies corporatist-style relations, according to these views. So does informal coordination within private networks linking the LDP, bureaucrats, and interest groups. Many interest group officials sit as members of the Diet affiliated with both political parties, and their presence fits some corporatist models. As many as four out of five SDPJ members of the Diet had labor union backgrounds in some sessions; group representation within the upper house contingent of the LDP was almost as high.[4]

Structural relations like these are necessary but not sufficient indicators of corporatist relations as far as the purposes of this book are concerned. Instead of taking the existence of close ties alone as evidence of corporatism, I examine whether seemingly close relations are openly conflictual. Where close ties between interest groups and government are conflictual, I conclude that the relations are not corporatist but pluralist.

I prefer to discuss corporatism mainly in terms of behavior, fitting the authoritarian version of the term; there, corporatism seems to be quiet cooperation in exchange for government favors. This is the most frequent sense in which the term has been used in Japan. Also, democratic corporatism involving "treaties" between business and labor on major economic policies has not existed in Japan to the degree that it has in Europe. I have avoided the problem of drawing a precise line between what is sometimes called bargained corporatism, on the one hand, and bargained pluralism, on the other, simply because it was too hard to fit empirical evidence to such a distinction. Instead, I have pointed to cases where there were *relationships* that seemed to fit a corporatist model, but disagreement and conflict that suggested *pluralism*. I have optimistically called them examples of pluralism.

Corporatism has also been used in a macrosocietal sense in Japan to characterize the seeming lack of direct political influence by labor. In the 1950s new mass-level interest organizations were formed, and existing economic organizations began to assume political roles. When the LDP was consolidating its interest coalition at this time, it entered into a series of social contracts with various population sectors, including farmers and small-business owners.[5] No less of a contract was written with big business. Later, the concerns of social welfare groups were added to the programmatic commitments of LDP.[6] In contrast, the labor movement seemed to be excluded from close ties with the ruling party by its alliance with opposition parties.

This view of the situation of labor is valid up to a point. The parties supported by labor unions were, until 1993, always in the minority. They had less of a chance to influence public agendas than groups allied with the LDP. Nevertheless, there are important examples of union influence on policy that weaken the exclusionist argument as applied to labor. Unions protested and lobbied government, sometimes successfully, on coal, shipping, education, welfare, employment, tax, and privatization policy. Labor was also at times represented in the Diet by the opposition parties participating in quid pro quo exchanges with the LDP. Behind-the-scenes contacts between LDP politicians and people in the labor movement existed as well; recent instances are documented at various points in this book. The exclusionism of the LDP interest coalition seems to have been more apparent than real, and some scholars even argue that private-sector labor entered into a social contract with the LDP.[7]

Overall, interest intermediation in Japan is a mixture of close relations and social contracts plausibly characteristic of some version of corporatism, plus a great deal of adversarial participation and influence on the part of interest groups. What mix of pluralism and corporatism best characterizes Japan, and the implications of this mix for Japanese democracy, are central to the concerns of this book. At issue is the extent to which some interest groups have privileged access to, and highly cooperative relations with, government decisionmaking bodies at the expense of other interests. Is the system of interest group relations, especially during LDP hegemony, so internally cohesive that some vital interests are totally excluded from influence—an indication of an authoritarian corporatism? Or has there been sufficient pluralism in politics that even less than perfect representation of some groups has been somehow balanced by access for issues of true concern? What kind of corporatist and pluralist influences are found, and has this changed under coalition government?

My second concern lies with the focus of Japanese interest intermediation. Major interest groups in advanced democracies are allied with political parties, and they usually seek representation of their interests through legislative action. Less visible, often equally important contacts bypass party and parliamentary politics to focus on government ministries. The dominant mode of communication between interest groups and the government in some European countries, most prominently Britain and France, is by way of relations between interest groups and government bureaucracies. Some scholars have gone so far as to say that these relations form a political system parallel to parliaments. They describe policymaking that involves interest groups and ministries as "segmented and complex" and as concerned with small, technical issues more than the broader designs discussed in legislatures. According to one study: "The process of governing in this perspective is a process of government relations with groups. . . . The major established interests are often pursuing marginal adjustments to policy in non-public, routinized relations with civil servants who share a commitment to that policy area. . . . The agenda of the group-government world is not that of the parliament and the media."[8]

Many Japanese interest groups have close ties with ministries like those described for Europe. Most groups are also affiliated with one or another political party. The quality and patterns of these relations tell whether Japanese politics fits a vertical or horizontal model. Whether policymaking that involves interest groups is corporatist or pluralistic and how much interest intermediation has focused on parliamentary or bureaucratic processes is important to defining Japanese political style. Here I examine interest group roles in the 1980s in two major policymaking areas: farm policy and tax reform. Mainly but not exclusively LDP clients are involved in both, as were opposing alignments of different interest groups and of different interest groups and government ministries. The ensuing public debates were pluralistic. The alignments were representative of large-scale interest group conflicts. In the next chapter I will deal separately with issues that involve business groups, the LDP, and the government — areas of activity most often said to closely fit a corporatist model of interest group intermediation.[9]

Farm Policy

Although there have been major postwar changes in the size and make-up of the rural population, farmers remain politically important. Immediately after World War II, nearly half of all Japanese lived and worked on farms. Since then, the proportion of the population in agriculture has declined substantially, as sons and daughters of farm families emigrated to the cities to work in offices and factories. Today around 11 percent of that population still live on farms, and a much smaller percentage are engaged in farming on a full-time basis.[10] But among the industrialized democracies Japan still ranks with France as having one of the largest farm sectors.[11] Although there are far fewer farmers and far fewer full-time farmers than before, farmers still form a vocal group in Japanese politics.[12]

Agriculture remains economically important. Japan grows all of its rice and produces virtually all of its dairy products as well. In addition, it grows oranges and other citrus fruits in large quantities. As a percentage of gross domestic product, agriculture is more important than in most other major industrialized countries, including the United States and Britain.[13]

Life in rural districts has changed in many ways since the end of World War II. Industry began moving into rural areas as early as the 1960s in order to tap the surplus labor force in farm households. As a result, by the 1980s around 85–90 percent of farmers depended on outside work for most of their income. Employment in nearby industries and favorable government farm policies have created a rural population more affluent than its urban counterpart. Although right after the war, some in the conservative government were worried about farmers' lower incomes compared with those of urban dwellers, the situation is now reversed. Farm household incomes currently average 30 percent higher than the incomes of worker households in urban areas, whereas in 1960 they were 10 percent lower. In addition, farm household savings are now more than twice those of worker families. Although land values have not been as high in rural areas as in the cities, rural land inflation has been considerable until recently. Because of inflated land values and higher savings, farm household assets exceed those of urban families. By the mid-1980s farmer affluence had reduced the credibility of requests for maintaining farm price subsidies.[14]

Other aspects of rural life have also changed since the war and, in some instances, continue to change. Even though the opportunities for work have increased in rural areas, many sons and daughters still leave for life in the cities. Young people no longer want to live and work on the farm, a trend symbolized by the practice of importing women from other Asian countries to marry young farmers. (Usually their husbands are eldest sons, who by custom inherit the family farm and feel a concomitant obligation to farm.) Because of the exodus of young people to the cities, the rural workforce has aged dramatically. Compared with earlier periods, farmers today are fewer in number, better off, older, and likely to be part-time blue-collar workers — all of which shapes their political needs and views.

Farmers have been very important in politics since the war. They have always been a major group in the electoral coalition of the LDP. Farm districts were overrepresented in the electoral system in existence between 1946 and 1994; although overrepresentation is often exaggerated, in some cases rural votes counted as much as three times as votes from urban districts. Most farmers were also represented by one of the largest interest organizations in the world, Zenchu, the political arm of the National Federation of Agricultural Cooperatives (now called JA [Japanese Agriculture] Zenchu). The largeness of the cooperative movement and the adversarial nature of its politics, as well as farmers' electoral overrepresentation and consequent importance to the conservative party, made farm policy an important concern of governments. As in other industrialized democracies, farm policy has continued to be important even after a decline in the size of the actual farm workforce.

Three major issues have concerned postwar agricultural interests: (1) price subsidies for agricultural products, (2) protection from imports, and, recently, (3) Ministry of Agriculture, Forestry, and Fisheries (MAFF) plans to change the acreage allotted to different major farm crops and expand the size of farms. Although each issue involves different aspects of farmer concerns, they are interrelated; and all three have aroused strong feelings on the part of farmers.

Rice and many other grain crops were heavily subsidized for a long time. Until recently, part of the rice production was collected through a food-control program established during World War II to ration limited food resources. The distribution system set up under the food-control program remained the means by which rice was resold by the government, although the proportion of the rice trade directly controlled by the government sharply declined in the 1980s. Both producer and consumer prices for government-purchased rice were set under these arrangements. The producer price for government rice was set annually on the basis of recommendations by the Rice Price Consultative Council, a consultative council of the MAFF. The battle between those upholding farm interests and other political actors over the rice price subsidy used to be a major annual political event. Rice price subsidies were increased in most years as the result of farm pressures and LDP support. After the mid-1980s, however, there were bumper rice crops nearly every year, at the same time that demand for rice declined because of changing consumer tastes. According to the MAFF, annual per capita rice consumption peaked in 1962 at 260 pounds per person. By 1986 the figure had dropped to 161 pounds. The shifting demand-supply relation plus farmer affluence combined to undermine the credibility of the group position. The government responded by freezing and later lowering rice price supports. Nevertheless, in deference to farm interests, the LDP-SDPJ coalition government continued and even expanded agricultural subsidies in 1994.[15]

Protection of farm markets from foreign imports was the second major concern of farmers. As a result, formal government quotas on farm imports were continued long after those on most industrial imports were dropped. Starting in the 1970s, even though Japan had fewer farm import quotas than France, it became a target of U.S. pressure to open its markets for farm goods. In the so-called lemon war of the early 1970s the United States requested Japan to open its domestic lemon market. Later, other products were the target of U.S. concerns. In 1984, after fifteen months of sometimes bitter negotiations, Japan agreed to increase imports of oranges and beef. A program for further liberalization of those imports was agreed upon in 1988.[16] In the 1980s the United States also pressed Japan to open its rice market to foreign imports. In each of the protected areas, farmer resistance to liberalizing imports was very strong, so negotiations between Japan and the United States have sometimes taken years to reach a conclusion. In some cases, a conclusion has yet to be reached, although Japan has now committed itself to liberalizing rice imports.

A third area of concern to farmers has been MAFF plans to decrease rice acreage by converting paddies to other crops. Targets have been set each year. The plan was formulated in part because of the declining demand for rice. A second long-term MAFF plan encouraged expansion of the amount of land managed by individual farmers. Through loans and other incentives, farmers have been encouraged to farm an area of at least ten hectares (24.7 acres). Land reforms right after the war called for small holdings averaging less than three hectares (7.3 acres) in size and discouraged consolidation of holdings by imposing limits on free transfers of land. At present most farmers work several dispersed landholdings. Various other plans for increasing farm productivity have been established, too, including a program that encourages consolidation of farmland ownership. Special programs were also set in place to subsidize crop reduction efforts in the areas affected when trade liberalization measures were finally agreed upon for beef and oranges.[17]

Zenchu recently responded to the MAFF initiatives and other trends by altering its policy priorities to favor programs to increase productivity. Though not completely abandoning the fight for price subsidies, Zenchu has had to face political reality.[18] The farm lobby felt that it was wise to go along with the rice prices existing in 1987 and 1988 in order to maintain the credibility needed to gain support for continued protection of agricultural markets.

Zenchu, a major actor in all of the political debates over farm policy issues, has developed a sizable inventory of tactics to advance farmer interests through political participation. It has participated in MAFF consultative councils, held press conferences and released reports to the media, developed linkages with consumer groups, conducted postcard and signature campaigns, developed public education programs, and held public demonstrations (farmers' demonstrations and sit-ins during rice price negotiations in the 1960s are legendary).[19] Zenchu's efforts have been supported by other closely affiliated farm groups, including the Federation of Fruit Growers' Cooperatives, the Federation of Horticultural Farming Cooperative Associations, the Japan Fruit Juice Association, and the National Dairy Farmers' Cooperative. Each of these groups has fought for government price subsidies and assistance programs and against liberalization of imports, justifying their appeals by citing

(1) the need for a secure national food supply, (2) the importance of agriculture to local economies, (3) the importance of rice culture to the fabric of religious and social life, and (4) the contribution of rice paddies to water conservancy. Protection has even been posited as one of the "rights" of an independent nation. In 1988 the head of Zenchu stated: "After Japan's 2,000 years of dependence on rice culture . . . if we don't defend rice, we will no longer be an independent state."[20]

The position of the farm movement on agricultural issues has been supported by other important interest groups and by elements of the government and ruling party. Zenchu was supported by the National Federation of Livelihood Cooperatives in its fight against liberalization in the 1980s. Other farm groups, such as the All-Japan Federation of Farmers' Associations and the National Federation of Farmers, have also been loosely allied with Zenchu on the liberalization issue. The Japan Federation of Housewives and at least sixteen other consumer groups endorsed the Zenchu positions on liberalization and farmers' income parity with urban workers on various occasions in the 1980s.[21]

In addition to other allies, farmers generally had broad support within the parliamentary caucuses of the LDP. Tsutomu Hata, who later left the LDP to form the Renewal Party, is well known for his comment in support of import restrictions on beef: "Since the Japanese have longer intestines than Americans, we are not suited for eating beef."[22] Pro-farmer LDP members of parliament were organized into such groups as the Dietmembers' League for Fruit Industry Promotion, the Dietmembers' League for Livestock Industry Promotion, the Japan League for Agricultural Innovation, and the Rural Village Promotion Council. In 1982 the Rural Village Promotion Council collected 242 signatures of Dietmembers opposed to farm product liberalization "so as not to let this evil threaten the independence of Japan and the future of its people." The Japan League for Agricultural Innovation was sometimes described as an "Apache" group because of its hard-line positions. Many members of leagues showed up at farm movement rallies opposing liberalization of beef, oranges, and other farm products. Still, the leagues themselves did not play a large policy role because they were not as well organized as the agricultural policy organs of the LDP Policy Affairs Research Council.[23]

Within the PARC, two policy organs dealt with farm issues, the Agriculture, Forestry, and Fisheries Division and the Comprehensive Agricultural Policy Investigative Council. These groups had more members than any of the other PARC divisions or councils, a sign of the political importance of farmer constituents. The Comprehensive Agricultural Policy Investigative Council has been described as an intra-LDP farm interest group, as was the smaller

Agricultural, Forestry, and Fisheries Products Import Liberalization Problems Subcommittee.[24]

Besides successful advocacy of farm subsidies, the internal farm lobby of the LDP was on several occasions able to secure passage of Diet resolutions opposing the liberalization of rice imports. Nevertheless, even though many LDP Dietmembers continued to support farmers, contrary views began to appear in the 1980s. Party members began to challenge heretofore unqualified support for farmers. In 1990 some Dietmembers from both the LDP and the opposition joined to support a resolution to accept the policies of the General Agreement on Tariffs and Trade (GATT) urging liberalization of Japan's agricultural imports, a clear reversal of the previous stand.[25]

The Ministry of Agriculture, Forestry, and Fisheries has been one of the farmers' strongest allies. During the 1980s it was often as protectionist as Zenchu. Indeed, the prosperity of the farm sector is one of the major concerns of MAFF, partly for the sake of its own survival; with a shrinking farm sector there would be less for the ministry to supervise. Other reasons for MAFF support for farmers arise from the multiple channels of contact between Zenchu and MAFF personnel because of Zenchu management of the food-control program and from the rural backgrounds and the training at agricultural schools and regional universities common to many MAFF personnel, who consequently sympathize with farmers' positions. The MAFF and Zenchu still sometimes differ on such issues as paddy conversion and rice price subsidies.[26]

Until the mid-1980s the ministry supported annual increases in rice prices. But the MAFF was sometimes more adaptable to new situations than Zenchu. Concern over the decline in the Japanese demand for rice, for example, led MAFF to advocate decreasing rice paddy acreage as early as the 1970s. Its shift in favor of increasing productivity to cope with freer imports is another example of ministry pragmatism.[27] MAFF nevertheless continued to serve its farmer clients with such traditional policy tools as subsidies and loans when trade liberalization threatened formerly protected markets. This was its response when fruit growers complained about the expansion of import quotas for oranges in 1984 and 1988. Like farm ministries in most countries, the Ministry of Agriculture, Forestry, and Fisheries has often been protective of its farmer constituents.

Japanese farmers had a number of other important supporters in their political efforts, including several consumer groups. They also had some very strong opponents. As early as the late 1950s, big business opposed farm subsidies. The Federation of Economic Organizations (FEO) has urged agricultural import liberalization many times in recent years. It and other big business groups stepped up criticism of farm policies in the 1970s and 1980s. Business organizations have especially lamented the effects of farm import protection on the international reputation of Japan and on U.S.-Japan relations. Big business has also been dissatisfied with the high cost of agricultural products used in food-processing industries. Others have criticized the government-established Livestock Industry Promotion Corporation program that imports meat and sells it at prices higher than purchase cost to support domestic cattle growers. As awareness of high food prices in Japan became more general, business increasingly championed urban consumers' interests.[28]

In a reflection of these concerns, the major big business groups — FEO, Federation of Employers' Associations, and Keizai Doyukai — have wanted to rationalize agriculture to make farms more productive and less dependent on government help.[29] Big business groups were joined in this position in the early 1980s by the government's important Second Provisional Administrative Affairs Reform Council (SPAARC) and by the Agricultural Policy Consultative Council, one of several consultative councils set up by Nakasone to help resist pressures from interest groups and from within his own party. The council called for higher farm productivity, to be brought about by concentrating farming among those of working age (the current practice is for older family members to farm the small, dispersed plots while younger ones work in nearby factories), increasing the scale of farm units, rotating crops, and basing rice price settlements on actual production costs plus storage expenses. One businessman known for his strong opinions, Toshio Doko — former head of the FEO and chief of the SPAARC — chided a prime minister for failing to hold the line against higher rice price subsidies: "It's no good! I have offered my advice to the government on agricultural policy for a period of ten years. Nevertheless, the government has continued to deceive me!"[30]

Another consultative council for Prime Minister Nakasone, the Research Council on Economic Structure Adjustment for International Cooperation, headed by the former governor of the Bank of Japan, Haruo Maekawa, also urged termination of farm supports. The Ministry of International Trade and Industry also advocated rationalization of the farm sector. MITI advised farmers to remember that their prosperity depended on the economic health of the country, which in turn depended on the success of industrial exports in markets threatened by trade issues involving agriculture. This was also MITI's answer to complaints by farm groups that Japan's success with exports of manufactured goods had made them an unfair target of U.S. demands for liberalization.[31]

The Ministry of Finance was also an active participant in many farm policy debates. Because price subsidies for rice and other farm products cost money, it usually tried to conserve government financial resources by advocating their reduction.[32] Ministry bureaucrats were reluctant to spend money on new farm programs, and the ministry protested the costs of processing and storing rice under the food-control program, proposing its curtailment in 1988.[33] In a strange twist of events, it twice opposed lowering the consumers' rice price when that would have entailed less revenue from the sale of already existing government rice stockpiles. The Ministry of Finance has always been involved in policymaking wherever agricultural policies have cost the government money.

These broad characterizations of farm policy debates mask the complexity of specific policy measures. Patterns in government farm policy decisions have nevertheless been clear-cut. Throughout the 1970s and 1980s the United States pressed Japan to liberalize farm markets. The demands were usually successful in opening markets, but only after years of debate and negotiation. Government decisions were slow to evolve because of the enormous resistance by farm interest groups and their supporters in the LDP. But Japan eventually gave in to virtually all the U.S. requests. Decisions to liberalize farm imports have typically led to assistance for farmers affected by liberalization, including loans for entering a different line of farming and subsidies to enhance productivity. Subsidies for conversion of farmland to other purposes were expanded in 1988 to forestall the effects of the anticipated liberalization on local economies. The MAFF also decided to provide subsidies to promote sales by farm cooperatives of products threatened by liberalization. Along the same lines, the MAFF promised in 1988 to promote sales of Japanese farm products to restaurants and domestic food processors and even began to try to stimulate Japanese farm goods exports.[34]

Most aspects of farm policy making in the 1980s were highly pluralistic. The MAFF, Zenchu, and elements of the LDP and the SDPJ usually supported farmers' interests, while the Ministry of Finance, MITI, and major business groups opposed farmers' groups and the LDP on both protection and rice price subsidies. Within the LDP coalition and between ministries there were differences on farm issues. Farm groups felt it necessary to lobby both the MAFF and the LDP; MAFF policies were close to Zenchu positions on some issues but not others. Some consumer groups were aligned differently on farm protection and subsidies. Both pro-farm and anti-farm coalitions existed. A horizontal model best fits farm policy issues in the 1980s.

The Tax Reform of 1988–1989

Tax and fiscal policy are among the most important areas of government policymaking. The high status accorded the Ministry of Finance and its officials and the importance given to passage of the annual budget in the Diet attest to this fact. In debates, tax and fiscal policy have always taken precedence over lesser matters. The quid pro quo strategy by which controversial legislation was withdrawn in exchange for opposition acceptance of high-priority LDP bills was occasionally used to pass budget bills.

In the early years after the war, the government practiced budgetary restraint, making tax revenues lower than in other industrial nations. The "cheap government" approach was continued because outlays on defense and welfare were low. High growth also increased revenues, so individual income tax rates could be lowered on several occasions without causing a shortage of public funds. Total tax revenues actually declined as a portion of the gross domestic product after 1950 and did not rise to the earlier level until 1980.[35]

Conservative spending policies and expanding revenues made it possible to maintain balanced budgets in most years.[36] But in the 1970s increasing outlays on public works and expenditures on new and maturing social programs placed heavy demands on the government. Raising taxes was politically difficult, although it was discussed.[37] Japan entered a decade of sizable budget deficits; sales of government bonds paid for the increasing outlays. The deficits were a matter of grave concern to Finance Ministry bureaucrats and some LDP leaders. In the late 1970s the rising interest outlays led to government consideration of proposals for new taxes. The option considered most frequently was some sort of tax on production and sales. The so-called indirect taxes were preferred because they would be easier to collect in full than income taxes were. Indirect taxes were also thought to be less vulnerable to opposition party requests for tax cuts, which were usually for cuts in income taxes. Endorsed by fiscal conservatives in the LDP and by leading business groups and pushed by the Finance Ministry, tax reform was an off-and-on priority as Japan entered the 1980s.

Another factor favoring tax reform in the 1980s was the widespread conviction that the existing system of taxation was unfair to salaried employees. As in other countries, salaried workers had to pay much higher taxes on their income than did small-business owners or farmers, who could conceal income more readily by underreporting or by citing fictitious costs. The income tax arrangements at that time were called the 9–6–4 system: salaried workers paid taxes on 90 percent of their income; small-business owners, on only 60 percent; and farmers, on 40 percent. (A National Tax Administration Agency survey in 1987 found that 77 percent of farm households had omitted some income from their tax declarations. The average household reported only 60 percent, and the most dishonest only 10 percent.) The commodity tax system needed reform, too, it was felt. High commodity taxes were levied on some products seen as luxuries in earlier periods but as necessities by the 1970s. Automobiles were in this category. The automobile industry favored elimination of the commodity tax because a tax rate of 30 percent discouraged car purchases. Big business in general complained that corporation taxes were higher in Japan than in other industrialized countries.[38]

Faced with revenue problems and criticism of the existing tax system, political leaders recognized that some kind of tax reform was desirable, even though it would be hard to achieve. There was a long debate on what to do and a series of tentative efforts at resolution followed by retreat. Discussion of a value-added tax in 1979 was aborted when the Liberal Democrats lost seats in the general election that year. Later, in 1983, Prime Minister Nakasone stated that there would be no new indirect tax, even though his government was considering just such a move.[39] Pressures for change from a variety of interested parties (including the Ministry of Finance) gathered momentum, and in 1987 a Nakasone-led cabinet submitted a sales tax bill to the Diet.

Local and national interest groups protested the tax proposal virtually from the start. Eleven national retail sales organizations set up a People's Council on the Tax System to place signs opposing the tax reform on twelve thousand shopping streets. Other interest groups followed. The twenty-thousand-member Retail Cosmetics Dealers' Association threatened to withdraw funding and electoral support for the LDP. Another opponent of the bill, the Japan Department Stores Association, actually canceled its annual contribution of political funds to the LDP. Even local governments opposed the tax bill; by mid-March 1987 thirty-three of the forty-seven mostly conservative-dominated prefectural assemblies had urged the government to go slow or to abandon the tax proposal.[40]

Within the LDP rank-and-file dissent over the tax proposal was widespread. Two Dietmembers were censured by the party secretary general for attending an antitax rally. One of them was a member of an LDP league promoting shopping district interests. A small-business-run survey identified 108 LDP Dietmembers who opposed the tax. On February 25, 1987, a meeting of a newly formed antitax group was attended by sixty Dietmembers, including some senior Liberal Democrats. Two days later, after several groups opposing the tax had been formed, newspapers reported that the LDP party leadership had banned LDP Dietmembers' attendance at antitax meetings. By March, however, opposition within the LDP was so great that party leaders discussed revision or retraction of the tax reform proposal.[41]

Massive opposition eventually led the LDP to withdraw the controversial tax proposal. Initially the bills were postponed as part of a quid pro quo strategy to pass the budget. The LDP decided on April 5 to postpone the sales tax bills as part of a strategy to have the budget pass the House of Representatives prior to a trip by Prime Minister Nakasone to the United States.[42] The decision to withdraw them completely came after the LDP lost a parliamentary by-election and after party support declined in prefectural elections across the country, where the opposition used the tax issue to gain support (the LDP lost ground in thirty-two of forty-four prefectures); the latter was seen as a sign of the extent of popular opposition to the reform. During the same period the opposition parties added political heat by proposing an income tax reduction and measures to remove unequal provisions in the existing tax system. All this demonstrates the extent of pluralism and conflict in Japanese politics when important interest groups or population sectors are threatened.

Noboru Takeshita replaced Yasuhiro Nakasone as prime minister late in 1987. Debate on tax reform was resumed under the leadership of the Takeshita cabinet. Discussions in the Finance Ministry, the government's Tax System Research Council, and the LDP Tax System Research Council indicated continued support for an indirect tax. In addition to the concern over revenue, these groups reiterated that the existing income tax procedures were unfair. In spite of opposition from both large and small business interests, a comprehensive tax reform package was finally submitted to the Diet in late 1988. The bills passed both houses in December, lowering individual income taxes for some people, lowering corporate taxes, and eliminating a commodity tax on some goods. In exchange, the reform package set in place a consumption tax on transactions and sales at different stages of production and distribution.[43] The changes to the tax laws went into effect by April 1989.

The reactions of many political actors to tax reform were complicated and multidimensional (alignments are outlined in Table 7.1). The tax reform package was strongly endorsed by the Finance Ministry, the government's Tax System Research Council, and some elements within the Liberal Democratic Party. Debate about the strategy, timing, and appropriate rates for the different reform components was nevertheless intense even within this core coalition because of strong opposition from the commerce and industry zoku of the LDP and from medium and small retailers and some other sectors.[44] The final package of bills represented compromises between the revenue concerns of the Finance Ministry and various political concerns represented within the ruling party. The ministry initially argued for a 5 percent consumption tax with few exempted categories; the LDP favored lower rates and wanted more exemptions.[45] Eventually both the party's important Tax System Research Council and finance zoku, as well as many party members, came to support the tax package. In contrast to the 1987 push for tax reform, this time strenuous efforts were made to signal to rank-and-file LDP opponents of the tax that the

Table 7.1. Tax Reform Coalitions, 1988

Support	Mixed/Accept Reluctantly	Oppose
Finance Ministry	Japan Automobile Manufacturers Association	Japan Social Democratic Party
Government Tax System Research Council	Japan Electronic Industries Association	Democratic Socialist Party
Liberal Democratic Party	Greater Japan Fisheries Association	Clean Government Party
LDP Tax System Research Council	Japan Securities Industry Association	Japan Communist Party
Federation of Economic Organizations	Japan Chamber of Commerce and Industry	All-Japan Private-Sector Labor Unions
Japan Iron and Steel Federation	General Federation of Private Railway Workers	Federative Council (Zenmin Roren)
Electric Power Industry Federation	Confederation of Electric Power Workers' Unions	Japan Telecommunications Workers
Japan Real Estate Association	Japan Automobile Workers Federation	Japan Chain Stores Association
National Association of Banks	All-Japan Metal Industry Workers Union Federation	Japan Department Stores Association
Federation of Employers' Associations	National Central Union of Medium and Small Enterprises Associations	National Federation of Shopping Districts Promotion Associations
Keizai Doyukai	All-Japan Truck Service Association	National Federation of Environmental Hygiene Enterprise Associations
Japan Commodities Traders Association	Natonal Federation of Fisheries Cooperatives	All-Japan Federation of Shopping Street Associations
Japan Medical Association	National Federation of Automobile Associations	
Beer Brewers League	International Tourist Hotels Association	

Sources: Nihon Keizai, June 1 and 15, 1988; Nihon Keizai (E), June 15 and October 18, 1988.

party leadership supported the proposals. Top party officers and cabinet members were more unified because factional competition had temporarily abated with the appointment in late 1987 of Takeshita to replace Nakasone as prime minister. Leaders of all of the main LDP factions declared a de facto truce and announced their support for the proposals.[46]

Some major business interest groups supported the tax reform proposals. The Federation of Economic Organizations and Keizai Doyukai, which had long advocated reducing national dependence on deficit financing, were generally behind the reform package. However, the Keizai Doyukai proposed that corporate income taxes should be reduced further than was called for in the reform plan. Several key members of the FEO also supported a decrease in corporate tax rates and other features of the reform package.

Several industry associations favored the reforms. The Japan Iron and Steel Federation indicated satisfaction with the promised corporate tax reduction, as well as a provision in the bills for continued deductions for maintenance of "bonus reserve funds" by businesses. The Electric Power Industry Federation was satisfied that the tax on electricity would be reduced from 5 to 3 percent by substituting the consumption tax for the former electricity tax. Real estate interests were said to support the proposed increase in mortgage interest deductions, and the National Association of Banks endorsed the planned exemption of financial instruments from the new consumption tax. Insurance and commodity traders' interests received similarly favorable treatment. Breweries were reportedly satisfied with a reduction of the liquor tax imposed on each bottle of beer.[47]

A second cluster of business interest groups indicated satisfaction with some provisions of the reform but opposed others. Automobile and electronics manufacturers welcomed the elimination of the commodity tax. But the former opposed a consumption tax on trucks, which had hitherto not been taxed; and the latter were said to be concerned about how to incorporate the consumption tax into their pricing. The Japan Chamber of Commerce and Industry went along with tax reform, though reluctantly, on the belief that the consumption tax would have a broad but light impact.[48] Several unions reserved unqualified endorsement because they represented constituencies with conflicting or opposing views.

Small retailers continued to reject the consumption tax. The opposition of such small-store groups as the All-Japan Federation of Shopping Street Associations and the National Federation of Shopping District Promotion Associations was especially strong. Large-scale retailers, like those in the Japan Department Stores Association, also opposed the reform. Both large and small retailers felt that the tax might depress sales, and small retailers were worried about the labor costs involved in collecting and reporting the tax. Retailers and medium- and small-business owners exploded with frustration after the tax bill passed. Their opposition was a major contribution to the partial collapse of the electoral coalition of the LDP in 1989.

The traditional opposition parties generally opposed the consumption tax. They felt that Japan should have a more progressive tax system, including taxation of capital gains and stock sales, and asserted further that government operations should be more efficient, requiring less revenue. They also wanted to tax groups slated for partial or full exemption from paying taxes, such as doctors, religious organizations, and public corporations, and supported a tax on politicians' fund-raising efforts.[49]

The tax reform process is a clear example of pluralistic politics. There were many views within the Liberal Democratic coalition of supportive interest groups, as well as in non-LDP groups. Alignments were varied and sometimes complex; and many groups intensely opposed tax reform. And because pluralistic interests and intense feelings aroused all around had to be reconciled, the tax reform process is also a good example of the extent to which Japanese politics is characterized by highly formalized, sometimes ritualized efforts to bridge conflict through consultation. At each stage of the tax reform debate, politicians set up formal consultative committees or engaged in informal discussions to include as many relevant groups as possible in decisionmaking talks. At all levels there were step-by-step discussions designed either to enlist the support of relevant political actors or to resolve or defuse their opposition.

Coordination of tax proposals within the respective tax councils of the government and the LDP was the first visible sign of consultative procedures in the tax reform process. (The government's Tax System Research Council, a consultative council attached to the Office of the Prime Minister, set up to coordinate between the Finance Ministry and the Ministry of Home Affairs on matters involving national and local tax systems, was the location of heated debate. The head of the council, Takekazu Ogura, argued publicly that there were multiple defects in the Finance Ministry proposal.) There was a great deal of disagreement over tax reform in the council, even though ministerial consultative councils have often been seen in the past as hostage to bureaucratic influence. Consultations within the Ministry of Finance and between the ministry and the LDP undoubtedly took place as well, but these were less open to public scrutiny than later stages of the process. The Ministry of Finance and the Ministry of Home Affairs also negotiated with each other on parts of the reform package.[50]

The need to build and maintain a coalition supporting the tax reforms dictated that multiple groups be brought into the process via informal consultations, bridging committees, and the like, so after the government's tax council debated the tax reform package, the LDP tax council held hearings within a wide circle of organizations affected by the proposed reforms. The list of groups invited to testify included over forty professional, industrial, and distribution organizations.[51] Tax reform was also discussed in a meeting of secretaries general of LDP factions in an effort to mobilize widespread party support for the bills. Further consultations were conducted between the LDP secretary general, deputy secretary general, Diet policy committee chair, and lower house Steering Committee chair. The Government-LDP Consultative Council also discussed the proposals at several junctures.

The ruling LDP and the opposition parties consulted extensively across party lines in the months preceding passage of the tax reform package. Still, because some consultations bypassed the opposition parties, one opposition Dietmember said that they were like "starting a train without all of the passengers aboard."[52] A consultative council on tax reform, which included representatives of all of the main parties in the Diet, was set up in 1986. A later group called the Tax System Special Consultative Council was established during the discussion of tax reform proposals in the Diet in the summer of 1988. Given the political importance of the proposals, each party in the Diet named senior politicians to the council. The opposition SDPJ named a thirteen-year veteran of the lower house Finance Committee experienced in local administration as its senior representative to the council. The Clean Government Party named a party leader who had good ties with the LDP and with Prime Minister Takeshita.[53] The thirty-member LDP contingent included five who had experience both as cabinet minister and as secretary general of a faction, which served the need for not just expertise but also factional balance. The five major factions were also given balanced representation in the rank-and-file council assignments, a further bridging effort. Four senior LDP members from the party's Tax System Research Council were included in the government's council, providing more expertise, as well as overlapping membership with an important intraparty policy coordination group. The best-known behind-the-scenes arranger in the LDP, a leader of the prime minister's own faction, Shin Kanemaru, was selected as chair of the consultative council.

Besides discussions within the council, there were also coordination talks between the secretaries general of all five main parties in the Diet.[54] LDP representatives also held private talks with opposition Dietmembers; the LDP chair of the lower house Steering Committee, Hiroshi Mitsuzuka, met with the chair of the Democratic Socialist Diet Policy Committee, and Finance Minister Kiichi Miyazawa met with various Democratic Socialist Dietmembers.[55] The overall consultative style of Prime Minister Takeshita led to inclusion of opposition party leaders in the pre-legislative consultative process. All these meetings presumably played an important role in moving the often-delayed tax reform forward.

Efforts to include all relevant actors in the political process helped paved the way for passage of the tax reform package in 1988. But the consultations did not result in acceptance of the measures among interest groups opposed to them — to wit, the near collapse of the interest group coalition of the LDP in 1989. Nor did consultations dissipate opposition party antagonism to the new tax system. Several interest groups — including those representing medium and small businesses — and the opposition parties made repeal or amendment of tax reform the leading issue of the 1989 House of Councillors election. As a result, several exemptions to the new consumption tax were written into a revision of administrative rules on taxes in 1991.[56] Consensual procedures are useful in resolving political conflict, and the degree to which they are used in highly visible ways in Japan is extraordinary. But use of consensual procedures does not eliminate disagreements underlying and producing conflict. Because conflict often persists even after extensive consultation and coordination, it is incorrect to see widespread efforts at coordination as corporatist intermediation between interests and government.

The Significance of Case Studies

Both farm policy and tax reform caused major conflicts between political actors in the 1980s. In each case, behavior conformed to the pluralistic model of interest group politics. Even where there were long-standing ties — between farmers, small-business owners, large business, and the LDP and between the government and the LDP — autonomous groups from these sectors openly lobbied the LDP and the ministries. Both issues also gave rise to opposing coalitions and alignments. Big business and MITI criticized protection of farm markets and subsidizing agricultural prices. Small business plus some large firms, the opposition parties, and labor unions opposed the Ministry of Finance and the LDP on tax policy. Specific industry groups expressed favorable, mixed, or unfavorable opinions when invited before the PARC. Interest groups were in some cases aligned with different coalitions on different issues. For example, Japan's three leading big-business interest groups supported the government on the tax issue but opposed it on farm policies. There was conflict rather than a corporatist agreement within consultative councils. Even labor unions, which have been said to have restricted access to government councils, participated in some consultative councils. Lobbies, conflicting views, and shifting coalitions are all features of pluralism. Divisions between ministries could also be seen. Neither interest group politics nor the bureaucracy was monolithic.

Research indicates that the practices assumed in the corporatist model do not hold for major issues in Japan. There have been contested issues like tax and farm policy ever since the war. Big business and MITI have generally favored a weak antitrust law but were opposed on several occasions by medium and small businesses, farmers, labor unions, opposition parties, and the Fair Trade Commission. Business opposition to rice price subsidies dates back as far as 1952, although business displeasure with LDP farm policy was muted then compared with the 1970s and 1980s. The debate in the early 1960s over a MITI-sponsored Interim Special Measures Law for the Promotion of Designated Industries involved MITI and the Keizai Doyukai on one side and the Ministry of Finance, Federation of Economic Organizations, banking industry, and elements of the LDP and the opposition parties on the other. Policies for depressed coal-mining regions, for repatriates (who lost property abroad when Japan was defeated), and for former landlords who claimed that they had not been fully compensated for land lost in the postwar land reform also demonstrated pluralistic patterns.[57] Intercamp fights over constitutional reform, police powers, centralization of schools and police administration (after occupation-sponsored decentralization), ratification of the International Labor Organization convention, teacher and university autonomy, national security policy, and relations with the Soviet Union and Korea typically involved some of the labor unions and, at times, business and education groups as well.[58]

Many of these pluralistic conflicts involved strong upward pressures from interest groups with numerous members at the mass level. Indeed, the presence of a mass following inevitably heightened the visibility of policy conflict and may even have led to more intense conflict. Interest groups of, say, small-business owners may have voiced their claims all the more aggressively because they perceived their own weakness. But even groups like the farmers, who have a long history of favorable contacts with the LDP and bureaucracy, engaged in adversarial behavior. For some groups, taking an adversarial position was probably motivated occasionally by the desire of leaders to demonstrate their dedication vis-à-vis potential internal critics.

Policymaking participation and power were more decentralized than predicted by corporatism in both cases that I have cited. Nor were there lasting policy agreements between centralized interest groups or interest groups and government, as envisioned by some corporatist approaches. For the most part, relations among interest groups and interactions between interest groups and the government conformed more to pluralistic than to corporatist models. The hypothesis advanced by corporatist theory that large countries with complex economies are not a natural breeding ground for corporatism was supported in the Japanese case.[59]

The many examples of close relations between interest groups and government ministries might have caused Japan to have a "parallel" parliament such as is discussed in European research. But the degree to which Japanese interest groups openly seek influence in Diet processes by way of the LDP makes Japan different from some European countries where a "parallel" interest group politics prevails, notably Britain and France. The presence and importance of intra-LDP policymaking procedures reflect three considerations absent in the European cases: (1) long dominance by a single party, (2) the generally decentralizing effects of the electoral institutions on the political process and the related politicization of the nexus between mass interest groups and politics, and (3) the inclusiveness of the interest coalition of the LDP, which for both political and cultural reasons has sought to represent most of Japanese society. (Following Confucian precepts, the LDP repeatedly cast itself as concerned with the welfare of all Japanese.)

Whether and how coalition government will affect patterns of interest representation is, as yet, unknown. The extensive involvement of the LDP in interest group politics through the PARC system of committees and subcommittees increased the visibility of interest group politics and contributed to the development of stable policy communities that transcended institutional boundaries.[60] Under coalition government some of the same effects may be derived by the practice of setting up interparty policy teams in major issue areas. Alternatively, coalition government may so weaken the political center that interest groups will come to depend on the bureaucracy for political access, as in Europe.

Thus far, the history of three coalition governments does not clearly indicate whether ministries or government will consistently prevail in relations with interest groups. The government's Tax System Research Council debated national tax system requirements through the fall of 1993 and on into the spring of 1994 without concluding what balance of income, consumption, and assets taxes would best accommodate the aging Japanese society. The head of the council, a businessman, complained of bureaucratic manipulation, yet politics prevailed when Prime Minister Hosokawa was forced to abandon the proposal to double the consumption tax advanced by the Finance Ministry.[61] The tax policy debate in various councils continued throughout 1994 without major decisions being made.

Farm policy decisions were also dominated by politics: U.S. pressure finally compelled the Japanese government to agree in 1993 to remove quotas on imported rice as part of its support for GATT policies on international trade, although actual imports under a proposed tariff system would not begin for several years.[62] Administrative reform was also discussed under the new government structure, but promises of deregulation had not proceeded in line with Federation of Economic Organization demands by the end of 1995. Promised cuts in administrative staff had likewise failed to materialize, and the weakness of the LDP-SDPJ coalition was frequently cited as the cause of this state of affairs.[63]

Japan has not had soft authoritarian government, as some claim. Confirmation is found in the failure to uncover widespread evidence of corporatist styles of interest intermediation in important policy decisions; the abundant ministerial pluralism shown in Chapter 5 constitutes additional proof. The ministries exercise some autonomy vis-à-vis societal interests, indicated by both the dogged pursuit of tax reform by the Ministry of Finance and the partial implementation by the Ministry of Agriculture, Forestry, and Fisheries of programs to change farmland usage. But ministerial power has also been frequently qualified by political party and interest group — that is, societal — power. Democracy in Japan has been different from democracy in countries with alternating parties, especially parties paired with bureaucracies more committed to neutrality than the Japanese one is. Japan is nevertheless a functioning democracy.

8

Business Interests and Political Life

An alliance between business and the Liberal Democratic Party has been seen as a keystone of postwar Japanese politics by many interpreters. The two largest big-business federations — the Federation of Economic Organizations and the Federation of Employers' Associations — have consistently supported the conservative camp, but with a few deviations. Other business groups, like the Keizai Doyukai and the Japan Chamber of Commerce and Industry, which includes small business members, have been more independent but have usually supported the conservatives. Specific industry associations have also supported the LDP, although some disagreements have occurred.

During the period of the 1955 system, LDP-business relations were based on shared interests and values, paralleling similar interest group–political party alignments before World War II. Big business wanted to have a stable government that was tolerant of business interests, and the LDP wanted to stay in power. Political stability under a pro-business government made it easier for business to plan ahead and make long-term investments. Big business and the LDP agreed that economic growth and macroeconomic stability were a high priority, though frequently disagreeing on how stability should be maintained. Together, they opposed socialism and communism. The discussion in most of this chapter focuses on business and politics under the 1955 system. According to a 1994 interview with a director of the Federation of Economic Organizations, big business addressed requests to both the coalition parties and the LDP under the 1993–94 coalition governments, even though the latter was part of the opposition.

Medium and small business shared some of the preferences and conservative leanings of big business. Some small-business organizations, including the Japan Small and Medium Enterprise Political League, were closer to the LDP than to other parties. But the league was always more independent than big-business groups were. Some national medium- and small-business organizations were affiliated with other parties; at the constituency level, some supported LDP candidates, but some also supported nominees from other parties. There are thousands of small business organizations, and the the medium- and small-business sectors are not politically cohesive.

The ideological and policy alignment of the LDP and business, especially big business, is the basis for the vertical model tenet that Japanese interest intermediation is corporatist. But there is also a great deal of empirical evidence of disagreements between business and the LDP, which are more characteristic of pluralism.

Business-LDP Interactions

One source of the belief that big business and the LDP were unusually intimate was the frequency and regularity with which they held meetings (Table 8.1). In the 1980s, and probably earlier as well, the party leaders and the heads and senior officials of the four leading business groups — Federation of Economic Organizations, Federation of Employers' Associations, Keizai Doyukai, and Japan Chamber of Commerce and Industry — met each month for breakfast.[1] The LDP secretary general and other senior party officials attended regularly; only the party president (the prime minister) did not. These meetings provided an opportunity for those in big business to express their views and for government leaders to hear them. The regularity of the meetings attests to the value that both sides attached to their relations.

In addition to the top-level breakfast meetings, the LDP also sponsored policy seminars where business leaders and LDP politicians could share opinions. There were also summer seminars run by the LDP jointly with the FEO at which the secretary general, chair of the executive council, chair of the PARC, and even sometimes the party president gave talks. Meetings to solicit funds from business groups were another opportunity for exchanges of views. When the fund manager for the LDP met with FEO leaders and company representatives to request support for the House of Councillors election campaign of 1989, for example, the business people warned the LDP to correct its negative public image and improve tax policy.[2]

There were not only party-level contacts with business leaders; senior LDP

Table 8.1. Meetings Between Business and Political Leaders, 1954–1990

1954	FEO Officials Meet with Liberal Party PARC to Explain Foreign Trade Policy
1955	FEO Leaders Meet with Liberal Party PARC Officers on 1956 Budget Needs
1955	FEO Invites Democratic Party PARC Leaders to Meet/Discuss New Budget Plan
1957	Three Business Organizations Hold Luncheon for Kishi Cabinet Ministers
1959	LDP PARC Economic Affairs Research Council Discusses Plans with Environmental Protection Agency and Business Leaders
1959	FEO Invites Foreign Minister to Discuss Japan-PRC Rapprochement
1960	FEO, Prime Minister Ikeda, and Cabinet Members Meet on High Economic Growth
1966	Business Groups Hold Talks with LDP Leaders on Supporting Sato
1972	Prime Minister Tanaka Meets with Business Groups to Discuss Posture on Economic Problems
1973	FEO and Electronics Industry Chairmen Meet with Prime Minister on Liberalization
1975	Business Organization Leaders Meet with Top LDP Executives
1975	Prime Minister Miki Invites Business Organization Leaders to Meet
1983	Business Group Leaders Have Breakfast with Top Four LDP Officers
1984	Leader of Federation of Employers' Associations Meets with Top LDP Officers to Propose Assembly Reform
1990	Leaders of Business Groups Meet with LDP Political Reform Committee Head
1990	FEO Leader Meets with LDP Secretary General to Discuss Political Reform

Sources: Asahi, October 12, 1955, and September 25, 1957; *Yomiuri*, June 15, 1954, April 5, 1955, October 1 and December 12, 1960, November 29, 1983; *Nihon Keizai*, January 20, 1956, August 27, 1959, March 15 and May 17, 1973, October 5, 1975, February 3 and April 12, 1984; *Sankei*, October 21, 1966, December 18, 1975 (E); *Mainichi*, June 19, 1990 (E); *Tokyo Shimbun*, April 28, 1982 (E); *Tokyo Times*, February 3, 1959; *Nihon Kogyo*, July 14, 1972.

Notes: The meetings cited here are representative of many more cited in newspapers in different periods. FEO = Federation of Economic Organizations.

politicians cultivated relationships with heads of business organizations and company presidents to raise money for their factions. When a politician became prime minister his personal connections in the business world were described in great detail by national newspapers, with the implication that these constituted important communication channels between business and the LDP. In the 1960s party leaders were usually former bureaucrats whose ties with business reflected contacts made during ministry careers. Hayato Ikeda's (1960–64) contacts with banks and stock brokerage companies reflected his Finance Ministry background, just as Eisaku Sato's (1964–72) came from a career in the Transportation Ministry.

In the 1970s and 1980s the presidency of the LDP was divided evenly (in terms of years in office) between former bureaucrats (Fukuda, Ohira, Nakasone, Miyazawa) and former local politicians (Tanaka, Miki, Suzuki, Takeshita). As in earlier years, former bureaucrats were described as having extensive ties with business supporters. Even those who were not former bureaucrats were usually said to be so affiliated. Sometimes there was indeed a longstanding relationship; at other times, the claim simply reflected the desire of those in business to have political access. In such a case, those anxious to have links to the center of political affairs formed support groups after the election of a prime minister. Two large groups were formed after Takeshita (1987–89) was elected. One, the Chikuseikai, was composed of leaders of the four major business organizations and headed by the chair of the Federation of Economic Organizations and their affiliates in Osaka and surrounding regions; the second group, the Mokkeikai, was made up of business leaders from the Keizai Doyukai (Table 8.2). Takeshita also had ties with several other smaller groups of business people, bureaucrats, and Waseda University graduates.[3]

Scholars and newspaper reporters have long asserted that the personal ties between business leaders and LDP prime ministers and faction heads exemplified an elitist or corporatist style of politics. This belief was strongest in the 1950s and 1960s. Although the substance of the connections was not known, inter-elite ties were usually seen as evidence that big business was favored over other interests.[4] For instance, a nine-part series running from June 15 through July 23, 1952, in the now defunct *Tokyo Nichinichi* cited various confidants of Prime Minister Shigeru Yoshida, calling them "political merchants"; they were leaders in the power, shipbuilding, shipping, and coal industries. The same industries received large Japan Development Bank Loans at this time. On the other hand, for LDP leaders, personal relationships with people in business functioned like a brain trust, providing them with information on the economy and particular industries. Close LDP-business ties continued to be part of political folklore until the early 1990s; after that, corruption scandals and political realignments made interest group ties with political parties more fluid and harder for outsiders to fathom.

In spite of the obvious utility to both LDP politicians and business leaders, connections were not as intimate as they seemed, or so some evidence suggests. Gerald Curtis has shown that Prime Minister Sato had only about twenty

Table 8.2. Business Leaders' Support Groups for LDP Prime Ministers, 1982–1989

Yasuhiro Nakasone (1982–87)	*Noboru Takeshita (1987–89)*
Nakaikai	*Chikuseikai*
President, Mitsui Shipping Co.	Chair, Federation of Economic Organizations
CEO, Mitsui Petroleum Development Co.	Chair, Federation of Employers' Associations
Kokikai	President, Japan Chamber of Commerce and Ind
Adviser, Fuji Bank	Secretary, Keizai Doyukai
President, Japan Chamber of Commerce	CEO, Kansai Federation of Economic Organizat
and Industry	Chair, Osaka Chamber of Commerce and Indust
Adviser, Japan Precision Industry	CEO, Komatsu Industry
CEO, Tokyo Gas Co.	CEO, Sumitomo Bank
Adviser, Nisshin Textile Co.	*Mokkeikai*
Other	CEO, Komatsu Industry
President, Mochida Pharmaceutical Co.	CEO, Nomura Securities Co.
CEO, Mitsubishi Real Estate Co.	President, Aoki Construction Co.
CEO, SONY Co.	CEO, SECOM
CEO, Federation of Economic	CEO, Ushio Electric Machinery Co.
Organizations	President, Recruit Co.
President, Tokyo Electric Co.	CEO, Japan Times Co.
CEO, Kansai Electric Co.	Vice President, Industrial Bank of Japan
CEO, Sumitomo Metals Corp.	President, Fuji Xerox Co.
CEO, New Japan Steel Co.	Vice President, Mitsui Bank
President, Asahi Chemicals Co.	President, Tokyo Electric Power Co.
CEO, Kajima Construction Co.	President, Mitsubishi Trading Co.
Deputy CEO, Fujitsu Corp.	CEO, Chichibu Cement Co.
Adviser, Mitsui Bank	Supreme Adviser, Mazda Corp.
President, Tokyu Railways Co.	President, Takenaka Engineering Co.
Adviser, Itochu Co.	President, Fukuda Gumi
	CEO, JUSCO

Sources: Nihon Keizai, November 26, 1982, October 20, 1987 (E), November 26, 1987, May 10, ▮
Mainichi, December 3, 1987; *Tokyo Shimbun,* December 9, 1987.

Note: CEO = chief executive officer, or *kaicho.*

contacts with business leaders each year, and these were limited to brief appearances at meetings of business organizations and supporter groups. Private meetings with individual businessmen were rare. In Curtis's view, contacts between interest groups and the LDP and connections between business leaders and the prime minister were more superficial than was usually assumed.[5]

Contacts between business people and government and LDP leaders apparently declined as more former local politicians became party leaders. Although relationships in the late 1980s were similar to those in earlier periods, they fit Curtis's model better. For example, businessmen's support groups for Takeshita were formed in the usual way after his appointment as prime minister, but actual meetings between him and business leaders were infrequent. Takeshita attended the inaugural meeting of the Chikuseikai and the Mokkeikai (see Table 8.2) and listened to the views of business group heads. But, according to one account, his most frequent contacts as prime minister were with prefectural leaders, the opposition parties, and labor unions. During his first two months in office he was visited by no fewer than twenty-three prefectural governors and eleven Socialist, Democratic Socialist, Clean Government Party, and labor union leaders. His only business contacts were with people from the construction industry, the main business sponsor of the Takeshita faction.[6] There is no public evidence of extended contacts between Takeshita and top business leaders from the support groups formed when he entered office.

Details of relationships between those in business with conservative party and government leaders since 1989 are harder to locate because of the extended political turmoil before and after the LDP's loss of power. The former bureaucrat Kiichi Miyazawa, who was prime minister from 1991–93, reportedly had close ties to businesses associated with the Finance Ministry, as could be expected. The first post-LDP prime minister, Morihiro Hosokawa, had few contacts with business leaders at the national level—a sharp contrast with past trends. The heads of Fuji Xerox and Kyocera (a high technology ceramics firm) were reportedly acquainted with Hosokawa, as was the head of the Seibu Railway group, Yoshiaki Tsutsumi, and the chief executive office of Chichibu Cement, Ken Moroi. Hosokawa also had ties with the head of the Osaka branch of the Federation of Economic Organizations and the nationwide Federation of Employers' Associations. But these were Hosokawa's only major business connections, and only Moroi, who headed a study group of which Hosokawa was a member, was on intimate terms with the prime minister. Hosokawa's main external ties were apparently with people from his native prefecture of Kumamoto.[7] Hosokawa's successor, Tsutomu Hata, was connected mainly with farm interests, and his successor, Tomiichi Murayama, comes from a labor union background. Neither is deeply involved with business elites.

In addition to various personal and group relations, the large business federations and their member industrial associations and firms were a major source of funding for the LDP throughout its stay in power. The figures on contributions by specific industries to the LDP indicate different patterns of giving over time. In the 1950s the most generous industries were the electric power, coal, iron and steel, and shipbuilding industries. In the 1970s automobiles and electrical equipment and electronics were heavy givers; the main donors from the 1950s also continued to make substantial contributions. However, banks were the biggest single donors in the 1970s, and by the 1990s banks and other financial institutions accounted for nearly 50 percent of all business donations.[8] The trend substantiates the general understanding about the influence of specific industries at different times since the war.

The LDP's long-standing dependence on big business for support was acutely evident at the time of the Diet elections in 1989–90. With members' backs to the wall after an unpopular tax reform and a sizzling political scandal, the LDP was able to get ninety million dollars from business groups for its conduct of the House of Councillors election campaign in 1989. As was customary, the Federation of Economic Organizations and its member associations were important conduits for big-business contributions.[9] After losing the election and prior to the lower house election in 1990, the LDP launched an additional fund-raising campaign. Because many party members felt correctly that losses in the upper house election had created a partywide emergency, extraordinarily large amounts of funds were solicited from the richest industrial associations in the FEO, in addition to the funds requested from the FEO itself. This campaign reportedly netted $186 million in 1989–90.[10] Still, big business contributed heavily to LDP coffers year in and year out. Even after the LDP lost power, it continued to receive sizable business donations. But the FEO's decision in 1993 to abstain from funding commitments to the LDP, as well as the LDP corruption scandals, did lead to some shrinkage of contributions. A major business recession in 1992–93 reinforced the trend.

Business-LDP relations have been treated folklorically as if *all* businesses were equally close to the conservative party and its leaders. Home Ministry figures on political contributions tell a slightly different story. Fewer than 8 percent of the top 620 companies listed by the stock market gave $300,000 or more to the LDP in 1990.[11] Whereas most of the very largest firms and industrial associations contributed some money, many important firms did not make large donations. Some businesses were much closer to the LDP than others, which fits the growing awareness of the complexity of government-firm relations and the inherent pluralism of the business sector described in this book.

Relations between small-business organizations and the LDP are less well documented than those pertaining to the *zaikai,* or "financial world." Constituency-level affiliations between Dietmembers and small business are of legendary importance, as the discussion below of the Large Store Law indicates. Medium- and small-business organizations have also been listed on some occasions among major donors to the LDP. But a very large number of small-business groups exist, and many of them are organized at a local level or within a specific industry. Available information on the political role of small business taps only a small part of this activity.

Certain aspects of LDP-business relations merit qualification. Personal relationships between senior LDP members and business executives and regular meetings between LDP officials and leaders of business federations served as channels of communication throughout LDP rule, but business-government relations were not always smooth or amicable. Business leaders were frequent critics of LDP politics (Table 8.3). The FEO often took stands on macroeconomic policies in opposition to conservative governments. It was more internationalist than the LDP and, among other things, urged liberalization of protectionist trade policies as early as 1958. It attacked LDP farm policy intermittently as far back as the mid-1970s; some criticisms surfaced as early as the 1950s. The long-term commitment of big business to the general values of the conservative party notwithstanding, business criticism of LDP policies and internal party affairs was common, illustrating once again how conflict can exist within even important coalitional alignments.

The perennial concern of big business with political stability led the FEO and other business organizations to deplore factional infighting all the way from the early years after the war until 1993. Other indications of LDP weakness or loss of external credibility were similarly criticized. Business backed the formation of the LDP in 1955 after repeatedly lamenting the instability that resulted from conflict between the two existing conservative parties.[12] Its criticism of the LDP was intense with every succeeding party crisis.[13] It was never shy in condemning LDP factionalism and other examples of party disorder. Like other coalitions, the LDP–big business relationship was reciprocal: business supported the conservative party in exchange for the LDP's guarantee of a stable, pro-capitalist political environment. Had there been plausible alternatives, business groups and leaders might well have turned to other parties when disagreements, election losses, and scandals soured their dealings with the LDP. But a Socialist commitment to nationalize major industries kept that party from being a viable alternative in the 1950s and 1960s; and the general inability of the opposition parties to cooperate among themselves undermined their credibility within the business community. Until very recently business had to be satisfied with criticizing the LDP, because none of the opposition parties were as supportive of business interests as the LDP.

Business leaders' statements during the turbulence of 1989 exemplify the centrifugal potential in LDP-business relations. The leaders repeatedly deplored the lack of ethics among top LDP politicians and called for political

Table 8.3. Business Criticism of Conservative Politics, 1952–1989

1952	Business Groups Petition Liberals to Stabilize Party and Government
1952	Businessmen Want Stable Anticommunist Regime
1952	Financial Circles Despair of Ever Having Stable, Unified Government
1953	Business Leaders Want Stable Conservative Government
1954	Business Circles Welcome Possibility of a Conservative Merger
1954	Business Circles Want Yoshida Cabinet to Resign over Sato Bribery Scandal
1954	Business Organization Leaders Criticize Government's Lack of Responsibility
1954	Economic Organizations Send Request to Parties to Settle Diet "Fracas"
1954	FEO Directors Decide Business Should Push Parties to Reform
1954	Business Circles Want New Conservative Party
1954	Business Circles Moving Toward Overthrow of Yoshida Government
1956	Business Circles Want Prime Minister Hatoyama to Resign
1956	Business Groups Petition LDP to Select New Prime Minister to Stabilize Politics
1957	Keizai Doyukai Requests Prime Minister Kishi to Avoid Factional Conflict
1959	Business Leaders Disgusted with Kishi Government's "Teahouse" Politics
1959	Business Leaders Disgusted with LDP Cabinet-Party Reshuffle
1960	Business World Claims Kishi Cabinet Responsible for Social Disorder
1960	Financial Circles Disgusted with LDP Factional Strife
1960	Business Circles Disgusted at Internal Strife and Delayed Cabinet Formation
1973	Banking Circles Critical of Government Attitude of "Evading Responsibility"
1973	FEO Criticizes Prime Minister Tanaka for Violating Election System Rules
1974	Business Circles Welcome Establishment of LDP "All-Faction" Cabinet
1975	Businessmen Express Dismay with and Distrust of Weak Miki Leadership
1976	Business Circles Ponder and Lament Near Split in LDP
1982	Business Leaders Prefer That the LDP Select Party President in Informal Talks
1983	Business Leaders Shocked by LDP Election Losses, Urge Political "Stability"
1984	Business Groups Seek Reform of Diet and Reduction of Local Assembly Size
1984	Business Group Heads Want Nakasone Reelected to Continue Stability
1989	Keizai Doyukai Leader Urges Drastic Political Reform and Desires Resignation of Prime Minister
1989	Business Worries over LDP Election Loss

Sources: Nihon Keizai, October 3, 1952, March 21, 1953, June 8 and September 15, 1954, January 24, February 1, September 6 and October 7, 1956, January 19, 1959 (E), February 3, 1984, April 22, 1989; *Asahi*, October 8, 1952, April 22, June 9, and December 1, 1954; *Yomiuri*, October 18, 1952, September 19, 1954, July 12, 1957, June 11 and December 12, 1960 (E), May 15, 1973, July 25, 1989; *Mainichi*, March 30, 1954, June 18, 1959, October 20, 1983; *Tokyo Shimbun*, October 13, 1954 (E), June 25, 1960, July 5, 1975, September 12, 1976, December 19, 1983 (E), October 17, 1984; *Sankei Jiji*, September 8, 1956; *Sankei*, December 8, 1960, December 23, 1972, October 23, 1982 (E); *Nihon Kogyo*, April 18, 1973.

Notes: Examples are representative of business behavior as documented by large numbers of newspaper accounts. FEO = Federation of Economic Organizations.

reform. In May, at the height of the turmoil created by the Recruit scandal, leaders of the four major business organizations issued a joint "emergency" statement calling for resolution of the LDP's leadership crisis and development of a plan for party reform. The statement was drawn up at a meeting of chairs or vice chairs of the groups and was handed personally to the LDP secretary general. A month later, they issued an even stronger statement, sensing that the crisis was more serious than party leaders were aware or willing to admit.[14]

In 1989 the strongest criticism of the LDP came from the director of the Keizai Doyukai, Takashi Ishihara, who was also chief executive of Nissan Motor Company. Ishihara urged Prime Minister Takeshita and other LDP members of parliament involved in the ongoing Recruit scandal to resign. He forecast (accurately) that LDP would lose the upper house election because of its failure to take responsibility for its ethical problems. Ishihara also belittled former Prime Minister Nakasone's token resignation from the party because of involvement in the scandal, saying it was only "the garnish on the raw fish." Some LDP leaders responded by branding Ishihara a "class A war criminal" (a reference to postwar Allied war crimes trials of major Japanese leaders in World War II).[15]

Friction between the Liberal Democrats and business groups or individual business leaders increased during the House of Councillors election campaign in mid-1989. One sore point was an apparent breakdown of business support for the LDP in certain industries. A newly unified union movement, Rengo, had decided to run candidates in several House of Councillors prefectural constituencies. Key elements in the Rengo effort were Jidosha Roren and Denki Roren, industry unions from the automobile industry and the electrical equipment and electronics industries, respectively. LDP leaders were irate when they discovered the unions were mobilizing for Rengo candidates support that had formerly gone to LDP candidates. They became angrier when Honda and some other firms refused to speak out in support of the LDP. Some Liberal Democrats later attributed the party's bad showing in the election to lack of support from these industries.

On several occasions during the 1989 crisis, prominent business executives openly discussed alternatives to LDP rule. One suggested that Japan should have a two-party system with LDP-SDPJ parity. Ishihara of the Keizai Doyukai urged a comprehensive reform: the Liberal Democrats should (1) undertake a total review of party funding practices, (2) impose a ban on business contributions to both factions and individual politicians, (3) promote disclosure of Dietmembers' assets, and (4) dissolve party factions. When clear signs of an LDP commitment to reform failed to appear, Ishihara argued for abandonment of the dominant party system. Reflecting his views, the Keizai

Doyukai held meetings with each opposition party to discuss the possibility of forming a coalition government. Other business leaders joined Ishihara in his critique. At an FEO meeting, a former head of the National Association of Banks, after noting that ten of the twenty-one nations in the Organization for Economic Cooperation and Development had Socialist governments, said that a Socialist-led government was no longer an impossibility. At the same meeting, the vice chair of the FEO stated that the "historic mission" of single conservative party dominance had ended, and advocated a two-party system.[16]

Widespread business criticism of the LDP in 1989 and other years — even soon after the party was formed — suggests that business-LDP relations were more adversarial than is commonly believed. As with other aspects of Japanese politics, seemingly well institutionalized relationships concealed considerable conflict. Big business was both close to the LDP and distant from it, depending on when and where their connection is examined. The business-LDP coalition survived because there were no alternatives, but it was hardly an example of corporatist consensus. In the following section, we will look further to see whether conflict and pluralistic competition were the dominant mode in specific policy processes where business interests were at stake or whether the interactions were mainly examples of closely coordinated cooperation, as the corporatist school has argued.

The Large Store Law: Pluralism in the Business Sector

Enacted in 1973, the Large Store Law requires that companies wishing to open stores occupying a space larger than 1,500 square meters (approximately 100 feet by 150 feet) must go through a complicated procedure of government approval.[17] The purpose of the law is to limit the establishment of new department stores, large convenience stores, and supermarkets. Under the law's initial procedures, gaining approval for a new large store required an explanation of the plans to retailers in the area where the store is to be built. A series of review meetings were held, beginning with a hearing of the local Commercial Activities Adjustment Council (Jizen Shochokyo).[18]

Because the adjustment councils were part of branches of the Japan Chamber of Commerce and Industry, a group whose local organs are usually dominated by medium and small business interests, the system operated to discourage the opening of new large stores. At any stage of the lengthy review process, small retailers in the areas affected by the proposed large-scale store could slow down or block approval. Until recently, conclusion of the review process could take as long as ten to twelve years.[19] Large stores were also required to report their closing and holiday hours to local chamber authorities in advance of their initial opening, or later if changes were made. There were many barriers to the operation of large stores.

The restrictions on large stores were the result of earlier LDP concessions to smaller merchants. Although the LDP was not the only recipient of small-business electoral support, many medium and small businesses and their trade associations leaned toward the LDP and received a multitude of loans, subsidies, and special privileges as a result.[20] A Medium- and Small-Business Agency was established under the Ministry of International Trade and Industry in 1947, and it was followed by the Medium- and Small-Business Finance Corporation in 1953.[21] Medium and small businesses were permitted to form cartels to foster exports, and small businesses received special subsidies for technological improvements, as well as assistance during economic slowdowns. Small businesses also benefited on multiple occasions from regional development policies. In fact, in most periods medium and small businesses received considerably more government support than the vaunted large industries (see Chapter 9).

In the late 1980s, in spite of the political clout of small business, the government considered a revision in the Large Store Law or modification of its implementation procedures. The stimulus was mainly foreign pressure (*gaiatsu*). In 1985 the U.S. government requested that the Japanese government modify the law as part of what came to be called the SII (Structural Impediments Initiatives) negotiations. Elimination of distribution system barriers to trade was discussed again at the G-7 government leaders' summit in Toronto in 1988. The United States made the "structural impediments" to trade a major issue again in the U.S.-Japan Trade Committee talks in September 1988.[22]

U.S. businesses and supporters of their interests in Washington asserted that the Large Store Law inhibited sales of American products in the Japanese consumer market. It was believed, correctly, that many exclusive alignments between small businesses with Japanese manufacturers meant that the small businesses would never carry American imports.[23] In contrast, most department stores and some discount stores and supermarkets carried foreign products as a matter of course. Eventually the Japanese government agreed to take measures to improve the procedures by which applications for new stores were reviewed under the Large Store Law machinery. A revision of the law was promised.

The second stimulus to change came from the Takeshita government's Provisional Administrative Reform Consultative Council. Anticipating more foreign requests for changing the administration of the Large Store Law, the council recommended in June 1988 that major changes be made in the retail distribution system. It also reflected big business views in favoring less governmental regulation of economic activities as a matter of principle. The government's General Affairs Agency drew up a thirty-two-point proposal for easing the Large Store Law procedures in response to the council's suggestions. In September 1988, MITI created a new senior position, commercial distribution councillor, to study and coordinate changes in Large Store Law and distribution system regulations. The Japan Chamber of Commerce and Industry also began its own investigations of the impact of the Large Store Law.[24]

Once the commitment to the United States was made, MITI set about changing the review procedures under the Large Store Law. But the government's decision brought forth storms of protest from small-business associations across Japan. Interest groups opposed to changes in the approval procedure claimed these would cause "confusion" and "disorderly competition," which are favorite terms among bureaucrats and other Japanese concerned with stable markets. Local chambers of commerce and industry protested against the proposed changes, as did several other small-business groups, including the Japan Specialty Stores Association, the National Federation of Shopping Districts Promotion Association, and the All-Japan Federation of Shopping Street Associations. The interest groups opposing changes in the law represented mom-and-pop retail stores, which dominate the shopping streets of Japanese cities and small towns. The frustrations of the small-business groups quickly reached the ears of Liberal Democratic politicians, with the result that local party groups in various parts of the country joined in opposing the move to change the procedures. Opposition by small-business groups and by LDP Dietmembers in the commerce and industry zoku repeatedly delayed MITI's efforts to move forward with changes. Large LDP losses in the House of Councillors election reflecting defections by small-business owners reinforced LDP anxieties.[25]

Efforts to achieve some kind of agreement on Large Store Law changes proceeded slowly as different interest groups were consulted or otherwise made their claims public. The voices of proponents of change were heard, as were those of opponents. One of MITI's first steps toward changing the procedures was to study current practices. An unforeseen problem was the discovery of regulations in many communities that were more restrictive than the Large Store Law itself. Twenty-three of Japan's 47 prefectures and 991 of its 3,223 cities, towns, and villages were found to be enforcing "expanded" regulations.[26] Local authorities had responded to the interests of medium and small business with stricter regulations than those embodied in the national legislation. MITI's decision to investigate local conditions, together with the necessity of consulting with the Home Affairs Ministry (the ministry most concerned with local government affairs), meant that changes were delayed even longer.

MITI produced a new set of regulations for applying the Large Store Law on May 24, 1990, roughly two years after the commencement of its study of the implementation procedures under the law.[27] Under the new regulations, applications would be processed within one and a half years, a drastic shortening of the time involved in the multilevel process of application and review. In addition, MITI's Large Store Consultative Council would become the principal body for reviewing applications; it would replace the usually biased adjustment councils in local chambers of commerce.[28] Finally, large stores would be able to change their hours of operation with a minimum of bureaucratic intervention and reporting requirements. Expansion of existing store space for the purpose of placing imported merchandise on sale was to be automatically approved.

Revision of the approval procedures in the Large Store Law was a blow to medium and small retail businesses, which are a very important part of Japanese life. There are twice as many small retailers relative to the population in Japan as there are in the United States.[29] Shopping streets with dozens of tiny stores can be found next to train and subway stations in large cities or in smaller city and town neighborhoods. Most housewives shop for necessities on a daily basis, with the unanticipated result that small retailers often serve as a direct communication channel with ordinary voters. Because of the long-standing relation between the LDP and some small-store interest groups, the decision to change the application procedures of the Large Store Law in the face of small-store opposition was quite remarkable.

The political costs of deciding that the Large Store Law or its implementation procedures should be amended were high. But there was some political support for change, in addition to the very considerable opposition. The chief large-business group, the Federation of Economic Organizations, already supported changes in the large-store procedures (its views were reflected in the stand of the Second Provisional Administrative Affairs Reform Council on this issue). The FEO appreciated the need to respond to foreign pressure to open the domestic market and had long taken a broad-gauged view of international trade issues and the political costs of the Japanese overseas export surplus. FEO support of changes in the law also reflected the position of two of its important large-business constituents, the Japan Department Stores Association and the Japan Chain Stores Association.[30]

In the late 1970s and 1980s Japan was in the midst of a major change in retail business practices, not unlike the earlier experience in the United States. Starting in the 1970s, a number of new, relatively large chain stores selling merchandise at often discounted prices appeared in various places in Japan. Many of the new stores were located outside towns and cities where land prices were cheaper and where the store owners could convince local small businesses that competition would not overwhelm their interests. The large-store movement gained momentum when housewives — especially those living outside areas of high population density — shifted to using automobiles for shopping trips, instead of walking to nearby shopping districts.[31] The changes in the way people shopped and related trends in the organization of the retail store industry coincided with the interests of American businesses in promoting large-store development in the Japanese market. To some extent, these changes created an opportunity for modifying Large Store Law procedures.

A third factor encouraging revisions in the Large Store Law was an alteration in popular attitudes toward consumption. Consumer groups in Japan, like those in other countries, have not had as much political power as other interest groups. Their members are dispersed within the population at large, and members' livelihood does not depend on organizational activity. Small merchants, in contrast, are geographically concentrated, which fosters an exchange of opinions about common problems, and their livelihood is seen to depend at least in part on political success. Nevertheless, despite obvious drawbacks, consumerism has been growing. Many people have become aware of the high cost of merchandise sold in small stores. Increased consumer awareness of price issues closely paralleled the development of chain stores, discount stores, and catalog sales, all of which provide goods at a lower price than traditional small stores or even department stores. As a result, in many media accounts in the 1980s, government support for private-sector interests, including small retailers as well as large producers, was blamed for high consumer prices. The LDP government accordingly became more sensitive to its own role in consumer matters, as the following statement by a former LDP secretary general indicates: "Store owners are the center of the basis of support for our party. I want to give full explanations to them. At the same time, . . . we must establish stores that will respond to changes in consumption activities in Japan and the diversities of consumers' needs."[32]

A final factor that probably influenced conservative party thinking was that owners of small businesses increasingly tended to be older people. The children of small-business owners often do not want to work in family-owned stores; compared with the payback from other opportunities, compensation is low and the hours are long. Until the 1993–94 recession the severe labor shortage in medium and small businesses, sometimes including retail outlets, reflected these and other trends. As shopping streets dominated by mom-and-pop stores become a less distinct part of the social fabric, their political importance will decrease.

MITI's move to change Large Store Law implementation procedures was a milestone in government policies toward small business. Still, events after the 1990 directive demonstrate the continuing power of small-business interests. When MITI proposed to revise the law to institutionalize the changes, small-retailer opposition was again intense and widespread. Throughout the country LDP Dietmembers faced resistance:

> Medium and small shopping centers in areas ranging from Hokkaido to Okinawa have held meetings at the store association or chamber of commerce level, one after another, to oppose the proposed revision or abolition of the Large Store Law. . . . The Tokyo Metropolitan Assembly, the Osaka City Assembly, the Kyoto City Assembly, and shopping district associations in Shiga, Mie, and elsewhere have adopted resolutions or expressed opinions such as these: "Consideration ought to be given to local merchants and industrialists. . . . We seek the continuation of the Large Store Law." . . . "The U.S. trade deficit with Japan is due to automobiles and electric products. . . . Why should medium and small retailers bear the consequences of the actions of big firms?"[33]

After LDP losses in the July 1989 upper house election, the party took petitions by small-business owners very seriously. Even though big-business support for revision of the Large Store Law continued, the revision was stalled within the LDP policy council as a result of small-business opposition. Implementation of MITI's procedural changes was also frustrated by existing local ordinances constraining construction of large stores. Small-store opposition persisted, and despite an increase in new large-store applications in 1992–94, the Large Store Law was not abandoned. Because of the recessed economy, department stores were also forced to cancel expansion plans in some cases, causing the Large Store Law issue to lose momentum by 1994.

In any event, some shopping districts dominated by small stores found it useful to have a large neighborhood store, much as department stores anchor U.S. malls by attracting large numbers of customers.[34] Despite frequent opposition to the presence of new large stores among coalitions of local leaders and small-business interests, some communities have also seen large stores as a development opportunity. Tsugaru in Aomori prefecture invited developers to build a 130,000-square-meter shopping center, even though there was opposition from chambers of commerce in fourteen surrounding towns and villages. Recently Ogawa in Kumamoto prefecture, Hamamatsu in Shizuoka, Hirosaki in Aomori, Matsumoto in Ehime, and Kyoto were all engaged in the same kind of effort in one or another way.[35]

The disagreements between big and small business on the Large Store Law issue demonstrate that conflict can occur within interest sectors in Japan as it does in other countries. Conflict over the Large Store Law was intense within the business sector, an arena otherwise united on some economic policy issues. Internal sector discipline, normally seen as a prerequisite for corporatism, was weak. Big and small businesses are concerned with different kinds of markets. They also have distinctive capital needs and different kinds of labor relations. These broad differences, as well as industry size, location, and other factors, result in different policy preferences. The business sector has been divided and pluralistic on many other postwar issues, even though it is also united on broad principles.

The issues examined in Chapter 7 and so far in this chapter — farm policy, tax reform, and large-store procedures — have been highly politicized. The positions of interest groups, parties, and ministries received a lot of publicity, many political actors were involved, and political processes were adversarial. Are these issues representative? Are there possibly pockets of corporatist policymaking within a system prone to heavily politicized, pluralistic competition on major issues? In policy areas where the issue impact has been narrow — that is, where the affected groups are few in number and channels for interest group involvement in government decisions (such as those provided by ministry consultative councils) are readily available — are relations more often corporatist? Are corporatist arrangements more likely in interest groups with few members? Are the sectors themselves sufficiently cohesive so that negotiated agreements are binding, as corporatism requires? In such cases, do different groups, or groups and government, negotiate their differences with each other in collegial ways that make sustained conflict unnecessary? In short, are the requirements for corporatist-style group-state linkages and policymaking present?

Let us turn to industrial policy for answers. An influential body of Japan scholars sees industrial policy as a preserve of corporatist styles of integration.[36] Business interests are represented on such important ministerial advisory councils as MITI's Industrial Structure Consultative Council, and informal interaction between industry leaders and ministry officials has been extensive. Industrial policies have also seemed to meld a popular interest in economic growth with the wishes of chosen industries to expand markets. Even though the corporatist model can be qualified in regard to major political issues, it remains a potentially plausible paradigm in some kinds of policy settings.[37]

To test the proposition that corporatism sometimes prevails, I examined the character of industrial policy processes in twenty-one different cases, basing my analysis on both primary and secondary sources. Variations in time, economic context, industry concentration, market relations, government policy goals, and business interests resulted in different types of interest intermediation. There were at least four clearly identifiable types; as the following accounts demonstrate, one was corporatist, the other three were some variant of pluralism.

Industry Policy Type I: Corporatist Cooperation. Relations between the iron and steel industry and the government in the 1950s and 1960s generally fit a corporatist model. The government wanted industry to produce adequate supplies of basic industrial commodities like power, coal, and steel to support economic recovery and growth, and it wanted to lower prices for basic commodities to both encourage domestic growth and help exports compete in world markets. In pursuit of these goals, MITI orchestrated capacity expansion plans allocating market shares to individual firms, oversaw price and production agreements, and promoted productivity increases through two technology-induction programs.[38] The major iron and steel firms generally cooperated with MITI and each other; interactions between MITI officials and iron and steel corporation officials were intimate, with give-and-take on both sides. When Sumitomo Metals tried to invest in more capacity than MITI had approved, the company was forced to give up its plans because of MITI threats to limit its imports of coking coal.[39] All the components of corporatism were present: sustained, cooperative interaction, support for industry interests, and occasional government coercion. At times, as in the Sumitomo Metals example, government actions were closest to the authoritarian variant of corporatism.

Industry Policy Type II: Pluralistic Resistance or Avoidance. Although a resource-poor country overall, Japan has significant coal deposits. Domestic coal, despite its low energy content, was an important source of energy in Japan until the 1960s. After 1958 the demand for Japanese coal declined as petroleum became a cheaper, often better source of energy. Stereotypes label Japanese industrial policy as perennially growth oriented, but in the case of coal, the MITI invested large sums of money (Japan Development Bank loans) in the recessed coal industry to maintain its viability.[40] MITI also issued seven Five-Year Coal Rationalization Plans designed to preserve the most productive parts of the industry while permitting decline in less productive areas.[41]

In spite of MITI's long-term efforts to save the coal industry, the high value of the yen after the G-7 Plaza accords in 1985 turned out to be a death knell for Japanese coal. In the early 1980s, Japan was already importing U.S. and Australian coal while still using the output of domestic collieries. Both the U.S. and Australian governments were pressing Japan to increase coal imports. MITI was able to resist these demands because of favorable (albeit subsidized) prices for domestic coal until 1985. But after the yen leapt in value relative to the dollar, the subsidized price advantage of Japanese coal disappeared. It became cheaper for the three major coal users of Japan — the power, iron and steel, and cement industries — to import foreign coal than to buy domestic coal.[42] The major coal producers of Japan very quickly lost money.

In developing an eighth coal plan in 1986, MITI tried to halt the decline of the coal industry by pressuring the main coal users to buy domestically. In meeting after meeting of MITI's Coal-Mining Industry Consultative Council, iron and steel industry representatives indicated their preference for foreign coal. Power and cement industry officials also resisted MITI pressure, although power companies eventually agreed to buy Japanese coal because the higher cost of domestic coal was already built into utility rates. When the Eighth Coal Industry Rationalization Plan was finally completed, the iron and steel industry had agreed to buy a limited amount of Japanese coal, but only after MITI agreed that their purchases of Japanese coal would be phased out by 1991. Other users, including the cement, paper and pulp, textile, and chemical industries, accepted the same conditions.[43]

Unlike the automobile and electronics industries, several other manufacturing industries were structurally depressed after the mid-1970s.[44] Two industrial stars of the 1960s, iron and steel, and shipbuilding, were in this group, as were petrochemicals, some kinds of textiles, and aluminum. All experienced declines after the early or mid-1970s. In some cases, the recessions were temporary; in others, they have been more or less permanent. A main cause of decline was the high cost of petroleum after the oil crisis in 1973, induced by the oil-producing nations. Expensive oil hurt the petrochemical industry directly while raising production costs in industries dependent on petroleum for generating heat or electricity. The two oil crises in the 1970s also depressed world demand for new oil tankers, reducing the demand for iron and steel in Japan. Excess capacity in iron and steel after rapid facilities expansion in the 1960s also contributed to the structural recession. Competition from new, low-cost producers in newly industrializing countries like Korea and Taiwan shrank sales in some industries, too, especially iron and steel and textiles.

Of the sick industries, aluminum smelting was one of the worst off from the 1970s on. Large amounts of electrical power are used in aluminum refining. In spite of multiple efforts to reduce costs and develop technologically advanced processes in some plants, aluminum refining simply became too expensive after the cost of oil used in power generation more than quadrupled from price rises imposed by oil-producing countries. MITI responded to the floundering aluminum industry much as it had responded to depressed industries as far back as the early years after the war: by setting targets for reduced output, curtailing plant capacity, and encouraging firms to merge in order to improve their financial condition and lower costs.[45] MITI's plans did not help, nor did its concession to requests from the Japan Aluminum Federation for cheap power rates and elimination of customs duties on imported raw materials. Production dropped below government targets as individual firms failed to conform to MITI's plans. Firms made independent decisions about market exit: one firm moved its production to Australia, another left the aluminum business, and a third declared bankruptcy.[46] Interfirm industry-level discipline was lax.

Both Type II examples, coal and aluminum, show the Japanese manufacturing sector failing the corporatism test. In one case, there were irreconcilable conflicts of interest between coal producers and coal buyers; in the other, idiosyncratic decisions by individual firms.[47] Firms did not follow state initiatives, and intra-interest sector control was weak.

Industry Policy Type III: Arbitrated Pluralism.   Disagreements between industries that purchased commodities and those that sold them were the source of still another pattern of state-business interaction. In the 1970s policy disagreements between aluminum refiners and companies that rolled aluminum and similar arguments over refined petroleum products like naphtha required MITI's role to be at least partly that of an arbiter. Coal programs, too, called for arbitrated negotiation over prices between buyers and sellers. In some cases, MITI was a direct party to the negotiations. In others, it accepted the results of arbitration by the Federation of Economic Organizations.[48] In either case, MITI was the arbiter of last resort in inherently pluralistic processes.

Industry Policy Type IV: State Pluralism.   In the coal industry there are examples of a process of state pluralism that is common to both industrial policymaking in Japan and Japanese policymaking in general. Loose coalitions of state ministries and private-sector actors, plus at times political parties or segments thereof, have been aligned against each other in policy disputes. A bipolar confrontation involving state ministries, interest groups and firms, and sometimes party politicians took place in the late 1940s during the debate over a "priority production plan" for coal, as well as later in several energy industry policy debates. In the early case, the Economic Stabilization Board and the Ministry of Commerce and Industry were allied with the Socialist Party, the public-sector trade union movement, and consuming industries against portions of the Democratic Party, the Liberal Party, and coal producers.[49] In a celebrated case in the 1960s, the proposal of an Interim Special Measures Law for the Promotion of Designated Industries, MITI and the Keizai Doyukai were opposed by the Federation of Economic Organizations, the automobile industry, the National Association of Banks, the Fair Trade Commission, and the Ministry of Finance. This state pluralism model also fits some farm policy debates, Anti-Monopoly Law revision processes, and other cases cited in this book where ministries, interest groups, and political parties took opposing sides.

The business sector is not homogeneous. True, most businesses have wanted political and economic stability and have often preferred conservative parties over Socialist or Communist alternatives. Agreement on some general principles notwithstanding, there are numerous examples of issues over which business has significant divisions and issues for which the interests of industry are contrary to those of government ministries (Table 8.4).

Cleavages have been found between firms in the same industry, as in the case of aluminum. Kawasaki and Sumitomo steel companies and other steel firms had internal differences that led them to oppose government-monitored intra-industry agreements.[50] Likewise, Toyota and Nissan responded differently to merger proposals from MITI than did Honda and some other smaller auto-makers. Different trading companies had distinct views on Sino-Japanese ties in the 1950s and 1960s; and medium and small machine-tool makers have been frequently divided among themselves in response to government initiatives throughout the postwar era.[51]

Purchasers and sellers of products have repeatedly disagreed over prices in the iron and steel, nonferrous metal, power, and petrochemical industries. Big firms generally have different interests from small firms: small firms are suppliers for large firms in many industries and constitute retail outlets for large-firm products. When big business lobbied for an easing of the Anti-Monopoly Law to permit flexible use of market agreements during recessions, small business argued for retention of the law on the grounds that big business should not have too great a concentration of market power. Big business also opposed legislation permitting small businesses to organize and bargain collectively.[52] A cleavage between big and small firms was also evident among retailers in the Large Store Law case.

Large and small businesses have responded differently to government initiatives for reasons separate from self-interest. Industries in which there are a few large firms, such as iron and steel, have found it easier to cooperate with MITI, other things being equal, than have industries with many (often small) firms. Industrywide control is much more difficult to achieve with small firms, as the ineffectiveness of some MITI policies toward the machine tool industry indicates. Nor do all Japanese industries support cartels; many medium and small businesses prefer to ignore industry agreements of this kind or even reject membership in industry organizations.[53]

Business-government differences of opinion over industrial policy have

Table 8.4. Intra-Business and Business-Government Conflict, 1954–1984

Business

Big vs. Small

1954   Big Difference in Large Firm vs. Small Firm Support for Textiles Cartel
1954   Small Textile Firms Ask for MITI Import Finance Help, Big Firms Indifferent
1954   Small Firms Oppose Government Tight Money Policy, Big Business Supports It
1955   Large Firms Want Anti-Monopoly Law Amended, Small Firms Want It Continued
1957   Large Firms Oppose Small Enterprises on Small Business Organization Bill
1982   FEO Wants Administrative Reform but Small Business Wants Public Works
1984   Interest Groups of Big and Small Business Opposed over Anti-Monopoly Law

Buyers vs. Sellers

1966   Machinery Industries Oppose Titanium-Refining Industries over China Exports
1975   Automobiles, Shipbuilding, Machinery Circles Protest Steel Price Increases
1975   Petrochemical, Cement, and Power Firms Opposed to Oil and Naphtha Price Increases

Other

1959   Major and Minor Business Firms Clash over China Trade
1959   Shipbuilding Circles Split on Whether to Export Ships to Philippines
1966   Electric Power, Iron and Steel, Textiles, Banking, Securities Favor Early Capital Liberalization, Which Automobiles, Electronics Oppose
1967   FEO Firm on Capital Liberalization, Industry Circles Hesitant
1983   Depressed Industries Welcome New Special Industries Bill but Differ on Details

Business-Government

1960   Machinery Industry Circles Opposed to MITI Plan for Machinery Adjustment Fund
1960   Financial Leaders Dissatisfied With Government for Not Coordinating Domestic Industry Structure with Projected Liberalization
1966   Industry Circles Opposed to Capital Liberalization
1966   Trade Circles Dissatisfied with Government Stand on Japan-China Trade
1967   Industrial Circles Against MITI Policy on Construction Rationalization Cartel
1967   Ordnance Industry Dissatisfied with Government View on Weapon Exports
1967   Business Circles Opposed to Full-Scale Tight Money Policies
1968   Business Circles Express Dissatisfaction with Raise in Money Rates
1972   Textile Industry Circles Opposed to MITI over Restrictions on Facilities
1972   Industry Circles Upset That Government Yielded to U.S. Pressure on GATT
1973   Industry Circles Reject Finance Ministry Surplus Balance Adjustment Measure
1973   Business Circles Disagree with MITI, Want to Keep Export Restrictions

Sources: Nihon Keizai, March 7, 1953, June 18, 1966, October 8, 1982; *Shakai Taimusu*, April 7, 1953, October 3, 1955; *Yomiuri*, April 13, December 9, 1954, February 26, 1960, March 6, 1968, July 9, 1975, February 4, 1983; *Tokyo Shimbun*, April 15 and 16 (E), 1954, July 23, 1966; *Asahi*, October 10, 1955, June 7, 1957, January 13, 1959, January 20, 1971, May 30, 1972; *Sankei*, August 15, 1967, February 15, 1973, August 7, 1983; *Nihon Kogyo*, February 5, April 12, and August 4, 1966, March 14, April 5, and April 27, 1967; *Tokyo Taimusu*, March 31, 1960; *Mainichi*, January 18 and February 6, 1959, October 2, 1973.

Note: Examples are representative of different types of conflict from a much larger listing.

been common. When times were bad or specific problems came to the fore, business often hoped for government help. When times were good, firms were more likely to prefer independence from government intervention or regulation. In the early 1950s big business asked government for help in getting the economy out of the post–Korean War depression by supporting industrial rationalization. Even then, business sought to keep control by the ministries at a minimum. When economic conditions were better, the desire of business to avoid bureaucratic control increased. The fear of greater intervention was one motivation for opposition by the FEO and automobile industry to MITI's proposal of an Interim Special Measures Law for the Promotion of Designated Industries in 1962.[54] Even where businesses such as iron and steel had close ties with MITI for several decades, opposition to government policies could be seen at times.

Not surprisingly, businesses were pleased to cooperate with the government when their interests were consistent with government goals. When encouraged to increase productivity and expand production, they were usually more willing to cooperate with government plans than when asked to curtail capacity. Firms operating in capital-short markets or needing large capital inputs when capital was in short supply worked more closely with the government than did firms in markets where capital was readily available. Threats to company integrity, like those implicit in the mergers proposed for the automobile industry in the 1970s, were unpopular, especially among the firms that would lose the most in the merger. Big business may be closer to government in Japan than in the United States, as is usually believed. But Japanese big business is not docile, nor does it welcome close government supervision as much as many Americans and Europeans who criticize the government-business relationship believe. Indeed, the concept of American business independence used to evaluate Japanese business-government relations is unexplored folklore. In the United States the so-called military-industrial complex and corporatist relations between U.S. regulatory commissions and the industries that they regulate both suggest closer business-government relations than is described for the American model in American folklore. Business-government relations in Japan are much more complex than the typical American thinks, as Richard Samuels has shown so clearly in *The Business of the Japanese State.*

Patterns in Interest Politics

Empirical evidence on a variety of policy issues and interest group activities indicates widespread pluralism in Japanese politics. Policymaking coalitions vary depending on the issue. Interest groups are autonomous and lobby the LDP and government ministries on policy matters. At times, interest sectors display prominent internal differences. Thus, the requirements of corporatism are not met in most of the policymaking processes that we have examined. But two practices could meet corporatist criteria: direct representation of interest groups on ministerial advisory councils and devolution of government functions to interest groups. Both can be seen in the interest arenas examined in this and the last chapter, as well as elsewhere in politics.

Interest groups are represented on many of the 154 consultative councils attached to ministries. Zenchu, for example, the political arm of the giant farm cooperatives movement, was represented on the Rice Price Consultative Council and eleven other Ministry of Agriculture, Forestry, and Fisheries councils in 1990.[55] MITI has twenty councils on which business federations, industry associations, and sometimes labor unions are represented. The presence of these direct channels to ministerial policymakers suggests a kind of corporatist integration, as it does for similar European practices. Still, the extent of cooperation varies with different issues. There are departures from a pure corporatist model when interests so dictate. Representation of Zenchu on the Rice Price Consultative Council and other important councils, for instance, did not keep the farm cooperatives from lobbying LDP governments on rice price and other issues.[56] Nor was the relation between the cooperatives and the government one of tightly constrained mutual deference, as corporatism would lead us to expect. Instead, contacts between the two were highly politicized, reflecting, among other things, frequent differences in substantive views. Extensive business representation on MITI, Ministry of Finance, Ministry of Transportation, and Environmental Protection Agency consultative councils has not kept FEO and other major business groups from publicly criticizing government policy. Even if intermediation relations have some corporatist characteristics, policymaking is adversarial.

Devolution of public functions to interest groups is also potential evidence of a corporatist style of integration between groups and their ministry regulators. In a long-standing arrangement under the Food Control Law by which farm cooperatives implemented portions of the rice collection system, Zenchu's role was clearly corporatist, according to microcorporatist concepts. Administration of the Large Store Law by committees in local branches of the Japan Chamber of Commerce and Industry is another example of the same kind of microcorporatism, although recent changes in the implementation of the Large Store Law may terminate this practice.

The presence of interest groups carrying out government functions invites caution in branding interest group politics in Japan as unremittingly pluralistic. But Zenchu and local chambers of commerce both attacked government policies with which they disagreed, and the existence of corporatist ties did not prevent them from doing so. We must realize that the same group can have varying relations with the government at any one or different times; patterns of influence and communication can vary accordingly.[57] The pluralism-corporatism dimension is important, but it is sometimes hard to tell where ideal types fit, given the intricacy of government-group relations. The corporatist-pluralistic distinction is substantially more complex than it appears to be in the bold, somewhat mechanical statements of political science.

Comparative research shows that there are many possible relations between interest groups and government offices. The degree of conflict and pattern of influence are often hard to determine precisely. One European study, for example, identified three different kinds of group-government relations that came under the rubric of consultation. In each type, either the government or the groups may be more influential. The mechanical corporatism-pluralism distinction is hard to capture when these differences and subtleties are recognized. Some other scholars make much the same distinction. As Harry Eckstein has stated: "Negotiations take place when a governmental body makes a decision hinge upon the approval of organizations interested in it, giving the organizations a veto over the decision. Consultations occur when the views of the organization are solicited and taken into account but not considered to be in any case decisive."[58] Nor are interest intermediation systems static; practices continually change and relations evolve.

Interest group–government relations in Japan combine fragments of corporatism with generally pluralistic tendencies. Pluralistic position taking is frequent in actual policy processes. Adversarial alignments by autonomous interest groups existed in most of the cases examined in this and the preceding chapter. Interest groups have opposed each other, coalitions of interest groups and ministries have opposed each other, and, as in the aluminum-smelting industry, firms have opposed MITI. Interest groups have also taken different sides from the government on different issues or different sides relative to past alignments. Medium and small business, which had been aligned at times with the LDP, opposed the government over both the Large Store Law and tax reform. Big business, normally seen as an ally of the government and the LDP, criticized the traditional farm policies of the LDP and MAFF. Big business did not win on farm issues. Regardless of American visions of a consensual Japan, Inc., business was generally unable to move the LDP on farm issues. Farm interests possessed enough votes essential to LDP survival to neutralize opposition. Business groups were also divided over coal policy. Which pattern of pluralistic interaction prevailed depended on interest group concerns regarding specific issues.

The LDP's history of adversarial as well as cooperative relations with business leaders supports the theme of interest group pluralism. Business executives were as prone to criticize as praise LDP behavior. Criticism was especially intense at the time of the intraparty crises. It seems unlikely that business leaders would publicly announce their frustration with LDP leadership if relations were as intimate as is sometimes asserted. Besides, in some situations business circles were unable to influence the LDP; in others, they could.[59]

Where government functions were delegated to the local affiliates of interest groups, more obviously corporatist practices have existed. There are also many examples of informal coordination and consultation in interest politics, as in political life generally. Efforts at bridging conflict or promoting intra-coalition coordination might be seen as corporatist-style integration if the dominant pattern of participation in interest intermediation processes were not pluralism. I concur with the contention that large countries with complex industrial economies are not a natural breeding ground for large-scale corporatism.[60] The autonomy of the state has not generally been unqualified; societal power and state power have interacted in a variety of ways — depending in the issue, the interest sector, and the time.

Japanese and European versions of interest group politics differ in a crucial way. Those researching interest group politics in Britain and France describe interest groups as interacting more with ministries than with political parties with just a few exceptions. (In Britain groups lacking ministry connections or presenting new social agendas are more likely to seek relations with parties than are old, well-established groups. Even well-established groups may approach parties on big issues.)[61] Conditions more like those in Japan are found in Italy — a country that I identify in Chapter 10, along with Japan, as a decentralized bargained democracy. Generally speaking, the long stay in power of the Japanese conservatives and the overall decentralization of party power created a more permeable environment for interest group politics than exists in political systems where parties are more centralized and autonomous. In Japan, contacts between interest groups and parties are decentralized, and parties are internally more open to interest group contact. The factors that led to the strong institutionalized involvement of the LDP in interest group politics also gave those politics a degree of openness and politicization not found in some other parliamentary democracies.

9

The Government and the Economy

The vertical model of Japanese politics is closely connected to interpretations that emphasize the directive role of the state in economic development. Japan rose from the ashes of wartime destruction and neglect to establish the second largest economy in the world. Because the economy grew while the state appeared to intervene in economic affairs, many believe that the government contributed significantly to the growth. In fact, some see Japan as the most successful example of government-directed economic development in the world.[1] Admirers argue that a Japanese model of government growth strategies and government-business cooperation can be used in other countries to improve productivity and competitiveness.[2] Critics accept the role of the government as crucial but see the Japanese economic miracle as a threat to the survival of other economies.[3] Both groups in the "developmental state" school believe that the government had a directive role in economic development, as would conform to a vertical metaphor for Japanese politics.

The developmental state approach is based on two premises. Government ministries are seen as making decisions independently. Government may consult with business in order to better understand market conditions, but the government in this relationship is independent of external political influence. In earlier chapters of this book such a view has been severely qualified. Confirming that Japanese economic policymaking is often pluralistic would undermine the claims of developmental state theory.

Developmental state ideas are also based on the assumption that a government's commitment to economic growth exerts a strong influence over the normal market behavior of the economy, including the behavior of individual firms. Bureaucratic elites are seen as highly competent and insulated against influence from private-sector interests by a "safety valve" political process and therefore able to set economic priorities and implement them using such tools as government loans and tax incentives.

Economic reality has worked differently from the developmental state paradigm. Many factors normally affect the implementation of economic policy, and Japan is no exception. Economic conditions frequently changed, frustrating planners' intentions. Even granting the developmental state tenet that the state bureaucracy was pragmatic and therefore revised plan estimates in response to market conditions, state plans and targets became out of date far more quickly than developmental state theorists have assumed. Money markets also operated in less predictable and more complicated ways than idealized versions of the developmental state would suggest. Some targeted industries needed vastly more money than others, either because they were capital intensive or because they were recovering from the destruction of World War II or were trying to expand when private capital was scarce. Individual firms responded in terms of their perceived opportunities and costs, not solely on the basis of government-orchestrated incentive programs. Policy outcomes, then, were affected by a variety of mostly economic variables and decisions.

Changing economic conditions meant that Japanese governments were often more accommodationist than developmental state formulas suggest. Government plans and targets were often modified as a result of economic conditions, not doggedly pursued regardless. State and society were interdependent, and private actors debated with government policymakers about what was workable. State ministries not only tried to propel the economy according to their independent designs but also responded to articulated societal needs. This was especially apparent in the tendency of the developmental state to turn into an economic welfare state attentive to the needs of sick industries or even a "party clientelistic" state over time. Thus, the postwar political economy was more a bundle of loose, partially connected threads than a neatly woven tapestry of state-designed results. Industries initially favored by the state did not always succeed, and industries that were not recipients of state help sometimes did quite well. Examining the implementation and effects of government economic and industrial policies is revealing. Determining when state development priorities consistently promoted growth and, relatedly, whether the government always picked winners is important. If government efforts failed, we want to know the reasons for failure—that is, the limitations of the developmental state model.

The Economic Role of the Government

In the 1950s and 1960s a combination of rapid economic growth, sharp production gains in important industries, and export successes, on the one hand, and extensive macroeconomic and microeconomic planning by the government, on the other, indicated to many observers that the state played a big role in economic development. The coincidence of government intervention — specifically, the apparently successful provision of government incentives for private-sector firms to modernize production — and dynamic growth made Japan seem unique among major economies. To some, the success reflected state policies that conformed to market conditions.

One of the best-known characterizations of Japanese government economic policy from the developmental state viewpoint is in the work of Chalmers Johnson. In his pioneering study of the Ministry of International Trade and Industry, Japan is seen as a state with special priorities and influence. "The priorities of the Japanese state derive first and foremost from an assessment of Japan's situational imperatives . . . [which] include late development, a lack of natural resources, a large population, a need to trade and the constraints of the international balance of payments. . . . Nurturing the economy has been a major priority of the Japanese state because any other course of action implied dependency, poverty and the possible breakdown of the social system."[4]

Johnson sees the developmental ideology of the state (mainly MITI) as the major driving force in industrial plans. He believes that the ministries have been unusually capable of successfully guiding economic growth, having imposed their own version of economic rationality or based economic policies on a synthesis of technocratic formulas and market information. His view has become the mainstay of popular knowledge about the economic role of the Japanese government among both admirers and critics of Japanese policy. U.S. and European Community politicians have, as a consequence, frequently accused Japan of engaging in economic practices that tilted the playing field of international trade.

Some economists take a radically different view. Hugh Patrick, Henry Rosovsky, and others have written that the role of the state is less important than private-sector initiatives and that Japan is much like European mixed economies as a result.[5]

A third group of investigators feel that the governmental role in economic and industrial policymaking lies somewhere between the poles represented by Johnson's interventionist state and the economists' conventional state, limited to the usual fiscal and monetary tools. The authors of these accounts see state-economy linkages as complex and government actions as mixed in effect.[6] In their interpretations of government economic policy, they emphasize that (1) most important economic decisions are politicized, (2) policy inputs by interest groups and firms are often as influential as or more influential than policy inputs by the government, and (3) industry interests and government rationales are not always complementary. Richard Samuels is a leading proponent of the view that firms and industrial associations, not just state concerns, influence policymaking.

Growth was the motivation for most economic policy under the developmental state paradigm. According to a broader view, however, policies were not based on a single economic growth formula. Instead, multiple rationales emerged in policy debates. Policies were as often problem driven as growth motivated. Ministries and private interest groups approached economic policy choices with different, often incompatible goals. The same interest group or ministry had different concerns at different times. Political parties, local governments, and trade unions also made policy inputs reflecting their own goals and needs. Actor alignments varied with issues and context.

For the ministries, goals often corresponded with the economic problems and potentials of the day. Some policies were designed mainly to increase production, others to stimulate productivity, others to conserve foreign exchange, and still others to relieve burdens on fiscal resources. In some cases, ministries proposed economic policy formulas that would conserve or expand their own control.

The policy goals of business owners reflected economic conditions at any given time, as well as their primary concerns of survival or growth. They wanted to acquire a stable or growing market share, avoid bankruptcy, and increase profits. These and other goals led them to make demands for production subsidies, regulations to limit market entry, and government-supported price mechanisms, among other aids. Many in business also wanted to avoid direct government control.

Other political actors had diverse concerns depending on the time and setting. Trade unions wanted to establish, maintain, or expand employment, unemployment benefits, retraining programs, and participation in management and, in some periods, to nationalize particular industries.[7] Local governments wanted to procure subsidies for industrial infrastructure while maximizing local employment and prosperity. Politicians made demands based on the concerns advocated by constituency groups.

Given the diversity of interests and economic rationales, economic policies were made in what Norton Long has called an ecology of games.[8] Policies were the outcome of a negotiated intersection of various economic rationales and interests, not the imposition of a single economic growth rationale on private-sector actors. As a result, there was much more to government policymaking and its implementation than solely a bureaucratic drive for growth. There have also been many departures from initial ministry intentions in the policies that emerge from negotiations between the government and interest groups. The ends of state policy have sometimes been subverted by the behavior of firms or unanticipated market trends.

Economic conditions played a much bigger role in policymaking and implementation than was assumed in the developmental state approach.[9] Both private and public lending decisions were as much a product of a variety of risk assessments as government intentions. The fulfillment of economic plans and industrial targets was more a function of general economic conditions than a response to interventions by talented bureaucrats. Recessions resulted in programs responding to economic needs and political imperatives that usually far exceeded the scope of developmental policies. The needs of industry were a complicated matter of economics, with policy priorities being tailored in different industries at different times.

A Record of the Economic Miracle

The economic performance of Japan since World War II is one of the truly dramatic trends in recent world history. Starting with an economy disrupted by war and more dependent on raw material from abroad than that of any other major power, Japan in some years registered the highest annual growth rates experienced in the modern history of the major world economies.

The postwar record was also impressive in light of Japan's own past experience. The country had made major strides in economic growth before World War II. In 1939, Japan was the most advanced industrialized nation outside western Europe and North America, although it retained some characteristics of an underdeveloped economy—among them, extensive rural poverty and exports dominated by the products of light industry. Six years later, devastated by war, Japan had an economic capacity reduced by more than two-thirds. Yet by the mid-1950s, Japan had recovered prewar production levels, and by 1990 economic output in constant prices was over six times output in the late 1950s; nominal gross national product itself increased seventy-five times between 1960 and 1991. The performance of heavy industry, like iron and steel, automobiles, machinery and electronics, was especially strong.

Trends in the GNP provide a good way to measure postwar economic success. In 1955 (roughly the beginning of the era of high growth), the nominal GNP was $19 billion. By 1960 it was $39 billion, and by 1990 it was $2.9 trillion (Table 9.1), with very high growth rates in some years.[10] The peak

Table 9.1. *Japan's Postwar Economy, 1955–1990*

	Japan	United States	West Germany	Britain
	Nominal GNP (in billions of U.S. dollars)			
1955	19	328	34	43
1960	39	504	71	72
1965	89	688	115	100
1970	203	992	186	124
1975	498	1,549	421	234
1980	1,040	2,626	824	542
1985	1,340	3,974	970	463
1990	2,940	5,423	1,501	974
	Per Capita Nominal GNP (in U.S. dollars)			
1955	213	2,185	527	856
1960	458	2,804	1,325	1,358
1965	704	3,142	1,687	1,585
1970	1,961	4,789	3,055	2,198
1975	4,499	7,148	6,781	4,082
1980	8,902	11,536	13,383	9,280
1985	11,100	16,610	15,900	8,250
1990	23,800	21,690	23,740	17,020

Sources: Most figures on nominal GNP are from Keizai Koho Center, *Japan 1981: An Economic Comparison* (Tokyo, 1981), p. 9, and Keizai Koho Center, *Japan 1992: An International Comparison* (Tokyo, 1992), pp. 12–13, and are based on United Nations estimates. Data for 1955 are from Prime Minister's Office, Statistical Bureau, *Japan Statistical Yearbook* (Tokyo, 1961), p. 550. Per capita data for 1960–75 are from United Nations, *Statistical Yearbook* (Tokyo, various years), and per capita data for 1980–90 are from Keizai Koho Center, *Japan 1992: An International Comparison.*

Note: Nominal GNP estimates are not adjusted for the effects of inflation.

years were 1960, 1961, and 1964, when 13–14 percent real growth was observed. Growth in 1968–69 was almost as rapid. These growth rates are higher than those in other major industrial economies at that time.[11]

The economic success of Japan can be seen even more clearly in a comparison of per capita GNP for industrialized countries (see Table 9.1). In 1952, Japan's per capita GNP was $188, roughly one-twelfth that of the United States and one-half that of West Germany. By 1960 it had risen to $458; by the mid-1970s, to well over $4,000, which was 62 and 66 percent, respectively, of American and German levels. By 1980, reflecting changes in currency values as well as continued growth in most years, the Japanese figure soared even closer to the levels registered in the United States and West Germany. By 1990 the levels in both Japan and and the former West Germany surpassed the level in the United States and Britain. Per capita nominal GNP in Japan had increased 126 times from 1952 to 1990.[12] If postwar growth is added to prewar experience, in slightly over one century Japan was transformed from a predominantly poor, agricultural country into one of the world's most successful industrial nations.

Postwar growth in production in specific industries provides more concrete testimony to Japan's success. Increases in steel production are an excellent indicator of industrial growth. Japan was already unique in the non-Western world before World War II by virtue of its high levels of steel production. In 1896 steel output was only an estimated 100 tons, but by 1936 it had reached 3.6 million tons. After World War II steel production grew virtually exponentially. By 1960, in roughly the middle of the high-growth period (1955–72), output was a much greater 22 million tons, and in 1973, it peaked at 119 million tons. Since then, Japan has ranked second in the world in crude steel output behind the former Soviet Union.

Even GNP/GDP and crude steel figures do not tell the whole story.[13] Much of the success has been due to growth and enormous export sales in specific industries. In the 1950s and early 1960s these industries included shipbuilding and steel. Later, the automobile, electronics, and machine-tool industries took the lead in exports. The automobile industry, in particular, is a striking example of both growth and export success. In the early years after the war automobile production was very small—minuscule in comparison with that in the United States and Europe. In 1960, for example, Japan produced only 165,000 automobiles and 308,000 trucks, whereas U.S. production exceeded 7,000,000 vehicles. By 1970, however, automobile production alone exceeded 3,000,000 units, and by 1990 the figure was nearly 10,000,000, a sixty-one-fold increase in production over thirty years. By 1980, passenger car production in Japan exceeded that in the United States, the world leader until then.[14] In recent years roughly half of the automobiles produced in Japan have been exported, with a large share going to North America. Production data for several other modern manufactures indicate similarly successful trajectories. As is well known, Japan is currently the world's largest exporter of automobiles and consumer electronics, as well as a major exporter of many other industrial commodities.

Japan's economic miracle is all the more impressive in view of its traditional dependence on foreign imports for many of the raw materials needed in industrial production. Currently Japan imports nearly all of its energy needs.

Imported crude oil contributes 99.5 percent of petroleum requirements; imported coal, 92 percent of coal requirements. Other minerals are likewise scarce in Japan: the dependency ratio for iron ore is 100 percent, and for copper — the only metal of importance mined in Japan — 98.9 percent. About half of food needs are also met by imports. Feed grains, corn, wheat, and soybeans are at the top of the list.[15]

Government Economic Plans and Investments

The government's penchant for formulating elaborate plans for both general economic growth and specific industry development is often seen as evidence that the economy is state led. Early postwar plans addressed the need for reconstruction. The economy was severely weakened during World War II: plants and facilities were damaged or destroyed, and work was disrupted by both wartime mobilization and by the flight of the population from the bombed cities. The initial economic plans after the war dealt with the repair of facilities and revival of an economy whose physical base was in disarray. Japan also suffered from lack of access to former sources of critical raw materials.

After the most difficult of the reconstruction tasks had been completed, the government turned to economic growth. From the 1950s on, it endeavored to promote growth through various macroeconomic plans and by programs aimed at specific industries. Economic tools, including government bank loans, tax incentives, and trade protection, were developed and deployed to foster modernization and growth. An alternative proposal for rearmament was rejected after an intense debate by politicians concerned with Japan's economic versus its military strength.[16]

Indicative economic planning — that is, making plans that set economic goals but do not provide sanctions for noncompliance — began in the 1950s.[17] Five major plans were developed and promulgated by the Economic Planning Agency from 1955 to 1967 (Table 9.2); other macroeconomic plans have followed. The plans, which are broad outlines for guidance of public and private economic activity and not compulsory programs, are essentially large-scale development forecasts buttressed by elaborate statistical references and supplemented by programs for growth in specific sectors. The documents in the plans contain target figures for most kinds of economic activity, with special attention being paid to outputs from selected major industries. The plans also contain goals for developing infrastructure, public works, and social programs. Each plan has had a special focus and target slogans, such as "Catching up with Britain" (1953–57) or "Doubling income" (1960–67). As time went on and the economy prospered, the concerns addressed by the plans shifted to noneconomic goals: quality of life and welfare. Planning continues today, although plans are given much less public attention than in the early years after the war.

The general economic plans were supplemented by policies designed to shape developments in specific industries and promote foreign trade. The Ministries of International Trade and Industry and Transportation orchestrated a wide range of supports to encourage qualitative improvements and, in the 1950s and 1960s, competitive viability in international markets. As can be seen from the examples in Table 9.2, different industries were emphasized at different times. The programs of the 1950s addressed infrastructure needs and the growth of the power, coal, shipping, steel, and petrochemical (especially fertilizer) sectors. Later, interest shifted more to automobiles, machine tools, and electronics. These are precisely the sectors that experienced high growth in those periods, respectively.

Most of the laws and plans developed along with these programs were very general and can best be seen as policy frameworks. General goals were indicated by the frameworks; more specific programs emphases and policy tools — government bank loans, accelerated tax depreciation allowances, special tax-free reserve funds, and tax deductions — were developed and deployed under the umbrella that they provided. MITI's power to license imports of raw materials and technology was used to allocate materials and technologies to industries slated for development. In the 1950s industrial policies mainly encouraged productivity gains through technology improvements. In the 1960s increasing firm size was emphasized in the New Industrial Order program. Mergers were encouraged on the assumption that concentration would increase international competitive power. Other policy instruments included protective tariffs and import quotas and the sanctioning of cartels. Table 9.3, which shows the cluster of policy tools developed to support the computer and information industry under specific framework legislation, demonstrates the many facets of government efforts.

The macroeconomic policies and institutions supported growth in most years. In spite of a widespread view abroad that the government has a large economic role, it actually favored severe fiscal restraint until the 1970s. In the previous decade Japan had had the lowest level of taxation of any major industrial power. In 1965 taxes, excluding social security contributions, amounted to 18 percent of the gross domestic product, in contrast with 27–35 percent for the United States, Britain, the former West Germany, and France. Public expenditures also carried out the theme of limited government. In the 1950s and 1960s government outlays on the current account represented only 13–14 percent of GDP, whereas in other industrialized countries outlays ranged as high as 30 percent.

Constraint in government expenditures facilitated savings and investment. Less was extracted from the national income and allocated to public expenditures in Japan than in other industrialized nations, especially early in the postwar era (Table 9.4), which permitted allocations of financial resources to other purposes. Lower outlays on social programs and defense were one reason for the differences in government expenditures between Japan and other industrialized countries. The Japanese government, after an intense debate in the early 1950s over defense outlays versus economic development, decided to place growth at the top of its agenda. Defense outlays were as high as 6 percent of national income in the 1950s but have hovered around 1 percent in most years since then. Prime Minister Takeo Miki (1974–76) formally committed the government to not exceed the 1 percent level; the commitment has been honored, with the exception of the mid-1980s, when personnel expenditures forced the percentage up slightly. In contrast, the United States has spent around 6 percent of its GNP on defense in most years. Other major industrialized countries have normally spent between 3 and 6 percent.[18] In the mid-1960s, Japan also spent a little less on social welfare than the United States and roughly one-third of the amounts committed to social programs by European countries. The picture is much the same today, except that Japanese expenditures on social security are much higher than before because of policy changes in the 1970s and the maturing of the pension system. The government pension and health-care programs are now as comprehensive as those in some western European countries. Expenditures will continue to grow in this area as time passes and the population becomes older.

In addition to a constrained fiscal policy, the government encouraged investment by maintaining low interest rates in some periods. In the early postwar years policymakers raised interest rates only when the economy overheated to the point where demand for imports exceeded the amount of exports, creating a negative trade imbalance.[19] The Organization for Economic Cooperation and Development estimates that gross fixed investment in Japan averaged 38 percent of GDP each year by the late 1960s, while comparable figures for other major industrialized countries ranged between 16 percent for the United States and 26 percent for France.[20] In addition to government policies, high individual and corporate savings rates facilitated investment. A disposition to save was encouraged by tax exemptions for small savings deposits, including those made through the vast postal savings system.[21] Savings levels today are still slightly higher than those in the former West Germany and France and twice those in the United States.[22]

Table 9.2. Economic Plans and "Framework" Legislation, 1949–1978

Plan/Law/Program	Year	Goals/Actions
Early Postwar Economic Plans		
Five-Year Plan for Economic Self-Support	1956–60	Economic self-sufficiency via balanced trade, stable prices, full employment
New Long-Range Economic Plan	1958–62	Strengthened industrial base, stable high growth, full employment
National-Income-Doubling Plan	1961–67	Expanded, stable growth/living standards, improvement in social capital
Medium-Term Economic Plan	1964–68	Improved small firm efficiency, improved technology, improved quality of life
Economic and Social Development Plan	1967–71	Balanced social/economic development, improved social infrastructure
Major "Framework" Programs and Legislation		
Foreign Exchange and Trade Control Law	1949	Rationed foreign exchange for imports using a quota and licensing system
Foreign Capital Law	1950	Limited foreign investment in Japanese industries
First–Third Steel Plans	1951–66	Promoted technological modernization of steel industry

Enterprise Rationalization Promotion Law	1952	Gave tax incentives, loans, and other supports to modernizing firms
Five-Year Plan for Synthetic Fiber Development	1953	Same
Five-Year Petroleum Resources Development Plan	1954	Established joint public-private company to develop new oil sites
Coal-Mining Industry Interim Promotion Law	1955	Encouraged lowering of coal costs via purchase of old mines, new equipment subsidies, legitimization of some cartels, other help
Petrochemicals Promotion Plan	1955	Sales of military fuel-storage facilities plus rationalization support
Machine Industry Temporary Promotion Law	1956	Framework for industry-level rationalization programs
Fifteen-Year Auto Parts Rationalization Plan	1956	Provided modernization loans and encouraged concentration of production
Electronic Industry Temporary Promotion Law	1957	Initial efforts to support computer industry development
Basic Machine-Tool Industry Promotion Plan	1968	MITI "guidance" for increasing scale of production
Electronic Industry Temporary Promotion Law	1969	Provided a rationalization framework for electronic industry
Special Electronics and Machine Industry Law	1971	Government-subsidized computer leasing started, numerically controlled machine tools promoted
Special Information and Machine Industry Law	1978	Computer industry superprojects

Sources: Japan Institute of International Affairs, *White Papers of Japan: 1972–73* (Tokyo, 1974), pp. 275–382; Tsusansho, *Tsusansho 25 gonenshi* (Tokyo, 1979).

Note: The information in this table ends with 1978; industrial plans after the early 1970s are less significant as evidence of a developmental state than earlier information is. The examples here are representative selections of different industry plans and frameworks; there are many more frameworks than I have listed.

Table 9.3. Policy Frameworks in the Computer Industry

Major Policy Framework	Electronics Industry Promotion Special Measures Law, 1957	Electronics and Machine Industry Special Measures Law, 1971	Information and Machinery Industry Framework: Special Measures Law, 1978
New Institutions	MITI Electronics Industry Division Electronics Industry CC JECC Japan Information-Processing Center	Electronics and Machine Industry CC	
JDB Loans	Support for new firms Support for JECC	Loans for startup, specialization, cost reduction, expanded output Support for JECC	Software development JECC loans
Tax Incentives	Tax incentives for computers	Numerically controlled machinery AD	Computer repurchase reserves tax break

	EX for R & D reserves Computer repurchase reserves Software engineers training EX	New industrial technology AD Computer repurchase reserves EX Software development reserves EX Local tax on computers EX Tax incentives for mergers	
Protection	Mainframe computer quotas High tariffs Foreign investment limits NTT domestic maker purchases AML exemption for computers	Mainframe computer quotas High tariffs Foreign investment limits NTT domestic maker purchases Specialization urged	Mainframe import "guidance" High tariffs until 1980 NTT domestic maker purchases Cartels for numerically controlled machines promoted
Structure	Peripheral-makers cartels Computer research subsidies Public-private research projects	Guidance on standards, technology Computer research subsidies Large-scale research projects	State-of-art projects Superprojects
Research and Development			

Sources: Marie Anchordoguy, *Computers Incorporated* (Cambridge: Harvard University Press, 1989); and Eugene J. Kaplan, *Japan: The Government-Business Relationship* (Washington, D.C.: Department of Commerce, 1972).

Note: AD = accelerated depreciation. AML = Anti-Monopoly Law. CC = Consultative Council. EX = exemption from tax. JECC = Japan Electronic Computer Company. NTT = Nippon Telephone and Telegraph Company.

Table 9.4. Government Revenues and Outlays and Societal Savings, 1965–1987

	Japan	France	West Germany	United Kingdom	United States
Taxes as Percentage of GNP					
1965	18	35	32	32	27
1978	24	30	32	37	28
1987	28	34	30	42	26
Central Government Expenditures as Percentage of GNP					
1960	13	30	28	29	25
1984	18	25	14	32	24
1989	15	23	13	26	22
Social Security Outlays as Percentage of GNP					
1965	6	17	19	14	8
1978	10	24	20	10	10
1990	11	26	21	9	9
Defense Expenditures as Percentage of GNP					
1965	1	6	4	3	7
1980	1	4	3	5	5
1988	1	4	3	5	6
Savings as Percentage of GNP					
1960	25	16	20	11	9
1970	27	21	18	13	8
1980	18	11	10	6	6
1987	18	7	11	5	2

Sources: Data on taxes from OECD, *Revenue Statistics of OECD Member Countries, 1965–79*; Keizai Koho Center, *Japan 1981: An International Comparison* (Tokyo, 1981), p. 65, and *Japan 1991: An International Comparison* (Tokyo, 1991), p. 84. Data on expenditures from United Nations, *Yearbook of National Accounts* (1980); Keizai Koho Center, *Japan 1985: An International Comparison* (Tokyo, 1985), p. 83, and *Japan 1991*, p. 82. Data on social security from Harold Wilensky, *The Welfare State and Equality* (Berkeley: University of California Press, 1975); Keizai Koho Center, *Japan 1981*, p. 65, and *Japan 1991*, p. 84. Data on defense from Gabriel Almond and G. Bingham Powell, Jr., *Comparative Politics* (Boston: Little, Brown, 1978); Keizai Koho Center, *Japan 1981*, p. 67, and *Japan 1991*, p. 85. Data on savings from United Nations, *Yearbook of National Accounts* (1977 and 1989).

Note: Years do not always match across categories because the sources of information are different.

As in other countries, individual and corporate savings generated funds that could be used for investment via the banking system. In addition, personal savings deposited in the popular postal savings system were funneled into capital investments by a government-run institution, the Fiscal Investment and Loan Program (FILP). The FILP also drew funds from social security deposits. FILP investments ranged between 27 and 55 percent of the government budget. Because most FILP funds came from nontax sources, the program was not the same as a public budget, even though the use of funds was sometimes comparable to budget expenditures elsewhere. FILP makes the government role more significant than budget information alone indicates.

The FILP funded investment loans to industries by way of such institutions as the Japan Development Bank. In 1955–62 between 11 and 21 percent of the FILP funds were designated for large-scale industrial development. Since that time, the direct role of FILP in funding the large-firm sector has steadily decreased. Currently only 2.5 percent of FILP funds directly support large-scale industry. But its role in financing medium and small business has grown substantially (see Table 9.9); the programs contribute to overall economic growth and stability, not in high-profile large industries, but in different sectors. The FILP investment in roads, railways, ports, housing, and other social and industrial infrastructure projects (many of which facilitate growth) has been heavy since the late 1960s and early 1970s. Government infrastructure development may be its most important contribution to economic growth.

FILP and economic plans notwithstanding, a belief that a dominant state successfully directed economic growth after the war is not supported by evidence on the scale and priorities of government economic intervention. To begin, the size of government financial interventions in specific industries, as well as in the economy generally, has been exaggerated. "Many of the writings about Japan are very short on numbers, and thereby slip into an exaggeration of this role by failing to understand the relative size of government financing of the private sector."[23] Chalmers Johnson's assessment that the government provided between one-quarter and one-third of all industrial capital in the 1950s and a sizable percentage of funds in the 1960s is an example of such exaggeration.[24] Elsewhere, Ira Magaziner and Thomas Hout wrote incorrectly that "the greater part of investment capital [in the steel industry] — roughly 65 percent — was financed . . . primarily through government institutions."[25] But government lending accounted for only 12 percent or so of the borrowing of the steel industry even in peak periods (see Table 9.6). Besides providing misleading figures, many studies have cited yen data for government investments and subsidies, which inevitably appear larger than the same information in dollars.

Table 9.5 presents data on (1) the government share of all loans to industry and (2) its share of loans for industrial equipment. Both measures are based on widely available statistical series published by the Japanese government and are good indicators of the government role in financing enterprises. The figures in the table are substantially smaller than those claimed by developmental state theorists. Specifically, the Japan Development Bank and the Export-Import Bank, the government banking institutions closest to big business, made only between 3 and 8 percent of all industrial loans in the 1950s and roughly the same share in the 1960s, not the much higher contributions asserted by Johnson and others. The Export-Import Bank figures might be left out, for EIB loans were not directly used for growth but in support of ship and later industrial plant exports. I include them here simply because the comparison is with all bank loans to industry, which does not differentiate with regard to purpose. Also, EIB loans did support growth where they funded overseas demand, as was the case for shipbuilding.

In some cases, the share of government lending peaked in the 1970s, a time when recessed industries made heavy claims on government, not a period of government support for growth. The Japan Development Bank, the main government bank directly supporting the modernization of the production facilities of large firms, provided industry only between 5 and 6 percent of its equipment investment needs in the 1950s, roughly the same in the 1960s, and between 3 and 5 percent thereafter. Although the amount of government lending is not insignificant, it was considerably smaller in scale than earlier information indicated.

The discrepancy between my figures and those of some other scholars reflects the misleading inclusion of loans to agriculture and small business in the aggregated government loan data. Overall, government loan figures normally combine government bank loans, which include loans from the People's Finance Corporation, the Medium and Small Business Finance Corporation, the Environmental Sanitation Finance Corporation (after 1968), and the Agriculture, Forestry, and Fisheries Finance Corporation, along with the figures for Japan Development Bank lending. However, with the exception of Japan Development Bank lending and some loans by the Medium and Small Business Finance Corporation to small machine-tool and automobile parts producers, all of these institutions lend to small businesses or farmers for nondevelopmental purposes. Very large loans were directed to the small-business sector, mainly for social policy purposes or because of LDP intervention on the behalf of clients. This lending should not be seen as government support of targeted growth industries. Move carefully calculated statistical series, then, indicate a much more modest state role in direct investment than that suggested by development state theorists.[26]

Table 9.5. Government Share of New Lending to Large Firms, 1955–1985
(in billions of U.S. dollars)

Year	New Loans to Industry			New Industrial Equipment Loans		
	Total	Government Banks	% Government Banks	Total	JDB	% JDB
1955	1.8	.1	6	.9	.05	6
1956	3.7	.1	2	1.4	.02	1
1957	3.8	.1	3	1.6	.10	6
1958	3.9	.2	3	2.0	.12	6
1959	4.9	.2	3	2.4	.12	5
1960	6.9			3.4	.12	3
1961	7.9	.2	3	3.9	.20	5
1962	9.1	.4	4	4.4	.30	7
1963	13.7	.3	4	6.1	.32	5
1964	11.5	.5	4	6.5	.41	6
1965	12.2	.4	4	7.8	.53	7
1966	13.8	.6	4	8.4	.61	7
1967	17.9	.7	4	10.9	.62	5
1968	18.8	.9	5	15.9	.74	5
1969	25.7	1.0	4	19.7	.76	4
1970	31.3	1.2	4	22.8	.92	4
1971	45.1	1.3	3	31.8	1.15	4
1972	61.2	2.0	3	39.4	1.09	3
1973	73.3	1.6	3	45.2	1.60	4
1975	57.2	2.9	5	50.5	1.80	5
1980	77.3	1.2	2	66.4	2.80	4
1985	12.0	1.7	1	118.2	4.97	4

Sources: Prime Minister's Office, Statistical Bureau, *Japan Statistical Yearbook* (Tokyo, various years); Economic Planning Agency, *Monthly Economic Statistics* (various years).

Notes: "% Government Banks" refers to the share of government loans among all new loans and is the sum of loans made by the Japan Development Bank and the Export-Import Bank, the two principal government banks lending to large business firms.

"% JDB" is the share of Japan Development Bank loans for new equipment. The Export-Import Bank does not function in this area.

Loans made by the Small Business Finance Corporation, the People's Finance Corporation, the Agriculture, Forestry, and Fisheries Finance Corporation, and, after 1968, the Environmental Sanitation Finance Corporation are omitted. They are reported as "industrial" loans in some government data series even though farmers and small businesses are the loan recipients and not large firms.

I provide more detail on JDB lending because it was the government's main institution for lending to large firms. Percentages were calculated before conversion to dollars.

A second important qualification of the belief about state-directed economic growth concerns the priorities represented by government bank loans to specific industries. Here two kinds of information are relevant: the shares of Japan Development Bank Loans provided to specific industries and the degree to which these industries were dependent on government compared with commercial bank loans (Table 9.6). The former figures indicate government priorities, the latter industrial dependence on government support. Four industries — shipping, electric power, coal, and iron and steel — received the bulk of government loans in the 1950s. These same industries were also more dependent on government financing than other industries were. The other industries generally received a very small share of government loans and were not especially dependent on the Japan Development Bank as a result.

Because Japan has a government development bank that makes loans to targeted industries, developmental state theorists have asserted that government loans were (1) a direct source of investment funds or (2) an indicator of government priorities, which stimulated private lending to industries targeted for growth.[27] In reality, government lending priorities were, in the early years after the war, as often a policy response to the needs of the economy as a guide to growth. The four industries that provided important inputs or services for other industries and that needed very large loans received the most government bank support (compared with all other industries) and in turn depended the most on government lending. Each industry among the four also had special needs, some of which were not directly related to growth goals.

Shipping capacity was limited right after the war by the wartime loss of ships, and in the 1950s large government loans were provided to replace the losses. Shipbuilding was encouraged both by loans to domestic shipping companies that placed orders for new ships and by loans from the Export-Import Bank to support the export of Japanese-made ships. Both the shipping and the shipbuilding industries needed very large loans to become and stay viable. Electric power also received considerable funds from the Japan Development Bank; it was important to Japan's economic viability as well as its growth, and the high cost of the new hydroelectric capacity required support. Power industry loans were in some cases also indirect subsidies for continued use of domestic coal in power generation. In the 1970s substantial bank loans to the industry were part of efforts to control industrial pollution — another rationale for government policy besides simply growth and development.[28] The coal industry itself received a sizable share of government financing to increase productivity so that domestic coal could compete with imported oil, which would both maintain employment in the coal industry and help conserve foreign currency.[29] The iron and steel industry was given funds because of the importance of steel to other industries, as well as because of its potential as an export industry.

Table 9.6. *Government Bank Lending Priorities and Industry Loan Dependency Ratios,*
1950s–1970s

	1950s		1960s		1970s	
Japan Development Bank Loans and Their Composition						
Electric Power	$ 595.7	(44%)	$ 584.1	(12%)	$ 3,466.8	(23%)
Shipping	$ 371.3	(27%)	$1,606.6	(33%)	$ 2,791.9	(4%)
Coal	$ 99.9	(7%)	$ 301.0	(6%)	—	
Iron and Steel	$ 58.9	(4%)	$ 15.6	(-)	—	
Computers and Electronics	—		$ 87.5	(2%)	$ 1,456.1	(6%)
Total Loans	$1,363.5	(100%)	$4,886.9	(100%)	$22,944.0	(100%)
Japan Development Bank Loans as a Share of All Loans						
Electric Power	55.4%		52.2%		NA	
Shipping	48.6%		59.9%		44.3%	
Coal	24.6%		33.8%		—	
Iron and Steel	12.2%		1.4%		3.8%	
Electric Machinery	.3%		.6%		.8%	

Sources: Nihon Kaihatsu Ginko (Japan Development Bank), *Nihon Kaihatsu Ginko 25 nenshi* (Tokyo, 1982), appendix, pp. 42-49; and Nihon Ginko, *Keizai Tokei Nenkan* (various years).

Notes: Percentages in the upper half of the table are shares of JDB loans to specific industries. Figures for industries having small shares are not shown. Percentages in the lower half of the table are shares of all loans to specific industries accounted for by JDB loans. NA means "not available" and refers to situations in which total loan and JDB loan aggregates are not comparable. Dollar amounts are in millions of U.S. dollars.

— = no amounts indicated or category deleted.

The basic or infrastructure industries, especially electric power and shipping, unquestionably needed very large funding at a time when private banks were unable or reluctant to provide loans on the scale needed. For a combination of reasons, three of the four basic industries — power, coal, and shipping — continued to receive priority attention even after the early postwar justifications were less important. Meanwhile, several of the industries targeted by government plans in the 1960s did not receive substantial government loans, even though developmental state ideas would lead us to expect it.

Automobiles received a negligible portion of government bank loans, with a resulting dependency ratio of less than 1 percent in the period in which it was a targeted industry.[30] Other machinery industries likewise failed to come near the leading infrastructure industries in terms of either shares of Japan Development Bank loans or dependency on government funds. The machinery industries, including manufacturers of automobile parts and machine tools, received only $285 million from the bank while a targeted industry in the 1960s.[31] The computer industry was lent only $39 million in the 1960s, when it was first targeted as part of the electric machine industries.[32] In contrast, loans provided to the shipping, coal, and power industries totaled $2.49 billion in the 1960s and $3.56 billion between 1951 and 1969, the time span during which industrial development received the greatest government attention.

Government lending priorities and industry dependence on government loans imply that from the 1960s on, the state was as much a problem solver for sick industries as a leader, which is the opposite of developmental state ideas. (There was an element of responding to the problems of specific industries in the 1950s, too, but the problems of coal and shipping also increased and became more politicized over time.) Once lending patterns were established in the 1950s, they were hard to change, partly because of the large amounts of the loans (such as those provided to the power industry) and partly because of the difficult times facing coal and shipping. The increasingly shaky economic situation made commercial bank loans hard to procure in these two industries, and increased risk made them expensive. Government bank loans to the affected industries were essential under these conditions, and in the 1960s and later, the government became a lender of last resort. Pressures from political parties, private enterprise, and labor unions to rescue industries and concerns for preventing unemployment also favored continued lending to these industries.[33] The rational priorities of the 1950s became the political priorities of the 1960s. Meanwhile, as economic prosperity increased and the future looked more certain, most healthy industries — automobile and machinery, for instance — were able to obtain commercial loans without recourse to the government banks.[34]

Because of the distortion and politicization of government lending priorities, many economists judge that government lending did not normally play an indicative role in investment decisions. In fact, government bank lending was constrained by the effects of the early bias in favor of making funds available for the power, coal, and shipping industries. Government bank loans were also prevented from having indicative effects by the complexity of bank lending decisions and increasing access to commercial loans by all industries as growth advanced.[35] As time went on, FILP funds were used more and more to support development of the infrastructure (roads, ports, industrial parks) and other priority concerns. As a result, lending to targeted growth industries generally failed to reach significant indicative levels.[36]

The overall impact of the government on economic growth, above and beyond the role played by government bank lending, is another subject of controversy. Some specialists point out that plan targets were not reflected very well in subsequent economic reality. Others cite government support for industries that became losers. Still other researchers have pointed out that state programs for recessed industries and economic policies designed to satisfy LDP clients outpaced supports for high growth as a share of government subsidies. Once again, both the variety of economic rationales and the inherent uncertainty of economic trends suggest weaknesses in the developmental state model of the political economy.

Some research has discounted the direct effects of planning on economic growth because the fit between planned and actual outputs was usually poor. Output was often double or more the size of GNP goals in the periods covered by economic plans.[37] Production also deviated from plan goals in specific industries. According to David Friedman's account of the machine-tool industry, "Actual results varied wildly from plans. Output in 1960 was ¥45 billion ($125 million), or 225 percent of planned value, whereas output in 1965 was only 52 percent of the plan." Friedman also points out that targets for machine-tool specialization were not met, government loans correlated more with recessions than with growth, and government plans for restructuring were not followed. Writing in the same vein about 1957–58, Richard Samuels states, "Government planners, who had failed completely to anticipate the recovery, projected increasing demand for coal. They were off by 9 million tons."[38] The responses of business firms to economic cycles and general demand determined outputs in these examples, not just government policy.[39]

Under these circumstances, some Japanese economists have been loath to grant the plans an influential role in economic behavior. According to Toshimasa Tsuruta: "The modernization of the industrial structure, and the strengthening of industrial competitiveness were not the result of industrial policy, but rather of the relatively smooth operation of the price mechanism and the ability of firms through their own decisions to adapt. The initial objectives of industrial policy could not be realized, and they remained empty plans."[40] These words may be unduly severe. Economic planning played a positive role by raising popular expectations of growth and providing enormous amounts of valuable information about markets. Plans simply did not work the way they were supposed to do quite a bit of the time. The economic plans corresponded to Japanese political and economic behavior in areas of uncertainty. They represented efforts to reduce uncertainty but could not guarantee the future. They also constituted a coalitional agreement between government and the private sector.

Other aspects of economic performance indicate further problems with the ability of the government to anticipate events or set alternative priorities. Many recent commentators on Japanese economic policy doubt that the government was able to allocate resources to specific industry winners in the ways indicated in the developmental state theory. Among the industries supported by the government in the 1950s, steel is typically seen as representing the most successful application of industrial policy.[41] Other industries addressed by the policies of the 1950s were either less uniformly successful or harder to judge by success-failure standards.

Various policy tools were used to stimulate modernization of steelmaking facilities: loans, tax incentives, protection, and coordinated production and sales. Iron and steel received $74.5 million in rationalization loans from 1951 to 1965. Although this is a fairly small amount of money compared with government loans to power, coal, and shipping, it was still considerably more than the amounts given to other industries. The main goal of government policy was improvement of steelmaking processes to enhance productivity and lower prices. Lower prices in the steel industry, it was felt, would facilitate growth for domestic manufacturers that depended on steel inputs. Lower prices would also lead to more competitive exports. Productivity did increase during the period of government-supported investment, and steel prices declined until the first oil crisis in 1973.[42]

Two of the most highly successful industries, consumer electronics and automobiles, were given very little direct government support relative to both the infrastructure industries of the 1950s and the recessed industries of the 1970s. Consumer electronics received only $6 million in government loans during the 1960s. The government even initially opposed technology imports destined for the industry.[43] The government role in the automobile industry was mixed. Government lending provided 8 percent of the borrowing needs of the industry in 1955 but less than 1 percent to 2 percent in most other years. It is possible, in fact, that automobile firms *sought* fewer supports than some other industries. The well-known resistance of the industry to the MITI policy of promoting mergers symbolizes the independence of outlook of some firms. Some automobile companies, including Honda, consistently distanced themselves from the government.[44] Tax incentives, government-licensed technology imports, and protection had a modest positive effect on the industry in the 1950s and 1960s. Government support and protectionist barriers played a modest role relative to such economic factors as domestic and world demand and improvement of the Japanese road system.[45] Perhaps the loans and other incentives provided to auto parts producers were the most important government support given to the automobile industry. Lending to this part of the industry encouraged lower costs and higher-quality products in medium and small firms, which in turn improved inputs to the assembly lines of large firms.[46]

Some argue that support for the computer industry had positive effects on its development. Nevertheless, the overall evaluation of government computer policy is somewhat mixed, like that of industrial policy in general. Early in the development of the computer industry the government allowed IBM to enter the Japanese market in exchange for sharing its technology with Japanese firms.[47] Government support of technology induction was supplemented by the establishment of a quasi-government firm, Japan Electronic Computer Company (JECC), in 1969 to lease Japanese computers to end users.[48] This measure, a direct response to IBM's use of leasing to develop mainframe computer markets, helped produce a stable, predictable demand for Japanese-made computers. Government procurement of Japanese computers for public offices and universities had a similar effect. But government support for high-visibility research and development projects involving cooperation between the government and the private sector may or may not have had unalloyed benefits for the computer industry and its various spinoffs. Some scholars evaluate these programs highly; others say little of significance was carried out within the cooperatively run laboratories. For example, Glenn Fong reports that computer firms in the very large scale integrated circuits (VLSI) project routinely carried out their most important research in locations separate from the government-sponsored laboratories set up for cooperative work. As in other areas of industrial policy, scholars who actually look at policy implementation and impact were more pessimistic than those who examined only policy goals and instruments.[49] In addition, the government's emphasis on hardware development at the expense of systems design and software innovation may well have contributed to lags in Japanese industry in these areas.

Of the industries targeted for support in the 1950s and 1960s, electric power is not normally evaluated in terms of success or failure. Electricity output kept up with growth in most periods, and the industry can be seen as performing its infrastructure role credibly for this reason. The infrastructure argument, plus the high costs of nuclear power development, led the Japan Development Bank to continue disproportionately high levels of support for the industry. Japan does, however, have higher electricity rates than other industrialized countries — the rate was 24 percent higher in Tokyo than in New York in 1991.[50] The experience with coal and shipping policy shows both the difficulties of designing successful programs for recessed industries and the tendency for politics to intrude even after old economic rationales have lost relevance.

The developmental state model of the Japanese political economy has generally ignored the unintended consequences of some government economic programs. In spite of allegedly high levels of business-government communication and claims of a corporatist consensus on economic policy, case studies indicate frequent private-sector resistance to government policy proposals and programs. Private firms have also exploited and manipulated government policies in ways not congenial to government intentions. Sometimes companies have totally evaded government policy directives. The pluralism evident in policymaking settings and the diversity of economic rationales engaged by government policies has ensured that many of the government's industrial supports were not fully successful, judging by intentions.

Examples of private-sector subversion of government programs are easy to find. Subsidies provided to coal companies under the Priority Production Program of 1947 did little to improve mine efficiency, which was one of the goals of the program. Coal firms mined marginal fields because production costs were paid by the government. They were thus able to save their better fields for use after government subsidies were no longer available.[51] Under the same program, government funds intended to encourage coal firms to install productivity-enhancing equipment were used to purchase equipment that was stored until after cost-based remuneration ended. Although this may have promoted efficiency in the long run, it hardly demonstrates successful industrial policy in the usual sense of the term.[52] Later the goal of the coal rationalization plan of 1955 — retiring inefficient mines — was subverted when firms sold old, depleted mines to the government while simultaneously opening new facilities without regard to efficiency.[53] In some years, large mining companies even bought coal from small-scale, less efficient firms in order to take advantage of high prices while simultaneously receiving government supports designed to enhance their own efficiency.[54]

Just as government programs were subverted in the coal industry, so, too, were they subverted in the textile industry, where the government hoped to reduce production capacity. Textile makers kept obsolete machinery that they would normally have abandoned in the hope that the government would buy the old equipment under purchase-and-scrap programs.[55] Likewise, government directives to machine-tool makers about product concentration and other kinds of cooperation were often ignored; production corresponded more to market demand than to government plans.[56] Other examples of private-sector noncompliance, such as resistance to MITI's plans for industrial restructuring in the automobile and computer industries, are well known. So is resistance to MITI-supervised steel capacity plans in both the 1950s and 1960s.[57] Even when government policies should have been easy to implement because the number of firms was small (as in steel, automobiles, and computers), some firms resisted government technocrats when it suited them to do so.

Some scholars assert that the industrial policy of the government worked better for growing industries than for declining ones. Addressing decline is often difficult, and industry and government interests were much less closely aligned in recessed than in developing industries. Other things being equal, firms in developing industries can benefit from stimulation of growth or support for investments in new equipment. In declining industries government-supported downsizing is a bitter pill for individual firms to swallow, making policy agreement and compliance more difficult. Overall, policymaking has been more politicized and more intensely pluralistic with recessed industries; at the same time, policy implementation has been more complicated and, in some cases, unsuccessful. For a variety of related reasons, the need for government funds is usually greater in recessed than in developing industries.

Government-endorsed economic growth has had negative effects on some aspects of the quality of life even while making positive contributions to real wealth and shared affluence. Urban overcrowding is a major consequence of high economic growth about which not very much can be done beyond regional deconcentration of industry and service centers. Japan is a crowded nation with little space and ranks with South Korea, Indonesia, the Netherlands, and Belgium as one of the most heavily populated places on earth. Population movement to the cities and development of regional industrial centers in the 1950s and 1960s brought more people to already overcrowded areas. The population concentration is especially burdensome in large cities and their surrounding regions. The population density of Tokyo prefecture in 1990 was 14,064 persons per square mile, a figure dramatically higher than the national average of 860.

Population increases in the cities and suburbs had many consequences. Japan, which has one of the best urban rapid-transit systems in the world, made many improvements in train and subway lines in the 1960s and 1970s. Yet the rapid urbanization that accompanied high economic growth meant no end to overcrowded trains. Commuting times for many people became longer as the suburbs grew. Statistics are inadequate indicators of the scale of this problem. People living as far as two hours from Tokyo must scramble for standing space on trains during the rush hour. Roads and highways are also enormously overcrowded, even though the government has spent a great deal on highway construction. The proportion of paved roads in Japan ranks substantially below that for other major industrialized countries — another indicator of the difficulty of keeping up with growth.

Japan's waste disposal systems are hard put to keep up with need. The lag in sewage disposal facilities compared with other industrialized countries has been especially severe. In 1973 only 31 percent of Japanese homes had flush toilets; about 90 percent in Britain, the United States, France, Sweden, and West Germany did. Only 42 percent of homes in Japan were connected to sewer lines in 1989; again, the figures for other industrial countries were substantially higher.[58] Conditions in Osaka, Tokyo, and other major cities are much better than the national average, but country comparisons are still important indicators of nationwide lags in public infrastructure formation. Finally, cities have little space for parks, and high growth reduced ratios of park land per capita. In 1989 there were only 2.1 square yards of park space per resident in Tokyo, compared to 31 in Bonn, 25 in London, and 20 in Chicago.[59]

Deficiencies in public infrastructure were matched by a growing water and air pollution problem in the late 1960s. With most of the population and all of the industrialized centers concentrated on only 20 percent of the land, Japan had the highest concentration of industrial output and energy use per kilometer in the industrialized world (Table 9.7). The output figures were substantially greater than those for Europe, which is also crowded, and were very much higher than those for the more sparsely populated United States.

The painful consequences of overcrowding in urban and industrial districts were flagrant by the late 1960s and early 1970s, when high growth brought more factories, cars, and homes to the most heavily populated areas. The polluting effects of industrial growth even spread to remote areas. As trees died and birds disappeared from the cities and as people suffered from air, water, noise, and even "sunshine" pollution — the shutting off of direct sunlight by the construction of high-rise apartment buildings — several thousand citizens' movements sprang up around the country, organized by people opposed to pollution and regional growth.

One of the immutables of the Japanese physical setting is the shortage of usable land and space. The land-population ratio is reflected very directly in the pollution problems. It is also at the root of severe overcrowding and astronomical land prices. Land speculation has made the costs of land even higher. Neither of these problems was new to Japan before economic takeoff after the war, but they became much more acute, even though houses grew in size over time.

In 1963 the average dwelling had just under four rooms and a total area of 41 square yards (roughly 19 by 19 feet). Twenty-five years later there had been a 40 percent increase in the size of homes. Construction of slightly larger homes in city suburbs and rural areas plus shrinkage of family size resulted in an even greater increase in space per person. Whereas each person had a little more than 9 square yards of space in 1963, they had 19 square yards by 1988.[60] While this growth was salutary, Japan was still an extremely crowded place by comparative standards, and population pressure on housing remains a constant problem.

Table 9.7. Industrial Concentration per Square Kilometer

	Industrial GNP (in millions of U.S. dollars)	Output (in millions of U.S. dollars)	Energy Consumption (thousand TEP)	Number of Cars
Japan	2.33	0.75	1.59	117
United States	0.12	0.03	0.14	10
United Kingdom	0.40	0.10	0.39	28
France	0.34	—	0.18	18

Source: Data from the Organization for Economic Cooperation and Development.
Note: TEP = thermal energy units.

In most years in the 1970s and the 1980s, land price inflation exceeded general inflation trends. In addition, in comparative terms, both land and housing prices were and remain extremely high in Japan. In 1979 one square meter (1.2 square yards) of residential land in Tokyo cost $43,000 on the average, roughly the cost of a typical 1,500-square-foot lot in an expensive suburb in many cities in the United States in the same year. Even in remote areas like southern Kyushu, a square meter of land cost roughly $15,000. Meanwhile, in the late 1980s average new home prices were 5.6–7 times average household income; in Tokyo, 8.7 times. In comparison, they were 3.4 times household income in the United States; 4.4 times household income in Britain; and 4.6 times household income in the former West Germany. Many married couples were unable to purchase homes until their mid-forties, if then.[61]

Because of the chronic shortage and high cost of land for homes, demand for public housing has remained high despite substantial national and local expenditures on housing over the years. Applications for housing units in public projects have ranged as high as eighty-five requests for one vacancy in Tokyo in some years.[62] Enormous improvements have been made in housing, especially outside large cities. Housing nevertheless still joins other public and private infrastructure investments as a major continuing problem for the government, as well as being an example of the largely uncontrollable effects of economic growth.

Beginning in 1972, decentralization was also a public policy to lessen the pressure of population growth in large cities. More recently, plans for moving Japan's capital to a rural district have been discussed for the same reason. Although industry in peripheral regions has actually grown, building plants in rural areas has done little to alleviate existing population concentrations in developed parts of the country. Population pressure is still great as the result of the heavy concentration of people relative to the land.

Economic Welfare and Party Clientelism

Most political economy research on Japan has emphasized and provided explanations for the phenomenal postwar growth. But not all industries have been successful at all times, and economic welfare policies — specifically, support for small firms or areas where recessed industries were concentrated — have often resulted in higher levels of government expenditure than growth supports. Several major industries, including shipbuilding, iron and steel, petrochemicals, and aluminum, were structurally depressed in the 1970s and sometimes later because of the effects of oil price increases on production costs and demand. Competition from newly industrializing countries, including South Korea and Taiwan, also diminished demand for some Japanese products.

Contrary to folklore about Japan's economic prowess, some industries were in trouble for long periods of time. One or another segment of the textile industry has been depressed virtually since the war because cycles of innovation have undermined competitiveness in different segments at different times. The shipping and coal industries have likewise been in difficulties much of the time.[63] As I discussed above, enormous government loans and other incentives were provided to the coal industry in ultimately unsuccessful efforts to make domestic coal competitive with foreign oil.[64] Initially, government policies helped shipping recover after heavy wartime losses; but from the 1970s on, shipping was usually inefficient and high-cost, hence uncompetitive. Government supports thereafter were a response to political pressures from owners and labor, as a well as clientelism on the part of the Transport Ministry and the desire to maintain a merchant fleet under the Japanese flag.[65] The textile industry received a lot of government attention, although far less money than coal or shipping.

Shipbuilding was helped by the early postwar shipping programs, and Japan was a world leader for two decades due to strong domestic and foreign demand. High quality and low production costs made Japanese-built ships competitive overseas. Not only did the government provide subsidies to shipowners and loans to support the export of ships but labor costs were low in those early years, and the costs of steel inputs were lower than for European and American competitors beginning in the late 1950s. Prewar and wartime experience had also given Japan substantial shipbuilding capacity and know-how.[66] But shipbuilding declined in the 1970s because of reduced world demand and competition from low-cost shipbuilders in South Korea and elsewhere. As a result, government shipbuilding policies in the 1970s and 1980s followed the model for a recessed industry more than a development model.[67] Business, labor, and Liberal Democratic politicians were active in seeking funds for the declining shipping and shipbuilding industries. The policies for shipping and shipbuilding indicate the general importance of recession measures in the political economy.

The government responded to industrial decline with an elaborate inventory of measures, including encouragement of capacity reduction (frequently involving government purchase of excess equipment), employee retraining, and programs for regional economic renewal. In other remedial programs the government encouraged reductions or transfers in the labor force, promoted antirecession cartels, and offered special recovery loans. Government antirecession measures sometimes affected as many as one in every five workers. Medium and small businesses, many of which were chronically weak financially, have also received substantial government support over the years.

The magnitude of attention given to weak and sick industries by postwar governments is shown statistically by the number of major recession policies and the amount of resources allocated to problems of weak industries. Tallying the number of MITI plans and programs dedicated to growth and recessed industries between 1955 and 1980 (using annual ministry reports) gives a total of 125 growth programs versus 108 recession policies (Table 9.8). If the purpose of another category, market interventions, was known in all instances, recession programs would probably slightly outnumber growth programs.

Table 9.9 shows that the actual amounts of FILP program funds used for small-business loans far exceeded lending to big business. Because quite a bit of the financial support given to small business has addressed economic woes, these data also indicate the degree to which industrial distress motivated policy. Taken together with the data in Table 9.8, these figures show policy concern for each area: farming and small and big business. The two sets of data provide evidence that the government has paid almost as much attention to recessed and less economically promising economic sectors as to encouragement of successful industries.

The ratios of government lending to production and the value added in specific growing versus recessed industries tells the same story as the data on policy types and related funding in Table 9.10. In successful industries like automobiles and consumer electronics, the ratio of government bank borrowing to all borrowing has remained low ever since the war. In addition, borrowing

Table 9.8. *Government Actions for Specific Industries, 1952–1982*

	Development Policies		Recession/Depression Policies		
	Development Frameworks	Rationalization Cartels	Recession Frameworks	Recession Cartels	Market Intervention
Infrastructure Industries					
Electric Power	9				3
Gas	8				4
Nuclear Power	17				
Petroleum	18		4	1	6
Developing Industries					
Aircraft	4				
Automobiles/Parts	3			1	
Electronics	12				1
Machinery	15	1		1	
Developing/ Problem Industries					
Iron and Steel	10	2	3	6	12
Chemical Fertilizer	4		3	4	
Nonferrous Metals	2		4	1	3
Petrochemicals	4			1	2
Problem Industries					
Cement				2	1
Chemicals			3	4	
Coal	11		37		4
Pulp and Paper			2	1	1
Textiles	3	2	21	9	31
Total	120	5	77	31	68

Sources: Tsusansho Nempo (various years).

Notes: Frameworks are MITI and MITI Consultative Council plans/laws/programs, cartels are MITI sanctioned interfirm agreements, and interventions are normally MITI actions to set prices. Blanks = no policies.

In any given year 80 percent of the cartels listed in Fair Trade Commission reports are in the categories of medium and small business and health and sanitation — which are also small businesses (Kosei Torihiki Iinkai *Nempo Hokoku* [Tokyo, various years]).

Table 9.9. *Government Support for Farmers, Small Businesses, and Large Businesses* (in millions of U.S. dollars)

	Farmers				Small Businesses			Large Businesses
	Programs	Price Supports	Loans	Total	Programs	Loans	Total	Total Government Loans
1955	.13	.02	.07	.22	.01	.07	.08	.13
1960	.24	.09	.12	.45	.01	.22	.28	.23
1965	.61	.36	.29	1.50	.03	.57	.59	.44
1970	.53	.52	.41	2.38	.14	1.53	1.67	.77
1975	1.43	3.28	1.28	5.79	.35	4.03	5.30	.93
1980	3.96	4.34	2.98	12.01	.82	11.45	12.27	2.41
1985	3.68	2.90	3.73	10.30	.88	15.75	16.63	2.52
1990	6.06	2.72	6.04	14.77	1.33	29.90	31.26	3.25

Sources: Prime Minister's Office, Statistics Department, *Japan Statistical Yearbook* (Tokyo, various years); Takafusa Nakamura, *The Postwar Japanese Economy: Its Development and Infrastructure* (Tokyo: University of Tokyo Press, 1981), p. 137.

Notes: Figures for loans are net new loans from government financial organs affiliated with the Fiscal Investment and Loan Program. "Programs" refers to budget allocations.

from the Japan Development Bank usually declined when gross output and added value were increasing, which implies that firms needed less from government banks as they became more successful. (Occasionally even successful industries borrowed from the Japan Development Bank, but this was usually a reflection of decisions to increase capacity rather than the result of problems.) But in industries like iron and steel and nonferrous metals, dependence on Japan Development Bank loans has increased in times of recession. Both industries actually received more assistance relative to output or value added when they were in decline than in earlier high-growth periods.

Japan is as much an economic welfare state as a developmental state. Special programs for sustaining employment in industries affected by (1) oil price "shocks," (2) cyclical downturns, (3) declines in export sales caused in part by the high yen, and (4) removal of protective tariffs tell a similar story of concern for weakened economic sectors. Rather than addressing unemployment by providing welfare for the unemployed, the Japanese approach has been to keep people in problem sectors of the economy at work. It is possible that Confucian values are the basis for this policy. As Derk Bodde has noted, under Confucianism "the welfare of the social organism as a whole depends on

Table 9.10. Japan Development Bank Lending Compared with Industry Success, 1960–1985

	JDB Loans	% Industry Borrowing	JDB Loans: Output	JDB Loans: Value Added
Industries Successful in the 1970s				
Transport Equipment				
1960	3	1	.8	1.5
1965	15	2	5.8	16.6
1970	43	2	5.8	17.7
1975	82	2	5.6	19.0
1980	82	2	3.3	12.3
1985	48	1	1.3	4.9
Electrical Equipment				
1960	1	0	.6	1.5
1965	5	1	1.9	5.1
1970	17	2	2.3	5.8
1975	20	1	1.8	4.7
1980	31	1	1.4	3.5
1985	106	2	2.6	7.3
Industries Depressed in the 1970s				
Iron and Steel				
1960	10	2	5.8	24.8
1965	12	1	4.6	19.4
1970	25	1	3.8	14.6
1975	111	3	9.8	44.1
1980	251	6	14.0	47.8
1985	306	5	17.2	58.9
Nonferrous Metals				
1960	1	0	1.1	4.4
1965	4	1	3.4	16.5
1970	22	4	7.2	33.9
1975	84	6	21.4	96.3
1980	63	3	7.7	32.3
1985	88	3	13.8	56.2

Source: Prime Minister's Office, *Japan Statistical Yearbook* (Tokyo, various years).

Notes: JDB (Japan Development Bank) loans are stated in billions of yen. "% Industry Borrowing" is the share of all outstanding loans accounted for by JDB loans. "JDB Loans:Output" is the amount of JDB loans in millions of yen needed to generate one billion yen of output. "JDB Loans:Value Added" is the amount of JDB loans in millions of yen needed to generate one billion yen of value added. (Value added is the difference between the costs of inputs [including labor] and the value of production.)

Transport equipment includes automobiles, and electrical equipment includes computers and consumer electronics.

I lack detailed loan data at the industry level before 1960, hence could not provide analyses for some years when Japan Development Bank lending was directly intended to promote growth in iron and steel.

harmonious cooperation among all of its units. . . . Society should be like a magnified family, the members of which, though differing in their status and functions, all work in harmony for the common good." All sectors of society thus have an economic role, and the state is obligated to think in holistic terms about their economic health and general security.[68]

The economic welfare state is the outcome of political processes that are competitive and pluralistic. It is not the product of corporatist interactions involving only elites from big business and the bureaucracy. Japan under Liberal Democratic rule was also a "party clientelistic" state. Programs targeted at weak sectors were often motivated by a political concern for aiding conservative party supporters. In some cases, clientelism superseded economic welfare as a policy motivation; drawing a line between the two kinds of motivations would certainly be unrealistic in many cases. Interest groups, individual Dietmembers, and LDP zoku endlessly sought help from the government on behalf of traditional LDP clients, including small-business owners and farmers (see Table 9.9). Representatives of local governments of areas where recessed industries were located also asked for help. Funding of public works projects, which was a common response to both local economic problems and cyclical downturns, also favored another LDP client, the construction industry. By the early 1980s the number of workers employed in the construction industry was higher than the number in agriculture. Often, however, construction workers were part-time farmers. The development of public works infrastructure in rural areas thus served two LDP constituencies simultaneously.[69] Much of the domestic policy agenda was affected by the needs of political clients. A conservative view that keeping people employed is an appropriate social welfare strategy probably motivates the same kind of policy preferences. But normative concerns are hard to separate from purely political motivations in this case.

Farmers were another major LDP client who did well compared with big business (see Table 9.9). If support for farm programs is added to the programs and loans provided to medium and small businesses, the enormous role of the state as a combined economic welfare and party clientelistic state becomes clear. (Heads of small-business interest groups are quick to point out, however, that farmers have received far more subsidies, and small businesses are given more loans, which they have to repay.) Outlays to clients or declining sectors have always exceeded amounts directly provided for industrial growth, with ratios between the two varying from 2:1 in the 1950s to as high as 12:1 later. The popular image of Japan as a developmental state obviously needs qualification, and recent research has in fact modified earlier images drawn without detailed attention to the clientelistic and economic-welfare-oriented aspects of the political economy.[70]

Table 9.11. *Government Support for Large-Scale and Small-Scale Industry,*
1955–1988

Year	FILP Loans to Industry (%)	Tax Losses from Incentives (%)	Import Quotas	Import Tariffs (%)	Cartels Small Business	Other
1955	20.2				89	14
1956	21.4					
1957	15.7					
1958	13.4				273	177
1959	10.7					
1960	12.7					
1961	10.6					
1962	8.5		466			
1963	8.9		197	7.3	556	354
1964	7.8		136	7.7		
1965	6.6		122	7.3		
1966	6.6		126	7.1		
1967	5.9	7.4	121	7.1	572	431
1968	5.7	6.9	118	6.9		
1969	5.4	7.0	90	6.6		
1970	4.7	7.4	33	6.3		
1971	3.5	7.9	32	5.0	439	406
1972	3.0	9.0	31	2.7	604	372
1973	3.0	6.4	30	2.9	607	372
1974	2.8	5.4	27	3.3	591	317
1975	2.4	5.0		3.3	511	277
1976	2.9	5.1		4.1	395	259
1977	2.6	3.9		3.1	279	249
1978	2.6	2.6		3.5	290	245
1979	2.6	3.4	22	2.5	274	232
1980	3.0	2.2		2.5	267	224
1981	3.0	1.9		2.5		
1982	3.0	1.8		2.7		
1983	3.0	2.7		2.5		
1984	3.0			2.6		
1985	3.0			2.7		
1986	3.0			3.3		

Table 9.11. Continued

Year	FILP Loans to Industry (%)	Tax Losses from Incentives (%)	Import Quotas	Import Tariffs (%)	Cartels Small Business	Other
1987	2.0			3.4		
1988	2.0			3.4		

Sources and Notes: FILP loan percentages are the share of loans to industry (industry *and* technology in the 1980s) in total FILP loans. The data are from Hajime Nakamura, *The Postwar Japanese Economy* (Tokyo: University of Tokyo Press, 1983), p. 137; Prime Minister's Office, Statistics Bureau, *Japan Statistical Yearbook* (various years); Japan Economic Institute *Report* series, various numbers. The tax losses are percentages of losses from total corporate taxes due to special tax exemptions for industrial development. The data are from unpublished Ministry of Finance data. The import quotas are the number of item categories for which there are import restrictions. The data are unpublished MITI figures. The tariff data are percentages of the total import value represented by duties and are from unpublished Ministry of Finance figures and Keizai Koho Center, *Japan: An International Comparison* (various years). Cartel information is raw numbers from Kosei Torihiki Iinkai, *Kosei Torihiki Nempo Hokoku*, various years. Before 1971 figures are averages for 1953–55, 1956–60, 1961–65, and 1966–70, respectively. Blanks mean that there was either no information or the government actions did not exist.

Developmental state theory was increasingly out-of-date by the 1970s as Japan began to formally terminate or shrink many of its earlier industrial programs. Foreign pressure hastened the process of dismantling industrial policy supports. Indicative economic planning has continued, although the rhetoric of plans from the mid-1960s on has increasingly stressed economic stability and quality of life. Growth rates in the 1970s and 1980s were considerably lower than those of the 1960s, but the economy has still prospered in most years. Support for industrial growth, structural change, and technology induction through policy frameworks and government incentives has declined over time as the economy has grown and other priorities emerged. Many of the industrial supports characteristic of the 1950s and 1960s have dwindled in importance.

As Table 9.11 indicates, FILP lending to big business (including funding for the use and development of industrial technology) has declined substantially and currently totals only about one-tenth of its share of lending in the 1950s. The offering of tax incentives for industrial development has taken a similar downward trajectory. So have cartel agreements between firms, although cartels are still a preferred instrument of market coordination during downturns in the economy especially in medium and small enterprises. At present, the government continues to support research projects designed to ensure the development of Japan as a high-tech, high-value-added twenty-first-century economic power. Otherwise, with only a few exceptions, industrial policy to encourage new industry development is pretty much a thing of the past.

Timetables for changing industrial policy have at times been influenced by foreign pressure in response to the growth of Japan's exports to other countries. This is especially true of criticisms of the protection of domestic markets. The growth of Japan's role in world trade matches the growth of the domestic economy. In 1958 exports totaled a nominal $2.8 billion. By 1975 the total was $55 billion, in 1980 it was $127 billion, and by 1990 it was a huge $287 billion. Measured in nominal currency values, exports quadrupled in the 1970s and doubled once again in the 1980s.

Even controlling for changes in currency values, we find that the share of total world trade, figured in terms of exports, increased from around 3 percent in 1960 to 12 percent in 1990. Foreign sales boomed even in the 1970s, when inflation in petroleum prices changed the structure of world commerce and depressed markets in many countries. In addition to other factors, success in trade was predicated on free and expanding world commerce. Increased external demand for specific Japanese products was also important. Interestingly, the high growth did not depend on exports in any simple sense. Early postwar economic growth reflected mainly domestic factors, although exports were the motor driving later economic growth, specifically in the 1970s and in part of the 1980s.[71] Although foreign trade flourished in the 1970s, a different product mix reflected changes in foreign markets and Japanese competitiveness. Automobiles and consumer electronics became more prominent while shipbuilding and iron and steel declined in importance.

Expanded trade permitted Japan to import the raw materials necessary to propel high growth, satisfy new food preferences among the population, and pay the huge oil bills of the 1970s. The long-term growth of foreign trade was in some senses, however, a mixed blessing. As early as the 1960s success in foreign markets led to requests to open the protected domestic market to manufactured goods. Even though huge internal demand for imported energy and industrial raw materials meant an adverse trade balance in some years, success in export markets still produced adverse reactions abroad. Foreign governments, including the U.S. administration, deplored the high tariffs and numerous import quotas in the 1960s. The Japanese government responded to requests by lowering tariffs, eliminating import quotas (see Table 9.11), and liberalizing restrictions on foreign investments in Japanese industries. By the mid-1970s only a handful of products were still protected by import quotas, and, as in other industrial countries, most of these were farm goods. By 1980 average tariffs were lower in Japan than in the United States and the European Community. High tariffs for a few nonagricultural products do exist, concealed within the overall averages. It is also important to appreciate that usually tariffs and barriers to foreign investment are reduced only after industries are competitive.[72] Still, in at least formal terms, the Japanese economy is open to the world in most product areas.

Conclusion

The Japanese economy grew dramatically between the 1950s and the present. During the first two decades, the government wrote industrial policies that developed infrastructure, achieved production and productivity gains in some industries, and promoted market concentration. More recently, government aid was provided to develop high technology by means of high-visibility cooperative research projects. Indicative economic plans calling for growth of the total economy have also been formulated. Because of the coincidence of government planning and economic success, Japan became known abroad as a successful example of government-led growth. But evaluations of the role of the developmental state depend on scholarly biases and methodology. Arriving at a balanced understanding of government policy impact is difficult in the face of the divergences. By focusing on the implementation and impact of government policies (rather than taking the developmental state approach of imagining effects without examining consequences), some evaluations of the postwar political economy can be made with confidence.

1. Government lending and some other instruments of development plans for key industries helped facilitate economic efficiency and growth in iron and steel and to a lesser degree in the auto parts and computer industries. Government investments in other successful industries were too small relative to private bank funding to have the indicative effects often attributed to them. Government bank lending likely played a fairly limited role after the 1950s, except in the shipping, coal, and electric power industries, where government loans were necessary because the amount of needed capital was large or because the industries were permanently depressed.

2. Protection may have helped some industries, but its general impact is unclear. For example, protection may have encouraged the growth of the domestic automobile industry in the 1960s, but the absence of foreign competition (due to protection) may have delayed increases in productivity and improvements in quality for at least a decade.

3. Government priorities often favored declining or problem industries with the result that considerable government funds were misallocated from an economic point of view, even though they served social and political imperatives.[73] When the extensive supports given to recessed industries, medium and small industries, and farmers are considered, Japan appears to be as much an economic welfare and party clientelist state as a developmental state.

4. The decisions of business firms reflected many concerns, and government policy was only one of them — a sometimes large, sometimes small part of the environment. Economic conditions were very important. They affected bankers' assessments of risk, which in turn determined the availability of funds for investment and growth in different industries at different times. The very large capital needs of some industries also affected firm strategies. Business cycles were another factor affecting how firms responded to government efforts to influence economic behavior.

5. Government support for economic growth was often welcome in expanding industries. In contrast, government requests to weak or recessed firms to reduce capacity or to merge with other firms were less welcome. There were unintended policy consequences reflecting the subvention, avoidance, and manipulation of government programs by private firms.

6. Economic and industrial performance showed the influence of political, social, and economic factors that were not exclusively under the direct control of the government: political stability, aggressive firm competition, high national savings and investment rates, the permanent employment system, stable labor relations, improved process technologies (such as Toyota's famed "just in time" inventory management), high levels of literacy and basic training in mathematics and science, modern communications systems, and consumer markets.[74]

7. The government shared vast amounts of information with industry while cheering on growth and provided a stable and supportive environment for business expansion and improvement. Businesses could invest without undue fear of nationalization or other major changes in the political environment. The perception in many firms that the government would stand behind specific industries may have led some firms to make daring investments.

8. The government's investments in infrastructure were enormous and may have constituted its single most important contribution to growth from the 1960s forward. Its development of industrial zones adjacent to deep water ports, for example, helped reduce the price of some raw materials to as little

as one-half the price for the same commodities shipped via the Great Lakes and private rail in the United States.[75]

9. The government's frequent policy adjustments were a plausible strength. Plans were reviewed before their terminal dates and new plans were promulgated as growth outpaced original targets, or other planning parameters changed. Pragmatic, market-oriented behavior was seen as an advantage of Japanese government planning regimes for this reason.[76]

Together, these conditions created an opportunity structure within which different factor combinations produced growth. The largely horizontal nature of government-business interactions can also be seen at several junctures. Multiple public and private rationales were invoked in economic policy design, reflecting a pluralistic pattern of policymaking participation, interest, and motivation. A horizontal pattern of public-private interaction is also apparent in the negotiational style of industry-ministry relations. The frequent deviation of individual firms from government policies had the same implication. A fundamental horizontalism can be seen very clearly where policy conformed to an economic welfare or clientelist state paradigm.

IO

Japan as a Bargained Distributive Democracy

Political power in Japan is fragmented and pluralistic. The parties are horizontally fragmented and partially decentralized. Interest intermediation has itself been mainly pluralistic. The traditionally assertive administrative bureaucracy has often been divided, which has kept it from making policy as a monolith. Both grass-roots and national interests have influenced the behavior of rank-and-file members of parliamentary parties and, through them, government elites and ministry officials. Political leaders and bureaucratic officials have been constrained by the multiple power centers and upward political pressures. The long-dominant Liberal Democratic Party accommodated the concerns of the opposition in the Diet on roughly one in three legislative issues. Overall, politics conforms better to the horizontal metaphor than to the vertical one.

The political processes demonstrate tendencies that I have characterized as opposing dynamics. A centrifugal tendency toward intense competition, conflict, and even fragmentation within existing coalitions and organizations is matched by a centripetal tendency toward cooperation, coordination, and integration. Individual political actors in Japan tend to be aggressively competitive whenever their interests are affected. What is unusual about Japanese politics has been the extent to which intense conflict immobilizes political processes. This has occurred within the LDP, between parties in the Diet, and even between interest groups and the LDP or the ministries. Sometimes LDP politicians publicly call interest group spokesmen "war criminals" or an interest group vows to "overthrow" the prime minister and cabinet, both of which indicate high levels of intergroup tension. Conflict was so intense on certain occasions that existing coalitional structures were threatened with collapse. At times new intraparty groups were formed to challenge existing groups, and the ruling party itself came close to splitting. In 1993 the conflict-fragmentation dynamic was once again dominant, and party collapse became real.

Although highly competitive, politics has often been integrated and bounded by patterned, sometimes even semi-institutionalized, inter-actor consultative and coalitional relationships. Efforts have been made to resolve differences and, where relevant, promote solidarity through a variety of informal face-to-face encounters and strategies that rely on small-group processes. Some of these efforts eventually led to development of procedures to control and channel conflict and to the formation of groups, making political life more predictable. The Government-LDP Consultative Council, the enormous LDP policy apparatus, ministry consultative councils, and interparty consultative councils for handling controversial bills in the Diet—all are examples of integrative organizing efforts to reduce or handle political conflict and uncertainty. Candidates for office have also mobilized voters using semipermanent personal electoral organizations; politicians and bureaucrats have formed consultative groups at many stages of policy processes; and party politicians have formed semi-institutionalized factions and policy groups and joined policy communities.

Informal consultation between politicians and local group and community representatives has been frequent. Interparty accommodation and cooperation within the Diet has been organized and orchestrated by the directors of Diet steering committees and at informal gatherings of Diet strategy committee heads or party secretaries general. Intra-LDP accommodation has been facilitated by elaborate formal policymaking machinery, by meetings of faction secretaries general, and by coordinating groups, such as party executive committees. Similar institutions exist in other parties, although small parties sometimes have less elaborate organizations. Most parties of the traditional opposition, because of their smaller size and limited constituencies, have tended to be less institutionalized. Abhorrent of uncertainty, politicians have frequently participated in, or fostered, coalitional arrangements and consultative contacts that promote order in political relationships.

The dual tendencies toward conflict and fragmentation and toward cooperation and integration are "dynamic" because these aspects of political process are characterized by intense activity and changing relationships at some times and relative stability at other times. Because the twin dynamics take us beyond structure, they afford a way to succinctly characterize heretofore puzzling and contradictory aspects of Japanese political style.

Political Elements and the Twin Dynamics

Political parties in all countries have formal organizations, certain properties as coalitions, and informal structures. In Japan informal intraparty structures are usually more important than formal organization. The two largest parties, the Liberal Democratic Party and the Social Democratic Party of Japan, were heavily factionalized until recently (though with some important differences), and factional competition affected both elite recruitment and policymaking. Factions are semi-institutionalized groups that perform important order-invoking, uncertainty-reduction functions for their members. Even now, both parties have numerous internal study groups, which are factions of a sort. There have also been many party policy groups, especially in the LDP during its long stay in power.

Conflict between factions and policy groups in the major parties was often so intense that it immobilized internal political processes. Conflict between informal factions, policy groups, and zoku frequently weakened the LDP's ability to take a unified stand on policy issues or parliamentary and election strategies. In 1987 intra-LDP policy differences stalled tax reform, and confrontations between intraparty policy groups delayed until 1972 the opening of diplomatic relations between Japan and the People's Republic of China. Factional feuds in the LDP also made it possible in 1980 and 1993 for the opposition parties to pass a nonconfidence motion in the Diet. Differences among SDPJ members over Japan National Railway reform weakened opposition influence on that issue.

Political parties are excellent examples of the twin dynamics of fragmentation and integration. The integrative dynamic was evident in the LDP's development of an elaborate internal organizational structure and procedures for resolving conflicts within the party. A steady flow of demands from the large number of interest groups aligned with the LDP and factional competition over high-level appointments during the party's stay in power encouraged the establishment of elaborate intraparty policymaking and recruitment norms. There were proper places and procedures for making party policies and designating party leaders. The resulting structures and procedures typically became institutionalized over time. The institutionalization of political recruitment and policymaking in the dominant LDP provided a considerable degree of internal party stability, which in turn potentially enhanced the ability of the LDP to dominate government. The long-standing opposition parties also had policymaking organs, though less developed ones; the same is true of the new parties today.

The elaborate internal policy arrangements of the LDP and the related decentralization of policy processes were virtually unique among political parties in industrialized nations. The level of organizational complexity in the LDP is not found in American parties, and in Japan there was more opportunity for parliamentary rank-and-file participation than in major European parties with the exception of the Italian Christian Democratic Party. The decentralization of the LDP provided politicians with an opportunity to articulate grass-roots interests made strategically important by the decentralized electoral system. I call the parties decentralized because there is a great deal of internal conflict and competition and an important flow of communications and demands from the party's rank-and-file members of parliament to the party's leadership. Electoral campaigns are also decentralized, all the way down to the level of interactions with ordinary voters. Configurations of power in the LDP and SDPJ differ from European examples as a result of LDP adaptation to its environment, plus the Japanese tendency to build elaborate organizations to control competition and conflict.

The two largest political parties have been more fragmented than their counterparts in major western European parliamentary systems. All political parties have internal groups and internal dissent. The largest parties in Europe, however, are more unified and centralized than those in Japan; only the former Christian Democratic Party of Italy displayed a crisis dynamic comparable to that of the LDP.[1] Among major parties in large industrialized democratic countries, only the factionalized parties of Italy and the stratarchical party organizations of Germany manifest internal fragmentation comparable to that in the LDP and the SDPJ.

Interest group politics during the era of LDP hegemony were generally more pluralistic than corporatist. There were multiple political actors and points of contention in most policy debates, and there was conflict in even the supposedly most privileged of political relationships: those among the ruling party, big business, and the bureaucratic ministries. Conflictual patterns involving coalitions of opposing groups, parties, and ministries could be seen in major debates over farm, tax, small-business, and industrial policies in the 1980s, as well as earlier in debates over revision of the antimonopoly law, formation and reform of the pension system, a proposed law for promotion of industries, basic laws for small business and farmers, rescue of the coal industry, and many other legislative proposals.

The long-term big-business allies of the LDP were frequently strong critics of the ruling party, especially during periods of party crisis. There were also disagreements within the business sector. Big-business and small-business interest groups took different positions on major political issues. Big-business groups were themselves divided over policies in some cases, reflecting intraindustry variations and other differences. Only a handful of policy processes demonstrated corporatist tendencies; a few displayed a mixture of corporatist integration and pluralistic intermediation.

Policy choices involving interests were usually decided on the basis of negotiations within and between coalitions of varying combinations of interest groups, individual firms, advisory councils, ministries, and political parties. Some policy decisions involved mainly private interest groups, the traditional paradigm for pluralism. Other examples fit the concept of state pluralism. In these cases, a state ministry was an active coalition participant, sometimes in opposition to a coalition including another government office. Variable interest-group alignments in policy processes in the 1980s likewise attest to the importance of pluralism. Nor was the pluralism observed in postwar policymaking unique or new. Researchers have documented similar examples as far back as mid-nineteenth century.

Major debates, like that over tax reform in 1987–88, demonstrated the ebb and flow of the twin dynamics of conflict-fragmentation and coordination-integration. Unable to persuade the interest group constituency and the party rank-and-file to support the proposed reform in 1987, the LDP backtracked and presented a new legislative proposal in 1988. After extensive consultation with both the interest groups and the rank-and-file and after changes in the bills, there was a short debate in the late autumn of 1988; then tax reform passed the Diet. If the conflict-fragmentation dynamic was evident in policy processes concerned with private interests, integrational impetus was evident in the presence of such practices as amending Diet bills and such institutions as policy communities, consultative councils, ad hoc cabinet-level and subcabinet-level task forces, and consultative groups in the Diet.

Political processes involving government ministries reflected horizontal pluralism and conflict to a marked degree. There were many issues that engaged the concerns of more than one ministry, so interministry conflicts were common, as were jurisdictional rivalries. Differences over interests or ideology were also evident. The gap between the Finance Ministry with its concern over the availability of revenue and other ministries with their desire to spend money is one example. Individual ministries were also sometimes internally divided, which further limited their influence.

Interministerial jurisdictional and programmatic jealousies and struggles were made more intense by employment practices: ministries recruit staff who spend most of their careers within the same ministry. As a result, ministry staffs are insular in outlook and have strong in-group identifications, which reflect Japanese cultural "groupism" as well as these recruitment patterns. Where ministerial ideologies and interests clash, policy agreement is delayed or derailed. Policy disagreements within ministries have similar effects. Conflicts both within and between ministries make the ministries less decisive and forceful than they might otherwise be.

Jurisdictional jealousies and competing views about policy have kept ministries from acting monolithically in many situations. Political imperatives and the Japanese propensity to consult widely have led ministries to seek allies in political parties and interest groups. Alliances formed in such circumstances have resulted in pressure on the ministries to accommodate group or party interests. Both of these conditions have limited ministry autonomy. These constraints on ministry autonomy notwithstanding, there were still instances of coercion in some government operations, as when ministries used administrative guidance to control particular firms or groups. The weights and limits of bureaucratic power depend on the circumstances.[2]

Even though ministries were sometimes coercive, I did not find widespread evidence of a soft-authoritarian style of governance. Japanese ministries behave like their counterparts in other parliamentary systems. They have ideologies, interests, ties to clients, concerns for survival, and long-lasting feuds with other ministries. They can be assertive and autocratic in pursuit of their own views and goals. But there are too many examples of ministry negotiations and alliances with political actors outside the bureaucracy and too many examples of conflict between ministries and other actors for soft authoritarianism to apply to Japanese politics. Coercion is not unheard of, but negotiated cooperation is much more common. In spite of a seemingly intimidating array of jurisdictional responsibilities and an aura of strong authority, the shape of ministerial power fits a horizontal metaphor of governance.[3]

The government (prime minister and cabinet) are empowered by the constitution to submit bills to the Diet, exercise control and supervision over the administrative bureaucracy, manage foreign relations, and conclude treaties. It must also prepare the budget, enact cabinet orders, and declare general amnesty. Single-party rule after 1955 potentially enhanced the influence of the political elite to dominate political processes even further. But in reality, the government was often constrained by a wide array of partially decentralized political forces. Its dependence on a coalition of factions in the ruling party was a major source of political constraint during the period of LDP dominance. Rank-and-file elements of the LDP influenced party and government decisionmakers and forced them to accede to the demands of special interests on many occasions. Organized in zoku, for example, they and sympathetic members of the party elite succeeded for many years in authorizing new subsidies for farmers, even though farm prices were already way above world market prices. Interest group and LDP Dietmember coalitions also countered efforts to liberalize farm imports, promoted the interests of small-business owners, former landlords, and repatriates, and influenced party decisionmaking on many other issues.[4]

The LDP's upward flow of influence extended to the bureaucratic ministries. The conservative party and coalitions of party members and interest groups often overcame ministerial inertia or resistance. Party politicians and party organs provided independent policy pressures, such as when the LDP Special Committee on Okinawa Problems pushed a recalcitrant bureaucracy to speedily resolve Okinawa reversion issues.[5] Where issues were highly politicized and the LDP was supported by powerful outside allies, the LDP and its internal groups were a forceful component in policymaking. Even though multiple factors, including recruitment of former bureaucrats to high LDP positions, implied great ministry influence, the party was supreme in many instances.

Rank-and-file members of the LDP's parliamentary caucus can exert influence on policy decisions. In contrast, rank-and-file members of parliamentary parties in several European countries play only a limited role in interest articulation. There, interest groups tend to work directly with bureaucrats on many matters or to press party elites on broad issues that are heavily politicized. Critical interactions take place at higher levels, and politics is more centralized than in Japan. Only the former West Germany and Italy have appeared to be as decentralized as Japan in this aspect of political relationships.[6] In the LDP, factionalism and policy group pluralism opened the party to upward influences. The decentralization of electoral mobilization, especially where candidates ran their own campaigns, also widened the opportunities for rank-and-file influence. The development of an enormous party policymaking apparatus, the importance of consultational norms, and the decentralization and parochialism inherent in electoral mobilization were all important to the differences between the LDP and parties in other countries.

Many accounts of Japanese politics have characterized the Diet as a ratifying body that rubber-stamped legislation prepared by the bureaucracy and accepted by the leaders and internal organs of the LDP in 1955–93. It is true that most legislation is drafted by the bureaucratic ministries and submitted to the Diet by the cabinet. Contrary to Japanese political folklore, however, ministry influence at the drafting stage is not exclusive to Japan nor even necessarily reflective of ministry dominance. A similar tendency can be seen in other parliamentary systems. As was shown in Chapter 6, in the British House of Commons 97 percent of the bills passed recently originated in the government, a figure higher than that for the Diet. Until now, most judgments of the performance of the Diet were based on comparisons with the U.S. Congress or an idealized legislature, rather than on comparisons with systems similar to the Japanese one. They were misleading for this reason.

The Diet has amended or rejected bills much more often than is implied in many studies of Japanese politics. I showed that only 60 percent of the government bills submitted to the Diet between 1950 and 1990 were passed without some kind of modification, withdrawal, or delay; 15 percent of the bills considered by the Diet were amended in committee; and 23 percent were postponed or withdrawn in response to opposition party pressures — an exercise of a de facto veto.[7] When the actual nature of Diet actions is examined, rather than simply the origin of legislative bills, the Diet appears to have been a fairly activist legislature.

The processing of legislative bills in the Diet during the period of LDP hegemony reflected the operation of both conflict-fragmentation and coordination-integration dynamics. Legislative impasses, opposition boycotts, and even physical violence in the 1950s and 1960s serve as evidence for legislative conflict. Conflicts were also resolved — via bill amendments, postponements, and withdrawals — more often than not as part of a quid pro quo between the LDP and the opposition. The behavior of the LDP in these instances reflected a desire to pass other legislation in exchange for removal or modification of bills that the opposition parties did not want to pass. Its ability to move bills through the Diet was hostage to the rule of the Diet steering committees requiring interparty consensus on legislative schedules. In other instances, the LDP wanted to restore or maintain order in the Diet by reaching an accommodation with the opposition, thereby also enhancing its own legitimacy and credibility.

Such Diet actions were orchestrated by the secretary general of the LDP working with the Diet Policy Committee of the party or its chair and counterparts in the other political parties. Often the most significant actions were taken in consultative encounters outside the formal processes of the Diet. In contrast, bill amendments in Britain normally reflect intervention by government ministers.[8] The same situation prevails in France. Politics is more decentralized in Japan, and the parliament is a more assertive body as a result. From what I can discern, Japan is more like Germany and the United States than either France or Britain in this regard, even though the Diet is nowhere as active as the U.S. Congress.

Bargained Distributive Democracy

Confirming the importance of a horizontal model of Japanese power is a major step toward negating vertical model interpretations. But I have still to address the views of those who feel that Japanese politics is inherently irresponsible. To do this requires further consideration of how Japan fits in different models of democratic systems.

Empirical research on contemporary industrialized democracies suggests two basic concepts of how a democratic political system works. One is the Westminster model of alternating two-party government. Parties compete in elections on the basis of overall programs. Party-led governments, once elected, instruct neutral bureaucracies to carry out their electoral mandates. Ministries are accountable to cabinets and prime ministers selected by the winning parties. Some parliaments are also granted direct powers of administrative oversight. Such a model could be called centralized programmatic democracy, given its focus on national redistributive issues — which involve something being taken away from one part of society (for example, well-to-do people) and given to another (poor people) — and the responsibility of parties to carry out electoral programs.

Japanese politics does not fit the centralized programmatic democracy model very well. There have been times when strong leadership or politicized issues have overshadowed decentralized influence, especially in the areas of foreign and security policy and, in the 1980s, administrative reform. More typically, some combination of individual politicians, parties, interest groups, ministries or ministry sections, and local interests has contributed to policy outcomes. A model of democratic government that takes these more complex relations into account could be called decentralized bargained democracy. In such a democracy, politics is a matrix of high-level, middle-level, and low-level decisions. There are many decision points and many channels through which popular concerns can be expressed and the government made accountable. Political actors bargain over matters of specific interest to policy communities or other interest groups at different decision points, rather than having a simple centralized confrontation between alternative programs. Allocations of political resources — laws, regulations, subsidies, and programs — look less like redistributional choices, in which one side loses and another wins, and more like distributive decisions, in which interests get favored treatment without this being seen as taking something away from other groups.

A decentralization of decision points results in mutual constraints on the behavior of individual actors. Decentralized decisions involve trade-offs and obligations that extend far beyond the present. Bargains are made by political actors who consider the implications of their actions for other actors with regard to past, present, and future issues. Rather than a simple, direct competition between aggregative party programs, there are complex bargaining patterns that result in a matrix of mutual obligations among decentralized political actors. The government is responsible to the electorate and its interest groups, but responsibility comes most often in fragmented, decentralized bargains and less often by way of programs.

A brief summary of decision points for policy choices in German politics illustrates the concept of decentralized bargaining.[9] In post–World War II West Germany, legislative powers have been centered in a unicameral elected parliament, the Bundestag. Even though the Bundestag has considerable power, its actions, not unlike those of Japanese government organs, are constrained. Proposed legislation has to be reviewed by an appointed upper house, the Bundesrat, whose members come from state governments. The political interests of subnational power centers thus have to be considered during the crafting of national legislation. Some leading politicians who occupy positions as heads of particular states also have input into national legislation.

The legislature and the bureaucracy are dependent on each other. Legislative bills are generally drafted by government ministries, which brings bureaucratic participants and interests into political processes. Further interpenetration of bureaucratic and legislative processes is encouraged by the presence of substantial numbers of civil servants in the Bundestag. Thirty-seven percent of Bundestag members were civil servants in 1990, and unlike in Japan, they were not retired officials but people temporarily detached from active official duty.

The parties represented in the Bundestag are well organized and have internal policymaking processes somewhat like those in Japanese parties. In addition, the Bundestag has a strong committee system, which is the domain of specialist members of parliament, who are in turn linked closely to external interest groups. The specialist parliamentarians, not unlike members of zoku in the LDP, frequently receive appointments as cabinet ministers in their areas of expertise.

The many other power centers and decision points reflect the decentralization of interests and influence characteristic of federal systems. The degree of decentralization in Germany compared with the British and French cases is remarkable. A similar decentralization can be outlined for Italian politics.[10]

Britain is very different from Germany and Japan. The British government is highly centralized.[11] The prime ministers choose cabinet ministers with less deference to the preferences of intraparty groups than in the Japanese case. Some scholars say that they can hire and fire whom they please. Because cabinet ministers do not have a party base of support as institutionalized and influential as the LDP factions, they tend to be beholden to the prime minister for their appointments. They are reluctant to differ with the prime minister, because dismissal would damage their careers.

British prime ministers have considerable influence over the government and over the performance of their party in Parliament. They are able to set the agenda of the cabinet through their influence over the cabinet secretariat, which reviews ministers' policy proposals before they are placed on the agenda. A prime minister can also set up cabinet committees, which he or she chairs, as another means of controlling policy choices and can influence the cabinet ministers through informal talks. The civil service, however much committed to political neutrality, is generally responsible to the prime minister, because the Home Civil Service is administered by the First Lord of the Treasury, who is closely associated with the prime minister.

The prime minister and his appointees normally control the parliamentary party. Prime ministers have the power to make and break the careers of MPs through their control over party patronage, which includes not only government appointments but also recommendations for peerages, knighthoods, honors, and decorations. Major legislative bills, called policy bills, are controlled by the prime minister as head of the party. The party whip, who reports to the prime minister, explains the prime minister's wishes and positions on policy matters in order to impose discipline on parliamentary voters. Rank-and-file members of parties have some chance to influence policy on party committees, which, like the PARC divisions of the LDP, parallel the organization of the government. But the upward flow of pressure in no way matches that existing in the LDP in its heyday.

As a system, British governance is quite different from Japanese governance. In Britain the electorate chooses between programs advocated by centralized parties, which in turn control ministries and parliamentary backbenchers far more than is possible in Japan. Parliaments in Japan, Germany, and Italy exercise some influence over executives, and executives and bureaucratic ministries are constrained by decentralized power centers more than in Britain and France. Japan is more like the United States in the permeability of its political parties and legislative politics to the influence of interest groups, although American politics is a mixed system because of the centralizing influence of the American presidency.

Most democratic governments have some of the characteristics of bargained democracy, and all have some of the characteristics of programmatic democracy. But postwar Italy, Germany, and Japan fit the decentralized bargained democracy model more than other major democratic governments do. The

U.S. government has a strong element of bargained democracy, though more of a programmatic democracy element than Japan because of the leadership potential of the American presidency.

Determinants of Political Style

The patterns of Japanese politics, including the twin dynamics of conflict-fragmentation and coordination-integration, reflect the influence of political institutions, the social and economic setting, and culture. Each factor has had an impact on some aspects of politics. But causality is hard to establish in a deterministic sense; politics is more part of an interdependent system of factors, conditions, and experiences than the result of the influence of specific identifiable independent influences.

Three postwar government institutions in Japan are especially important to the shape of politics. The combination of a parliamentary system and a fragmented ruling party exposed the government to the constraints of informal political forces to a marked degree. Coalitional support is important to a government in any kind of democratic system, especially where a leader or party wants to achieve an ambitious legislative program. But a president is less immediately dependent on the balance of power in party politics; a prime minister, in contrast, is much more vulnerable. When the leadership of a parliamentary system is based on the support of an interparty coalition or, as in the case of the LDP, an interfaction and intergroup coalition with a strong upward flow of communications from rank-and-file Dietmembers, it can be weak and constrained. The presence of a strong bureaucratic tradition and a cultural heritage of consensualism adds to these constraints.

A second important political institution has been the medium-sized multimember election district. Election systems alone seldom cause anything. They interact with too many other variables for this to be true. But they may permit certain tendencies to occur if other factors so dictate. The Japanese system makes it possible for election campaigns to be decentralized rather than centralized and for individual candidates to develop their own power bases and contacts with interest groups. The system does not cause decentralization, but it does permit it. Prevailing styles of electoral mobilization based on the congeniality of local society to penetrative organization are also important.

The administrative bureaucracy is itself an exceedingly important institution, or set of institutions. Bureaucratic rule became an invaluable instrument of state and domain power during the latter part of the feudal period. The practice was continued into the early modern era, although after the introduction of constitutional government in 1890, political parties, too, were sometimes major political actors. Party-led governments influenced policy from roughly 1918 until the rise of military power and the outbreak of war in China in the mid-1930s. Later, Japan's military involvement in China and in the Pacific during World War II brought a full return to administrative government. The long acquaintance with administrative rule and the resultingly high social status of the corps of bureaucratic officials is an important factor in governance, even though bureaucratic influence has sometimes been overestimated. The ministries are largely immune to the kinds of external legal and judicial controls found on the European continent. Bureaucratic accountability in Japan is political, not legal.

In spite of the development of some centralized political and economic institutions, modern Japanese society remains decentralized and parochial in significant ways. Farm ownership and management is decentralized to a remarkable degree. There have been government efforts to increase the scale of farming, but most farms are still minuscule and are owned and managed by individual families rather than larger entities. The size of the average farm is 3.2 acres per person engaged in agriculture. The average in France is 40 acres; in Germany, 15 acres; in Britain, 31 acres; and in the United States, 178 acres.[12]

There has been no wholesale abandonment of the traditional household farm in Japan, even though the size of farm households and the active agricultural workforce has dwindled since the early postwar years. Because of these trends there are proportionately more small farmer-capitalists in Japan than in any other major industrialized country. In absolute terms Japan has three times the number of farmers as France, the major west European country with a large agricultural sector; in relative terms, the rural sector in Japan has a larger share of the workforce than the rural sector in France does: one and a half times larger.[13] A large portion of the population in Japan still lives in areas considered to be rural or small-town urban.

Decentralized farming is paralleled by decentralized, small-scale wholesale and retail sales. The small towns and cities are dotted with tiny, often family-owned shops. The ratio of retail outlets to population in Japan is double that in the United States, and a large proportion of these stores are very small, having only one or two employees. To some degree, the same conditions hold true for wholesale businesses. In both sectors Japan is markedly different from the major European cases in the proportion of small-scale enterprise. In the late 1980s, Japan had 132 retail stores and 36 wholesale firms per every 10,000 persons in the general population — roughly double comparable figures for the United States, Great Britain, Germany, and France.[14]

Japan also has a considerably larger proportion of its employed workforce engaged in manufacturing in small-scale units than any other major industrialized country. Three of four Japanese manufacturing workers are employed in firms having fewer than 300 employees. In the United States, in contrast, 47 percent of employed persons work in firms with 250 workers or fewer, and in Britain and Germany, 50 percent work in firms with 500 or fewer.[15] Even leaving out agriculture, small capitalists and their employees make up a larger portion of the Japanese population, and therefore of the voting public, than in the United States, Britain, or Germany. Small-scale capitalists form a very large potential voting bloc in Japan. There are dramatically more votes in the highly decentralized small-enterprise sector than in any other economic category.

The social and political horizons of Japanese farmers and small-business owners are still much narrower than those of large-firm employees. In both rural areas and in large cities, in the districts with small shops and small-scale manufacturers, social relationships overlap, group memberships are redundant, and few people commute far to work. In politics, these people pay more attention to local and occupational interests than to remote affairs, and under the medium-sized multimember constituency electoral system, political inputs were often highly decentralized.

The appeal of conservative farm and small-business programs and the nonunionization of the small-enterprise labor force explain conservative strength up to now. One factor that will affect future politics is the extent to which the voting blocs of small capitalists in local communities and neighborhoods remain an organized and mobilized political force. On one hand, social changes over time may have undermined traditional electioneering techniques more than scholars or Japanese journalists have realized (see Chapter 2). On the other hand, conservative small-business voting blocs exist in other countries, which are not known for Japanese-style communal voting, so the social structural changes in Japan may not change the direction of politics very much.

In this setting, individual Dietmembers have played a critical role in articulating local interests and the interests of small firms and farms in their constituencies. Figures on government allocations of funds to agriculture and small business show, in turn, that these voters with small enterprises had considerable political influence under LDP rule.

Hamlets — small communities of a few hundred to no more than fifteen hundred — constitute the main form of community organization in rural areas. Even in modern, industrialized Japan the hamlet still serves as the setting for some local self-rule and a handful of cooperative caretaking and ceremonial activities and continues to exercise some kind of residual influence over residents. The hamlet, more than other, larger entities, is a focus for people's extrafamilial public attachments, despite the eroding effects of several factors on community life: (1) the presence of small industrial plants in many rural areas, (2) a remarkable increase in personal mobility (reflecting increased wealth, improvements in roads, and the diffusion of personal automobiles), and (3) dramatically increased household ownership of farm tools.[16] Much the same can be said for the district organizations in the traditional small-business districts of large metropolises and provincial cities.

Although I have shied away from assuming that culture is deterministic, culture does influence politics at many points. I also believe that its effects are less homogeneous and internally consistent than has been suggested by many. Culture as viewed here grants legitimacy to competitiveness but favors consultation and group solutions. I also see a strong aversion to uncertainty and a preference for order as central cultural components of politicians' motivations.

Outside business relationships, Japanese society is not normally known for its competitiveness. Many accounts have identified a collectivist preference for harmony as the most conspicuous trait of Japanese culture. But Japanese life does contain a great deal of sanctioned competition. Middle-class children compete to enter high schools and universities under the current examination system, and there is enormous parental pressure for them to succeed. Graduates compete to enter prestigious firms, and employees, for good positions within the firms that accept them. Exemplary careers are admired as much in Japan as anywhere else, perhaps even more so, given the importance of social status and titles.[17] Individual accomplishment is also valued; some interpretations of Japanese life posit a strong sense of self.[18]

Individual and group self-interest is an important component of Japanese political life and generates intense competition on many occasions. Lively disputes stemming from interhamlet or intervillage conflicts of interest are recounted in anecdotes. Competition between different localities for new schools, roads, and other kinds of public works can reach very high emotional levels, as can enmities between different blocs of voters in local elections. In some hotly contested mayoralty elections, supporters of different candidates in different districts in some small cities have even refused to have commercial dealings with each other.[19]

Occupational interests are strongly felt by farmers and small-business owners, along with those in many other lines of business. This is the implication of the tax, farm, and Large Store Law conflicts in the 1980s and the breakdown of LDP support in the upper house election of 1989. Economists studying the sources of early postwar growth and later industrial overcapacity have also said that large firms are intensely competitive. The competitiveness of small manufacturers has been cited as inhibiting intraindustry cooperation among machine tool makers (Chapter 9). MITI's often-mentioned measures to prevent excessive industrial competition recognize the societal tendency to compete. Relatedly, a recent comparative evaluation of management strategies concludes that Japan's reputation for aggressiveness in foreign markets reflects the rush of individual firms to compete when new business strategies are invented.[20]

Pursued by highly ambitious and aggressive people, politics itself generates a plethora of conflicts, beginning with the intensely competitive behavior of subfaction leaders in the LDP and of candidates in elections. Collectivist and parochial tendencies likely add to the severity of intergroup conflict in many instances. Interministerial feuds are common and reflect both the aggressive defense of ministry interests and in-group feelings of solidarity stemming from insular recruitment practices.[21] Institutionalized factionalism has had similar implications within political parties. In the Japanese style of individualistic leadership, ruthlessly competitive behavior is sanctioned for those who represent particular collectivities in wider arenas of politics.

Equal to competitiveness in importance is a desire for order and routine that is also operative in Japanese politics and Japanese life in general.[22] Whereas competitiveness leads to conflict and fragmentation, a concern for order contributes to the coordination-integration dynamic. Order means that relationships should be stable and conflict kept to levels that do not threaten the integrity and smooth operation of normal social and political processes. Order also means the reduction of uncertainty to tolerable levels in a society where people are more concerned about uncertainty — they feel more discomfort in unstructured situations — than in most other countries, according to surveys in 104 nations. IBM conducted the surveys among its own employees. The researchers defined "uncertainty avoidance" to mean to what extent a culture "programs" its members to feel uncomfortable . . . in unstructured situations. . . . Uncertainty-avoiding cultures try to minimize the possibility of such situations by adhering to strict laws and rules."[23]

Japanese politics has been an ordered world for the most part, especially during LDP hegemony. In an ordered world, procedures and norms govern the allocation of scarce resources to encourage predictability and stability. Policies have emerged from established routines and procedures within ministries, between ministries, between the cabinet and the LDP, within the LDP and other parties, and within the Diet. In an ordered world, members of political parties expect to be assigned to party, Diet, and cabinet positions on the basis of their factional seniority, and most cabinet positions are rotated annually to give senior politicians a chance to hold ministry portfolios. Ministry officials themselves move to higher positions in a predictable sequence. In an ordered world, informal cooperation and negotiation among parties keeps Diet processes from paralysis or collapse, and networks of local supporters and support organizations produce wins in elections. Even if specific events are unpredictable, procedures and processes encourage predictable and routinized patterns. Uncertainty is reduced.

Predictability and routine are broadly valued in Japanese society, not just in politics. Several features of economic life indicate a preference for ordered, institutionalized relationships. Many men are employed for life in large firms, a practice taken up in earnest after World War II. Careers in large business firms and the bureaucracy until now have followed a more or less predictable course in regard to the match between level of seniority and assignment of authority and responsibility. Seniority has been the usual norm for career development and compensation in large Japanese organizations. But this in no way rules out competition or recognition of ability in promotions to high positions. Various subterfuges are used to remove incompetents from positions of authority or importance. Merit, which has always been recognized, is apparently also growing in importance in making job assignments and determining compensation.[24] Long-lasting vertical interfirm alignments between assemblers and suppliers or between producers, wholesalers, and retailers known as *keiretsu* are common in some industries and markets. There are also horizontal keiretsu alignments between banks and clusters of firms that are manifested in lending and borrowing arrangements, exchanges of directors, and sometimes purchases and sales.[25] Companies themselves recruit employees systematically from certain high schools, much as some firms and ministries recruit senior personnel only from selected universities.[26]

In each of these examples, the practices emerged in the context of specific historical conditions and sometimes explicit choices. Any implication of cultural determinism should be avoided. At the same time, the existence of broadly similar patterns in different areas of activity is striking; patterned institutionalized relationships that exist in Japan are not found in many other places. Individuals, political groups, and firms behave in certain ways for rational reasons while choosing organizational forms and behavioral repertoires that reflect common cultural themes.[27]

The reactions of individuals and organizations to breakdowns in order help us appreciate its importance. The LDP's crisis dynamic is a good example. Politicians from the LDP and its predecessor conservative parties have been involved in corruption scandals intermittently since the war. Most of the major scandals have led to periods of considerable fluidity in intraparty processes and coalition arrangements (Chapter 4). Factional coalitions were very fragile at the time of coalition fragmentation, and rumors that certain factions might withdraw their support for a particular LDP government (which actually happened in 1980 and 1993) were common. During these crises, Dietmembers elected only once or twice feared that internal disagreements and corruption scandals would so weaken party credibility as to damage their chances for reelection. They were also concerned that chaotic conditions in the party would destroy their chances for predictable advancement to high party or government positions. These "young" Dietmembers formed groups to press party seniors for reforms that would restore stability and predictability to intraparty processes. A similar pattern of intermittent organizational crisis, factional breakdown or realignment, appeals for reform from groups of junior Dietmembers, and requests for unity from supportive interest groups could also be seen in the SDPJ.

The typical response of the LDP to party breakdown was to try to renew internal organizational integrity and external credibility by negotiating a new interfactional leadership coalition. Faction leaders also sought to ensure continued solidarity in their own groups by holding meetings for members of different lengths of tenure or by taking other tacks, such as making ceremonial gifts of money to faction members. They emphasized their strength and therefore the value of their faction as a predictable gateway to high-level positions. The efforts to ease feelings of uncertainty that arose from LDP factional and coalitional crises resembled, in many instances, efforts to end interparty disagreements in the Diet. The warring parties often agreed to replace the upper or lower house speaker or to make some other symbolic gesture, or to implement a specific legislative quid pro quo, as a means of getting Diet deliberations back on track after a breakdown in normal processes (Chapter 6). Parliamentary disorder often resulted in criticism from an anxious business community, which, as in intra-LDP crises, was concerned with preserving conservative hegemony and, relatedly, political order and predictability. It is from behaviors such as these that we can infer both a strong concern for order and the motivation for developing norms and procedures for its attainment.

Collectivism, an aspect of Japanese culture that manifests itself in both the fragmentation and the integration dynamics, refers to a tendency at all levels of society for people to form or enter groups to accomplish instrumental goals, including, in some cases, stabilization of a disorderly environment.[28] There are many examples of collectivism in the accounts of political parties in this book. The largest party, the LDP, contained factions, subfactions, policy groups, groups of retirees, groups of former leaders, groups of members concerned with particular economic or noneconomic interests, reform groups, and groups of politicians at different levels of electoral tenure. The SDPJ, the second largest party, has also had many of the same kinds of internal groups at one time or another. Not all of the groups are so small as to allow regular face-to-face encounters. But with these large parties, the groups are much smaller than the parties within which they are found.[29] Various groups are also found in interest organizations and in the bureaucracy, although they are not as well documented as those in the LDP.

Collectivism and related in-group and out-group distinctions have been widely cited in descriptions of Japanese society. For some observers, they constitute the predominant tendency in Japanese culture and reflect early school training.[30] For others, collectivism reflects a dependent personality orientation.[31] Groups are also formed on the basis of mutual exchange; that is, much as in factions, people become group members to attain some goal or other, providing a service to the group or its leader in exchange for the leader's and the group's support of their own needs.[32] Each of these explanations has merit, but in politics the basis for collectivist behavior is more often than not the achievement of instrumental goals. The exchange model fits politics best.

The tendency to form or join groups also contributes to a strong element of parochialism in parties, labor unions, and other organizations. In this case, groups smaller than the formal organization or the local administrative entity in which they are located become the basic units in the definition and expression of political interests. These groups are often the focus of political identities and feelings of solidarity. Examples are party factions and many other small groups found in large organizations. The main organization or setting in which the smaller groups are situated is sometimes of only secondary importance to small-group members. A parochial tendency within organizations can lead to centrifugal competition and conflict and, in some instances, even the breakdown of the host organization. Or, if the organization itself is permanent, as is the case for bureaucratic ministries and corporations, immobilism may result. Because a tendency for informal groups to form inside large organizations can be seen in any culture, I hasten to point out that in Japan these groups tend to take on identities and names and to even become partially formalized to a degree rare in other settings.

An element of mutualism in Japanese politics is at least in part related to the more general collectivism. It is this side of collectivism that contributes to the existence of a coordination-integration dynamic in politics. We have seen that mutual accommodation constitutes the most legitimate solution to parliamentary conflicts. Elsewhere in politics, a typical outcome when different groups or parties have conflicting interests is an agreement based on reciprocal consent — that is, all parties give up something and achieve at least a part of their original goals.[33] The tendency to negotiate is also compatible with what some have felt is the exchange basis of Japanese social relationships.[34] A related "fair shares" norm has been described as guiding budgetary allocations to different ministries.[35] Some say that negotiated solutions reflect the expansion of in-group (uchi) relationships to include all of the original parties to a conflict.[36] This tendency to accommodate is the basis for my emphasis on the bargained nature of Japanese democracy.

Informality is the fourth major category of politically relevant orientations in Japanese culture, after the desire for order, collectivism, and mutualism. Informality refers to behavior that is not prescribed by constitutions, legal frameworks, or formal, purposive aspects of social organization. Informality and the social embeddedness of Japanese politics (mentioned in the introductory chapter) are closely related. Widespread person-to-person and small-group consultation and coordination in forming and maintaining coalitions, as well as in resolving conflicts, exemplify informal behavior in politics.[37] In parties, therefore, informal groups are often more important than formal organization, and informal ad hoc procedures more important than formal rules. This is why Japanese parties tend to be decentralized and fragmented, whereas some European parties are much more centralized. In the Japanese case, informal small-group-based behavior prevails; in the European case, formal procedures are more important, or informal practices are brought into line with them.

Somewhat similarly, Japanese bureaucrats prefer informal arbitration and negotiation over formal legal procedures. Informality in this case results from a desire to preserve ministerial influence by avoiding delegation of control to laws and the courts.[38] Bureaucrats are able to influence the behavior of firms more easily this way than if firms were able to challenge bureaucracies in the courts. The preference for informality here conforms to general cultural patterns while serving other purposes and is an excellent example of the blending of cultural and instrumental elements of behavior.

Culture suggests ways to get things done rather than simply determining what politicians do. Japanese politicians form small groups more often than politicians in some other countries — and for a purpose. They join in groups to advance their career, consolidate power, and articulate interests. Forming or joining a group is a purposive, instrumental response to a perceived need, not just a determined behavioral response. The tendency for Japanese to relentlessly engage in some kind of coordination has similar origins. Japanese culture appears to be more a menu of possible behaviors than a simple deterministic force. In politics, most culturally influenced behaviors are purposive and rational, even though the manifestation of cultural forms is different from the manifestation of those same forms in other societies.

Who Wins and Who Loses

In this book I have been largely concerned with political processes—specifically, what power centers are involved, whether policymaking is pluralistic, and whether the behavior of politicians leads to stable or unstable politics. I have asserted and defended the idea that Japanese politics is democratic, pluralistic, and decentralized. To stop at this point and not think about the effects of Japanese-style politics on different segments of the population and different social or economic actors would be remiss. Some population sectors may have consistently won, and some may have more often lost; identifying them will make this assessment of Japanese democracy more complete.

Various summary interpretations of Japanese politics are relevant to this discussion. Some scholars, for example, say that postwar Japanese politics has been oriented toward producers and that consumers' interests have been ignored. According to the Japan, Inc., metaphor—the assertion that Japan is run by MITI, big business, and the LDP—other population sectors were excluded from influence. Some interpreters have stated that labor was excluded from meaningful political participation. In all three of these approaches, big business is a major player in politics and the recipient of government largess.

In Chapter 9, I suggested alternatives to these models: the Confucian welfare state and the party clientelistic state. I used the term *Confucian welfare state* to call attention to the fact that, reflecting Confucian holism, all sectors of society were considered important. I also wanted to point out that the policy of the government was to keep people actively employed, hence the welfare component. By *party clientelistic state* I mean a government that cares for the groups that are clients of the governing party—in this case, the LDP.

Following this perspective, in Table 9.9 I demonstrated that government financial and fiscal support for large firms was overshadowed by support for small firms and farmers. In 1990, for example, each small firm "received" $6,866 through government programs, each farm "received" $5,487 in government support, and each large firm (with more than 300 employees) in theory "received" only $84.[39] In effect, two of the most inefficient economic sectors received the most support. In reality, a concern for political benefits and social harmony was greater than a concern for large producers or the elements of Japan, Inc.

The most privileged population sector in postwar Japan has been the farmers. Although more government resources are allocated to small enterprises than to farmers, farmers have more often received price subsidies and other direct government program support, which does not require repayment. In contrast, small businesses have mainly been given loans, which have to be repaid (see Table 9.9). Farmers also pay lower taxes than other occupational groups if the 9–6–4 formula described in Chapter 7 is accurate. At the same time, farmers have on the average more wealth than urban dwellers (Chapter 7).

These disparities favoring farmers are borne out in the ownership of consumer durables. Residents of Toyama prefecture on the Japan Sea coast, one of the more isolated places in Japan, have 1.6 cars per household, well above the national average of one car per household. In Tokyo the figure is 0.6 car per household. The high cost of parking space and the crowded roads in cities are a factor in these urban-rural differences. But with other consumer durables — color televisions are a case in point — there are much the same differences. Government revenue equalization policies also result in rural prefectures receiving more financial assistance from the national government than urban prefectures do. In 1990, Tokyo prefecture received just 28 percent of its total revenue needs from the national government; the figure for Shimane, a rural prefecture in western Japan, was 87 percent.[40]

If journalistic folklore is to believed, small businesses have a similarly privileged position regarding taxes. In addition, the Large Store Law discussed in Chapter 8 was obviously designed to favor medium and small businesses, as are many related local regulations in the same category. The alignments permitted between manufacturers and small retail stores also favor smaller enterprises, as well as generate higher prices for shoppers preferring local stores over discount stores in central urban locations.

It is much harder to assess government policy from the perspective of employees, unions, and large businesses than from the viewpoint of farmers and small businesses. Employees have no large organizations to assert their interests other than unions. In spite of labor's traditionally less direct access to power centers because of its affiliation with parties opposed to the LDP, tax burdens — that is, lowered income taxes — favor employees in general at the expense of large businesses. Corporate taxes are high in Japan relative to other countries even after the various tax incentives described in Chapter 9 are considered. The effective corporate tax rate (adjusted for deductions) is 49 percent, which is much higher than the comparable rates for the United States and France: 33 percent. The corporate tax burden in Britain is just 20 percent. Corporate taxes account for 24 percent of all taxes in Japan; the figures for the United States, Britain, Germany, and France are 15 percent, 5 percent, 10 percent, and 10 percent, respectively.[41]

Individual income tax rates are much lower than corporate taxes in Japan. At most income levels the income tax rate for individuals is about half that in the United States. Taxes are also more progressive in different income categories than in the United States. Individual income taxes range from o percent for married couples with incomes under $28,000 to 44 percent for those with incomes of $471,000 or more. The latter tax bracket is the highest one, and the tax is much higher than that for the highest income tax bracket in the United States: 36 percent. The income shares of taxes paid by individuals and corporations in other major democracies also show that ordinary Japanese pay less than their counterparts abroad. The lower individual income taxes in Japan, along with union successes, indicate how opposition agendas were implemented even under LDP hegemony. Sometimes the LDP co-opted opposition programs; sometimes the opposition used its de facto veto in the Diet. Sometimes there were behind-the-scenes bargains between unions and the LDP.

There is other evidence of employees having won in Japanese politics. Even after some cutbacks in commitments in the 1980s, Japan now distributes more in social security payments relative to GNP than the United States or Great Britain.[42] The social security system reflects much the same co-optative political formula as taxes, as well as a commitment to a comprehensive pension system on the part of one LDP leader in the early postwar period.[43] Since 1970, in response to several thousand local antipollution and antigrowth citizens' movements, fairly strict pollution controls have been developed and deployed in urban and industrial areas. Automobile emissions of carbon dioxide, sulfur oxide, and nitrogen oxide are now substantially lower than those in other major countries. Air pollution (sulfur oxide and nitrogen oxide) from stationery sources has also been reduced significantly. On the loss side, consumers have had to pay high prices for many products, especially food and goods from inefficient economic sectors. But many aspects of life that affect consumers and other population groups are better than they are represented to be in foreign media.

The treatment of big business by the government is itself a very complicated matter. In spite of the alliance between big business and the conservative movement, evident in the large political contributions from big firms and frequent meetings between big-business and government leaders, big business has been a frequent critic of the government on macroeconomic policy issues and political corruption. Industrial policies and protectionist barriers designed to help particular industries figured large in the policy repertoire of the government in some periods; remnants of these policies exist even today, although more has usually been spent on sick industry rescues than on growth (Chapter 9). Businesses collectively lose because of the high corporation tax, although they have presumably won because of consistent government attention to infrastructure development. Ironically, it is the extensive supports given to inefficient economic sectors, including farmers and many small businesses, plus big businesses in trouble, that have cost ordinary citizens the most in material terms.

It is true that there is little explicit concern for consumers as such. But the motivation for much policy has been to keep people in all economic sectors employed. Because employees and shopowners are also consumers, Japan seems to have approached the question of the material quality of life from a different, more basic perspective than some other countries have: by facilitating the survival of small firms. Ordinary people have not been ignored (although this is a common foreign interpretation). Rather, the emphasis has been on employment and social harmony, not on consumption in its own right.

Future Patterns

Japan was ruled by one political party or by a coalition dominated by one party (1983–86) from 1955 until that party lost the House of Representatives election in 1993. Liberal Democratic cabinets ran Japan until then, and intra-LDP processes to some degree took the place of legislative processes. After July 1993, Japan was led by a coalition of three small moderate conservative groups, two Socialist parties and the Clean Government Party. The ruling coalition changed in 1995, and the LDP returned to power in a coalition that included the Social Democratic Party of Japan and the Harbinger Party. It is useful to see whether the patterns of politics during LDP rule can help us understand the new political environment.

To begin, let us characterize LDP rule as an era of intense pluralism within a party framework. The organization of the LDP and its component processes made up a system not unlike that of the government in many countries. Intraparty factions struggled for influence and government positions much like parties in a highly competitive multiparty system. Intraparty policy families operated like interest groups in the pursuit of access and influence, in many cases representing groups outside the party. Government leadership was subject to multiple constraints as the result of this pluralism, and intraparty policymaking partially replaced Diet deliberations as the center of political competition and policymaking. Politics operated within a party framework as much as or more than it operated on the basis of interactions between parties; the latter is more typical in democracies, but the result is potentially the same.

Under today's coalition governments, politics remains highly pluralistic. The prime minister and cabinet are chosen by multiple political actors; their power is constrained by multiple constituencies. The difference between LDP rule and the present government lies in the involvement of several parties in an external framework of interaction. Other aspects of politics — including interest intermediation, legislative competition, and interactions between parties and interest groups and the bureaucracy — must shift to focus on an external political process, rather than on the process within one party. Interactions are likely to remain highly pluralistic. Some interactions will be even more pluralistic than before, for some former institutionalized relationships based on an ongoing, semi-institutionalized exchange of resources will be replaced by frequently renegotiated understandings.

Predictions of political patterns are as risky in the Japanese case as in any other. The strong influence of the coordination-integration dynamic under LDP rule suggests, however, that some newly established political relationships may over time achieve a degree of inertia such as was observed with those centered on the LDP. Policy communities will be reoriented toward new relationships involving multiple parties; these relationships could become highly institutionalized. As policy communities adjust to new power configurations, bureaucratic actors will confront newly configured interests and pressures. If there should be immobilism in the cabinet, ministries may emerge as stronger actors than under LDP rule. On the other hand, the bureaucracy may be constrained even more than in the past because of the multiplicity of parties and complexity of positions that must be dealt with to build a policy coalition. Institutionalized channels and procedures for political recruitment will certainly reassert themselves within parties and perhaps even between parties, if multiparty coalitions stay in power long enough for this to happen.[44] Interparty accommodations will be made in the Diet in adjusting to new structures of power, but by using channels and processes of accommodation like those used in the past. The government will be different, but not all that different. It will remain highly pluralistic, and most relations will fit a horizontal model of power and process.

It is also likely that politics will be less stable in the future. We have already seen how a party that was internally more or less stable for a long time could collapse rather quickly under the influence of the conflict-fragmentation dynamic. We have also seen that there is a clear potential for volatile voting among some population sectors. The electorate lacks both the sociological anchors of societywide cleavages and the psychological anchors of full-blown party attachments, and even candidate machines sometimes fail under pressure of compelling events. Experiences in 1989 and 1993 have also shown that salient issues and interest group defections could suddenly derail long-established patterns of support.

The lack of a cleavage in Japanese society is probably itself conducive to volatility in an interesting way. If we discount the idea of a value cleavage, the support of small-business owners and their employees for mainly conservative parties has been based solely on representation of their interests. The resulting demographic patterns look like one side of a class cleavage, because these people are property owners. However, the interest-based support of the small bourgeoisie was not reinforced by strong class loyalties, antagonism to other classes, or periodic manipulation of class symbols in the way traditional class attachments have been in Europe. Nor was there the same degree of economically derived alienation among groups that has traditionally existed between lower and upper classes in Britain and some other countries. These lacks, together with rural prosperity in the 1980s, made the attachments of many small enterprisers and farmers fungible under the pressure of high-level corruption and appeals for political reform in 1993.

The decision to introduce proportional representation as the method for selecting nearly 40 percent of the members of the House of Representatives could increase the potential for volatility by substituting manipulation of remote symbols and images in future election campaigns for the existing practice in many districts of activating political networks in communities and local interest groups. Past electoral instability may breed future instability if old ties are broken and not replaced with new attachments. Communal electoral mobilization and weakly anchored psychological images have made electoral outcomes fairly stable until now, in part because politicians' ties to parties were very stable. There have been pockets of instability — for example, in metro-suburban constituencies after the early 1970s. Much of the true movement in the 1993 vote (votes for candidates of the Japan New Party in contrast with votes for old LDP members who ran under new labels) took place in metro-suburban districts where volatility was already an established precedent.

Multiparty government is not likely to work as smoothly as intra-LDP government, even given time for new cooperative norms and procedures to develop. Intra-LDP conflict was, to a considerable degree, conflict over positions and interests. Ideological differences were less formal and rigid, and therefore less pervasive and important, than in the opposition Social Democratic Party. In addition, the LDP's claim on power — and, relatedly, the well-established opportunities for advancement through frequent reallocations of top positions — held a highly fragmented party coalition together. In an inter-party coalition with ideological fracture lines between and within some parties — as is now the case to a mild, but still potentially significant, degree — there is a greater possibility for eventual immobilism and coalitional collapse.

Immobilizing intracoalition conflict would once again make the future look less certain to career-oriented politicians. Given the typical workings of the conflict-fragmentation dynamic, if the present political arrangements continue in force, Japan will have pluralistic political rule and a much less stable political system than under LDP domination.

Notes

Chapter 1: Postwar Politics

1. The works upon which the vertical model and its horizontal counterpart are based are cited at many points in this book. Three especially useful sources in the development of the vertical and horizontal metaphors are Michio Muramatsu, "Center-Local Political Relations: A Lateral Competition Model," *Journal of Japanese Studies* 12 (1986), pp. 303–27; Richard Samuels, *The Politics of Regional Policy in Japan: Localities, Incorporated?* (Princeton, N.J.: Princeton University Press, 1983); and Frank Upham, *Law and Social Change in Postwar Japan* (Cambridge: Harvard University Press, 1987).

2. Although quite a bit of the vertical-integrative metaphor for Japanese politics reflects patterns during the 1955 system, some components of the model — most obviously a strong bureaucracy — have outlasted the LDP's reign of power. Throughout the book I use verbs in the past tense to describe characteristics of Japanese politics that ended with the LDP's defeat in the 1993 general election and the present or present perfect tense to denote continuing themes in Japanese governance.

3. For an analysis of the alleged "soft authoritarianism" of Japanese politics see Chalmers Johnson, "The Institutional Foundations of Japanese Industrial Policy," in Claude E. Barfield and William Scambra, eds., *The Politics of Industrial Policy* (Washington, D.C.: American Enterprise Institute, 1986), pp. 187–205. For an analysis congenial with Johnson's see also James Fallows, "Containing Japan," *Atlantic Monthly,* May 1990, pp. 40–54; and Karel Van Wolferen, *The Enigma of Japanese Power* (New York: Vintage Books, 1989). Fallows, Van Wolferen, Clyde Prestowitz, and Johnson are known as the revisionist school of interpretation of contemporary Japan. In spite of differences in

emphasis, each believes Japan is a social, political, and economic system fundamentally different from systems in the West.

4. See Daniel Okimoto, *Between MITI and the Market: Japanese Industrial Policy for High Technology* (Stanford: Stanford University Press, 1989), pp. 35–36.

5. Yung H. Park, *Bureaucrats and Ministers in Contemporary Japanese Government* (Berkeley: Institute of East Asian Studies and Center for Japanese Studies, University of California, 1986), chap. 6.

6. See Muramatsu, "Center-Local Political Relations." According to Steven Reed, neither the centralized model of national-local relations nor the local autonomy model is uniformly accurate. See Reed, "Is Japanese Government Really Centralized," *Journal of Japanese Studies* 8 (1982), pp. 133–64.

7. Since World War II there have been a variety of conceptual concerns in comparative politics. Macro-structural-functionalism and systems "theory," political economy, corporatism-pluralism, institutionalism, and rational choice — each has contributed to the vocabulary of comparative analysis. But none of the favored approaches, with the exception of corporatism-pluralism, addresses the distribution of power centrally. Nevertheless, despite the appeal of new paradigms and methods, middle-range views of power and process are often the basis for empirical comparative research. On pluralism and corporatism see David Truman, *The Governmental Process* (New York: Knopf, 1951); Robert Dahl, *Who Governs?* (New Haven: Yale University Press, 1961); Philippe Schmitter and Gerhard Lehmbruch, eds., *Trends Toward Corporatist Intermediation* (London: Sage, 1979); Andrew Cox, "Corporatism as Reductionism: The Analytic Limits of the Corporatist Thesis," *Government and Opposition* 16 (1981), pp. 78–95; Peter Katzenstein, *Small States in World Markets: Industrial Policy in Europe* (Ithaca, N.Y.: Cornell University Press, 1985); Ilja Scholten, ed., *Political Stability and Neo-Corporatism: Corporatist Integration and Societal Cleavages in Western Europe* (London: Sage, 1987); and John Keeler, "Corporatism and Official Union Hegemony: The Case of French Agricultural Syndicalism," in Suzanne Berger, ed., *Organizing Interests in Western Europe: Pluralism, Corporatism and the Transformation of Politics* (Cambridge: Cambridge University Press, 1981), pp. 185–87.

For descriptions of distributions of power in party systems see Jean Blondel, "Party Systems and Patterns of Government in Western Democracies," *Canadian Journal of Political Science* 1 (1968), pp. 180–203; Giovanni Sartori, *Parties and Party Systems: A Framework for Analysis* (New York: Cambridge University Press, 1976). For descriptions of distributions of power within parties see Robert Michels, *Political Parties* (Glencoe, Ill.: Free Press, 1949); Maurice Duverger, *Political Parties* (London: Methuen, 1951); Samuel Eldersveld, *Political Parties: A Behavioral Analysis* (Chicago: Rand McNally, 1964); and V. O. Key, *Parties, Politics and Pressure Groups* (New York: Thomas Y. Crowell, 1958), chap. 12. Government power relations are described in many places. For a recent analysis of the democratic state's need for power see Eric Nordlinger, *On the Autonomy of the Democratic State* (Cambridge: Harvard University Press, 1981); and for similar concerns about the capabilities of parties vis-à-vis government bureaucracies see Richard Rose, "The Variability of Party Government: A Theoretical and Empirical Critique," *Political Studies* 17 (1969), pp. 443–45.

8. For pioneering considerations of the importance of conflict in Japan see Ellis

Krauss, Thomas P. Rohlen, and Patricia G. Steinhoff, eds., *Conflict in Japan* (Honolulu: University of Hawaii Press, 1984); Susan J. Pharr, *Losing Face: Status Politics in Japan* (Berkeley: University of California Press, 1990); and Tetsuo Najita and Victor J. Koschmann, *Conflict in Modern Japanese History: The Neglected Tradition* (Princeton, N.J.: Princeton University Press, 1982).

9. Immobilism is a major theme of J. A. A. Stockwin et al., *Dynamic and Immobilist Politics in Japan* (Honolulu: University of Hawaii Press, 1988).

10. Arend Lijphart, "Consociational Theory: Problems and Prospects," *Comparative Politics* 13 (April 1981), pp. 355–60.

11. A detailed treatment of Japanese political culture is deferred until later in this book for methodological reasons. I infer political cultural themes from elite behavior reported in newspapers or in the secondary literature on Japanese politics. Except in Chapter 2, I lack independent measures of political culture (such as those provided by survey interviews) that would permit a more rigorous causal interpretation of the effects of culture on behavior.

12. Edward Banfield, *The Moral Basis of a Backward Society* (Glencoe: Free Press, 1958).

13. Negotiation and accommodation are identified in Richard Samuels's term, "reciprocal deference." See Samuels, *The Business of the Japanese State: Energy Markets in Comparative and Historical Perspective* (Ithaca, N.Y.: Cornell University Press, 1987), chap. 1. A frequent resort to negotiation by Japanese politicians also reflects what some describe as the lack of a clearly defined center of political power. On the importance of order in Japanese culture see Thomas Rohlen, "Order in Japanese Society: Attachment, Authority and Routine," *Journal of Japanese Studies* 15 (1989), p. 32. A normative preference for balance, which means fairness in allocation of resources and is related to consensual ideals, also contributes to an emphasis on negotiation and accommodation. John Campbell discusses balance in *Contemporary Japanese Budget Politics* (Berkeley: University of California Press, 1979), pp. 3–4. Even the interventionist tendency of the central Japanese ministries contributes to a reliance on negotiation. Because government actors frequently lack fully specified coercive powers and prefer informal guidance, they rely on negotiation and accommodation to gain support for their policies. See Frank Upham, "The Man Who Would Import: A Cautionary Tale About Bucking the System in Japan," *Journal of Japanese Studies* 17 (1991), pp. 324–25.

14. For excellent treatments of Japanese postwar political history see Junnosuke Masumi, *Postwar Politics in Japan, 1945–55* (Berkeley: Institute of East Asian Studies, and Center for Japanese Studies, University of California, 1985); and the same author's *Contemporary Politics in Japan* (Berkeley: University of California Press, 1995).

15. Throughout this book, I use the general Western order for names—first names precede family names—although the reverse is the Japanese custom.

Chapter 2: Political Culture and Electoral Behavior

1. Bradley Richardson, "Stability and Change in Japanese Electoral Behavior," *Journal of Asian Studies* (1977), pp. 675–93.

2. After the early 1970s, voting in House of Councillors elections was similar to

voting in House of Representatives elections. Elections for prefectural and local (city, town, and village) assemblies were usually dominated by conservatives or conservative independents as well. In the 1980s city, town, and village mayors were usually supported by multiparty coalitions; centrist coalitions that included the LDP were the dominant mode. Mainichi Shimbunsha, *'91 Toitsu Chiho Senkyo* (Tokyo, 1991), pp. 10–20. Information on local elections was provided by the Chiho Jiji Sogo Kenkyujo, an organ of the Jichiro (local government employees) labor union.

3. Seymour M. Lipset and Stein Rokkan, eds., *Party Systems and Voter Alignments: Cross-National Perspectives* (New York: Free Press, 1967). For evidence from Britain and Germany see Anthony Heath, Roger Jowell, and John Curtice, *How Britain Votes* (London: Pergamon Press, 1985); and Hans-Dieter Klingemann, "Soziale Lagerung, Schichtbewusstein und politisches Verhalten: Die Arbeitschaft der Bundesrepublik im historische und internationalen Vergleich," in Rolf Ebbighausen and Friedrich Tiemann, eds., *Das Ende der Arbeiterbewegung in Deutschland? Ein Diskussionsband zum sechzigsten Geburtstag von Theo Pirker* (Opladen: Westdeutscher Verlag, 1981). For documentation of cleavage decline in the Netherlands, Spain, and more generally in western Europe see Seymour M. Lipset, *Political Man: The Social Bases of Politics* (Baltimore: Johns Hopkins University Press, 1981), Warren E. Miller and Philip Stouthard, "Confessional Attachment and Electoral Behavior in the Netherlands," *European Journal of Political Research* 3 (1975), pp. 219–58; and José Ramón Montero, "Iglesia, Secularización y Comportamiento en España," *Revista Española de Investigaciones Sociológicas* 34 (1986), pp. 131–60.

4. Farmers and small-business owners are always hard to define in terms of social prestige, one of the bases for class membership. They are often prominent members of the middle class in small communities, even though they lack similar status in national prestige rankings. But if social class is defined, more realistically, on the basis of property ownership and related political interests, Japanese farmers and small-business owners are members of the middle class. See Heath et al., *How Britain Votes*, pp. 15–16, for an interest theory of class voting.

5. Heath et al., *How Britain Votes*, chap. 2. Both occupational groups are also directly vulnerable to market forces. Since the war this has meant they have sought subsidies and loans to help insulate themselves from these vulnerabilities.

6. Heath et al., *How Britain Votes*, pp. 16, 20–21.

7. Scott C. Flanagan and Bradley Richardson, *Japanese Electoral Behavior: Social Cleavages, Social Networks and Partisanship* (London: Sage Contemporary Political Sociology Series, no. 06–24, 1977). From 1970 to 1990 union membership declined from 35 percent of the workforce to 25 percent. There are important differences in levels of unionization in different employment sectors: 30 percent of employees in the manufacturing sector are unionized, 15 percent of employees in the service sector, and 75 percent of those in the public sector. Japan Institute of Labor, *Japanese Working Life Profile* (Tokyo, 1991), p. 48.

8. A majority of Japanese are essentially secular, according to national character studies. See Tokei Suri Kenkyujo, *Dai-go Nihonjin no Kokuminsei* (Tokyo, 1992), p. 522.

9. Joji Watanuki, "Social Structure and Voting Behavior," in Scott C. Flanagan, Shinsaku Kohei, Ichiro Miyake, Bradley Richardson, and Joji Watanuki, *The Japanese Voter* (New Haven: Yale University Press, 1991), p. 83.

10. Joji Watanuki, "Patterns of Politics in Present-Day Japan," in Lipset and Rokkan, *Party Systems and Voter Alignments,* p. 456.

11. Scott C. Flanagan, "Value Change and Partisan Change in Japan: The Silent Revolution Revisited," *Comparative Politics* 11 (1978), pp. 253–78; Flanagan, "Value Cleavages, Economic Cleavages and the Japanese Voter," *American Journal of Political Science* 24 (1980), pp. 177–206; and Flanagan, "Value Cleavages, Contextual Influences and the Vote," in Flanagan et al., *Japanese Voter,* pp. 84–142.

12. These are the rural districts of prefectures outside major metropolitan and industrialized areas adjacent to the Tokaido and Sanyo main train corridors. Using data from rural districts removes most of the effects of Jichiro union concentration in prefectural capital cities. I also avoided including cases from rural constituencies with prominent company towns, like Hitachi in Ibaragi and Ube in Yamaguchi, where there are concentrations of workers.

13. Some Socialist candidates from prestigious rural families are supported on ascriptive grounds, according to informants that I interviewed in Shimane prefecture. Bradley Richardson, "Stability and Change in Japanese Electoral Behavior," *Journal of Asian Studies* 36 (1977), pp. 675–93.

14. Tokei Suri Kenkyujo, *Dai-go Nihonjin no Kokuminsei,* pp. 509 ff.

15. Another problem of the cultural cleavage approach has been missing data. Up to 30 percent of the public has no clear opinion regarding some values.

16. For revisionist and more recent views on party identification see Gregory B. Markus and Philip E. Converse, "A Dynamic Simultaneous Equation Model of Electoral Choice" *American Political Science Review* 73 (1979), pp. 1055–70; and Benjamin I. Page and Calvin C. Jones, "Reciprocal Effects of Policy Preferences, Party Loyalties and the Vote," *American Political Science Review* 73 (1979), pp. 1071–89. For a recent statement of the continuing importance of party identification see Warren E. Miller, "Party Identification, Realignment and Party Voting: Back to the Basics," *American Political Science Review* 85 (1991), pp. 557–71.

17. As in the United States, the concept has sometimes had a rough reception in European scholarly circles. For evidence indicating the relevance of psychological partnership in western Europe see Bradley Richardson, "European Partisanship Revisited," *American Political Science Review* 85 (1991), pp. 751–75.

18. Angus Campbell, Philip E. Converse, Warren E. Miller, and Donald E. Stokes, *The American Voter* (New York: Wiley, 1960), pp. 121–67; and David Butler and Donald Stokes, *Political Change in Britain* (New York: St. Martin's, 1969), pp. 37–43.

19. Bradley Richardson, "Party Loyalties and Party Salience in Japan," *Comparative Political Studies* 8 (1975), pp. 32–57.

20. The calculations were based on 1976 study data collected by Joji Watanuki, Bradley Richardson, Ichiro Miyake, Scott Flanagan, and Shinsaku Kohei.

21. Ichiro Miyake, "Seito Shiji to Seijiteki Imeji," in Joji Watanuki, Ichiro Miyake, Takashi Inoguchi, and Ikuo Kabashima, *Nihonjin no Senkyo Kodo* (Tokyo: Tokyo Daigaku Shuppankai, 1986), p. 79.

22. Miyake, "Seito Shiji to Seijiteki Imeji." The intervals between surveys were very different in the different countries. In Japan the period was just six months. In contrast with the Japanese case, 68 percent of American respondents were stable partisans over a four-year period in the turbulent 1970s, and 73 percent of British voters were stable

partisans over five years in the same decade. If defection increases as time intervals lengthen, the Japanese patterns are extremely fragile.

23. Bradley Richardson, "Japan's Habitual Voters: Partisanship on the Emotional Periphery," *Comparative Political Studies* 19 (1986), pp. 675–93.

24. Gabriel A. Almond and Sidney Verba, *The Civic Culture: Political Attitudes and Democracy in Five Nations* (Princeton, N.J.: Princeton University Press, 1963); and Almond and Verba, eds., *The Civic Culture Revisited* (Boston: Little, Brown, 1980).

25. Philip E. Converse and Georges Dupeux, "Politicization of the Electorate in France and the United States," in Angus Campbell, Philip E. Converse, Warren E. Miller, and Donald E. Stokes, *Elections and the Political Order* (New York: Wiley, 1966), pp. 269–91; and Sidney Tarrow, "The Urban-Rural Cleavage in Involvement: The Case of France," *American Political Science Review* 65 (1971), pp. 344–46.

26. Martin P. Wattenberg, *The Decline of the American Parties 1952–80* (Cambridge, Mass.: Harvard University Press, 1984).

27. Leonardo Morlino and José Ramón Montero, "Legitimacy and Democracy in Southern Europe," in Richard Gunther, P. Nikiforos Diamandouros, and Hans-Jurgen Puhle, eds., *The Politics of Democratic Consolidation: Southern Europe in Comparative Perspective* (Baltimore, Md.: Johns Hopkins University Press, 1995), pp. 231–60.

28. Roper Center, *The Public Perspective* 4 (July–August 1993), p. 86.

29. Bradley Richardson, *The Political Culture of Japan* (Berkeley: University of California Press, 1974), chap. 3.

30. Akarui Senkyo Suishin Kyokai, *Dai-39kai Shugiin Giin Sosenkyo no Jittai* (Tokyo, 1991), pp. 381, 388–89.

31. Richardson, "Constituency Candidates vs. Parties in Japanese Voting Behavior," *American Political Science Review* 82 (1988), pp. 705–12. There is some debate in Japan and elsewhere on the durability of party images. For evidence of short-term fluctuation see Miyake, "Seito Shiji to Seijiteki Imeji," p. 110. For evidence suggesting long-term stability in some imagery see Jiji Tsushinsha, *Sengo Nihon no Seito to Naikaku* (Tokyo: Jiji Tsushinsha, 1981), pp. 146 ff.; and Akarui Senkyo Suishin Kyokai, *Sosenkyo no Jittai* (Tokyo, 1972-) series.

32. A view that partisanship is based as much on cognition as on affect fits research based on the assumption that voting is driven by partisan schema, that is, memory structures that incorporate, classify, and evaluate cognitive substance. Richardson, "European Party Loyalties Revisited," pp. 705–7. Overall levels of party saliency (based on answers in open-ended questions) are also lower in Japan than in the United States and some other countries. Richardson, "Party Loyalties and Party Saliency in Japan" and "European Partisanship Revisited."

33. The constitution expressly forbade Japan to have military forces. But after the Korean War broke out in 1950, this clause was interpreted to mean only denial of an offensive military capability. Japan's military arm is still labeled the Self-Defense Forces for this reason.

34. Shinsaku Kohei, Ichiro Miyake, and Joji Watanuki, "Issues and Voting Behavior," in Flanagan et al., *Japanese Voter*, chap. 7.

35. Richardson, "Japan's Habitual Voters."

36. Much the same patterns can be seen in the Netherlands, West Germany, and Spain.

Richardson, "European Partisanship"; and Richardson, "The Development of P: Commitments in Post-Franquist Spain," paper presented at the annual meeting American Political Science Association, San Francisco, August–September 1990. I iavit-ual voting is also implicit when majorities of Japanese say that they have "voted for the same party" for a decade or more. In the 1990 general election study, 56 percent of the respondents answered this way. Akarui Senkyo Suishin Kyokai, *DA-39kai Shugiin Giin Sosenkyo no Jittai,* p. 346.

37. Some Japanese qualify as negative partisans because they lack positive identifica-tions but feel negatively toward nonpreferred parties. Ichiro Miyake, "Types of Partisan-ship, Partisan Attitudes and Voting Choices," in Flanagan et al., *Japanese Voter,* chap. 6. On quite a few dimensions — habitual voting, intermittent partisanship, and negative partisanship — Japanese voters are more like their counterparts in Europe than like Amer-ican voters. Authoritarian traditions followed by a period of widespread mobilization of the vote by candidate machines (Japan) and social cleavages (Europe) have shaped con-temporary loyalties differently in Japan and western Europe than in North America.

Up to now, followers of small parties, specifically Democratic Socialist sympathizers and identifiers with new parties (in 1976, the New Liberal Club), have had weaker party ties than followers of big parties, much as is the case in Europe. Their weak partisanship also made aggregate national levels lower than they would be otherwise. Bradley Rich-ardson, *The Party Type Principle* (Madrid: Centro de Estudios Avanzados en Ciencias Sociales, Instituto Juan March de Estudios e Investigaciones, 1993).

38. Richard K. Beardsley, John W. Hall, and Robert E. Ward, *Village Japan* (Chicago: University of Chicago Press, 1959), chap. 13.

39. The following description of candidate machines and their activities draws heavily from Bradley Richardson, "Japanese Local Politics: Support Mobilization and Leader-ship Styles," *Asian Survey* 7 (1967), pp. 860–75.; Gerald Curtis, *Election Campaigning Japanese Style* (New York: Columbia University Press, 1971); and recent Japanese news-paper and magazine articles. Theodore Bestor's description of urban community life and local candidate machines in *Neighborhood Tokyo* (Stanford: Stanford University Press, 1989) was also very useful.

40. Masayuki Fukuoka, "Tanaka Kakuei's Grass Roots," *Japan Echo* 10 (1983), p. 36.

41. This tendency was reported in Curtis, *Election Campaigning Japanese Style,* chap. 5; and Richardson, *Political Culture of Japan.*

42. *Yomiuri,* May 1, 1989.

43. *Asahi,* November 26, 1989. Because it is the custom in Japan for a political figure to make a gift of money to support local events, Dietmembers' participation in these local activities is different from the participation of politicians in the United States and most Western democracies, where money is often collected at local events rather than being paid out.

44. *Tokyo Shimbun,* January 29, 1989.

45. *Tokyo Shimbun,* January 30, 1989.

46. *Mainichi,* November 26, 1989. The Etsuzankai's maximum total membership was 98,000 persons. Fukuoka, "Tanaka Kakuei's Grass Roots."

47. Chalmers Johnson, "Tanaka Kakuei, Structural Corruption and the Advent of Machine Politics in Japan," *Journal of Japanese Studies* 12 (1986), p. 8. Public works

projects employ farmers in many places, to the extent that the construction industry has been said to have replaced agriculture as the main rural occupational base for the LDP. *Asahi,* April 11, 1983, reported that "farm and fishing villages were being turned into construction villages" and identified 80 percent of construction workers as part-time farmers.

48. These data are from the same source as Table 2.4, but party percentages were calculated from information not shown in the table. Replies total more than 100 percent because of multiple answers. The figures were actually 561 percent for candidate aspects of the campaign, 138 percent for party-related activities, and 109 percent for media exposure (the total for *multiple* answers was 806 percent). Some of the reported emphasis on candidates might have been artifactual, for party and media parts of the campaign were addressed in only nine of the total thirty-one aspects of the campaign covered by the standard Akarui Senkyo Suishin Kyokai battery of questions. But the emphasis also reflected the nature of the real world. For 1990 figures, see Akarui Senkyo Suishin Kyokai, *Dai-39kai Shugiin Giin Sosenkyo no Jittai* (Tokyo, 1991), p. 4.

49. The general expectation in the early years after the war was that "traditional" voting centered on the character of candidates would eventually be replaced by "modern" choices based more on self-interest, including party affiliation. Robert A. Scalapino and Junnosuke Masumi, *Parties and Politics in Contemporary Japan* (Berkeley: University of California Press, 1962), p. 124. Now we see that candidate-based choices have been remarkably resilient over time, even though party-based voting has also increased somewhat.

50. One reason that farmers became better off was government price supports for farm products, the result of Dietmembers' pressure on behalf of their farmer constituents. Nowadays most farm families depend on outside employment for most of their income. New job opportunities in many areas reflect industry penetration into rural districts, which, in some cases, has been motivated by government programs.

51. The electorate may also be becoming more open in their answers about campaign activities as the result of these same processes of social change. The total percentage of multiple replies about all kinds of electoral campaign activities has increased from slightly more than 600 percent to more than 800 percent in the twenty-year period covered by Akarui Senkyo Suishin Kyokai surveys.

52. Richardson, *Political Culture of Japan,* chap. 5, esp. pp. 108–17.

53. Even voting on the basis of seemingly ascriptive qualities may reflect underlying instrumental concerns, as I have shown elsewhere. Richardson, *Political Culture of Japan.*

54. Slight majorities (55 percent) favor national over local politics in the United States. Inter-University Consortium for Political and Social Research, *The American National Election Studies Series: 1972, 1974, and 1976* (Ann Arbor, Mich., 1979), vol. 2, p. 274.

55. Akarui Senkyo Suishin Kyokai, *Dai-38kai Shugiin Giin Sosenkyo, Dai-14kai Sangiin Giin Tsujo Senkyo no Jittai* (Tokyo, 1986), p. 5; and the same sources as for Table 2.6.

56. See Richardson, *Political Culture of Japan,* chap. 5.

57. Fukuoka, "Tanaka Kakuei's Grass Roots." But there were sizable aggregate defections from the LDP in the July 1993 election. These reflected both votes taken from the party's total by defecting candidates who ran under new party labels, typically in rural

areas, and rejection of LDP candidates due to the party's prominence in ongoing corruption scandals — defections that were most clearly visible in urban districts.

58. For an example of similar sentiments in an earlier United States see Herbert Gans, *The Urban Villagers* (New York: Free Press, 1962), p. 164.

59. Thomas Rochon, "Electoral Systems and the Basis of the Vote: The Case of Japan," in John Creighton Campbell, ed., *Parties, Candidates and Voters in Japan: Six Quantitative Studies* (Ann Arbor: Michigan Papers in Japanese Studies, 1981), pp. 1–28.

60. By personalism is meant the tendency in many areas of daily life to depend on face-to-face contacts between known people within small networks and groups more than on formal intermediaries. Parochialism invokes Chie Nakane's famous vertical society thesis that Japanese communities and groups are highly insulated from each other and vertically linked with national affairs. Nakane's observations on the importance of small units within in Japanese society are widely echoed in Japanese community and organization studies, even those in large, metropolitan areas, where parochial institutions were sometimes self-consciously created, as Theodore Bestor has documented in *Neighborhood Tokyo*. For Nakane's views see Nakane, *Japanese Society* (Berkeley: University of California Press, 1970), pp. 120–40.

Uchi-soto (inside-outside) distinctions in Japanese society, and especially a preference for uchi ties, also has a parochial connotation. Although uchi boundaries can be flexible, dependence on personal relationships seems to restrict their size. See Takeshi Ishida, "Conflict and Its Accommodation: Omote-Ura and Uchi-Soto Relations," in Ellis S. Krauss, Thomas P. Rohlen, and Patricia G. Steinhoff, eds., *Conflict in Japan* (Honolulu: University of Hawaii Press, 1984); and Thomas Rohlen, "Order in Japanese Society: Attachment, Authority and Routine," *Journal of Japanese Studies* 15 (1989), pp. 5–40.

61. The Communist Party has also received voting support from interest groups, usually from organizations closely affiliated with the communist movement, such as the Churitsu Roren unions and the Minsho, a group formed by the party to represent small-business people. The Minsho (Minshushokokai, or Democratic Commerce and Industry League) is discussed briefly in Curtis, *Election Campaigning Japanese Style*, p. 70.

62. Enterprise unions are the typical form of private-sector labor organization in Japan. The term *enterprise union* refers to unions formed within companies, like Toyota or Honda, rather than on an industrywide basis, for instance, among all auto workers. The latter kind of organization exists in Japan but is less influential than in the United States.

63. For example, see Bradley Richardson and Scott Flanagan, *Politics in Japan* (Boston: Little, Brown, 1984), pp. 305–6.

64. For an appreciation of the extent of this complexity and of the "shadow" role played by party affiliations in people's psychological responses to requests for cross-cutting votes see Bradley Richardson, "Social Networks, Influence Communications and the Vote," in Flanagan et al., *Japanese Voter,* esp. pp. 362–64. Richardson, "Constituency Candidates vs. Parties in Japanese Voting Behavior," pp. 695–718, sets forth a model of the Japanese vote and provides evidence that one in three people vote on the basis of the effects of candidate campaigns and related motivations, whereas the remaining two-thirds vote on the basis of party. Here, based on the ASSK findings in Table 2.5, I assume that, among those who vote regularly, roughly equal shares of the electorate

would respond to candidate versus party, other things being equal. These two sets of results, which reflect different statistical methods and questions, can be seen as upper and lower limits to the candidate vote.

65. See Table 2.5; and Richardson, "Constituency Candidates vs. Parties in Japanese Voting Behavior."

66. Campbell et al., *American Voter,* chap. 7; and David Butler and Donald E. Stokes, *Political Change in Britain* (New York: St. Martin's, 1969), pp. 45–55.

67. For anecdotes about these events, plus statistical evidence on the scope of change and related shifts in party support see Bradley Richardson, "Stability and Change in Japanese Voting Behavior." See also Gary Allinson, *Suburban Tokyo: A Comparative Study in Politics and Social Change* (Berkeley: University of California Press, 1979), esp. chap. 5.

68. Gerald Curtis, *The Japanese Way of Politics* (New York: Columbia University Press, 1988), p. 25.

69. Miyake, "Types of Partisanship, Partisan Attitudes and Voting Choices," pp. 206–20.

70. Japan has tens of thousands of shopkeepers' associations formed on the basis of location—an address district (*chome*), for instance, or proximity to a train or subway station or a particular street corner. (Chome are city blocks within which addresses are assigned arbitrarily on the basis of the sequence by which land was subdivided historically; street addresses do not exist in Japan.)

71. Bradley Richardson, "A Japanese House of Councillors Election: Support Mobilization and Political Recruitment," *Modern Asian Studies* 1 (1967), pp. 383–96.

72. In spite of the traditional affinity between farmers and the LDP, agricultural interest group support for the LDP has long been of a mixed and complicated nature. Zenchu, the political arm of the National Federation of Agricultural Cooperatives, has at times been critical of the Liberal Democrats, even while supporting the LDP in many places and consistently looking to the LDP for help. As is characteristic of Japanese organizations, there were some local farm cooperatives whose support did not go to the LDP. The cooperative movement has supported Socialist or independent left-wing candidates on quite a few occasions. *Yomiuri,* May 12, 1992. Social Democratic Party penetration of *unions* of farm cooperative employees was also reported in the 1970s. *Sankei,* June 4, 1974.

73. *Nihon Keizai,* April 23, 1989.

74. *Asahi,* April 22, 1989.

75. *Asahi,* April 22, 1989; *Mainichi,* April 4, 1989; *Asahi,* April 7, 1989.

76. *Nihon Keizai,* April 23, 1989; *Asahi,* May 2, 1989.

77. Akarui Senkyo Suishin Kyokai, *Dai-15kai Sangiin Giin Tsujo Senkyo no Jittai* (Tokyo, 1989), pp. 174–75; and Akarui Senkyo Suishin Kyokai, *Dai-38kai Shugiin Giin Sosenkyo, Sangiin Giin Tsujo Senkyo no Jittai* (Tokyo, 1986), pp. 304–5.

78. Seiji Koho Senta, *Seiji Handobukku* (Tokyo, 1992), pp. 281–82.

79. Interestingly, the interest group reactions in 1989 fit an often posited Japanese model of protest in which people at lower levels of hierarchical relationships signal their frustration to superiors with temporary disruptive behavior. See Richardson, *Political Culture of Japan,* pp. 99–100. It is also notable that the defections occurred in a House of

Councillors election, an arena of little apparent consequence for many voters, according to a variety of measures. The House of Councillors has been (1) the least interesting or relevant election for many Japanese (see Table 2.6), (2) the election for which party—a weak motivator—most exceeds candidate as a determinant of voting (see Table 2.6), and (3) an arena where the LDP traditionally did not do as well as in lower house elections.

80. The near collapse of the LDP's interest coalition in 1989 stands out as one of the major political crises since the war. From time to time specific interest groups have challenged the LDP. Criticism from big business has been especially conspicuous. In 1971, textile manufacturers were so opposed to Prime Minister Sato's deference to U.S. pressures for a volunteer limit on Japanese textile exports to the United States that they vowed to "overthrow the Sato government." Even if this statement was made partly for internal interest group consumption, it constitutes a severe critique of LDP leadership. *Nihon Seni Shimbun,* September 28, 1971.

81. Akarui Senkyo Suishin Kyokai, *Dai-32kai Shugiin Giin Sosenkyo no Jittai* (Tokyo, 1970), p. 211; and Richardson, "Party Loyalties and Party Saliency in Japan."

82. Akarui Senkyo Suishin Kyokai, *Shugiin Giin Sosenkyo no Jittai* (Tokyo, 1991 and 1994).

83. In Tokyo and surrounding areas alone, Socialists were displaced in fifteen of twenty-five constituencies.

84. *Asahi,* July 15, 1993.

85. *Yomiuri,* October 21, 1993; *Nikkei Weekly,* May 30, 1994; *Sankei,* November 29, 1994.

86. For the "social contract" idea see Sheldon Garon and Mike Mochizuki, "Negotiating Social Contracts," in Andrew Gordon, ed., *Postwar Japan as History* (Berkeley: University of California Press, 1993), pp. 145–66. By "social contracts" are meant long-term relations in which particular social sectors are favored by a political party. The central idea is that relations are stable; the partners may disagree over details, but the overall relationship continues. The idea that Japanese electoral politics is based on explicit stable exchanges between major voting blocs and conservative parties and politicians accords with the view that exchange relationships are a central feature of Japanese society. See various works by Harumi Befu, including "Four Models of Japanese Society and Their Relevance to Conflict," in S. N. Eisenstadt, ed., *Japanese Models of Conflict Resolution* (London: Kegan Paul International, 1990), pp. 213–38.

87. The small-enterprise sector of farmers, small-business owners, and small-business employees did decline slightly over time as a relative proportion of the total electorate. The total figure for the three sectors was 72 percent in 1950, 67 percent in 1990.

88. Data limitations make it hard to be specific about how many blue-collar and white-collar employees from large firms were attracted to the LDP during its period in power. Workers who answer surveys (which are the only way to gather this kind of information) often know the size of their workplace in rough terms but not—in the case of large firms with multiple plants or offices—the size of the firm that employs them. Still, there is some fragmentary evidence of LDP inroads into even the ranks of organized labor. *Yomiuri* reported on September 20, 1985, that a Tekko Roren survey of thirty-nine thousand of its steelworker members showed the LDP leading all other parties in support (opposition parties collectively still had broader support than the LDP.)

Chapter 3: Parties Under the "1955 System"

1. Technically speaking, the two parties did not merge, for both were disbanded just before formation of the LDP. The most comprehensive study of the Liberal Democratic Party in English is Haruhiro Fukui, *Party in Power: The Japanese Liberal Democrats and Policymaking* (Berkeley: University of California Press, 1972). See also Nathaniel Thayer, *How the Conservatives Rule Japan* (Princeton, N.J.: Princeton University Press, 1969), for an insightful description of the LDP and its internal processes in the 1960s. For a view of the party in more recent times consult Nobuo Tomita, Akira Nakamura, and Ronald J. Hrebnar, "The Liberal Democratic Party: The Ruling Party of Japan," in Hrebnar, ed., *The Japanese Party System: From One Party Rule to Coalition Government* (Boulder, Colo.: Westview, 1986), pp. 235–82; Haruhiro Fukui, "The Liberal Democratic Party Revisited: Continuity and Change in the Party's Structure and Performance," *Journal of Japanese Studies* 10 (1984), 385–435; Gerald Curtis, *The Japanese Way of Politics* (New York: Columbia University Press, 1988), chap. 3; and Seizaburo Sato and Tetsuhisa Matsuzaki, *Jiminto Seiken* (Tokyo: Chuo Koronsha, 1986).

2. On the organizational structure of the Liberal Democratic Party see Seiji Koho Senta, *Seiji Handobukku* (Tokyo, 1991); and Fukui, *Party in Power*, chap. 4.

3. LDP membership was 2,963,312, according to *Asahi*, September 17, 1989. Two years earlier the LDP reported a membership of 1.7 million; in 1983 the figure was said to be 1.26 million. See *Nihon Keizai*, August 22, 1984; *Tokyo Shimbun*, August 2, 1987.

4. The factions fit Duverger's idea that every party has prototypical basic units. See Maurice Duverger, *Political Parties* (London: Methuen, 1951), chap. 1.

5. *Sankei*, January 13, 1989. Takeshita and Kanemaru also had different visions of appropriate coalition strategies for the LDP after its loss of the 1989 upper house election. Kanemaru proposed a grand coalition with the SDPJ, and Takeshita was inclined to support a right-centrist coalition. *Sankei*, December 24, 1989. Kanemaru's son is married to Takeshita's daughter. At the time of Takeshita's rise to power, Kanemaru was reported to be Takeshita's "guardian," that is, main ally and spokesman.

6. *Asahi*, September 7, 1989, June 19, 1990, and May 3, 1991; *Sankei*, December 29, 1989.

7. *Tokyo Shimbun*, June 14, 1989; *Asahi*, June 24, 1990. *Asahi*, February 1, 1985, provides an excellent account of the formation of the Soseikai. Subfactions existed before the 1980s. Earlier in the development of the LDP, Kakuei Tanaka and Takeo Fukuda led subfactions of the Sato faction.

8. *Nihon Keizai*, February 13, 1985 (E). Throughout, "(E)" refers to evening edition.

9. A dramatic feud took place between Kiichi Miyazawa and Rokusuke Tanaka when Miyazawa succeeded as leader of the Suzuki faction. See *Nihon Keizai*, December 12, 1983.

10. *Yomiuri*, December 6, 1988; *Nihon Keizai*, June 10, 1990. See also *Asahi*, June 19, 1990, and July 7, 1991, for other examples of intergenerational tensions. See *Mainichi*, March 7 and 9, 1990.

11. *Asahi*, April 18, 1988.

12. For identities of LDP policy groups see Seiji Koho Senta, *Seiji Handobukku*, for the relevant year.

13. Haruhiro Fukui, "Tanaka Goes to Peking," in T. J. Pempel, ed., *Policymaking in Contemporary Japan* (Ithaca, N.Y.: Cornell University Press, 1977), pp. 60–102.

14. Takashi Inoguchi and Tomoaki Iwai, *Zoku Giin no Kenkyu* (Tokyo: Nihon Keizai Shimbunsha, 1987); Sato and Matsuzaki, *Jiminto Seiken*.

15. See also Leonard Schoppa, "Zoku Power and LDP Power: A Case Study of the Zoku Role in Education Policy," *Journal of Japanese Studies* 17 (1991), pp. 79–103. Schoppa argues credibly that the zoku enhanced party influence in specific policy arenas but diminished the ability of the party to provide overall leadership, set unified priorities, or engineer policy change.

16. The LDP interest coalition took form in the 1950s when important interest organizations were formed in several sectors, including small business and farming. See Kent Calder, *Crisis and Compensation: Public Policy and Political Stability in Japan* (Princeton, N.J.: Princeton University Press, 1988); Sheldon Garon and Mike Mochizuki, "Negotiating Social Contracts," in Andrew Gordon, *Postwar Japan as History* (Berkeley: University of California Press, 1993), pp. 145–66; and Michio Muramatsu and Ellis Krauss, "The Conservative Policy Line and the Development of Patterned Pluralism," in Kozo Yamamura and Yasukichi Yasuba, eds., *The Political Economy of Japan*, vol. 1: *The Domestic Transformation* (Stanford: Stanford University Press, 1987), pp. 516–54; Muramatsu and Krauss, "The Dominant Party and Social Coalitions in Japan," in T. J. Pempel, ed., *Uncommon Democracies: The One-Party Dominant Regimes* (Ithaca, N.Y.: Cornell University Press, 1990), pp. 282–305.

17. On the concept of the catchall party see Otto Kircheimer, "The Transformation of Western European Party Systems," in Joseph LaPalombara and Myron Weiner, eds., *Political Parties and Political Development* (Princeton, N.J.: Princeton University Press, 1966).

18. Nevertheless, the political arm of Zenchu, the association of large farm cooperatives, did not formally endorse the LDP at the national level because of differences in members' preferences in some parts of the country. The small-business sector was also divided. There are several thousand small-business groups in Japan. Some small-business owners' groups have preferred the Democratic Socialists and, in the 1970s, the Communists.

19. Interest group alignments were identified through data on the backgrounds of upper house parliamentarians, in Seiji Koho Senta, *Seiji Handobukku* (Tokyo, 1991).

20. T. J. Pempel and Keiichi Tsunekawa, "Corporatism Without Labor? The Japanese Anomaly," in Philippe Schmitter and Gerhard Lembruch, eds., *Trends Toward Corporatist Intermediation* (Beverly Hills, Calif.: Sage, 1979), pp. 231–70.

21. Michael Donnelly's descriptions of rice price subsidy decisions in different years show the variability over time of policymaking regarding just one kind of policy. See Donnelly, "Setting the Price of Rice: A Study in Political Decisionmaking," in Pempel, *Uncommon Democracies*, pp. 143–200.

22. A third reason for the LDP's continuity at the elite level was the strong anticommunist views of some party leaders and Dietmembers. For them, having the Self-Defense Forces and maintaining an anticommunist foreign policy were essential to national security. Keeping the Socialist and Communist parties out of power was a domestic imperative. Both goals required a conservative party majority in the Diet, a fact that reinforced other motivations for preserving the party's organizational integrity.

23. See Junnosuke Masumi, *Postwar Politics in Japan* (Berkeley: Center for Japanese Studies, University of California, Japan Research Monograph 6, 1985.)

24. One of the driving forces in Japanese culture is a desire to avoid uncertainty, according to comparative survey evidence in Geert Hofstede, *Cultures and Organizations: Software of the Mind* (New York: McGraw-Hill, 1991), chap. 5, esp. p. 113.

25. Some faction leaders were more skilled at raising and distributing funds than others. *Sankei,* May 29 and December 26, 1989.

26. See Fukui, *Party in Power,* chap. 5. A tendency for factions to draw more members from LDP contingents in the lower than the upper house should be kept in mind.

27. *Tokyo Shimbun,* June 3, 1983; *Nihon Keizai,* April 21, 1985. This was one of the aspects of factions that has led me to reject the idea that factionalism has reflected mainly (1) the existence until 1994 of multimember lower house constituencies and (2) candidate reliance on faction support in constituencies where more than one candidate stood from the same party. Factions simply did too much for their members to make this simple idea the sole explanation. Also, newspaper accounts have unanimously stressed the importance of handing out positions to the existence and survival of factions.

28. Leaders in the Abe and Nakasone factions gave New Year's presents worth as much as $23,000 per member to retain members' support during a leadership transition, according to *Sankei,* December 28, 1989, and *Asahi* July 23, 1991.

29. *Yomiuri,* October 5, 1993; Mike Masato Mochizuki, "Managing and Influencing the Japanese Legislative Process: The Role of Parties and the National Diet" (Ph.D. diss., Harvard University, 1982).

30. Factions were occasionally led by persons other than the faction leader. These matters are kept track of in Seiji Koho Senta, *Seiji Handobukku.*

31. Lateral entries by independents sometimes took place and were different from defections. For example, the Mitsuzuka and Watanabe factions both courted Noriyuki Sekine after his election in the Saitama local district in the 1992 upper house election. Various factions also sought after five other newly elected upper house independents in the weeks following the election. *Nihon Keizai,* August 2, 1992.

32. See Nelson Polsby, "The Institutionalization of the U.S. House of Representatives," *American Political Science Review* 62 (1968), pp. 144–68.

33. *Nihon Keizai,* January 16 and August 17, 1989.

34. *Sankei,* November 9, 1990.

35. The former Tanaka faction was often said to be especially well organized, even to the point of holding meetings for members' secretaries. *Tokyo Shimbun,* August 22, 1990. Faction leaders created organizations of regional supporters in some years in order to mobilize support in LDP elections. The extension of faction-based mobilization to the grass roots of the party is another example of the tendency of Japanese politicians to organize intraparty and extraparty relations thoroughly to avoid uncertainty. See *Asahi,* July 23, 1991; *Nihon Keizai,* June 11, 1985.

36. The seniority norm in the party parallels widespread usage of this principle in appointments to positions in corporations and the ministries. The seniority norm has existed in other political bodies for exactly the same reasons that it was found in LDP factions. For a clear statement of the seniority norm see *Asahi,* June 6, 1990. Having mechanisms like the seniority norm makes sense when one appreciates that many Japa-

nese politicians (like politicians elsewhere) are sensitive to even minor slights. Even though Shin Kanemaru was Takeshita's main lieutenant in forming the Takeshita faction, he refused to speak to Takeshita after feeling slighted by Takeshita. Similarly, SDPJ Vice Chair Takako Doi threatened to resign because she was not consulted on election reform plans that would affect her constituency. *Sankei,* June 16, 1985.

37. The accession to the headship of the Abe faction by Hiroshi Mitsuzuka, who was junior to nine other faction members in number of times elected to the Diet, is a good example of a violation of standing norms. *Asahi,* July 23, 1991. Ichiro Ozawa's rapid rise within the LDP was likewise criticized by older members of the Takeshita faction. *Yomiuri,* April 10, 1991. Perhaps the most bizarre example of the operation of the seniority norm was Takeo Nishioka's expulsion from the Miyazawa faction for having held too many important party positions for a person of his seniority. *Nihon Keizai,* December 29, 1990. Yohei Kono, a lateral entry after the disbandment of the New Liberal Club, was not welcomed into the Miyazawa faction by some members (and was said to be ineligible to run for party president in 1989 for this reason). *Yomiuri,* July 27, 1989; *Mainichi,* March 11, 1990.

38. *Nihon Keizai,* May 5, 1991, reports that Takeshita faction member and former party Secretary General Ichiro Ozawa met with groups of Takeshita faction members with different seniority ranks and "poured sake" for them as a means of solidifying his support within the faction.

39. In Japan people of the same age, same year of entry into a company, or same school class commonly form groups. The existence of seniority-based groups within LDP factions is consistent with general social practice. Stimulating solidarity with faction activities reflected both a response to the ambition rife among politicians and the importance of uchi or insider relationships. See Takeshi Ishida, "Conflict and Its Accommodation: *Omote-Ura* and *Uchi-Soto* Relations," in Ellis S. Krauss, Thomas P. Rohlen, and Patricia G. Steinhoff, eds., *Conflict in Japan* (Honolulu: University of Hawaii Press, 1984), pp. 16–38.

40. Both cultural principles and political pragmatism were the motivation for efforts such as those made to preserve balance in the former Takeshita faction between Ichiro Ozawa, Ryutaro Hashimoto, and Tsutomu Hata. *Sankei,* April 19, 1988.

41. Michio Watanabe's generous gifts to the members of the Nakasone faction upon his takeover reportedly eliminated bad feelings and consolidated his position as faction leader among even former Nakasone loyalists. In another case, Mutsuki Kato and Yoshiro Mori of the Abe faction gave subfaction followers monetary gifts. *Yomiuri,* August 15, 1990; *Sankei,* December 28, 1989.

42. Such was the mood within the Abe faction upon his death, according to *Asahi,* May 16, 1991. Earlier, when he was ill, faction senior Yoshio Sakurauchi suggested that the faction revert to being a study group because of its loss of politically meaningful status. *Yomiuri,* September 9, 1991.

43. In Figure 3.3 faction splits are ignored to some extent. In the 1960s and early 1970s several small factions were formed outside the five main factions when there were splits in the larger factions. For details see Asahi Shimbunsha, *Asahi Nenkan* (Tokyo, 1974), p. 256.

44. Most factions wanted to have at least one of their leading members capture a top

ministry appointment or one of the party's top positions. Sometimes particular faction members also wanted specific cabinet positions. The economic ministry portfolios — Finance, International Trade and Industry, and Transportation — were keenly sought. Foreign Ministry appointments were also valued. Often faction members wanted to be appointed construction minister to guarantee influence over public works projects, and over time the ministry's importance came to resemble that of Finance and MITI. *Asahi,* September 7, 1989.

45. *Asahi,* May 28, 1987; *Nihon Keizai,* May 3, 1989.

46. *Sankei,* October 20, 1987 (E). Takeo Fukuda's vendetta against Kakuei Tanaka and cabinets supported by the Tanaka faction surfaced every now and then from 1972 until Takeshita's takeover of the Tanaka faction in 1987.

47. Curtis, *Japanese Way of Politics,* p. 87.

48. The formal rules for choosing the party president were changed twice in recent decades. Between 1974 and 1989 party members could choose a president in a party convention vote or in a two-stage party election that included a first-stage direct primary. Under a more recent (1989) version of the presidential election rules, party members vote for candidates on the same day as members of the parliamentary party. The choices of party members are aggregated at the prefecture level through an arrangement resembling that of the American electoral college.

49. Informal negotiations often preceded formal votes. In most instances, the votes were ratified at a special party convention called for the purpose. But in six of twenty-three cases between 1956 and 1991, the party president was chosen only by the Diet caucus of the LDP. See Shujiro Kato, *Seiji no Shikumi* (Tokyo: PHP Kenkyujo, 1993).

50. *Nihon Keizai,* October 20, 1987.

51. *Nihon Keizai,* May 3, 1989; *Tokyo Shimbun,* May 16, 1991. Like the appointment of Miki in 1974 and Suzuki in 1980, the fine-tuned coalition strategies of the faction leaders Takeshita and Abe were thrown into confusion when a scandal forced Takeshita to resign in 1989. Abe's death in early 1991 provided an additional jolt to expectations. The sudden changes led to speculation that a turnover in leadership generations might take place and that the window of opportunity for leaders of the Abe, Takeshita, and Miyazawa age-group was closing. But Kiichi Miyazawa, a member of that generation, became prime minister in the fall of 1991. *Nihon Keizai,* May 5, 1991; *Asahi,* May 16, 1991.

52. *Tokyo Shimbun,* June 23, 1991. Since 1964 only two prime ministers, Eisaku Sato (1964–72) and Yasuhiro Nakasone (1982–87), had longer terms of eight and five years, respectively.

53. There were still some irregularities in assignments. In most cases, the faction of the incumbent prime minister (or sometimes the Tanaka faction, because of its huge size) did disproportionately well. Four of the twelve coalitions in 1980–90 excluded the smallest party faction, the Miki-Komoto group. The second Suzuki cabinet excluded Tanaka faction members from leading positions because of the problems associated with Tanaka's indictment for bribery. The first Kaifu government, formed in the late summer of 1989, excluded the Miyazawa faction because it had supported Kaifu's opponent for the party presidency.

54. The "fair shares" principle of Japanese political culture is described by John Camp-

bell, in "Japanese Budget Baransu," in Ezra Vogel, ed., *Modern Japanese Organization and Decision-Making* (Berkeley: University of California Press, 1975), pp. 71–100. The move to all-party coalitions is a departure from simple majoritarianism, argued to be the dominant principle of LDP coalition behavior in Michael Leiserson, "Factions and Coalitions in One Party Japan," *American Political Science Review* 62 (1968), pp. 770–87.

55. See Haruhiro Fukui, "The Policy Research Council of Japan's Liberal Democratic Party: Policy Making Role and Practice," *Asian Thought and Society* 11 (1987), pp. 3–30. See also Mike Masato Mochizuki, "Managing and Influencing the Japanese Legislative Process: The Role of Parties and the National Diet" (Ph.D. diss., Harvard University, 1982), chap. 3; Nihon Keizai Shimbun, *Jiminto Seimu Chosakai* (Tokyo: Nikkei Shimbunsha, 1985).

56. See Yung H. Park, *Bureaucrats and Ministers in Contemporary Japanese Government* (Berkeley: Institute of East Asian Studies and Center for Japanese Studies, University of California, 1986).

57. *Asahi*, May 16, 1984; *Sankei*, July 24, 1984 (E); *Tokyo Shimbun*, February 28, 1987.

58. *Asahi Nenkan.*

59. See John Campbell, *Contemporary Japanese Budget Politics* (Berkeley: University of California Press, 1979), pp. 128–33.

60. J. A. A. Stockwin, "The Japan Socialist Party: A Politics of Permanent Opposition," in Hrebnar, *Japanese Party System*, pp. 104–5.

61. *Nihon Keizai*, February 9, 1971. The Sone group was named the Democratic Socialism and Politics Research Council and nicknamed the Tameike Club, after a street intersection near the Diet. *Mainichi*, November 30, 1971.

62. *Tokyo Shimbun*, March 30, 1985. On June 30, 1985, both *Mainichi* and *Nihon Keizai* described a meeting that day of the "eastern" group, consisting of thirty-one of the fifty-one Democratic Socialist Dietmembers and headed by Ikko Kasuga.

63. *Sankei*, February 16, 1985. According to *Mainichi,* June 30, 1955, there was a group with the slogan Overthrow Rule by the Elders. As with the LDP, seniority was measured by number of times elected to the Diet.

64. Some famous divisions in the Japan Communist Party have been over ideology, such as the division between a pro-Soviet and an internationalist group in the 1950s. *Asahi*, February 27, 1973; Peter Berton, "The Japan Communist Party: The Lovable Party," in Hrebnar, *Japanese Party System*, p. 119.

65. Government employee labor unions and the recently formed united labor federation, Rengo, have been similarly fragmented.

66. On the organization of the Clean Government Party see Ronald Hrebnar, "The Komeito Party of 'Buddhist Democracy,' " in Hrebnar, *Japanese Party System*, pp. 158–63.

67. On party organization see Seiji Koho Senta, *Seiji Handobukku*, any year.

68. *Yomiuri*, October 5, 1993.

69. Robert Michels, *Political Parties* (Glencoe, Ill.: Free Press, 1949); Duverger, *Political Parties*; Sigmund Neumann, *Modern Political Parties* (Chicago: Chicago University Press, 1956); and Neumann, "Toward a Comparative Study of Political Parties," in Harry Eckstein and David Apter, eds., *Comparative Politics: A Reader* (New York: Free Press of Glencoe, 1963), pp. 351–67.

70. Hobby clubs, groups of retirees, sports clubs, and the like were established, as were functional groups for small-business owners, farmers, and those in other occupations. See Kurt Steiner, *Politics in Austria* (Boston: Little, Brown, 1976), pp. 119–54; and Keith Hill, "Belgium: Political Change in a Segmented Society," in Richard Rose, ed., *Electoral Behavior: A Comparative Handbook* (New York: Free Press), pp. 31–51.

71. Samuel Eldersveld, *Political Parties: A Behavioral Analysis* (Chicago: Rand McNally, 1964). See also V. O. Key, *Parties, Politics and Pressure Groups* (New York: Thomas Y. Crowell, 1958), chap. 12.

72. Kurt Shell describes the Austrian Socialist Party as highly centralized in both practice and formal organizational structure. See Shell, *The Transformation of Austrian Socialism* (Albany: State University of New York Press), pp. 95–111. But not all European parties are centralized to the same degree. Candidate nominations seem to be an aspect of party procedures where local influence can prevail. See Jeffrey Obler, "The Role of the National Party Leaders in the Selection of Parliamentary Candidates." *Comparative Politics* 5 (1974), pp. 157–84. Older models of European party organization are also less valid than they were as recently as the 1960s. Stefano Bartolini charts big declines in memberships in some European Socialist parties, in Bartolini, "The Membership of Mass Parties: The Social Democratic Experience, 1889–1978," in Hans Daalder and Peter Mair, eds., *Western European Party Systems: Continuity and Change* (Beverly Hills, Calif.: Sage, 1983). pp. 177–220.

73. David Hine, *Governing Italy: The Politics of Bargained Pluralism* (Oxford: Oxford University Press, 1993), chap. 4.

74. See Maurice Duverger, *Political Parties* (London: Methuen, 1951), chap. 1; Raphael Zariski, "Intra-Party Conflict in a Dominant Party: The Experience of Italian Christian Democracy," *Journal of Politics* 27 (1965), pp. 3–34; and Frank Belloni and Dennis Beller, *Faction Politics* (Santa Barbara, Calif.: ABC-Clio, 1980).

Chapter 4: Party Fragmentation and Coalition Dynamics

1. The essential coalitional nature of political parties is highlighted in a recent work by Angelo Panebianco: *Political Parties: Organization and Power* (Cambridge: Cambridge University Press, 1988).

2. Haruhiro Fukui, "Tanaka Goes to Peking: A Case Study in Foreign Policymaking," in T. J. Pempel, ed., *Policymaking in Contemporary Japan* (Ithaca, N.Y.: Cornell University Press, 1977), pp. 60–102.

3. *Asahi,* November 11, 1973.

4. *Mainichi,* March 28, 1974; *Asahi,* November 11, 1973.

5. *Tokyo Shimbun,* July 12, 1974; *Asahi,* July 16 and 27 and November 11, 1973; *Mainichi,* July 17, 1974; *Yomiuri,* July 13, 1974.

6. Two examples of Tanaka's use of his position to make favorable real estate investments were reported by *Asahi,* July 16–17, 1984. In one case, a Tanaka-owned real estate company purchased farmland that was undervalued because of intermittent flooding. After Tanaka bought the land, the Ministry of Construction built a protective dike, and he resold the now valuable farmland at an enormous profit. On another occasion, Tanaka used a tax loophole to exchange summer homes with a company president to avoid

paying high taxes on the sale of his original home, which had a higher valuation than one he traded it for.

7. *Asahi*, July 9, 1975.

8. *Nihon Keizai*, August 8 and 18, 1976.

9. *Nihon Keizai*, August 24 and 31 and October 22, 1976; *Yomiuri*, September 4, 1976; *Kanagawa Shimbun*, September 9, 1976; *Mainichi*, October 19, 1992.

10. Seiji Koho Senta, *Seiji Handobukku* (Tokyo, 1990); *Asahi*, October 2, 1993.

11. *Asahi*, April 5, 1989.

12. *Mainichi*, April 2, 1990.

13. *Asahi*, August 19 (E), and October 22, 1985.

14. *Asahi*, August 1, 1989; *Yomiuri*, March 29, 1989.

15. *Asahi*, August 1, 1989.

16. *Nihon Keizai*, April 4, 1991.

17. *Asahi*, June 13, 1988 (E); *Mainichi*, August 14, 1990.

18. *Asahi*, June 27, 1987.

19. Local SDPJ organizations have been the bastion of the ultra-left-wing Socialist Association. In the past, the value of the association as an organizational base often made intraparty agreement extremely difficult. Despite a decline in membership, the association is still active in some parts of the country.

20. *Tokyo Shimbun*, November 30, 1990; *Nihon Keizai*, February 7 (E) and May 23, 1991.

21. *Nihon Keizai*, November 15, 1992.

22. *Nikkei Weekly*, December 20, 1993; *Nihon Keizai* and *Yomiuri*, April 21, 1994. The Japan New Party changed its name to Kakushin (Reform) at this time. *Yomiuri*, April 6, 1994.

23. *Yomiuri*, March 24, 1994. This group appears to have changed names or spun off two other groups, in a way symbolic of the ferment of the times. Those who proposed electoral reform alleged that intra-LDP competition for seats in multimember constituencies led politicians to spend more money (sometimes collected by corrupt means) than they would if elections were based on a straight contest between candidates of two parties in single-seat constituencies.

24. *Yomiuri*, January 6, 1994.

25. *Yomiuri*, October 15, 1993, January 6 and March 24, 1994; *Sankei*, February 21, 1994; *Asahi*, June 30, 1994.

26. *Nihon Keizai*, July 20, 1989 (E); *Yomiuri*, July 25, 1993; *Tokyo Shimbun*, May 27, 1994; *Sankei*, June 11, 1994; *Nikkei Weekly*, May 30, 1994.

27. *Nikkei Weekly*, December 6, 1993, January 24, 1994. In the autumn of 1994 this group became the New Democratic League. *Nikkei Weekly*, October 3, 1994.

28. *Yomiuri*, April 4, 1994; *Nikkei Weekly*, April 25, 1994.

29. *Nikkei Weekly*, July 26, 1993; *Nihon Keizai*, August 22, 1993.

30. Moves to modernize the LDP have a long history. An intraparty group, the Party Organization Research Council (led by later Prime Minister Takeo Miki) recommended dissolution of the factions as early as 1963. The plea was repeated many times.

31. *Nikkei Weekly*, January 24, 1994.

32. *Nikkei Weekly*, April 25, 1994. Some factions formed study groups as a step

toward more legitimacy, according to *Tokyo Shimbun,* April 25, 1994. See also *Yomiuri,* September 9, 1994; *Nihon Keizai,* September 17 (E) and 19, 1994; *Sankei,* October 14, 1994. The Mitsuzuka faction thus became the Seiwakai, the Miyazawa faction the Kochi-kai, the Watanabe faction the Policy and Science Affairs Research Group, the Obuchi faction the Heisei Policy Research Association, and the Komoto faction the New Policy Research Association.

33. *Asahi,* September 18, 1993; *Nikkei Weekly,* September 20, 1993.

34. See Junnosuke Masumi, *Postwar Politics in Japan* (Berkeley: Institute of East Asian Studies and Center for Japanese Studies, University of California, 1985).

35. *Mainichi,* March 17, 1989; *Nihon Keizai,* March 18, 1989.

36. *Nihon Keizai,* March 18 and November 19, 1989, and March 23, 1990; *Asahi,* April 8, 1989. An opposition party summit was held in Kyoto on April 7, 1989. Eichi Nagasue of the Democratic Socialist Party was host. Nagasue was said to be a good choice because he was friends with a Doshisha University professor who had taught the head of the SDPJ, Takako Doi. Nagasue was also close to another professor who had taught the head of the Clean Government Party, Junya Yano. Japanese-style personalism is not solely the province of tradition-minded conservatives.

37. *Asahi,* April 8, 1989.

38. *Asahi,* April 22–25, 1994.

39. *Nihon Keizai,* August 6, 1994; *Asahi,* June 11, 1994. Ozawa maintained a close relationship with LDP faction leader Michio Watanabe, who, like Ozawa, was a supporter of a stronger military and foreign policy role for Japan. At one point, this relationship resulted in proposals for a "great conservative coalition," to include the Renewal Party, Clean Government Party, and Watanabe's faction from the LDP. *Mainichi,* January 14, 1994. It is symptomatic of the times that Watanabe was himself associated with an earlier idea to form a cross-party group called the Comprehensive Economic Policy Study Association. *Nihon Keizai,* September 23, 1993.

40. *Nikkei Weekly,* May 23, 1994.

41. *Tokyo Shimbun,* April 10, 1994; *Mainichi,* January 24, 1994.

42. *Yomiuri,* September 27, 1994. On September 26, *Sankei* said the new party was based on a desire for power, just like the LDP at the time of its formation, and lamented its lack of a clear policy basis.

43. *Yomiuri,* May 30, 1994. See also the announcement of the formation of the New Democratic Federation from this group, in *Nikkei Weekly,* October 3, 1994.

44. Michael Leiserson, "Factions and Coalitions in One Party Japan," *American Political Science Review* 62 (1968), pp. 770–87.

Chapter 5: Executive and Bureaucratic Power

1. Karel van Wolferen, *The Enigma of Japanese Power* (New York: Vintage Books, 1990), p. 28.

2. Ibid.

3. John Creighton Campbell, *How Policies Change: The Japanese Government and the Aging Society* (Princeton, N.J.: Princeton University Press, 1992); Richard J. Samuels, *The Business of the Japanese State* (Ithaca, N.Y.: Cornell University Press, 1987).

4. For variables affecting party control of government see Richard Rose, "The Variability of Party Government: A Theoretical and Empirical Critique," *Political Studies* 17 (1969), pp. 413–45.

5. A decentralized bargained democracy is a political system in which most interest intermediation takes place when rank-and-file members of parliament are bound by their constituencies to support arrangements to represent the interests of specific economic sectors, such as farmers, small-business persons, or workers. Political parties, and often interest groups as well, are themselves decentralized. A programmatic democracy is a democracy in which voters choose in elections the party they prefer to run the government on the basis of the policy programs of competing parties. Under this system, parties and policymaking are normally centralized, and often there are only two major parties, so that electoral alternatives are clear. Interest intermediation takes place between the headquarters of parties and interest groups. Rank-and-file members of parliament mainly react to government bill proposals and do not as commonly exert upward pressures on party or government leaders on behalf of narrow political interests.

6. For documentation of elitist and other views of Japanese politics see Haruhiro Fukui, "Studies in Policymaking: A Review of the Literature," in T. J. Pempel, ed., *Policymaking in Contemporary Japan* (Ithaca, N.Y.: Cornell University Press, 1977), chap. 2.

7. Yung H. Park, *Bureaucrats and Ministers in Contemporary Japanese Government* (Berkeley: Institute of East Asian Studies and Center for Japanese Studies, University of California, 1986), chap. 2.

8. There are many studies of coalitions in political science. For a set of studies that deal with coalitions in the more general way suggested here see Sven Groennings, E. W. Kelley, and Michael Leiserson, eds., *The Study of Coalition Behavior: Theoretical Perspectives and Cases from Four Continents* (New York: Holt, Rinehart and Winston, 1970).

9. Fukui, "Studies in Policymaking."

10. Robert A. Scalapino and Junnosuke Masumi, *Parties and Politics in Contemporary Japan* (Berkeley: University of California Press, 1962), chap. 5.

11. *Tokyo Shimbun,* February 23, 1983.

12. *Tokyo Shimbun,* April 25, 1987.

13. *Mainichi,* April 2, 1985 (E); *Asahi,* April 3, 1985.

14. *Nihon Keizai,* March 17, 1983; Hans Baerwald, *Party Politics in Japan* (Boston: Allen and Unwin, 1986), pp. 125–26.

15. *Sankei,* June 13, 1986.

16. *Sankei,* March 6, 1986; *Yomiuri,* March 19, 1986.

17. The green card issue concerned a system by which persons opening savings accounts in banks would have had to present a green identification card. Through this mechanism people would have been prevented from avoiding taxes on interest by opening accounts under false names. The Japanese do not have social security numbers like those used for identifying savers in the United States. *Nihon Keizai,* May 23, 1982; *Mainichi,* April 8, 1985; *Asahi,* October 3, 1986; *Tokyo Shimbun,* April 15, 1987.

18. Leonard Schoppa, "Zoku Power and LDP Power: A Case Study of the Zoku Role in Education Policy," *Journal of Japanese Studies* 17 (1991), pp. 79–103.

19. Michio Muramatsu, "Patterned Pluralism Under Challenge," in Gary D. Allinson and Yasunori Sone, eds., *Political Dynamics in Contemporary Japan* (Ithaca, N.Y.: Cornell University Press, 1993), pp. 57, 59. Policy communities are discussed by John Campbell in "Bureaucratic Primacy: Japanese Policy Communities in an American Perspective," *Governance* 2 (1989), pp. 5–22. In A. G. Jordan and J. J. Richardson's words: "There is a natural tendency for the political system in Britain to encourage the formation of stable policy communities, one of the primary purposes of which is to achieve a negotiated and stable policy environment. The underlying value is that, wherever possible, outcomes should be negotiated by policy professionals, with each participant fully aware of the needs and desires of the policy community. This is not to suggest an absence of conflict, but that conflict is, by agreement, kept within manageable grounds. . . . One of the rules of the game is that it is 'not done' to raise issues which are bound to cause bitterness and divide the policy community." Jordan and Richardson, *Government and Pressure Groups in Britain*, p. 181. A concept related to policy communities, "subgovernments," was introduced by Douglass Cater in *Power in Washington* (New York: Random House, 1964), p. 50, to describe the informal alliances between interest groups, congressional committees, and elements of the administrative bureaucracy. See also John Campbell, *Contemporary Japanese Budget Politics* (Berkeley: University of California Press, 1979), pp. 123–28, 268–72. The Japanese press has recently picked up another American term, *iron triangle,* to characterize intimate business, conservative party, and bureaucracy relations.

20. *Sankei,* February 19, 1987.

21. The Government-LDP Consultative Council was so named in July 1982. The group appears to have met at least monthly and maybe more often during Diet sessions. The party secretary general and policy council chair were included in the group. Depending on the issues of the day, various cabinet ministers were also present. *Nihon Keizai,* July 2 and December 24, 1982; *Sankei,* April 22, 1988.

22. See Park, *Bureaucrats and Ministers,* chap. 4.

23. See Chalmers Johnson, *MITI and the Japanese Miracle* (Stanford: Stanford University Press, 1982), pp. 261–62.

24. John Campbell, in *Contemporary Japanese Budget Politics,* chap. 6, lists some conditions under which ministers are dominated by their ministries, and vice versa.

25. The strongest academic supporter of the assertive LDP minister view is Yung H. Park; see his *Bureaucrats and Ministers,* esp. chap. 3. Newspaper accounts in recent years have also made this claim; for an example see *Yomiuri,* February 7, 1982. For a recent example of strong leadership by an LDP politician see the account of Rokusuke Tanaka's term as minister of international trade and industry in *Yomiuri,* July 16, 1982.

26. Rose, "Variability of Party Government," pp. 443–45, was helpful here. But Richard Rose's assertion that British ministerial appointees could only devote half their time to ministerial business owing to the necessity of their presence at parliamentary debates was not the case for Japan, according to aides of two major LDP leaders, whom I interviewed in 1990. One said that a large part of his job was to report what happened in legislative committee meetings to his boss.

27. Muramatsu, "Patterned Pluralism Under Challenge," pp. 59–60.

28. The Ikeda cabinet capitulated in the rice price negotiations in 1961. Ikeda's successor, Eisaku Sato, was sometimes likewise forced to capitulate to Liberal Democratic and farm group demands; at other times he was able to resist pressures from these groups. See Michael Donnelly, "Setting the Price of Rice: A Case Study in Political Decision Making," in Pempel, *Policymaking in Contemporary Japan*, pp. 171–72.

29. *Yomiuri*, January 5, 1988. See also Thomas Rohlen, "Order in Japanese Society: Attachment, Authority and Routine," *Journal of Japanese Studies* 15 (1989), p. 37.

30. For more on the frequently reactive role of Japanese prime ministers see Kenji Hayao, *The Japanese Prime Minister and Public Policy* (Pittsburgh: University of Pittsburgh Press, 1993).

31. For an example of the arbiter role in a ministry setting see Johnson, *MITI and the Japanese Miracle*, p. 263. The example involved an appointment at MITI; and a senior LDP leader, Etsuzaburo Shiina, played the role of arbiter.

32. Michael Donnelly, "Setting the Price of Rice," pp. 171–72. See also Donnelly, "Conflict over Government Authority and Markets: Japan's Rice Economy," in Ellis S. Krauss, Thomas P. Rohlen, and Patricia G. Steinhoff, eds., *Conflict in Japan* (Honolulu: University of Hawaii Press, 1984), pp. 348 ff., where the arbiter role is described and several more complex agenda-setting tactics and other decisionmaking roles are discussed. John Campbell also describes such roles in *How Policies Change*, p. 61. For earlier examples and the use of the term *arbiter* to describe leading executive bodies see Bradley Richardson, "Policymaking in Japan: An Organizing Perspective," in Pempel, *Policymaking in Contemporary Japan*, pp. 239–69.

33. *Asahi*, December 29, 1984. Tadashi Hanami discusses the concept of an arbiter role in "Conflict and Resolution in Industrial Relations and Labor Law," in Krauss et al., *Conflict in Japan*, pp. 117–18.

34. The Ministry of Finance traditionally had considerable say about allocations to specific ministries in the annual process of microbudgeting, even though party politics sometimes intervened to force ministry concessions. See Campbell, *Contemporary Japanese Budget Politics*, pp. 43–70.

35. Campbell, *Contemporary Japanese Budget Politics*, esp. pp. 160–62.

36. Johnson, *MITI and the Japanese Miracle*, pp. 259, 262–63.

37. See Hayao, *Japanese Prime Minister and Public Policy*, chap. 9.

38. Muramatsu, "Patterned Pluralism Under Challenge," pp. 63–69; Frank Schwartz, "Fairy Cloaks and Familiar Talks," in Allinson and Sone, *Political Dynamics in Contemporary Japan*, pp. 234–41; Hayao, *Japanese Prime Minister and Public Policy*, chaps. 3 and 4.

39. Haruhiro Fukui, "Tanaka Goes to Peking: A Case Study in Foreign Policymaking," in Pempel, *Policymaking in Contemporary Japan*, pp. 60–102.

40. See, among various sources, Scalapino and Masumi, *Parties and Politics in Contemporary Japan*, chap. 5.

41. Chalmers Johnson, "Japan: Who Governs? An Essay on Official Bureaucracy," *Journal of Japanese Studies* 2 (1975), p. 6. The figure is currently 10,942, according to *Sankei*, October 1, 1993.

42. See David Friedman's, *The Misunderstood Miracle: Industrial Development and Political Change in Japan* (Ithaca, N.Y.: Cornell University Press, 1988); and Richard

Samuels, "The Industrial Destructuring of the Japanese Aluminum Industry," *Pacific Affairs* 36 (1983), p. 499. Samuels comments: "The well-fabled bureaucracy is itself often dependent in the same way upon the industrial associations and firms with which it works so closely."

43. Michio Muramatsu, *Sengo Nihon no Kanryosei* (Tokyo: Toyo Keizai Shuppansha, 1981), p. 53.

44. From 1918 to 1936 ministers were more subject to the influence of political parties in the Diet than the constitution provided. But after the mid-1930s some military leaders took advantage of the constitution to reassert their ministerial authority over nonmilitary aspects of governance. See Peter Duus, *Party Rivalry and Political Change in Taisho Japan* (Stanford: Stanford University Press, 1968).

45. See Muramatsu, *Sengo Nihon no Kanryosei*, p. 56. The four bases for Japanese ministerial power that we have identified — legal authority, expertise, a statist tradition, and societal deference — correspond to four of the fifteen ways a state can enhance its autonomy in Eric Nordlinger's Type III category of state-society interactions. Nordlinger, *On the Autonomy of the Democratic State* (Cambridge: Harvard University Press, 1981).

46. For a discussion of the declining strength of economic ministries and shifting policy preferences and authority among noneconomic ministries in the 1980s see Muramatsu, *Sengo Nihon no Kanryosei,* pp. 64–66.

47. Chalmers Johnson concludes that the strong Japanese ministries have led to a "soft" version of authoritarianism. Johnson, "Political Institutions and Economic Performance: The Government Business Relationship in Japan, South Korea and Taiwan," in Frederic C. Deyo, *The Political Economy of New Asian Industrialism* (Ithaca, N.Y.: Cornell University Press, 1982), p. 137. See also Johnson, "MITI and Japanese International Economic Policy," in Robert A. Scalapino, ed., *The Foreign Policy of Modern Japan* (Berkeley: University of California Press, 1977), pp. 253–55; Johnson, *MITI and the Japanese Miracle;* T. J. Pempel, "The Bureaucratization of Policymaking in Postwar Japan," *American Journal of Political Science* 18 (1977), pp. 647–74; Marie Anchordoguy, *Computers, Inc.: Japan's Challenge to IBM* (Cambridge: Council on East Asian Studies, Harvard University, 1990).

48. See Samuels, *Business of the Japanese State;* Campbell, *Contemporary Japanese Budget Politics;* Haruhiro Fukui, "Economic Planning in Postwar Japan: A Case Study in Policy Making," *Asian Survey* 12 (1972): 327–48; and Park, *Bureaucrats and Ministers.* An important survey-based article by Michio Muramatsu and Ellis Krauss indicates that senior bureaucrats see politicians as slightly stronger than themselves. Muramatsu and Krauss, "Bureaucrats and Politicians in Policymaking," *American Political Science Review* 78 (March 1984), pp 126–46, esp. p. 135.

49. See Chapter 9; and Friedman, *Misunderstood Miracle.*

50. The sources of my information are Asahi Shimbunsha, *Asahi Nenkan* (Tokyo: various years); and newspaper reports.

51. See Park, *Bureaucrats and Ministers,* chap. 6. The decline in the ratios of cabinet bills as a percentage of all bills could mean that cabinet bills were restricted to those that would not contradict the concerns of the increasingly powerful opposition parties. See *Yomiuri,* July 6, 1982; Muramatsu, *Sengo Nihon no Kanryosei,* pp. 51–53.

52. On vague bills see Frank Upham, *Law and Social Change in Japan* (Cambridge: Harvard University Press, 1987), chap. 5.

53. Figures are based on Okurasho Insatsu Kyoku, *Horei Zensho Somumokuroku* (Tokyo, 1994). A comparison of legislative with administrative output in earlier decades in the postwar period can be seen in Bradley Richardson and Scott Flanagan, *Politics in Japan* (Boston: Little, Brown, 1984), p. 349.

54. Another tool for enhancing ministry influence is the manipulation of information to establish the frame of reference within which a policy is debated. The Ministry of Finance is widely mentioned for regularly underestimating yearly GNP growth and thus effectively capping demands for increased allocations to ministries and other agencies. Other bureaucratic actors, such as the Economic Planning Agency, usually predict a higher annual GNP, because they have different concerns. Ministries also sometimes manipulate political actors whose activities in one realm they are able to control in order to constrain their behavior in a second realm. Frank Upham describes actions of this kind in connection with efforts by MITI to force one company out of the oil import business, in "The Man Who Would Import: A Cautionary Tale About Bucking the System in Japan," *Journal of Japanese Studies* 17 (1991), pp. 323–43. Ministerial actions such as these also resemble Eric Nordlinger's examples of ways the state, that is, ministries, can achieve greater autonomy. See Nordlinger, *On the Autonomy of the Democratic State*, chaps. 3 and 4.

55. *Nikkei Weekly*, March 28, 1994.

56. Most Japanese management books indicate that typically appointments to managerial positions, and even to boards of directors, are made from inside. Rodney Clark, *The Japanese Company* (New Haven: Yale University Press, 1979), pp. 100–101.

57. *Economist*, May 6, 1995. In a seeming contradiction to the analysis in the *Economist*, the *Wall Street Journal* reported on January 19, 1996, that 64 of the nation's "top" banks had a former official as chair or president and that 159 Ministry of Finance alumni were on boards of the country's 118 publicly traded banks. The *Journal* also cited several examples of bad management by former Finance officials.

58. Newspaper reports contain evidence that many regional engineering and public works bureaucrats retire to become advisers to or officials in construction firms. *Yomiuri*, July 29, 1982, and July 6, 1993. There have been several prominent recent cases of official corruption involving public works contracts, that is, contracts based on private relationships like those represented by amakudari.

The ninety-two public corporations are a different matter from private companies. In 1992 former bureaucrats constituted 58 percent of the senior officials in those corporations. Seifu Kankei Hojin Rodo Kumiai Rengo, *Seiroren Amakudari Hakusho: Seifu Kankei Kikan ni okeru Amakudari Kanryo no Jittai* (Tokyo, 1993), p. 9. For a classic statement on amakudari see Chalmers Johnson, "The Reemployment of Retired Government Bureaucrats in Japanese Big Business," *Asian Survey* 14 (1974), pp. 953–65.

59. Richardson and Flanagan, *Politics in Japan*, pp. 269, 275; Goro Naka, *Kokkai Giin no Kosei to Henka* (Tokyo: Seiji Koho Senta, 1980), pp. 316–22.

60. Somucho, *Shingikai Soran* (Tokyo, 1988), pp. 1–9; and Frank J. Schwartz, "Shingikai: The Politics of Consultation in Japan" (Ph.D. diss., Harvard University, 1991), chap. 7.

61. *Yomiuri*, July 6, 1982.

62. Struggles between the Fair Trade Commission and MITI are discussed extensively in Johnson, *MITI and the Japanese Miracle*, pp. 282, 298 ff. See also Mike Masato

Mochizuki, "Managing and Influencing the Japanese Legislative Process: The Role of Parties and the National Diet" (Ph.D. diss., Harvard University, 1982), pp. 166–202; Upham, "Man Who Would Import," pp. 191–92, 196, 200–201.

63. See Yale C. Maxon, *Control of Japanese Foreign Policy: A Study of Civil-Military Rivalry, 1930–45* (Berkeley: University of California Press, 1957), pp. 21, 98–102.

64. See Eugene J. Kaplan, *Japan: The Government-Business Relationship—a Guide for American Businessmen* (Washington, D.C.: U.S. Department of Commerce, 1972), p. 97.

65. For more on this point see John Campbell, "Policy Conflict and Its Resolution Within the Government System," in Krauss et al., *Conflict in Japan*, pp. 335–74.

66. *Yomiuri,* July 11, 1982. The ideological factionalization of MITI is discussed in Johnson, "MITI and Japanese International Economic Policy," pp. 227–229; and Johnson, *MITI and the Japanese Miracle,* pp. 280–81.

67. See the excellent discussions of informality and consultational processes in Upham, "Man Who Would Import," pp. 210–12.

68. Haruhiro Fukui, "Foreign Policy Making by Improvisation: The Japanese Experience," *International Journal* 20 (1977), pp. 791–812. See also Park, *Bureaucrats and Ministers,* chap. 6; and Muramatsu, *Sengo Nihon no Kanryosei,* esp. pp. 59–60. In interviews that I conducted in Kanagawa and Shimane prefectures in the 1960s, local politicians bragged about their successful trips to Tokyo to follow through on local requests. The standard process was for a local delegation to join a constituency Dietmember in approaching a ministry official with the request.

69. Schwartz, "Fairy Cloaks and Familiar Talks," pp. 231–32.

70. *Yomiuri,* November 5, 1993.

71. *Sankei,* June 7, 1994.

72. *Asahi,* July 5 and 20, 1994; *Sankei,* July 9, 1994.

73. Upham, "Man Who Would Import," pp. 198–204, 210–11. Upham's assertion that consultation takes place in a vertical process involving dominant ministry officials and supplicant interest groups and companies does not, however, mesh well with newspaper accounts of intracoordination and intercoordination group conflict reported in this book. Scholarly research by John Campbell and Richard Samuels bears the same message as this book at many points. So does research by Frank J. Schwartz, including that reported in "Shingikai: The Politics of Consultation in Japan" (Ph.D. diss., Harvard University, 1991).

74. *Yomiuri,* November 5, 1993, and January 5, 1994; *Nihon Keizai,* June 2, 1994.

75. The main sources for comparisons were Dennis Kavanagh, *British Politics: Continuities and Change* (Oxford: Oxford University Press, 1990); Peter A. Hall, Jack Hayward, and Howard Machin, *Developments in French Politics* (London: Macmillan, 1990); William E. Paterson and David Southern, *Governing Germany* (Oxford: Blackwell, 1992); David Hine, *Governing Italy: The Politics of Bargained Pluralism* (Oxford: Oxford University Press, 1993).

76. See G. W. Jones, "The Prime Minister's Power," in Anthony King, ed., *The British Prime Minister* (London: Macmillan, 1985), pp. 198–99.

77. In 1976 Japan had 93 civil servants per thousand population, France had 150, the United States 169, Germany 179, and Britain 215. Keizai Koho Center, *Japan 1981: A*

Comparison (Tokyo, 1981), p. 67. In 1990 government employment accounted for 6 percent of all employment in Japan; in the United States, for 14 percent; and in Germany and Italy, 15 percent. The highest share of government in total employment is in Sweden, where the figure is 32 percent. The source is the Organization for Economic Cooperation and Development (OECD), quoted in *Financial Times*, March 15, 1993. Until recently, European countries had many more nationalized industries than Japan. Only salt and tobacco were nationalized in Japan. Citizens in Britain, France, Germany, and Italy were consequently seven to eight times more likely to buy a product that was produced in a state-owned industry. In Japan the two most pervasively important public corporations — until their privatization in the mid to late 1980s — were Japan National Railways and Nippon Telephone and Telegraph, but these had equivalents in Europe.

78. Kavanagh, *British Politics: Continuities and Change*, p. 186; and Vincent Wright, "The Administrative Machine," in Hall, Hayward, and Machin, *Developments in French Politics*, p. 128. In Germany the largest coalition parties normally have as many people in positions in government as hold around 8 percent of their proportion of seats in the Bundestag. Paterson and Southern, *Governing Germany*, p. 99.

79. Paterson and Southern, *Governing Germany*, p. 123; Vincent Wright, *The Government and Politics of France* (London: Unwin Hyman, 1989), p. 125. An index calculated for samples of national bureaucrats in various European countries from the 1970s indicated almost perfect inequality relative to the general populations. Joel D. Aberbach, Robert Putnam, and Bert A. Rockman, *Bureaucrats and Politicians in Western Democracies* (Cambridge: Harvard University Press, 1981), p. 63.

80. Peter Hall, "Pluralism and Pressure Politics," in Hall, Hayward, and Machin, *Developments in French Politics*, p. 80; and Wright, "Administrative Machine," in ibid., p. 117.

81. Upham, "Man Who Would Import."

82. Wright, *Government and Politics of France*, pp. 127–28.

83. Gerald L. Curtis, *The Japanese Way of Politics* (New York: Columbia University Press, 1988); Haruhiro Fukui, "The Policy Research Council of Japan's Liberal Democratic Party: Policy Making Role and Practice," *Asian Thought and Society* 11 (March 1987), pp. 3–30; Takeshi Inoguchi and Tomoaki Iwai, *Zoku Giin no Kenkyu* (Tokyo: Nihon Keizai Shimposha, 1983); and Seizaburo Sato and Tetsuhisa Matsuzaki, *Jiminto Seiken* (Tokyo: Chuo Koronsha, 1986).

84. *Nikkei Weekly,* June 1, 1992.

85. *Yomiuri,* July 6, 7, 9, and 10, 1982. One example cited in this series was the LDP's overruling of Ministry of Finance opposition to civil service raises, which left the 1982 supplementary budget in excess of revenues.

Chapter 6: Legislative Politics

1. Norihiko Narita of Surugadai University, formerly an official in the National Diet Library and a special assistant to Prime Minister Hosokawa, provided invaluable advice regarding Diet procedures. Junko Hasegawa of the Diet library helped me locate figures on legislative processes in the 1990s.

2. T. J. Pempel, "The Bureaucratization of Policymaking in Postwar Japan," *American Journal of Political Science* 18 (1974), pp. 647–64.

3. Ronald Dore, *Taking Japan Seriously: A Confucian Perspective on Leading Economic Issues* (Stanford: Stanford University Press, 1987), p. 195. For similar views see Hans Baerwald, *Japan's Parliament* (London: Cambridge University Press, 1974).

4. Shigeo Misawa, "An Outline of the Policymaking Process in Japan," in Hiroshi Itoh, ed., *Japanese Politics: An Inside View* (Ithaca, N.Y.: Cornell University Press, 1973), pp. 12–48, esp. p. 33.

5. Ellis S. Krauss, "Conflict in the Diet: Toward Conflict Management in Diet Politics," in Krauss, Thomas P. Rohlen, and Patricia G. Steinhoff, eds., *Conflict in Japan* (Honolulu: University of Hawaii Press, 1984), pp. 243–93.

6. Mike Masato Mochizuki, "Managing and Influencing the Japanese Legislative Process: The Role of Parties and the National Diet" (Ph.D. diss., Harvard University, 1982); and Seizaburo Sato and Tetsuhisa Matsuzaki, *Jiminto Seiken* (Tokyo: Chuo Koronsha, 1986), pp. 121–52, 277–91. Although parts of this chapter extend analysis of the Diet in new ways, my debt to Mochizuki, Sato, and Matsuzaki is also considerable.

7. Philip Norton, ed., *Parliaments in Western Europe* (London: Frank Cass, 1990). See also Michael Mezey, *Comparing Legislatures* (Durham, N.C.: Duke University Press, 1979); and Gerhard Loewenberg and Samuel Patterson, *Comparing Legislatures* (Lanham, Md.: University Press of America, 1988), pp. 197–99.

8. Mochizuki, "Managing and Influencing the Japanese Legislative Process," p. 67.

9. For example, bills could be amended on such trivial points as date of implementation without influencing policy content. Occasionally, bills were amended in such dramatic circumstances that the changes were discussed in the news media. Opposition-induced cuts in the defense outlays in the 1972 budget were one such case. A newspaper writer called the LDP concessions an "internal collapse in response to the opposition parties' 'Tet offensive,'" a reference to the success of North Vietnamese attacks on the more powerful U.S. forces during the Vietnam War. *Tokyo Shimbun*, February 23, 1972; Shigeru Ito, "Do or Die for the Socialists," *Japan Echo* 20 (1983), pp. 29–33. In the early 1990s highly publicized changes were made in the Diet to a bill concerning use of Japanese military forces in U.N. peacekeeping operations. Mike Mochizuki has estimated that roughly 50 percent of the amendments involved important substantive changes to bills in 1967–79. Mochizuki, "Managing and Influencing the Japanese Legislative Process," pp. 100–101.

10. See Thomas Rohlen, "Order in Japanese Society: Attachment, Authority and Routine," *Journal of Japanese Studies* 15 (1989), p. 37.

11. Asahi Shimbunsha, *Asahi Nenkan* (Tokyo, 1967). For information on the election law reform see Asahi Shimbunsha, *Asahi Nenkan* (Tokyo, 1983).

12. See Takeshi Ishida, "Conflict and Its Accommodation: *Omote-Ura* and *Uchi-Soto* Relations," in Krauss, Rohlen, and Steinhoff, *Conflict in Japan,* pp. 16–38.

13. *Tokyo Shimbun,* June 12, 1982; *Nihon Keizai,* June 19, 1982; *Asahi,* August 27 and September 1, 1983; *Nihon Keizai,* February 18, 1983; *Mainichi,* May 9, 1983.

14. Ehud Harari, *The Politics of Labor Legislation in the Diet: National-International Interaction* (Berkeley: University of California Press, 1973).

15. Noncontroversial bills were on the increase in Japan in the 1970s and 1980s, according to two separate research projects. Ellis Krauss reported that unanimous decisions were made for 45 percent of *all* bills in the early 1970s, increasing to 70 percent by the end of the decade. According to a different study that focused just on government

bills, unanimous support among the main political parties increased from 23 percent in the ordinary Diet session in 1985 to 45 percent in the ordinary session in 1988. These two sets of findings point in the same direction, although they are not strictly comparable because of a difference in statistical base. Both sets of evidence also conform to the declining trend in amendments and increase in postponements. See Ellis Krauss and Jon Pierre, "The Decline of Dominant Parties," in T. J. Pempel, ed., *Uncommon Democracies: The One-Party Dominant Regimes* (Ithaca, N.Y.: Cornell University Press, 1990), pp. 226–59; and *Asahi*, May 26, 1988.

16. Loewenberg and Patterson, *Comparing Legislatures*, pp. 225–26.

17. John Campbell, "Bureaucratic Primacy: Japanese Policy Communities in an American Perspective," *Governance* 2 (1989), pp. 16–17. See also Chapter 5.

18. See Norton, *Parliaments in Western Europe*, p. 6, for a discussion of the legitimation function of legislatures; and see Robert Packenham, "Legislatures and Political Development," in A. Kornberg and L. D. Musolf, eds., *Legislatures in Developmental Perspective* (Durham, N.C.: Duke University Press, 1970).

19. *Tokyo Shimbun*, May 5, 1984; *Mainichi*, April 8, 1985.

20. *Yomiuri*, May 10, 1983 (E). Interpellations in plenary sessions and budget committee meetings were also scheduled by these same committees. *Tokyo Shimbun*, March 4, 1983; *Nihon Keizai*, December 20, 1985.

21. *Nikkei Weekly*, August 23, 1993.

22. Mochizuki, "Managing and Influencing the Japanese Legislative Process," p. 62, is relevant here. The Diet as a whole meets for 80 to 100 days, whereas the U.S. Congress and the British and Italian parliaments meet for approximately 150 days, according to an Inter-Parliamentary Union report cited by Mochizuki. Committee meetings mainly involve ratification of decisions reached in informal discussions by committee directors, rather than lengthy debate by the committee members themselves.

23. In an *Asahi* report on May 16, 1984, the former LDP Policy Council chair, Masayoki Fujio, is quoted on his explanation of a putative point system by which government performance on different bills would be evaluated. Having a highly controversial health insurance bill passed would, he thought, net Prime Minister Nakasone sixty points; an important but less controversial education bill would net thirty points.

24. *Nihon Keizai*, August 2, 1984. This move followed an earlier LDP extension of the Diet session that had the same objective of getting major bills passed. *Tokyo Shimbun*, May 23, 1984.

25. *Tokyo Shimbun*, May 5, 1984.

26. *Nihon Keizai*, November 13, 1981 (E), and May 11, 1982; *Mainichi*, November 17, 1982 (E). See also Naoki Kobayashi, "The Small and Medium Enterprises Organization Law," in Itoh, *Japanese Politics*, p. 58.

27. *Asahi*, June 2, 1985. The Government-LDP Consultative Council was discussed in Chapter 5.

28. See Haruhiro Fukui, "The Policy Affairs Research Council of Japan's Liberal Democratic Party," *Asian Thought and Society* 11 (1987), pp. 3–30. At a microprocess level, LDP zoku members could also exert influence on the drafting of laws. Bureaucrats used them for support in interministerial struggles for influence, which naturally enhanced LDP members' ability to make claims on ministry counterparts.

29. *Mainichi*, May 9, 1983; *Sankei*, June 7, 1982. The agreement between the LDP and

the Socialist Party was never publicly acknowledged, but it was widely believed to exist. Both parties received electoral support from nationwide interest groups, which meant that neither would suffer from the proposed change as much as would parties that lacked broad support.

30. *Nihon Keizai,* May 23, 1982; *Tokyo Shimbun,* January 22, 1982; *Yomiuri,* May 27, 1984.

31. *Nihon Keizai,* June 16, 1984.

32. *Akahata,* April 3, 1992.

33. *Asahi,* August 9, 1984; *Nihon Keizai,* December 20, 1985. See also the discussion of the role of cross-party consultative committees in the Diet in Chapter 7. The LDP and the SDPJ worked out their differences on the Small and Medium Industries Organization Law of 1957 using this mechanism, plus there were meetings between the LDP Executive Council and SDPJ Diet Policy Committee members. See Kobayashi, "Small and Medium Enterprises Organization Law," pp. 58–59.

34. This example was provided by Terry MacDougall. The law in question was passed in the early 1960s.

35. The increasing use of postponements is another example of interparty accommodation; it is cited by Krauss as well. Ellis Krauss, "Conflict in the Diet: Toward Conflict Management in Diet Politics," in Krauss, Rohlen, and Steinhoff, *Conflict in Japan,* p. 265.

36. See Richard Rose, *The Post-Modern President: The White House Meets the World* (Chatham, N.J.: Chatham House, 1988), p. 80.

37. *Nikkei Weekly,* January 17, 1994.

38. *Yomiuri,* November 2, 1993.

39. Loewenberg and Patterson, *Comparing Legislatures,* p. 197; Norton, *Parliaments in Western Europe.*

40. Rose, *Post-Modern President,* p. 80. Most figures were from 1986.

41. Loewenberg and Patterson, *Comparing Legislatures,* p. 255.

42. See Kobayashi, "Small and Medium Enterprises Organization Law," pp. 57–62; Mochizuki, "Managing and Influencing the Japanese Legislative Process," pp. 74–78. For a critical view of committee debates see Baerwald, *Japan's Parliament,* chap. 4. Perhaps the vitality of committee debates during LDP rule has been underestimated. Committees in the prewar Diet were influential, according to James R. Bartholomew, *The Formation of Science in Japan: Building a Research Tradition* (New Haven: Yale University Press, 1989). See also George Akita, *Foundations of Constitutional Government in Modern Japan, 1868–1900* (Cambridge: Harvard University Press, 1967), esp. chap. 6.

43. Loewenberg and Patterson, *Comparing Legislatures.*

44. For an analysis of one-party dominance in Scandinavia, Israel, and Japan see Pempel, *Uncommon Democracies.*

Chapter 7: Interests, Policy, and Power

1. See Chalmers Johnson, *MITI and the Japanese Miracle: The Growth of Industrial Policy, 1925–75* (Stanford: Stanford University Press, 1982), pp. 196–97; T. J. Pempel and Keiichi Tsunekawa, "Corporatism Without Labor? The Japanese Anomaly," in Phi-

lippe Schmitter and Gerhard Lembruch, eds., *Trends Toward Corporatist Intermediation* (Beverly Hills, Calif.: Sage, 1979), pp. 231–70.

2. See Michio Muramatsu and Ellis Krauss, "The Conservative Policy Line and the Development of Patterned Pluralism," in Kozo Yamamura and Yasukichi Yasuba, eds., *The Political Economy of Japan*, vol. 1: *The Domestic Transformation* (Stanford: Stanford University Press, 1987), pp. 516–54.

3. See Aurelia George, "Japanese Interest Group Behavior: An Institutional Approach," in J. A. A. Stockwin et al., *Dynamic and Immobilist Politics in Japan* (Honolulu: University of Hawaii Press, 1988), pp. 106–40.

4. Bradley Richardson and Scott Flanagan, *Politics in Japan* (Boston: Little, Brown, 1984), p. 269; Richardson, "A Japanese House of Councillors Election: Support Mobilization and Political Recruitment," *Modern Asian Studies* 1 (1967), pp. 385–402.

5. See Kent Calder, *Crisis and Compensation: Public Policy and Political Stability in Japan* (Princeton, N.J.: Princeton University Press, 1988); Muramatsu and Krauss, "Conservative Policy Line"; and Sheldon Garon and Mike Mochizuki, "Negotiating Social Contracts," in Andrew Gordon, eds., *Postwar Japan as History* (Berkeley: University of California Press, 1993), pp. 145–66.

6. Michio Muramatsu and Ellis Krauss, "The Dominant Party and Social Coalitions in Japan," in T. J. Pempel, ed., *Uncommon Democracies: The One-Party Dominant Regimes* (Ithaca, N.Y.: Cornell University Press, 1990), pp. 282–305.

7. For examples of labor unrest that influenced policymaking in the coal and power industries see Richard Samuels, *The Business of the Japanese State* (Ithaca, N.Y.: Cornell University Press, 1987); and for examples of labor inputs on social welfare policy see John Campbell, *How Policies Change: The Japanese Government and the Aging Society* (Princeton, N.J.: Princeton University Press, 1992). See also recent evidence on the political activism and influence of labor in Gary D. Allinson and Yasuhiro Sone, eds., *Political Dynamics in Contemporary Japan* (Ithaca, N.Y.: Cornell University Press, 1993), specifically chaps. 2 (by Michio Muramatsu), 7 (Mike Mochizuki), and 8 (Yutaka Tsujinaka); and Garon and Mochizuki, "Negotiating Social Contracts."

8. A. G. Jordan and J. J. Richardson, *Government and Pressure Groups in Britain* (New York: Oxford University Press, 1987), pp. 8, 237,5–8. Ezra Suleiman makes much the same point when he argues that "the importance of the bureaucracy in the decision making process of modern societies has become almost axiomatic. . . . In France, the importance of the bureaucracy, insofar as interest groups are concerned, is probably greater than that of any other branch of governmental activity." Suleiman, *Politics, Power and Bureaucracy in France: The Administrative Elite* (Princeton, N.J.: Princeton University Press, 1974), p. 323.

9. Some political specialists in the 1960s saw Japanese postwar politics as an elitist triad of power based on the close relationships between senior persons in the LDP, big business, and the ministries. See Chitoshi Yanaga, *Big Business and Japanese Politics* (New Haven: Yale University Press, 1968). Journalists began to use the term "iron triangle" for these relationships in the early 1990s. Generally, these ideas of triads and triangles are meaningless unless qualified. There is some legitimacy to them if one means that there were three big groups of political elites from, respectively, the bureaucracy, the LDP, and big business under the 1955 system, although this typology ignores the importance of

farmer and medium-business and small-business organizations and the high frequency of their contacts with rank-and-file politicians rather than party elites. There was also movement from the bureaucracy into politics and to positions in interest groups, as I mentioned briefly in Chapter 5. See also the excellent treatment of this subject in Gary D. Allinson, "Citizenship, Fragmentation and the Negotiated Polity," in Allinson and Sone, *Political Dynamics in Contemporary Japan*, pp. 29–30. But to imply, as many seem to do, that there was a small set of elites all of whom were on intimate terms is unrealistic.

10. In 1984 people living in farm households totaled 20,495,000. *Asahi,* June 28, 1984. By 1992 there were 13,423,000. Asahi Shimbunsha, *Japan Almanac 1994* (Tokyo, 1995), p. 130.

11. In 1988 the proportion of the Japanese labor force employed in some way in agriculture was 7.2 percent; compare 5.8 percent for France, 3.5 percent for the then West Germany, 2.5 percent for the United States, and 2.1 percent for Britain. See the Economist, *Book of Vital World Statistics* (New York: Random House, 1990), p. 56.

12. For an excellent survey of Japanese agricultural politics see Michael Donnelly, "Conflict over Government Authority and Markets: Japan's Rice Economy," in Ellis S. Krauss, Thomas P. Rohlen, and Patricia G. Steinhoff, eds., *Conflict in Japan* (Honolulu: University of Hawaii Press, 1984), pp. 335–74. There are still around five million votes in the farm sector.

13. Agriculture accounted for 2.6 percent of the GDP of Japan in 1988 but only 2 percent of the GDP in the United States. Keizai Koho Center, *Japan 1992: An International Comparison* (Tokyo, 1992), p. 14. Japan is more dependent on food imports than Britain, the former West Germany, and Italy. Today roughly 50 percent of food needs are imported. A large share comes from the United States. Substantial amounts of wheat have been imported from the United States and Canada since the 1960s, reflecting changes in food preferences. Soybeans and sugar have been imported in large quantities for several decades, too. Data are from the Economist, *Book of Vital World Statistics.*

14. *Asahi,* June 28, 1984; *Nihon Keizai,* June 22, 1982, and July 31, 1986. Since the burst of the 1980s "bubble economy," land prices have declined in many areas, with obvious implications for what we have said here. Both urban and rural residents have thereby lost wealth.

15. *Nihon Keizai,* June 22, 1982, December 3, 1986, and September 29, 1987; and *Economist,* October 29, 1994. Bumper rice crops in 1984 through 1987 affected the demand-supply calculus used in MAFF plans. The autumn 1994 package included a six-year loan and grant commitment totaling $62 billion on top of $35 billion in annual subsidies and $14 billion in rural public works projects that employ farmers.

16. The details are reported in *Nihon Keizai,* February 11, June 20, and July 19, 1988.

17. *Mainichi,* July 23, 1982, and May 22, 1991; *Tokyo Shimbun,* November 14, 1986; *Nihon Keizai,* July 30 (E) and August 25, 1988; *Asahi,* August 8, 1986. See also Ronald P. Dore, *Land Reform in Japan* (Berkeley: University of California Press, 1959), pp. 138, 174–75.

18. *Nihon Keizai,* October 8, 1986.

19. See Michael Donnelly, "Setting the Price of Rice: A Study in Political Decisionmaking," in T. J. Pempel, ed., *Policymaking in Contemporary Japan* (Ithaca, N.Y.: Cornell University Press, 1977). In the 1980s the rice price movements were matched in intensity

by demonstrations on behalf of protection. Zenchu used many tactics to support its goals. It held rallies to oppose liberalization, with attendance reportedly reaching as high as six thousand, orchestrated a massive campaign to send six million postcards to Dietmembers, and tried to accumulate five million signatures on petitions to the government and LDP leaders. In 1988 it dispatched 250 representatives to Tokyo to talk to people in the streets about the need to fight liberalization. *Nihon Nogyo Shimbun,* March 25 and April 17, 1982; *Asahi,* October 23, 1988.

20. *Sankei,* December 15, 1988 (E); *Asahi,* January 4, 1987. Farmer organizations from Hokkaido were very active advocates of protection and cited the role of the prefecture as the breadbasket of Japan in their defense against liberalization and against the rice conversion plans of the MAFF. *Asahi,* June 26, 1986; *Yomiuri,* August 28, 1985, and February 4, 1988.

21. The consumer groups opposing agricultural market liberalization included the National Coordinating Council of Local Women's Organizations, Japan Consumers' League, Federation of Housewives' Associations, Association for Spreading Nutritional Development, Consultative Council of Youth Organizations, and Japan Confederation of Women Voters. *Nihon Nogyo Shimbun,* June 23, 1982, November 20, 1986, and April 22, 1987; *Nihon Keizai,* June 20, 1987. On November 13, 1986, the twenty-fifth National Rally of Consumers, held in Hibiya (Tokyo) and attended by 1,500 representatives of sixty-four organizations, also adopted a resolution opposing liberalization of rice imports. *Nihon Nogyo Shimbun,* November 14, 1986. Some consumer groups were divided on protectionist issues. The Federation of Housewives' Associations, for example, split over imports of beef. Women's groups in Osaka and surrounding cities favored freer imports, and units in other parts of the country supported Japanese farmers. *Sankei,* June 4, 1983 (E). Public opinion was divided roughly equally between those favoring or accepting imports and those supporting protection, according to one newspaper survey. *Mainichi,* December 16, 1986.

22. *Sankei,* December 19, 1987. *Asahi,* December 13, 1987, and other sources called Hata and Koichi Kato senior members of the agricultural zoku.

23. *Tokyo Shimbun,* March 9, 1988; *Sankei,* March 14, 1991. On Dietmember league activities see *Mainichi,* March 10, 1988.

24. Haruhiro Fukui, "The Policy Research Council of Japan's Liberal Democratic Party: Policy Making Role and Practice," *Asian Thought and Society* 11 (1987), pp. 22–23; *Nihon Keizai,* March 25, 1988.

25. As in earlier debates, the LDP, Democratic Socialist Party, and SDPJ were loath to court loss of farmer support, even though leaders in all three parties felt privately that some flexibility would eventually be necessary. Only the Clean Government Party openly indicated its acceptance of partial opening of the rice market, a posture motivated by its dependence on urban voter support. *Sankei,* August 15, 1990; *Nihon Keizai,* August 20, 1990 (E).

26. See Gerald Curtis, *The Japanese Way of Politics* (New York: Columbia University Press, 1988), chap. 2.

27. A full-scale review of the crop conversion plan and subsidy system was conducted by MAFF in the autumn of 1986. *Yomiuri,* November 14, 1986; *Nihon Keizai,* November 30, 1986.

28. *Nihon Keizai,* December 17, 1982, and September 21, 1983. The FEO proposals were often met by rebuttals from Zenchu. See *Nihon Nogyo Shimbun,* September 23, 1983.

29. This was the gist of a report issued by the Agricultural Administration Problem Discussion Committee of the FEO, according to *Nihon Nogyo Shimbun,* January 20, 1982. Later, in early 1987, the FEO released a major report calling for reform of the food control program and import of sufficient amounts of rice to allow rice prices to be determined by market principles. *Nihon Keizai,* January 6, 1987; *Sankei,* February 8 and July 22, 1987. All three major business groups have opposed procedures for meat imports. *Nihon Keizai,* January 26, 1988.

30. *Nihon Keizai,* August 2, 1981, and November 4, 1986. The Second Provisional Administrative Affairs Reform Council (SPAARC) was established in 1981 by the director of the Administrative Management Agency, Yasuhiro Nakasone, who used it to legitimize privatization of several major public corporations after he became prime minister in 1982. The SPAARC is discussed in Chapter 8.

31. *Mainichi,* June 9, 1982; *Nihon Nogyo Shimbun,* March 25, 1986. Like its predecessor, another consultative council set up by Prime Minister Takeshita, the Economic Structural Adjustment Promotion Headquarters, advocated agricultural market liberalization. *Nihon Keizai,* June 8, 1988. The SDPJ and Democratic Socialist Party waffled sometimes on whether to support farmers or consumers. *Mainichi,* October 3, 1986; *Asahi,* October 6, 1986. In 1991, Rengo, the newly established pan-union movement, went on record as supporting partial liberalization of the rice market. *Asahi,* April 19, 1991.

32. This policy applied to existing price subsidies and to new subsidies for producers of products that were to be liberalized. The Ministry of Finance proposed time limits to prevent the new subsidies from becoming "rights." *Nihon Keizai,* February 8, 1988.

33. *Mainichi,* December 17, 1988.

34. *Nihon Nogyo Shimbun,* August 24, 1984; *Nihon Keizai,* August 4, 16, 19, and 23 and September 27, 1988.

35. *Nihon Keizai,* March 27, 1986. See also Nihon Kokusei Zukai, *Suji de miru Nihon no 100nen* (Tokyo: Yano Tsuneta Kinenkai, 1991), p. 394.

36. John Campbell, *Contemporary Japanese Budget Politics* (Berkeley: University of California Press, 1977), p. 80; Yukio Noguchi, "Public Finance," in Yamamura and Yasuba, *Political Economy of Japan,* 1: 192.

37. *Asahi,* November 13, 1983. Consideration of an indirect general excise tax was begun in the 1970s.

38. *Nihon Keizai,* February 20, 1987, and January 13, February 6, and June 1, 1988; *Asahi,* October 30, 1987.

39. *Nihon Keizai* (E), June 13, 1983.

40. *Sankei,* February 6, 1987; *Tokyo Shimbun,* February 24 (E) and 25, 1987; *Nihon Keizai,* March 15, 1987.

41. *Nihon Keizai,* February 14, 1987; *Asahi,* March 18 and 19, 1987, and February 21 and 25, 1988; *Tokyo Shimbun,* February 27, 1988.

42. *Nihon Keizai,* April 14, 1987; *Asahi,* March 26, 1987. *Nihon Keizai,* April 5 and 8, 1987.

43. *Nihon Keizai,* January 12, June 1, and June 10, 1988; *Asahi,* July 30, 1988.

44. According *Sankei,* February 6, 1988, the same eleven retail organizations opposing the sales tax in 1987 were strongly opposed to the consumption tax proposal in 1988. Some local LDP politicians were also reluctant to endorse the tax bills. In gubernatorial election in Fukushima prefecture, the local LDP split over the tax issue, and a conservative candidate joined elements of the SDPJ in opposing the tax. *Asahi,* August 10, 1988.

45. *Nihon Keizai,* April 3 and June 10, 1988. There was also conflict between two zoku of LDP Dietmembers. Members of the commerce and industry zoku, who represented medium and small retailers, rebelled in meetings of the LDP Tax System Research Council. Members of the finance zoku supported the tax proposal. *Asahi,* May 24, 1988. The Finance Ministry was trying to avoid a return to the long list of tax exemptions that had been built into the 1987 reform. *Yomiuri,* March 3, 1987 (E).

46. *Nihon Keizai,* March 11, 1988; *Nihon Keizai,* August 27 and 30 and September 5, 1988. The LDP set up a coordinating group, the Tax System Reform Promotion Headquarters, to promote party support for the six tax bills. *Yomiuri,* July 2, 1988. For an earlier example of the effects of divided versus united party leadership see Mike Masato Mochizuki, "Managing and Influencing the Japanese Legislative Process: The Role of Parties and the National Diet" (Ph.D. diss., Harvard University, 1982), pp. 177–81.

47. *Nihon Keizai,* June 1 and 15, 1988.

48. Ibid.

49. *Yomiuri,* June 19, 1988 and *Asahi,* August 21, 1988.

50. *Nihon Keizai,* December 3, 1987, and January 12, 1988; *Asahi,* July 30, 1988. In 1988 the council included seven journalists, five company heads, two bank presidents, four private research group representatives, heads of two labor unions and a national women's group, two mayors, and one professor. Somucho, *Shingikai Soran* (Tokyo, 1988), p. 5. Its heterogeneous makeup conformed to the trend in the 1980s to appoint fewer bureaucrats to advisory councils and more people from diverse backgrounds. Frank Schwartz has presented *shingikai* in a new, more positive light in "Of Fairy Cloaks and Familiar Talks: The Politics of Consultation," in Allinson and Sone, *Political Dynamics in Contemporary Japan,* pp. 217–41.

51. *Nihon Keizai,* June 1, 1988. Here is a partial list of the participants: Japan Medical Association, National Federation of Shopping District Promotion Associations, All-Japan Federation of Shopping Street Associations, National Central Union of Federations of Medium and Small Enterprises, Japan Department Store Association, Japan Chain Stores Association, Japan Textile Industry League, Japan Petroleum Association, Japan LP Gas Federation, General Council of Japanese Trade Unions (Sohyo), All-Japan Private Labor Unions' Consultative Council, All-Japan Federation of Environmental Hygiene Enterprises, National Private Employment Exchange Association, Japan Business Administration Service Association, Association of International Tourist Hotels, National Federation of Automobile Associations, All-Japan Truck Service Association, Japan Bus Association, Japan Small-Shipping Industry Association, Greater Japan Fisheries Association, and National Federation of Fisheries Cooperatives.

52. *Mainichi,* July 18 and August 24, 1988; *Sankei,* August 27, 1988; *Nihon Keizai,* June 1, 1988 (quotation).

53. *Tokyo Shimbun,* September 13, 1988.

54. *Asahi,* July 17, 1988. Coordination among opposition parties took place several times in the lengthy tax reform process, and the four major labor federations and five opposition parties consulted in 1982. *Tokyo Shimbun* (E), November 16, 1982.

55. Both events are reported in *Mainichi,* July 18, 1988.

56. Education costs, rent, and "welfare" outlays (cremation, childbirth, wheelchairs, etc.) were exempted from the tax, along with certain business costs for running centers for handicapped people and older persons. *Asahi,* September 26, 1991.

57. For specific cases, see Mochizuki, "Managing and Influencing the Japanese Legislative Process," pp. 166–202; *Jiji,* October 25, 1952 (E); Johnson, *MITI and the Japanese Miracle,* pp. 159–60; Samuels, *Business of the Japanese State,* pp. 121–24; John Creighton Campbell, "Compensation for Repatriates: A Case Study of Interest Group Politics and Party Government Negotiations in Japan," in Pempel, *Policymaking in Contemporary Japan,* pp. 103–42; and Haruhiro Fukui, *Party in Power: The Japanese Liberal Democrats and Policymaking* (Berkeley: University of California Press, 1970), chap. 7.

58. Haruhiro Fukui, "Studies in Policymaking: A Review of the Literature," in Pempel, *Policymaking in Contemporary Japan,* pp. 22–59.

59. Peter Katzenstein, *Small States in World Markets: Industrial Policy in Europe* (Ithaca, N.Y.: Cornell University Press, 1985), pp. 21–22, 80–81.

60. Policy communities are loose aggregations of political actors who are concerned with particular functional interests. On Japanese policy communities in general see John Campbell, "Bureaucratic Primacy: Japanese Policy Communities in an American Perspective," *Governance* 2 (1989), pp. 5–22.

61. *Nihon Keizai,* November 3, 1993, February 7 and April 13, 1994.

62. *Mainichi,* October 14, 1993(E); *Nihon Keizai,* October 18, 1993.

63. *Nihon Keizai,* September 8, 1994; *Yomiuri,* October 8, 1994.

Chapter 8: Business Interests and Political Life

1. *Mainichi,* November 7, 1989.

2. *Asahi,* August 29, 1987; *Mainichi,* November 12, 1989.

3. *Asahi,* April 15, 1988; *Nihon Keizai,* October 20, 1987 (E).

4. See Chitoshi Yanaga, *Big Business in Japanese Politics* (New Haven: Yale University Press, 1968).

5. Gerald Curtis, "Big Business and Political Influence," in Ezra Vogel, ed., *Modern Japanese Organization and Decisionmaking* (Berkeley: University of California Press, 1975), pp. 33–70, esp. pp. 41–52, 50–51.

6. *Tokyo Shimbun,* December 9, 1987; *Yomiuri,* January 5, 1988. The importance of courtesy calls to people in new positions could be one reason for meetings of this kind, although protocol is also often interwoven with self-interest. As indicated earlier, Takeshita had extensive contacts with opposition leaders as well.

7. *Asahi,* August 6 and 7, 1993. The Japan New Party recruited several graduates from a reform-oriented political institute established by the founder of the Matsushita Electric Company. The Matsushita tie was another of Hosokawa's connections.

8. Funding data were provided by a private organization established by the late Fusae

Ishikawa with the assistance of Chinami Kondo. Most observers of Japanese politics feel that this information conceals much larger contributions. This caveat notwithstanding, the reported figures are widely used to describe funding trends. Big business also normally gave money to LDP factions (see Table 3.3).

9. *Asahi,* January 15, 1990. Conservative faction and subfaction leaders received money directly from individual companies. Individual LDP parliamentarians also received money from businesses, often from firms in their home constituencies. In some cases, local funding was more important than party or faction support. In an analysis of the finances of Dietmembers from different districts in the *Asahi Shimbun* (January 14, 1990), one candidate's money sources were described as follows: party funds (10 percent), faction leader support (15 percent), proceeds from a "seminar" held in Tokyo (20 percent), funds collected from supportive firms in Tokyo and his electoral constituency (40 percent), and unstated (15 percent).

10. *Mainichi,* April 10, 1991. Not all the money committed to finance the 1990 general election was received in 1989–90. Some of the money promised by industry associations was to be paid in installments over a three-year period in order to conform to the requirements of the election funds law. The LDP borrowed the funds used in the campaign from banks with this commitment as collateral.

11. The top 620 companies in aggregate value were determined from information in Toyo Keizai, *Japan Company Handbook* (Tokyo, 1989), pp. 1288–97. Interestingly, the large companies that did *not* make big contributions in 1990 were from the industries with the deepest pockets in the 1950s, namely, electric power firms.

12. Junnosuke Masumi, *Postwar Politics in Japan, 1945–55* (Berkeley: Institute for International Studies and Center for Japanese Studies, University of California, Japan Research Monograph 6, 1985), pp. 306–8.

13. The timing of party crises, in 1957–60, 1972, 1974, 1976, 1979–80, and 1989–93, was discussed in Chapter 3.

14. *Mainichi* June 19 (E) and November 3, 1989; *Nihon Keizai,* June 20, 1989. The statement called for election district reform, a political party law, and openness regarding political funding amounts and relationships. Reform always appealed to big business because, among other reasons, reform would reduce the demands for money from the LDP.

15. *Nihon Keizei,* June 20, 1989. Ishihara was a frequent critic of the LDP on other matters, including the weakness of the response by the government to the Tiananmen Square massacre.

16. *Mainichi,* November 3 and 6, 1992. Bankers were already angry with the Liberal Democrats because many LDP politicians, in debates over financial issues, supported the continuation of the postal savings system, which competes with banks for savings. Although they remained among the largest donors to the LDP, they allegedly reduced their contributions to the LDP starting around 1976 and began to support Democratic Socialist and other non-LDP candidates. See *Tokyo Shimbun,* February 6, 1989.

17. See the detailed discussion of the law in Frank Upham, "Privatizing Regulation: The Implementation of the Large-Scale Retail Stores Law," in Gary D. Allinson and Yasuhiro Sone, eds., *Political Dynamics in Contemporary Japan* (Ithaca, N.Y.: Cornell University Press, 1993), pp. 264–94.

18. *Nihon Keizai,* July 4, 1988.

19. Approval took ten years for a supermarket project in Saitama and had not yet been granted after eight years for a project in the Tokyo suburb of Kokubunji. *Yomiuri* on February 16, 1989; see also *Yomiuri,* April 5, 1990.

20. Medium and small businesses in some cities in the Osaka area support the Democratic Socialist Party. The Japan Communist Party was sometimes successful in organizing medium and small business support through the mechanism of its Democratic Businessmen's League (Minsho). See Kent Calder's discussion of the left vote of small business and the related rise and fall of Minsho, plus an extensive description of small-business policy. Calder, *Crisis and Compensation: Public Policy and Political Stability in Japan* (Princeton, N.J.: Princeton University Press, 1988), chap. 7. See also Naoki Kobayashi, "The Small and Medium Enterprises Organization Law," in Hiroshi Itoh, ed., *Japanese Politics: An Inside View* (Ithaca, N.Y.: Cornell University Press, 1973), pp. 53–55; and Sheldon Garon and Mike Mochizuki, "Negotiating Social Contracts," in Andrew Gordon, ed., *Postwar Japan as History* (Berkeley: University of California Press, 1993), pp. 145–66.

21. Chalmers Johnson, *MITI and the Japanese Miracle: The Growth of Industrial Policy, 1925–75* (Stanford: Stanford University Press, 1982), p. 223.

22. *Nihon Keizai,* July 4, 1988; *Mainichi,* August 23, 1988; *Asahi,* August 28, 1988.

23. Among the benefits that small merchants get from these alignments is an ability to return unsold merchandise to the manufacturer. *Nihon Keizai,* June 10, 1989. See also the informative ten-part series on the distribution system and its reform in *Yomiuri,* February 16–March 3, 1989, specifically the February 28 issue.

24. *Yomiuri,* June 26, 1988; *Tokyo Shimbun,* September 14, 1988; and *Mainichi,* September 23, 1988. The new MITI councillor's authority was said to be equal to that of a bureau director-general, a position second only to an administrative vice minister — Japan's highest administrative position — in rank.

25. *Tokyo Shimbun,* April 6, 1990; *Sankei,* December 7, 1989; *Nihon Keizai,* November 15, 1989.

26. *Sankei,* December 7, 1989 (E).

27. *Yomiuri,* May 25, 1990. Details of the proposed changes were set forth in an Industrial Structure Consultative Council (ISCC) report in June 1989 and in the first draft of MITI's "Vision for the 1990s," released the same month. The report was compiled by the Subcommittee on Medium and Small Enterprise Policy of the ISCC Distribution Department and was presumably written by MITI officials. A second MITI council, the Medium and Small Business Policy Consultative Council, also participated in this project. See *Asahi,* May 25, 1989; *Nihon Keizai,* June 10 and July 19, 1989. The Fair Trade Commission released a report proposing Large Store Law changes in February 1989, and the Foreign Ministry produced its own report and recommendations in March of the same year. See *Mainichi,* February 9 and March 5, 1989; *Sankei,* December 7, 1989 (E).

28. *Nihon Keizai,* December 20, 1990.

29. Japan Economic Institute, *The Japanese Distribution System,* JEI Report no. 28A (Washington, D.C., 1987). Retail stores with four or fewer employees account for 30 percent of the retail trade in Japan. *Asahi,* May 6, 1990.

30. *Yomiuri,* March 6, 1990 (E); *Nihon Keizai,* June 10, 1989, and April 6, 1990 (E).

31. According to MITI, department store sales increased at a faster rate than total retail sales from 1984; store space relative to number of employees per store nearly doubled between 1954 and 1985. The increase in store size paralleled increases in car registrations. See Japan Economic Institute, *Japanese Distribution System*; and Japan Economic Institute, *The Changing Japanese Consumer,* JEI Report no. 45A (Washington, D.C., 1988). During roughly the same period (1982–88) the number of small stores employing one to two persons declined 15 percent. *Asahi,* May 6, 1990.

32. Ichiro Ozawa, quoted in *Mainichi,* May 7, 1990.

33. *Asahi,* March 31 and May 4, 1990; *Nihon Keizai,* April 6 (E) and November 17, 1990.

34. *Mainichi,* June 23, 1994; *Nihon Keizai,* December 15, 1993 (E), July 23, 1994; *Yomiuri,* July 21, 1993.

35. *Nihon Keizai,* October 22, 1990.

36. See Johnson, *MITI and the Japanese Miracle,* pp. 196–97; T. J. Pempel and Keiichi Tsunekawa, "Corporatism Without Labor? The Japanese Anomaly," in Philippe Schmitter and Gerhard Lembruch, eds., *Trends Toward Corporatist Intermediation* (Beverly Hills, Calif.: Sage, 1979), pp. 231–70.

37. The corporatist metaphor, if not the concept itself, is the focus of Marie Anchordoguy, *Computers Inc.: Japan's Challenge to IBM* (Cambridge: Council on East Asian Studies, Harvard University, 1989).

38. For synopses of early postwar iron-and-steel policy and related matters see Johnson, *MITI and the Japanese Miracle,* chap. 6; Eugene J. Kaplan, *Japan: The Government-Business Relationship — a Guide for American Businessmen* (Washington, D.C.: U.S. Department of Commerce, 1972), pp. 137–58; and Frank K. Upham, *Law and Social Change in Postwar Japan* (Cambridge: Harvard University Press, 1987), pp. 176–83.

39. Upham, *Law and Social Change in Postwar Japan,* pp. 177–79.

40. See the general discussion of recession policy models in Gary Saxonhouse, "Industrial Restructuring in Japan," *Journal of Japanese Studies* 5 (1979), pp. 273–320.

41. See Richard Samuels, *The Business of the Japanese State* (Ithaca, N.Y.: Cornell University Press, 1987), chap. 3; *Yomiuri,* May 9, 1985.

42. *Mainichi,* February 21, 1986.

43. *Nihon Keizai,* July 13, 1986 (E); *Sankei,* August 3, 1986; *Asahi,* August 5, September 30, October 25,and November 5, 1986.

44. Saxonhouse, "Industrial Restructuring in Japan"; Richard J. Samuels, "The Industrial Destructuring of the Japanese Aluminum Industry," *Pacific Affairs* 36 (1983), pp. 495–509.

45. See Chapter 9; and Ronald Dore, *Flexible Rigidities: Industrial Policy and Structural Adjustment in the Japanese Economy 1970–80* (Stanford: Stanford University Press, 1986), chap. 9. MITI's traditional anxiety over the many ills attributable to excess competition was also present.

46. *Nihon Keizai,* April 19, 1982.

47. Both cases conformed to the intermediation patterns reported in depth by Samuels in *The Business of the Japanese State.*

48. *Sankei,* September 19, 1985; Samuels, *Business of the Japanese State,* pp. 114–16.

49. Samuels, *Business of the Japanese State,* pp. 95–102.

50. Kaplan, *Japan: The Government-Business Relationship*, pp. 141, 146–48.

51. Kaplan, *Japan: The Government-Business Relationship*, pp. 120–28; Sadako Ogata, "The Business Community and Japanese Foreign Policy: Normalization of Relations with the People's Republic of China," in Robert A. Scalapino, ed., *The Foreign Policy of Modern Japan* (Berkeley: University of California Press, 1977), pp. 175–204; David Friedman, *The Misunderstood Miracle* (Ithaca, N.Y.: Cornell University Press, 1988), pp. 96–97.

52. Kobayashi, "Small and Medium Enterprises Organization Law," pp. 53–55.

53. For support of this point, which is undoubtedly startling to some readers, I would urge comparison of Friedman, *Misunderstood Miracle*, esp. p. 84, with Johnson, *MITI and the Japanese Miracle*, pp. 236, 267–71. For a similar example of small-business organizational complexity see Suzanne Berger, "Regime and Interest Representation: The French Traditional Middle Classes," in Berger, ed., *Organizing Interests in Western Europe* (Cambridge: Cambridge University Press, 1981), pp. 83–102.

54. Kaplan, *Japan: The Government-Business Relationship*, p. 123.

55. Zenchu was represented on every MAFF general advisory council and most specialized panels with the exception of those where fishery or forestry group representation was more appropriate. See Gyosei Kanri Cho, *Shingikai Soran* (Tokyo, 1979), pp. 250–99.

56. Michael Donnelly, "Setting the Price of Rice: A Study in Political Decisionmaking," in T. J. Pempel, ed., *Policymaking in Contemporary Japan* (Ithaca, N.Y.: Cornell University Press, 1977), pp. 174–75.

57. Donnelly, "Setting the Price of Rice," pp. 164–68.

58. Harry Eckstein, *Pressure Group Politics: The Case of the BMA* (Stanford: Stanford University Press, 1960), p. 23. See Jordan and Richardson, *Government and Pressure Groups in Britain*, pp. 143–44, 197; and J. P. Olsen, "Integrated Organizational Participation in Government," in P. C. Nordstrom and W. D. Starbuck, eds., *Handbook of Organizational Design*, vol. 2 (Oxford: Oxford University Press, 1983), p. 166.

59. Curtis, "Big Business and Political Influence," pp. 39–40.

60. Peter Katzenstein, *Small States in World Markets: Industrial Policy in Europe* (Ithaca, N.Y.: Cornell University Press, 1985), pp. 21–22, 80–81. The economy and population of Japan are ten or more times larger than those of the countries cited by Katzenstein as the best examples of corporatist relations. The number of important business firms is also much greater. Even in Japanese industries dominated by oligopolies, the distribution of power is more pluralistic than that found in smaller countries like Austria and Sweden.

61. See Jordan and Richardson, *Government and Pressure Groups in Britain*, chap. 10; Ezra Suleiman, *Politics, Power and Bureaucracy in France: The Administrative Elite* (Princeton, N.J.: Princeton University Press, 1974), p. 323; and Joseph La Palombara, *Interest Groups in Italian Politics* (Princeton, N.J.: Princeton University Press, 1964), chap. 8 and pp. 307–16.

Chapter 9: The Government and the Economy

1. Chalmers Johnson, *MITI and the Japanese Miracle: The Growth of Industrial Policy, 1925–75* (Stanford: Stanford University Press, 1982), chap. 9.

2. Marie Anchordoguy, *Computers Inc.: Japan's Challenge to IBM* (Cambridge: Council on East Asian Studies, Harvard University Press, 1989), chap. 6.

3. Clyde Prestowitz, *Changing Places: How We Allowed Japan to Take the Lead* (New York: Basic Books, 1988); and James Fallows, "Containing Japan," *Atlantic Monthly* 261 (1989), pp. 40–54.

4. Johnson, *MITI and the Japanese Miracle*, chap. 9.

5. Hugh Patrick and Henry Rosovsky, eds., *Asia's New Giant: How the Japanese Economy Works* (Washington, D.C.: Brookings Institution, 1976), chap. 1, esp. pp. 47–48. See also Philip H. Trezise and Yukio Suzuki, "Politics, Government and Economic Growth in Japan," in the same volume, pp. 753–812. Differences in interpretation reflect different initial assumptions and different research concerns. Scholars who assert a strong government role normally have not examined policymaking and policy implementation in detail. Some studies in which the government role is downgraded also reflect normative preferences for free competition.

6. Richard Samuels, *The Business of the Japanese State: Energy Markets in Comparative and Historical Perspective* (Ithaca, N.Y.: Cornell University Press, 1987). See also David Friedman, *The Misunderstood Miracle: Industrial Development and Political Change in Japan* (Ithaca, N.Y.: Cornell University Press, 1988), chaps. 3 and 6. Both the developmental state and the negotiated policy models have an emphasis on the contribution that close relations between government and business make to policy formation. But the developmental state approach sees the state role as creative and directive, whereas the negotiated policy paradigm sees the state as a problem solver making bargains with firms that reflect the interests and goals of both parties.

7. Examples are drawn from Samuels, *Business of the Japanese State*, chaps. 3–6.

8. Norton Long, "The Local Community as an Ecology of Games," *American Journal of Sociology* 44 (1958), pp. 251–61.

9. Friedman, *Misunderstood Miracle*.

10. Keizai Koho Center, *Japan 1992: An International Comparison* (Tokyo, 1992), p. 13.

11. See Prime Minister's Office, *Japan Statistical Yearbook* (Tokyo, 1989), p. 792.

12. The increase was calculated on the basis of yen values to avoid the effect of appreciation of the Japanese yen especially after 1985.

13. Gross domestic product is an estimate of total economic activity within a particular country without consideration of whether the sources of income are domestically or foreign owned. Gross national product pertains to economic activity contributed by solely domestically owned sources, even if the location of production is outside the country. Before the 1970s Japanese firms had only limited overseas activity, so the overseas contribution to the GNP was not very great. Until recently Japan also had few foreign firms producing in its domestic market. Under these conditions the magnitudes of the GNP and the GDP are similar.

I use nominal GNP and GDP figures in most cases, that is, estimates for national income unadjusted for inflation. Real income figures, meant to represent actual income after considering the effects of inflation, are smaller than nominal figures in periods of high inflation, as in Japan in 1973–74. In general, inflation has distorted growth figures less in Japan than in some other industrialized countries in the postwar era.

14. Keizai Koho Center, *Japan 1981: An International Comparison* (Tokyo, 1981),

p. 20. Figures for 1960 are from Japan Automobile Manufacturers Association, *Motor Vehicle Statistics of Japan, 1994* (Tokyo, 1994), p. 14.

15. Keizai Koho Center, *Japan 1992*, p. 65.

16. Whether Japan should rearm or defer consideration of rearmament until later was hotly debated after the postwar Allied military occupation ended and Japan regained its status as an independent country in 1952. Prime Minister Shigeru Yoshida and his Liberal Party favored making economic growth the highest priority, whereas Ichiro Hatoyama, a conservative leader who headed a splinter group of the same party, supported rearmament. Their differences were one of the main issues in the 1953 general election. Junnosuke Masumi, *Postwar Politics in Japan, 1945–55* (Berkeley: Institute of East Asian Studies and Center for Japanese Studies, University of California, 1985), pp. 293–94.

17. There were precedents to the plans in the form of industrial production programs before and during the war and during the Occupation. See Johnson, *MITI and the Japanese Miracle*, chaps. 3 and 5; Samuels, *Business of the Japanese State*, chaps. 3–5.

18. Because of a large GNP, Japan was still third in the then noncommunist world in per capita outlays on defense after the United States and the former West Germany. See Gabriel Almond and Bingham Powell, *Comparative Politics Today: A World View* (Glenview, Ill.: Scott, Foresman, 1988), p. 124.

19. See Gardner Ackley and Hiromitsu Ishi, "Fiscal, Monetary and Related Policies," in Patrick and Rosovsky, *Asia's New Giant*, pp. 153–247, esp. pp. 161, 187 ff. A comparison of U.S. and Japanese rates in the 1970s and 1980s indicates that real rates were lower in Japan in some periods and higher in others. See Edward J. Lincoln, *Japan: Facing Economic Maturity* (Washington, D.C.: Brookings Institution, 1988), pp. 258–60.

20. Tsunehiko Watanabe, "National Planning and International Growth in Japan," in Bert Hickman, ed., *Quantitative Planning of Economic Policy: A Conference of the Social Science Research Council on Economic Stability* (Washington, D.C.: Brookings Institution, 1965), pp. 233–51.

21. Savings deposits in both the post office and commercial institutions were exempt from taxation in what was known as the *maruyu* system. Efforts to eliminate the system in the 1980s were unsuccessful. Individuals also opened many small accounts under their own and other names without fear of prosecution. There are different views on the reasons for the high levels of consumer savings. One study concluded that (1) the semiannual bonus system, (2) limited availability of housing credit, and (3) low levels of social security support in the early years after the war encouraged saving. The same study discounted most other hypotheses, including the effects of the dual economy (that is, people who own small businesses might save to meet the capital needs of their firms). See Henry Wallich and Mable Wallich, "Banking and Finance," in Patrick and Rosovsky, *Asia's New Giant*, pp. 258–59. But the Wallich and Wallich interpretation is dated. Access to housing credit has increased in recent years, and pensions are more adequate than in the past. After peaking in the mid-1970s, private savings ratios have declined as well, which may reflect these changes. See Kazuo Sato, "Savings and Investment," in Kozo Yamamura and Yasukichi Yasuba, eds., *The Political Economy of Japan*, vol. 1: *The Domestic Transformation* (Stanford: Stanford University Press, 1987), pp. 148–51.

22. Keizai Koho Center, *Japan 1992*, p. 85.

23. Japan Economic Institute, *Japan's Industrial Policies: What Are They, Do They*

Matter and Are They Different from Those in the United States? (Washington, D.C., 1984), p. 41.

24. Johnson, *MITI and the Japanese Miracle,* pp. 207 ff.

25. Ira Magaziner and Thomas Hout, *Japanese Industrial Policy* (London: Policy Studies Institute, 1980).

26. See also Seiritsu Ogura and Naoyuki Yoshino, "The Tax System and the Fiscal Investment and Loan Program," in Ryutaro Komiya, Masahiro Okuno, and Kotaru Suzumura, eds., *Industrial Policy of Japan* (San Diego, Calif.: Academic Press, 1988), pp. 121–23.

27. Johnson, *MITI and the Japanese Miracle,* p. 211.

28. See Ogura and Yoshino, "Tax System," p. 145.

29. See Komiya et al., *Industrial Policy of Japan,* chaps. 5 and 16.

30. See Hiromichi Mutoh, "The Automotive Industry," in Komiya et al., *Industrial Policy of Japan,* pp. 307–32; Ogura and Yoshino, "Tax System," pp. 146–47.

31. Machine tools also received support from the Medium and Small Business Finance Corporation, but I do not have information of sufficient detail to document those loans accurately.

32. See Komiya et al., *Industrial Policy of Japan,* specifically: Ogura and Yoshino, "Tax System," pp. 121–54; Hideki Yamawaki, "The Steel Industry," pp. 281–306; and Koji Shinjo, "The Computer Industry," pp. 333–68.

33. Interestingly, there were close ties between people in the power and shipping industries and leading conservative politicians, including Shigeru Yoshida; and industry associations made sizable money contributions along the lines of government bank lending priorities. In the 1950s newspapers carried many accounts of these matters; for example, according to the *Mainichi,* February 4, 1954, the Electric Industry Management Council and the Shipbuilding Association were the biggest contributors to the Liberal Party during the first six months of 1953, followed closely by the Coal Association.

34. Japan Economic Institute, *Japan's Industrial Policies,* p. 42. Because Japanese companies raise capital mainly by borrowing from banks, government lending could have had a greater indicative or leverage effect in Japan simply because borrowing was so important. Developmental state scholars have asserted that this is what took place, but many economists see other factors at work besides government leadership. See Koichi Hamada and Akiyoshi Horiuchi, "The Political Economy of the Financial Market," in Yamamura and Yasuba, *Political Economy of Japan,* 1: 232–35, 249–50.

35. Edward Lincoln says of the allegedly indicative role of the Japan Development Bank: "This statement could be true . . . but it remains a piece of unexamined mythology about Japan . . . the market for commercial loans is not more than marginally under the control of the Japan Development Bank." Lincoln, *Japan,* p. 41.

36. One of the leading economists in Japan has argued in a slightly different vein that firms saw government bank borrowing as a safety net and that corporate investment strategies were unusually daring as a result. Firms could take risks on the assumption that the government would bail them out if they had problems. See Takafusa Nakamura, *The Postwar Japanese Economy: Its Development and Structure* (Tokyo: University of Tokyo Press, 1981), p. 66.

37. At the end of each of the first five plan periods, nominal GNP was 168 percent of targeted growth (1956–60), 166 percent (1958–62), 280 percent (1961–67), 182 percent (1964–68), and 156 percent (1967–71). Note that plans appear to overlap because they were often superseded owing to changed economic conditions.

38. Friedman, *Misunderstood Miracle,* pp. 79–97; Samuels, *Business of the Japanese State,* pp. 112, 124.

39. On the tendency for business cycles to upset the calculations of plans and industrial policy frameworks see, among others, Samuels, *Business of the Japanese State,* esp. pp. 111–12, 117; Friedman, *Misunderstood Miracle,* pp. 81–84.

40. See Toshimasa Tsuruta, "The Rapid Growth Era," in Komiya et al., *Industrial Policy of Japan,* p. 83.

41. See Yamawaki, "Steel Industry," pp. 302–4. On the role of interfirm competition, Hideki Yamawaki states, "This was a reflection of vigorous investment competition by the individual steel makers . . . without real competition, such favorable market performance during this period could not have been expected."

42. Yamawaki, "Steel Industry." In spite of the successes in the 1950s, competition (and some say MITI policy as well) had produced overcapacity in the steel industry by the 1970s.

43. Magaziner and Hout, *Japanese Industrial Policy,* p. 44.

44. Mutoh, "Automotive Industry," p. 314; Eugene J. Kaplan, *Japan: The Government-Business Relationship — a Guide for American Businessmen* (Washington, D.C.: U.S. Department of Commerce, 1972), pp. 120–28; Johnson, *MITI and the Japanese Miracle,* p. 24; and interview with Soichiro Honda in September 1981.

45. Mutoh, "Automotive Industry," pp. 323–24.

46. See Kaplan, *Japan: The Government-Business Relationship,* pp. 116–20. But Takashi Yokokura, in "Small and Medium Enterprises," in Komiya et al., *Industrial Policy of Japan,* pp. 531–34, discounts policy for medium and small industry as generally unselective, so it is possible that the auto parts efforts were less successful than Kaplan states.

47. Kaplan, *Japan: The Government-Business Relationship,* pp. 83–86.

48. Anchordoguy, *Computers Inc.,* pp. 59–91.

49. See Shinjo, "Computer Industry," esp. pp. 354–56, for a guardedly positive view of the effects of government policy on the computer industry. For an essentially negative evaluation of the government-sponsored VLSI research project see Glenn R. Fong, "State Strength, Industry Structure and Industrial Policy: American and Japanese Experiences in Micro-Electronics," *Comparative Politics* 22 (1990), pp. 273–99. Gary Saxonhouse believes that cooperative research-and-development projects play a role like interfirm job mobility in the United States, that is, diffusion of knowledge across firms. Saxonhouse, "Tampering with Comparative Advantage in Japan," Testimony to the United States International Trade Commission, July 13, 1983, p. 4.

50. According to the Economic Planning Agency, electricity rates are 15 percent higher in Tokyo than in London and 9 percent higher than in Paris. Keizai Koho Center, *Japan 1992,* p. 74. The high cost of imported oil is a major factor in high electric power rates. Samuels, *Business of the Japanese State,* p. 183.

51. Samuels, *Business of the Japanese State,* pp. 92, 102.

52. See Samuels, *Business of the Japanese State,* p. 103.

53. Samuels, *Business of the Japanese State,* pp. 108–12.

54. Samuels, *Business of the Japanese State,* p. 103.

55. Ippei Yamazawa, "The Textile Industry," in Komiya et al., *Industrial Policy of Japan,* p. 410.

56. Friedman, *Misunderstood Miracle,* pp. 81–84.

57. Kaplan, *Japan: The Government-Business Relationship,* pp. 100–101, 120–28, 141, 146–47.

58. Keizai Koho Center, *Japan 1992,* p. 88.

59. Foreign Press Center, *Facts and Figures of Japan* (Tokyo, 1991), p. 82. The figures for other cities included 80 square meters per resident in Stockholm and 464 in Washington; see Bradley Richardson and Scott Flanagan, *Politics in Japan* (Boston: Little, Brown, 1984), p. 409.

60. Asahi Shimbunsha, *Japan Almanac, 1996* (Tokyo, 1995), p. 203.

61. See Japan Economic Institute, "Japanese Housing: The International Dimension," *Report* 30A, August 4, 1989, p. 2; Asahi Shimbunsha, *Japan Almanac, 1994* (Tokyo, 1993), p. 204; and Asahi Shimbunsha, *Japan Almanac, 1996,* p. 203.

62. Japan Institute for International Affairs, *White Papers of Japan, 1973–74* (Tokyo, 1975), p. 109. The government has been criticized for leaving some land undeveloped in urban centers through its taxation policies. Low taxes on farmland and low inheritance taxes are said to permit the holding of land for future profits without paying high taxes. Although these arguments are correct, their proponents often overestimate the extent of land in metropolitan areas that is suitable for development. Estimates of usable land in metropolitan Tokyo, for example, often ignore the fact that the western part of Tokyo prefecture is mountainous.

63. See Gary Saxonhouse, "Industrial Restructuring in Japan," in *Journal of Japanese Studies* 5 (1979), pp. 273–320; Merton J. Peck, Richard C. Levin, and Akira Goto, "Picking Losers: Public Policy Toward Declining Industries in Japan," *Journal of Japanese Studies* 13 (1987), pp. 79–123.

64. Samuels, *Business of the Japanese State,* esp. pp. 116–34.

65. Yoshie Yonezawa, "The Shipbuilding Industry," in Komiya et al., *Industrial Policy of Japan,* pp. 433 ff.

66. See, e.g., Yonezawa, "Shipbuilding Industry," p. 443.

67. See General Accounting Office, *Report to the Chairman, Joint Economic Committee, United States Congress, Industrial Policy: Case Studies in the Japanese Experience* (Washington, D.C., 1982), pp. 58–68.

68. Derk Bodde, "Harmony and Conflict in Chinese Philosophy," in Arthur F. Wright, ed., *Studies in Chinese Thought* (Chicago: University of Chicago Press, 1953), pp. 45–47.

69. See *Asahi,* April 11, 1983.

70. Kent Calder, in particular, has pointed to the importance of LDP clientelism. Calder, *Crisis and Compensation: Public Policy and Political Stability in Japan* (Princeton, N.J.: Princeton University Press, 1988), esp. chap. 11. See also Brian E. Woodall, "Pork Barrel Politics in Japan: Trade Friction, Public Works and the Triadic Syndicate, 1955–1988" (Ph.D. diss., University of California, Berkeley, 1990). Chalmers Johnson,

in his discussion of Kakuei Tanaka's career in corruption, makes a similar point. Johnson, "Tanaka Kakuei, Structural Corruption and the Advent of Machine Politics in Japan," *Journal of Japanese Studies* 12 (1986), pp. 1–28.

71. Yano Tsuneta Kinenkai, *Nihon Kokusei Zue* (Tokyo, 1980), pp. 140, 171; Keizai Koho Center, *Japan 1992,* p. 34.

72. Customs duties in Japan dipped below those in the United States and the European Economic Community as early as 1974, were lower than in the United States but slightly higher than in the EEC from 1976 to 1979, and were lower than in both from 1980. U.S. tariff duties now average 3.9 percent of imports, those for the EEC average 3.8 percent, and those for Japan average 3.4 percent. Keizai Koho Center, *Japan 1992,* p. 31.

73. Liberal economics allows government to play a remedial role in market failures but provides no precise indicator to suggest when public programs are desirable or when they lead to a waste of resources. See Robert Wade, *Governing the Market: Economic Theory and the Role of Government in East Asian Industrialization* (Princeton, N.J.: Princeton University Press, 1990.), p. 11.

74. Lifetime employment refers to the practice by which Japan's large companies hire most of their male workers and employees upon graduation from high school or college and retain them until the age of fifty-five or sixty. The system, though under pressure as many large firms have restructured their workforce in the early 1990s, still survives with modifications.

Process technologies are improvements in production processes, such as Toyota's just-in-time inventory management system and flexible manufacturing. Improvements in manufacturing processes were a major contributing factor in Japanese firms' ability to improve product quality and lower prices. These improvements helped some Japanese firms become more competitive both at home and abroad. For references and sometimes detailed discussion of these factors see Patrick and Rosovsky, *Asia's New Giant*; Komiya et al., *Industrial Policy of Japan.*

75. Magaziner and Hout, *Japanese Industrial Policy,* pp. 15–16.

76. Johnson, *MITI and the Japanese Miracle,* pp. 317–18; Anchordoguy, *Computers Inc.,* chap. 1.

Chapter 10: *Japan as a Bargained Distributive Democracy*

1. See the works of Maurice Duverger, Kurt Shell, and others cited in Chapter 3.

2. See Frank Upham, "The Man Who Would Import: A Cautionary Tale About Bucking the System in Japan," *Journal of Japanese Studies* 17 (1991), pp. 323–43; Chalmers Johnson, *MITI and the Japanese Miracle: The Growth of Industrial Policy, 1925–1975* (Stanford: Stanford University Press, 1982), chap. 7.

3. According to some views, bureaucratic ministries like those in Japan provide the kind of leadership needed in today's democracies to counter the domination of the state by private interests. See Eric Nordlinger, *The Autonomy of the Democratic State* (Cambridge: Harvard University Press, 1981).

4. John Creighton Campbell, "Compensation for Repatriates: A Case-Study of Interest Group Politics and Party-Government Negotiations in Japan," in T. J. Pempel, ed.,

Policymaking in Japan (Ithaca, N.Y.: Cornell University Press, 1977), pp. 103–42; and Michael W. Donnelly, "Setting the Price of Rice: A Study in Political Decision Making," in Pempel, *Policymaking in Japan*, 143–200. See also Haruhiro Fukui, *Party in Power: The Japanese Liberal Democrats and Policymaking* (Berkeley: University of California Press, 1972), pp. 173–97.

5. Bradley Richardson, "Policymaking in Japan: An Organizing Perspective," in Pempel, *Policymaking in Japan*, pp. 256–57. One of the best discussions of early Japanese macroeconomic policymaking also reports examples of party influence vis-à-vis the bureaucracy; see Haruhiro Fukui, "Economic Planning in Postwar Japan: A Case Study in Policy Making," *Asian Survey* 8 (1972) pp. 327–48.

6. See Joel D. Aberbach, Robert D. Putnam, and Bert A. Rockman, *Bureaucrats and Politicians in Western Democracies* (Cambridge: Harvard University Press, 1981), chap. 7; Ezra Suleiman, ed., *Bureaucrats and Policymaking: A Comparative Overview* (New York: Holmes and Meier, 1984); Jeremy Richardson, ed., *Policy Styles in Western Europe* (London: George Allen and Unwin, 1981).

7. Bradley Richardson and Scott Flanagan, *Politics in Japan* (Boston: Little, Brown, 1984), pp. 364–65.

8. See *Economist,* August 7 and November 27, 1976.

9. Among the several general works on contemporary Germany that I consulted, by far the most useful was William E. Paterson and David Southern, *Governing Germany* (Oxford: Blackwell, 1991).

10. See David Hine, *Governing Italy: The Politics of Bargained Pluralism* (Oxford: Oxford University Press, 1993). Detailed reference to Italy is omitted in view of the scope of recent changes in the political system of that country.

11. The following account of British institutions is based on Anthony King, ed., *The British Prime Minister* (London: Macmillan, 1992); Philip Norton, *Does Parliament Matter?* (Hempstead, Eng.: Harvester, Wheatsheaf, 1993); and Dennis Kavanagh, *British Politics: Continuities and Change* (Oxford: Oxford University Press, 1990).

12. Yano Tsuneta Kinenkai, *Sekai Kokusei Zue, 1995–96* (Tokyo: Kokuseisha, 1995), pp. 234–37.

13. Keizai Koho Center, *Japan 1992: An International Comparison* (Tokyo, 1992), pp. 6, 16.

14. See Japan Economic Institute, *Structural Changes in Japan's Distribution System,* JEI Report no. 43A (Washington, D.C., 1989). The number of small stores is declining, however; see Chapter 8.

15. Tokyo Chamber of Commerce and Industry, *Japan in the World in Statistics* (Tokyo, 1987), p. 52.

16. Ronald Dore, *Shinohata: Portrait of a Japanese Village* (London: Alleyn Lane, 1978); Robert Smith, *Kurusu: The Price of Progress in a Japanese Village, 1951–75* (Stanford: Stanford University Press, 1978).

17. See Harumi Befu, *The Group Model of Japanese Society and an Alternative* (Houston: Rice University Studies no. 66, 1980), pp. 69–87, for a discussion of the prevalence of competition and conflict in Japanese life.

18. See Ross Mouer and Yoshio Sugimoto, *Images of Japanese Society: A Study in the*

Social Construction of Reality (London: Kegan Paul International, 1986), chap. 5. Recent works by social scientists and historians on conflict in Japan are cited elsewhere in this book.

19. Local politicians and residents in Kanagawa and Shimane indicated, in my interviews with them, feuds between different hamlets over locations of public projects and other matters. Some hamlets also had local reputations for long-standing aggressiveness. On intense conflicts within rural communities see Smith, *Kurusu,* chap. 8.

20. George Stalk, Jr., and Alan M. Webber, "Japan's Dark Side of Time," *Harvard Business Review* 71 (1993), pp. 93–104.

21. This point has been made by John Campbell in several places; see, e.g., "Policy Conflict and Its Resolution Within the Governmental System," in Ellis S. Krauss, Thomas P. Rohlen, and Patricia G. Steinhoff, eds., *Conflict in Japan* (Honolulu: University of Hawaii Press, 1984), pp. 308–9.

22. Thomas Rohlen has written of the importance of order in Japanese culture and its sources in school experiences. There is a strong emphasis on routine in the classroom. See Rohlen, "Order in Japanese Society: Attachment, Authority and Routine," *Journal of Japanese Studies* 15 (1989), pp. 5–40.

23. See Geert Holstede and Michael Harris Bond, "The Confucius Connection: From Cultural Roots to Economic Growth," *Organizational Dynamics* 16 (1988) pp. 5–21.

24. See Rodney Clarke, *The Japanese Company* (New Haven: Yale University Press, 1979), pp. 112–25; and *Wall Street Journal,* June 17, 1993.

25. Like many things about Japan, the importance of these relationships is sometimes overestimated. See Michael Gerlach, "Twilight of the Keiretsu: A Critical Assessment," *Journal of Japanese Studies* 18 (1992), pp. 79–118.

26. Lawrence Olson, "Takehara: A Good Place to Be From," in Olson, *Dimensions of Japan* (New York: American Universities Field Staff, 1963), pp. 54–63; and B. C. Koh and Jae-on Kim, "Paths to Advancement in Japanese Bureaucracy," *Comparative Political Studies* 15 (1982), pp. 289–313.

27. Not all Japanese life is ordered and patterned, even though this is an important dimension of culture. Dwelling on the importance of harmony in Japanese society often means overlooking the rich variety of social forms and practices. Ross Mouer and Yoshio Sugimoto criticize the collectivist stereotyping of Japanese society in their *Images of Japanese Society.*

28. See Takie Sugiyama Lebra, *Japanese Patterns of Behavior* (Honolulu: University of Hawaii Press, 1976).

29. It is often suggested that the in-group can be extended to larger entities like corporations and nations. Though not denying that Japanese relate to and identify with larger groups, evidence suggests that much important behavior takes place in small groups. Even when, as some would argue, larger in-groups are formed by bridging consultation and coordination, such as takes place within the Diet, the main point of contact and focus for consultation is within small groups — for instance, among the directors of Diet steering committees, the heads of the Diet strategy committee of each party, and the secretaries general of each party.

30. Rohlen, "Order in Japanese Society."

31. Takeo Doi, *The Anatomy of Dependence* (Tokyo: Kodansha, 1973).

32. Befu, *Group Model of Japanese Society.*

33. See Richard Samuels, *The Business of the Japanese State: Energy Markets in Comparative and Historical Perspective* (Ithaca, N.Y.: Cornell University Press, 1987), pp. 8–9. The operation of reciprocal consent does not mean that all conflict gets resolved. Free-floating predatory conflict is certainly a well-known feature of some business environments, most notably those where there are many small firms.

34. Befu, *Group Model of Japanese Society.*

35. John Creighton Campbell, "Japanese Budget Baransu," in Ezra Vogel, ed., *Modern Japanese Organization and Decision-Making* (Berkeley: University of California Press, 1975), pp. 71–100.

36. Takeshi Ishida, "Conflict and Its Accommodation: Omote-Ura and Uchi-Soto Relations," in Krauss, Rohlen, and Steinhoff, *Conflict in Japan,* pp. 16–38.

37. In some settings, informal consultations represent an effort to expand in-group relationships to a larger set of people. See Rohlen, "Order in Japanese Society."

38. Upham, "Man Who Would Import."

39. The total amounts of loans and subsidies (Table 9.9) provided to the farm, small-business, and large-business sectors were divided by the number of farm, small-business, and large-business units to give a theoretical figure for per-unit "receipts" in each sector.

40. Prime Minister's Office, Statistical Bureau, *Japan Statistical Yearbook 1993–94* (Tokyo, 1994), pp. 516–17, 583. Distributions of national government monies to local governments followed a similar pattern.

41. Keizai Koho Center, *Japan 1995: An International Comparison* (Tokyo, 1995), p. 80.

42. Keizai Koho Center, *Japan 1995,* p. 81.

43. John Campbell, *How Policies Change: The Japanese Government and the Aging Society* (Princeton., N.J.: Princeton University Press, 1992), p. 65.

44. I am reminded of Arend Lijphart's concept of consociational democracy. He argues that a variety of elite-level understandings and consultative practices emerged that made political stability possible even when societies and party systems were strongly divided. Lijphart, *Democracy in Plural Societies* (New Haven: Yale University Press, 1977).

Index

Abe, Shintaro, 59–67 *passim,* 105
age cohorts, 41–42, 67
Agriculture, Forestries, and Fisheries,
  Ministry of (MAFF), 197, 198; and
  farm policy, 157–60, 162, 173; powers
  of, 117, 120, 122
alienation, political, 23, 24, 43, 44
amoral groupism, 7–8, 245
authoritarianism, 5, 72, 153, 154, 191;
  semi-, 1–2, 96; soft, 110, 173, 245

Blue Clouds (party), 82
Britain: bureaucracy in, 102, 109, 123,
  154; economy of, 156, 205–8 *passim,*
  214, 225, 227, 252, 253, 261, 262,
  265; executive power in, 105, 122; interest groups in, 172, 199; parliament
  of, 128, 139, 142, 148, 247; political
  system of, 8–9, 15, 22, 24, 64, 247,
  249–50
budget: accommodation on, 137–39,
  144, 259; allocation of, 11, 29, 46,

215; conflict over, 69, 83, 104–5, 133–
  34, 148; control over, 106–7, 118,
  124–25, 245; and Diet, 140–41; and
  ministries, 109–11; and tax policy,
  163–65
bureaucracy, 108–22, 256, 259, 264; and
  business, 10, 118, 177, 179, 196; constraints on, 122, 240; and corporatism,
  152, 153–55, 233; and Diet, 127–29,
  132, 148–50; and interest groups, 140,
  152, 171, 172; and LDP, 1, 2, 49, 125,
  246; in other countries, 122–24; and
  pluralism, 3, 241, 243, 245, 246, 248–
  52, 258; and policymaking, 48, 97,
  101–3, 110, 162, 201, 204; and political parties, 143, 173; power of, 96,
  109, 114, 170, 201; and tax reform,
  163, 168

Campbell, John, 152
candidates, political, 37, 92, 146, 255;
  and factions, 50, 60, 61, 63; and

candidates, political (*continued*)
  interest groups, 38–40, 55, 251; and
  voter mobilization, 29–36, 43–47,
  241, 246, 264
China, People's Republic of, 11, 146,
  194, 252; conflicts over, 49, 54, 77, 80,
  100, 107, 242
class, 16, 18, 19, 265
Clean Government Party (CGP;
  Komeito), 15, 19, 93; in coalitions,
  85–92, 138, 263; in Diet, 11, 14, 139,
  143–46; and LDP, 2, 44, 79, 179; organization of, 70, 71; support for, 17,
  37, 41–42; and tax reform, 166, 169
cleavage theory, 16, 18, 19, 21, 264, 265
clientelism, 3, 228, 233, 238–39, 260
coalition governments, 9, 119, 147, 172,
  184, 221, 264; changes under, 96, 100,
  102, 121, 125–26; Diet under, 128,
  131, 148; and horizontal model, 3, 4
coalitions: with business, 118, 174; conflict within, 90, 91, 181, 240–41, 266;
  constraints from, 107, 245, 251; and
  consultation, 241–43, 259; of factions,
  98–99, 245, 256–57; interest group,
  172, 189, 198–99, 246; with LDP, 97,
  173, 263, 265; within LDP, 80, 97–99,
  150, 162, 168, 170, 172; LDP-interest
  group, 153–54, 156–57; legislative,
  137–39, 143–45; between parties, 78,
  79, 84–88; within parties, 81, 89, 94;
  parties as, 74–76; and policymaking,
  96–97, 120, 165, 193, 196, 244
collectivism, 254, 255, 257–59
communism, 3, 9, 78, 80, 175
Communist parties, 16, 194. *See also*
  Japan Communist Party
competition, 66, 74, 255, 256; constraints on, 64, 67; and Japanese culture, 7, 8, 254; and pluralism, 5, 7,
  258, 263–64
conflict, 195, 243, 254, 255, 258, 265;
  within coalitions, 181, 184, 189, 266;
  and consultation, 121, 122, 139, 170;
  containment, 6–8, 241, 242; contain-

ment of, 94, 259; and corporatism,
  190, 193, 198, 199; legislative, 131–
  37, 140; over tax reform, 167, 168;
  and pluralism, 153, 155, 165, 171, 245
conflict-fragmentation dynamic, 7, 240–
  41, 244, 247, 251, 264, 266
Confucian values, 172, 231, 233, 260
consensualism, 7, 8, 104, 251
conservative parties, 25, 182, 194, 265;
  in coalitions, 9, 86, 256; and LDP, 12,
  13, 75, 181; new, 14, 41–42, 88, 92;
  and voting patterns, 15, 16, 18, 20, 35,
  46, 47. *See also particular parties*
constitutional reform, 2, 20, 25, 49, 54,
  80, 171, 245, 251
constitutions, 149; Japanese, 9, 97, 105,
  106, 109, 124, 127
consultative councils, 107, 185–86, 192;
  and farm policy, 157, 158, 161;
  Government-LDP, 125, 241; and interest groups, 190, 197, 241; and ministries, 111, 114, 120, 123; on tax
  reform, 168–70, 244. *See also* policy
  groups
coordination-integration dynamic, 7,
  244, 247, 251, 255, 258, 264
corporatism, 3, 5; in business-
  government relations, 177, 184, 190,
  191, 193, 223, 233; and interest
  groups, 152–55, 170–71, 173, 175,
  197–99, 243–44; in U.S., 196
culture, influence of, 21, 136, 150, 254,
  255, 257–59
Curtis, Gerald, 177–79

decentralization, 227, 252, 253; electoral, 49, 243, 251; of parties, 48, 52,
  260; political, 9, 73, 94, 96, 105, 122,
  125, 245–50
democracy, 1, 2, 5, 8; bargained, 8–9, 96,
  124, 199, 248, 250–51, 259; programmatic, 9, 96, 124, 248, 250, 251
Democratic Party, 50, 93, 193
Democratic Socialist Party (DSP), 2, 34,
  35, 70, 79, 93, 179; in coalitions, 15,

79, 85–92, 138, 139; in Diet, 11, 14, 143–46; support for, 17, 18, 41–42, 45; and tax reform, 166, 169

demonstrations, 10, 76, 158, 164

developmental state theory, 200–204, 216, 218–23, 231, 233, 235–38

Diet (parliament), 127–51, 247, 251; and bureaucracy, 109, 114, 123; coalitions in, 86, 87, 139; conflict in, 7, 134–37, 140, 256, 257; consultation with, 120, 121; elections for, 11, 15, 21, 23, 26; and horizontal model, 2, 3, 4; and interest groups, 46, 48, 153–54, 159–60, 172, 253; and LDP, 51–52, 54, 68–69, 72, 79, 84, 96, 128–29, 143; legislation in, 111, 112, 244–46; opposition parties in, 37, 71, 75, 77–78, 240–42, 262–64; and policy, 55, 97, 98; power in, 20, 95, 147–48; procedures in, 76, 255; and tax policy, 163–65, 169

Donnelly, Michael, 152

dynamics, twin, 75, 240–44, 247, 251, 255–58, 264, 266

economic development, 1, 3, 9, 236; government support for, 115–16, 200–209, 215–21 *passim*, 225, 227–38; and voting patterns, 36, 37

economic policy, 10, 203, 210–11, 220; indicative, 207, 235; pluralistic, 239, 262–63; resistance to, 223–24, 239, 262

education, 18, 114, 117, 133, 140

elections, 3, 5, 98–99, 164; and business, 175, 180–84 *passim*, 189; and coalitions, 87–90; future, 263–65; LDP losses in, 46, 49, 86–87, 147, 168, 170; of *1993*, 11, 76–84 *passim*, 88, 92, 94; and political culture, 12–48. *See also* local politics; voting patterns

electoral reform: accommodation on, 138, 139, 148; conflict over, 69, 90, 133, 134, 143; and factions, 60, 61; results of, 33, 34, 125; and voting districts, 15, 16, 251

elites, 3, 5, 13, 26, 27, 31, 47, 109

Etsuzankai organization, 27, 28, 29

Europe, 123, 125, 202, 226, 246, 265; economy of, 228, 237, 252; interest groups in, 153, 154, 172, 197–99, 246; parties in, 72–73, 150, 243, 259

executive power, 95, 96, 104, 122, 250

Export-Import Bank (EIB), 216–18

exports. *See* trade, foreign

factions: and business, 176, 181–83; and coalitions, 65, 74–94; and conflict, 6, 53, 54, 134, 142; constraints from, 98–100, 107, 108, 245; decline of, 82–84; and horizontal model, 49, 72; and informal processes, 50, 120; institutionalization of, 62, 94, 241, 242, 255; LDP, 52–69, 72–73, 75, 79–80, 102, 104, 243, 250; in opposition parties, 69–72, 81; and pluralism, 52, 66–67, 124–25, 144, 246, 263; and reform, 16, 167, 169; and stability, 63, 64, 76, 77, 257

farm cooperatives, 26, 31, 34, 38, 39, 162, 197

farm policy, 155–62, 198, 237; conflict over, 122, 133, 135, 243; and pluralism, 170–73, 190, 194

farmers, 16, 46, 55, 155–62, 163, 252, 265; government support for, 38, 216, 231–33, 238, 246, 252–53, 260–61, 263; and LDP, 10, 38–40, 54, 80, 103, 153, 181; voting patterns among, 16–19, 21, 29, 44, 46, 47, 253–54

Federation of Economic Organizations (FEO), 171, 173; on farm policy, 160, 161, 181; and foreign trade, 176, 187; and industry policy, 193–97 *passim*; and LDP, 174–84 *passim*; on tax reform, 166, 167

Federation of Employers' Associations, 161, 166, 174–79 *passim*

Finance, Ministry of, 120, 122, 177, 194, 197, 244; officials of, 114, 177, 179; and policymaking, 117, 160, 161, 171; and prime minister, 106, 107; role of, 109, 110, 118, 124–25; and tax reform, 134, 137, 162–73 *passim*

Fiscal Investment and Loan Program (FILP), 215, 220, 229, 234–35

Flanagan, Scott, 20

floating voters, 40, 44, 94

Fong, Glenn, 223

foreign policy, 2, 10, 88, 106, 115–17, 125

France: bureaucracy in, 109, 123, 124; economy of, 155, 157, 208, 209, 214, 225, 227, 252, 261; interest groups in, 154, 172, 199, 249; leadership in, 105, 122, 250; legislature of, 128, 148, 247; politics in, 23–24, 70

Friedman, David, 221

Fukuda, Takeo, 59, 61, 66, 78, 101, 146, 177; and Tanaka, 65, 77, 99

Fukui, Haruhiro, 152

General Agreement on Tariffs and Trade (GATT), 160, 172, 195

George, Aurelia, 153

Germany: bureaucracy in, 123, 124; economy of, 205–9 *passim*, 214, 225, 227, 252, 253, 261; legislature of, 128, 139, 142, 148, 149, 247, 249, 250; politics in, 19, 24, 84, 122, 243, 246

Harbinger Party, 11, 14, 70, 88–94 *passim*, 263

Hashimoto, Ryutaro, 66

Hata, Tsutomu, 59, 79, 82, 83, 159, 179; coalition government of, 88–94 *passim*, 121, 122

Hatoyama, Ichiro, 58, 106, 107, 182

Hirakawa Society, 54, 78, 80

horizontal-fragmented model, 2–4, 125, 150, 162, 239–40, 256, 264; and bureaucracy, 244, 245; and electoral politics, 13, 29, 45, 46; and factions, 49,

52, 72; and vertical model, 128, 155, 248

Hosokawa, Morihiro, 83, 148, 172, 179; coalition government of, 88, 90, 91, 94, 121, 122

House of Councillors, 33, 87, 101, 128, 129; elections for, 15, 34, 35, 183; and LDP, 13, 39, 40, 42, 51, 77, 147, 180, 186; representation in, 134, 143; and tax reform, 170, 175

House of Representatives, 33, 67, 95, 114, 128, 142, 165; elections for, 15, 32, 34, 35; and LDP, 11, 12, 13, 51, 263; representation in, 90, 265

Ichikawa, Yuichi, 91

ideology, 118, 175, 202, 244; and coalitions, 86–88, 94, 265; of factions, 54, 58; and party politics, 70, 80, 81, 84, 100, 135, 138, 146

Ikeda, Hayato, 10, 59, 77, 104, 106, 107, 176, 177

immobilism, 6, 7, 120, 258, 264–66

imports. *See* trade, foreign

industrial policy, 190–96, 204, 207–8, 221–25, 228, 243; foreign influence on, 235, 236

industrialization, 46, 156, 225, 227, 254

industry, 57, 166, 179–80, 183, 206, 237, 256; government support for, 10, 115–16, 185, 201–2, 217, 219, 234–37, 262; loans to, 215–20 *passim*, 231; nationalization of, 181, 203, 238; recessed, 229, 233, 238

informal processes, 73, 168, 242, 250, 251, 258, 259; consultation through, 121, 168, 190, 241, 256; and corporatism, 153, 199; in LDP, 50–53, 58, 153, 199, 241, 242; and legislation, 136, 141–48 *passim*, 247; and power, 95, 96, 104, 105

institutionalization, 61–63, 73, 242

interest groups, 152–73; and bureaucracy, 140, 152, 171, 172, 197, 245; under coalition governments, 94,

264; and conflict, 6, 10, 198–99, 241; constraints from, 98, 100, 124, 245; and farm policy, 155–62; and horizontal model, 3, 46; and LDP, 1, 2, 39, 40, 52–57, 68–72, 121, 178, 233; and legislation, 48, 111–12, 133, 153–54, 159–60, 172, 186–88, 253; local, 27–55 *passim*, 140, 248, 253, 265; pluralism of, 165–73 *passim*, 196–200, 243; and policymaking, 101–4, 109, 114, 190, 193, 194, 203–4, 246–50; and political parties, 71, 177, 242–44, 263; and power, 5, 47–49, 95–97; and stability, 40, 257; and tax reform, 162–70. *See also* occupational groups; voter mobilization

International Trade and Industry, Ministry of (MITI): appointments to, 107, 110; and business, 10, 185, 195; conflicts with, 115–18, 171, 222, 224, 229; on farm policy, 161, 162, 170; on industrial policy, 106, 186–202 *passim*, 208, 255; and legislation, 132, 145, 211; officials from, 114, 120; powers of, 108, 125, 260

interventionist state, 202

investment, 215–25 *passim*; foreign, 213, 236, 237; rates of, 209, 238

Ishihara, Shintaro, 66

Ishihara, Takashi, 183, 184

Italy, 19, 23, 84, 246, 249, 250; bureaucracy in, 124, 149; leadership in, 64, 122; parties in, 12, 70, 73, 199, 243

Japan Chamber of Commerce and Industry, 39, 167, 174, 175, 184, 186, 197

Japan Committee on Economic Development (Keizai Doyukai), 161, 166, 167, 171, 193; and LDP, 174, 175, 177, 182, 183

Japan Communist Party (JCP), 2, 70, 71, 93, 143, 166; in coalitions, 85–92 *passim*; in Diet, 11, 14, 15; support for, 17, 18, 35, 37, 41–42

Japan Cooperative Party, 93

Japan Development Bank (JDB), 10, 177, 191, 212, 215–19 *passim*, 223, 231, 232

Japan Electronic Computer Company (JECC), 212, 223

Japan Liberal Party, 93

Japan New Party, 11, 14, 70, 82–93 *passim*, 265

Japan Progressive Party, 93

Japan Socialist Party (JSP), 2, 10, 15, 93, 179, 181, 194; in coalitions, 85, 184, 193. *See also* Social Democratic Party of Japan

Johnson, Chalmers, 102, 152, 202, 215, 216

Kaifu, Toshiki, 66, 82, 145

Kajiyama, Seiroku, 83, 144

Kaku-Fuku war, 65, 68

Kanemaru, Shin, 11, 53, 65, 79, 80, 144, 145, 169

Kato, Koichi, 66

keiretsu (interfirm alignments), 256

Keizai Doyukai. *See* Japan Committee on Economic Development

Kishi, Nobusuke, 10, 59, 106, 107, 130, 182; opposition to, 76, 77, 98, 104

Kobayashi, Naoki, 152

Komeito. *See* Clean Government Party

Komoto, Toshio, 59, 61, 66, 89, 98, 99

Kono, Yohei, 83, 84

Korea, North, 90, 144

Korea, South, 192, 225, 228, 229; relations with, 10, 106, 133, 139, 171

Krauss, Ellis, 145, 152

labor unions, 171, 179, 197, 203, 220, 258, 262; and coalitions, 86, 193; conflict over, 20, 54, 133; exclusion of, 2, 154, 260, 261; and LDP, 36, 44, 56, 150, 153; and opposition parties, 25, 90; and tax reform, 166, 170; and voting patterns, 13, 18–19, 21, 26, 30–37 *passim*

Large Store Law, 180, 184–90, 194, 197, 198, 254, 261

legislatures, democratic, 148–55 *passim*, 249. *See also* Diet

Liberal Democratic Party (LDP), 1–4, 96–100; and bureaucracy, 1, 2, 49, 103, 109, 123, 125, 246; and business, 2, 10, 18, 39–40, 80, 83, 153, 174–87, 198–99, 216, 229, 253, 260; and cabinet, 7, 121, 125, 167, 255, 263; candidates from, 15–16, 29, 43; clients of, 221, 233; in coalitions, 85–95, 138, 139, 173; conflict with, 241, 255, 265; constraints on, 101, 104, 105, 124, 251; consultation with, 7, 120, 121; crises in, 75–80; in Diet, 14, 51–52, 54, 68–69, 72, 79, 84, 96, 127–51; dominance of, 1, 12, 13, 49, 145, 243, 263–66; factions in, 50, 52–69, 72–73, 75, 79–80, 84, 89, 94, 100, 102, 104, 242, 243, 245, 250, 257; and farmers, 10, 38–40, 54, 80, 103, 153, 156–60, 162, 181, 197; fragmentation of, 4, 74, 75, 81–83; informal processes in, 50–53, 58, 153, 199, 241, 242; and interest groups, 1, 2, 38–40, 46, 52–57, 68–72, 121, 152–55, 171–72, 178, 188, 196, 233, 244, 246; and labor, 36, 44, 56, 150, 153, 261; and Large Store Law, 186, 189; and legislation, 111, 130, 135–37, 247; losses of, 15, 46, 49, 76–83, 86–87, 147, 168, 170, 254; members of, 27, 114; as minority, 14, 126, 148; and opposition parties, 2, 4, 10, 44, 70–71, 77–79, 122, 179, 240, 242, 247, 262; organization of, 50–52, 73; pluralism in, 49–56, 58, 60–63, 69, 100, 124; policy groups in, 52, 72, 73, 76–78, 119, 242, 258; policymaking by, 8, 49, 56, 58, 68–69, 72, 106, 124, 172; and prime minister, 52, 53, 64, 65, 67, 106, 107; reform of, 78–80, 82, 84, 183; scandals in, 11, 24, 45, 66, 76, 77, 79, 83, 256; support for, 17, 20, 41–42, 44; and tax reform, 58, 163–70; voter mobilization by, 28, 30, 33, 44, 72; and voting patterns, 25–26, 37, 45

Liberal Party, 50, 82, 93, 193

loans, 215–20, 222, 229, 231–33, 237, 260

local politics: candidates in, 32–34, 47; and Diet, 48, 140; issues in, 164, 186, 189; and LDP, 38, 52, 55, 80; and local elections, 15, 254; and local government, 2, 3, 10, 33, 187, 203, 233; and national politics, 23, 47, 72, 73, 126; parochialism of, 252, 258; and voter mobilization, 26–29, 52; and voting patterns, 36, 37, 44, 246

local-mobilization model, 44, 45

MAFF. *See* Agriculture, Forestries, and Fisheries, Ministry of

Magaziner, Ira, 215

middle class, 16, 18, 25, 46

Miki, Takeo, 59, 61, 66, 101, 146, 177, 209; and business, 176, 182; and LDP, 76–78

military policy, 18, 88, 209, 214, 252; conflict over, 54, 69, 133, 135, 138, 207; and constitution, 9, 25

MITI. *See* International Trade and Industry, Ministry of

Mitsuzuka, Hiroshi, 53, 59, 61, 66, 89, 169

Miyake, Ichiro, 37, 40, 46

Miyazawa, Kiichi, 42, 65, 66, 67, 76, 79, 83, 169, 177, 179; faction of, 53, 54, 59, 61, 62, 80, 89

Mochizuki, Komei, 80

Moroi, Ken, 179

Muramatsu, Michio, 107, 152

Murayama, Tomiichi, 88, 121, 147, 179

mutualism, 258, 259

Nagasue, Eichi, 70

Nakasone, Yasuhiro, 66, 67, 141, 145, 146, 161, 177; and business, 178, 182; criticism of, 98–99, 101, 104, 183; faction of, 53, 54, 59–61, 142; and reform, 11, 106, 107, 164, 165, 167

National Federation of Agricultural Cooperatives. *See* Zenchu national security, 2, 49, 132, 133, 138, 171

Netherlands, 6, 19, 84, 225

New Frontier Party (Shinshinto), 14, 16, 44, 89–94 *passim*

New Liberal Club, 14, 75, 85, 86, 93, 97, 147

New Liberal Party, 92

New Power, 81

Nikaido, Susumu, 98, 99, 101

1955 system, 2, 4, 7, 49–73, 82, 127, 174

Obuchi, Keizo, 59, 61, 89

occupational groups, 261; voting patterns of, 13, 16–19, 37–39, 44, 46

Ohira, Masayoshi, 59, 66, 76, 99, 100, 146, 147, 177

Okinawa, 11, 106, 108, 133, 246

Onchikai, 53

opposing dynamics. *See* dynamics, twin order, 255–57, 259

Ozawa, Ichiro, 66, 79, 80, 82, 83, 91, 169

PARC. *See* Policy Affairs Research Council

Park, Yung H., 102

parochialism, 23, 252; of electoral politics, 32–36, 47, 72, 125–26, 246; within groups, 118, 255, 258

party identification, 22–26, 40–45 *passim*

party image, 25, 44, 46

Patrick, Hugh, 202

Pempel, T. J., 152

pluralism, 4–5, 149, 151, 233, 240–46; in business sector, 175, 180, 184, 190; under coalition governments, 263, 264, 266; in industry, 191, 193, 194; and interest groups, 152–73, 196–99; in LDP, 49–56, 69, 100, 124; in policymaking, 191, 200, 224, 225, 239, 260

Policy Affairs Research Council (PARC), 72, 73, 97, 98, 119, 120, 250; and

Diet, 140, 144, 149; and interest groups, 101, 159, 170–76 *passim*; organization of, 50–51, 68–69

policy groups, 54, 81, 98, 119, 241, 242, 246, 257; in LDP, 52, 72–78 *passim*; and power, 47, 48

policymaking: conflict over, 88–94 *passim*, 241–43; consultation on, 8, 120–22; in Diet, 127–51; and interest groups, 154, 155; by LDP, 49, 56, 58, 68–69, 124–25, 172, 246–47, 263; by ministries, 102, 110, 116–18; by opposition parties, 71, 72, 243; pluralist, 171, 190, 193, 196–97, 200, 224–25, 239, 244, 260; and power relations, 96–106 *passim*; by prime minister, 95, 107, 249–50. *See also particular types of policymaking*

political culture, 7, 23, 24, 32–34; and voting patterns, 12–48

political ethics, 58, 99, 135, 136

political parties, 4, 14, 17, 18, 74, 251; conflict in, 6, 243, 265; decentralization of, 48, 52, 260; factions in, 69–72, 81, 255; funding for, 69, 183; generational divisions in, 66, 70, 81–82; and interest groups, 71, 177, 199, 242–44, 250, 263; and twin dynamics, 242–47, 250, 257; in two-party system, 173, 183, 184, 248; and working class, 16, 18, 25, 35. *See also* coalitions; *particular parties and types*

power, 4, 5, 6, 122

prime minister, 23, 95–100, 106, 126, 128, 241, 249; British, 250; and bureaucracy, 4, 102, 103, 110, 114, 123, 248; and business, 175–79, 183; constraints on, 99, 100, 104–8, 245, 251, 263; consultation with, 120, 121, 168; former, 84, 100, 101; and LDP, 52, 53, 64, 65, 67; and legislation, 129, 142–43; power of, 20, 96–98, 122

progressive parties, 20, 25, 86

proportional representation, 15, 16, 35, 60, 90, 134, 143, 265

protectionism, 181, 207, 213, 222, 231, 237, 262
protest vote, 10, 38, 40, 43–46, 80
protests. *See* demonstrations

railways, 11, 99, 133, 135, 136, 143, 242
Recruit scandal, 11, 39, 54, 76, 78–80, 183
reform, 43, 81, 92, 243, 257; administrative, 11, 106, 172, 248; and coalition governments, 88, 90, 91, 94; groups for, 55, 74, 81, 82, 83, 92; land, 158, 171; of LDP, 78–80, 82, 84; political, 147, 148, 176, 183, 265; and prime minister, 11, 106, 107. *See also particular types of reform*
Reform Party, 93
regulations, 112, 113, 123, 203, 248, 261
religion, 16, 19, 44, 56
Renewal Party, 11, 14, 70, 79, 88–93 *passim,* 159
Rengo (pan-union movement), 35, 36, 39, 44, 91, 183
Rosovsky, Henry, 202
Ryukyu Islands, 11

salaried workers, 16–19, 35, 40, 46, 47, 163
Samuels, Richard, 152, 196, 203, 221
Sato, Eisaku, 10, 59, 106, 176, 177, 182
savings rates, 209, 214, 215, 238
scandals, 23, 180–83 *passim,* 262; and coalitions, 61, 86, 256, 257; conflict over, 134–36; and electoral reform, 16, 82; in LDP, 11, 24, 66, 76–80, 83, 143, 177; and voting patterns, 26, 27, 44, 45, 265. *See also* Recruit scandal
Self-Defense Forces (SDF), 86, 88, 133, 139, 144
seniority, 62, 63, 67, 84, 255, 256
shopping district associations, 38, 39, 167
social contracts, 10, 46, 153, 154

Social Democratic Party of Japan (SDPJ), 2, 4, 15, 72–73, 93; in coalitions, 79, 86–92, 94, 173, 263; in Diet, 11, 14, 134–39, 143–45, 147; factions in, 69–70, 71, 81, 86, 257; fragmentation in, 75, 82, 83, 243, 257–58, 265; and labor, 35, 153; and LDP, 78, 122, 132, 183; and policymaking, 71, 90, 157, 169, 242; support for, 17, 18, 41–42; and voter mobilization, 27, 30, 34; and voting patterns, 21, 37, 40, 43
socialist parties, 36, 43, 73, 150, 151; in coalitions, 79, 86, 137, 263; support for, 16, 21, 46. *See also* Democratic Socialist Party; Japan Socialist Party
Soka Gakkai sect, 37, 44, 92
Soviet Union, 10, 11, 106, 107, 171, 206
Spain, 15, 19
stratarchies, 72, 73, 80, 243
study groups, 84, 100, 242
subsidies, 3, 228, 248; for business, 185, 203; farm price, 156–62, 170, 171, 233, 246, 260; for industry, 191, 192, 215–24 *passim*
supporters' associations (*koenkai*), 27, 28, 30, 31
Supreme Advisers, 84, 100, 101, 120
Suzuki, Zenko, 59, 61, 66, 98, 101, 145–47, 177

Takemura, Kisayoshi, 91
Takeshita, Noboru, 104–5, 106, 185; and business, 177–79; faction of, 53, 54, 58–62 *passim,* 65–67, 89; leadership of, 145–47, 165, 167, 169; and scandal, 11, 79, 183
Tanaka, Kakuei, 66, 78, 106, 107, 146; and business, 176, 177, 182; campaigns of, 27–29, 34, 45; faction of, 53, 59, 61, 98, 144; and Fukuda, 65, 77, 99; and scandal, 76–77, 99, 134
Tanaka, Rokusuke, 145
tariffs, 213, 231–37 *passim*

tax incentives, 212–13, 234–35, 261
tax reform, 162–70; conflict over, 54, 98,
    100, 101, 242–44; in Diet, 58, 69,
    111, 132–37 *passim,* 180; and plural-
    ism, 49, 155, 173, 190, 198
Tax System Research Council, 144, 165–
    72 *passim*
Tax System Special Consultative Council,
    169
taxes, 208, 214, 254, 261, 262
trade, foreign, 38, 118, 185, 187, 204,
    206–8, 218; agricultural, 104, 157,
    161, 246; liberalization of, 158, 160,
    162, 172; policy on, 185, 191, 195,
    209, 216, 222, 236; restrictions on,
    159, 236. *See also* protectionism;
    United States: trade with

United Kingdom. *See* Britain
United Nations (U.N.), 10, 88, 139, 144,
    145
United States (U.S.): congress of, 128,
    139, 142, 149, 247; economy of, 156,
    205–6, 209, 214, 225, 227, 239, 252–
    53; political system in, 113, 123, 196,
    251; politics in, 15, 22–24, 72, 102,
    146, 243, 250; population of, 226,
    227; pressure from, 38, 107, 157–58,
    162, 185–86; relations with, 9, 25, 90;
    taxes in, 208, 261, 262; trade with, 11,
    99, 104, 161, 172, 185, 189, 191, 202,
    236–37
Upham, Frank, 124
urbanization, 10, 13, 36, 37, 155
U.S.-Japan Security Treaty, 10, 76, 98,
    106, 107, 133, 135

values, 24, 118, 133, 174, 181; Confu-
    cian, 172, 231, 233, 260; and voting
    patterns, 13, 19, 20–22, 44
vertical-integrative model, 2–4, 8, 200,
    240, 248; of Diet, 128, 149, 150; and
    electoral politics, 13, 29, 45; and inter-
    est groups, 155, 175, 256; shortcom-
    ings of, 9, 49, 72, 95, 124
voter mobilization, 13, 38, 54, 72, 125,
    251, 265; by candidates, 29–36, 43–
    47, 241, 246, 264; local, 26–29, 44,
    45, 52
voting patterns, 4, 12–48, 67; volatility
    of, 40, 42, 47, 94, 265
voting rights, 13, 40

Watanabe, Michio, 53, 59, 61, 66, 89
Watanuki, Joji, 19–21
welfare programs: economic, 137, 203,
    220, 228, 231, 233, 238, 239; social,
    11, 112, 153, 163, 207, 209, 214, 233
Westminster model, 124, 248
women, 13, 40, 43, 44, 156
working class, 17, 19, 40, 156; and polit-
    ical parties, 16, 18, 25, 35
World War II, 9, 117, 157, 201, 207, 252

Yoshida, Shigeru, 58, 107, 177, 182

Zenchu (National Federation of Agricul-
    tural Cooperatives), 38, 156–62 *pas-
    sim,* 197
zoku (interest families), 54–56, 100, 165,
    186, 233, 242, 246, 249; and bu-
    reaucracy, 103, 104, 109, 125; and
    PARC, 68–69, 73, 140